IFIP Advances in Information and Communication Technology

533

Editor-in-Chief

Kai Rannenberg, Goethe University Frankfurt, Germany

IFIP – The International Federation for Information Processing

IFIP was founded in 1960 under the auspices of UNESCO, following the first World Computer Congress held in Paris the previous year. A federation for societies working in information processing, IFIP's aim is two-fold: to support information processing in the countries of its members and to encourage technology transfer to developing nations. As its mission statement clearly states:

IFIP is the global non-profit federation of societies of ICT professionals that aims at achieving a worldwide professional and socially responsible development and application of information and communication technologies.

IFIP is a non-profit-making organization, run almost solely by 2500 volunteers. It operates through a number of technical committees and working groups, which organize events and publications. IFIP's events range from large international open conferences to working conferences and local seminars.

The flagship event is the IFIP World Computer Congress, at which both invited and contributed papers are presented. Contributed papers are rigorously refereed and the rejection rate is high.

As with the Congress, participation in the open conferences is open to all and papers may be invited or submitted. Again, submitted papers are stringently refereed.

The working conferences are structured differently. They are usually run by a working group and attendance is generally smaller and occasionally by invitation only. Their purpose is to create an atmosphere conducive to innovation and development. Refereeing is also rigorous and papers are subjected to extensive group discussion.

Publications arising from IFIP events vary. The papers presented at the IFIP World Computer Congress and at open conferences are published as conference proceedings, while the results of the working conferences are often published as collections of selected and edited papers.

IFIP distinguishes three types of institutional membership: Country Representative Members, Members at Large, and Associate Members. The type of organization that can apply for membership is a wide variety and includes national or international societies of individual computer scientists/ICT professionals, associations or federations of such societies, government institutions/government related organizations, national or international research institutes or consortia, universities, academies of sciences, companies, national or international associations or federations of companies.

More information about this series at http://www.springer.com/series/6102

Amany Elbanna · Yogesh K. Dwivedi
Deborah Bunker · David Wastell (Eds.)

Smart Working, Living and Organising

IFIP WG 8.6 International Conference
on Transfer and Diffusion of IT, TDIT 2018
Portsmouth, UK, June 25, 2018
Proceedings

 Springer

Editors
Amany Elbanna
Royal Holloway University of London
Egham, UK

Deborah Bunker
University of Sydney
Sydney, NSW, Australia

Yogesh K. Dwivedi
Swansea University
Swansea, UK

David Wastell
University of Nottingham
Nottingham, UK

ISSN 1868-4238   ISSN 1868-422X (electronic)
IFIP Advances in Information and Communication Technology
ISBN 978-3-030-04314-8   ISBN 978-3-030-04315-5 (eBook)
https://doi.org/10.1007/978-3-030-04315-5

Library of Congress Control Number: 2018964091

This Springer imprint is published by the registered company Springer Nature Switzerland AG
The registered company address is: Gewerbestrasse 11, 6330 Cham, Switzerland

Preface

The adoption and diffusion of information technology have gone through decades of developments and major shifts. It has progressed from developing and adopting single isolated systems to large integrated systems to cloud computing. It has taken major twists and turns with the adoption of mobile technology, Web-based services, wearable technologies, and the Internet of Things. The focus of Working Group 8.6 of the International Federation of Information Processing (IFIP) is the diffusion, adoption, and implementation of information and communication technologies.

This book presents the proceedings of the 2018 Conference of the IFIP WG8.6. IFIP WG 8.6 has a tradition of focusing on the new developments in the adoption and diffusion of technology, systems, and the resulting information that is produced and used for different purposes. The conference was held in Portsmouth, UK, and was hosted by the University of Portsmouth, which showed true academic spirit and generously offered all conference facilities free of charge and for this we are very grateful.

The theme of the conference was the adoption of new classes of technology that are being used everyday by individuals, organizations, sectors, and society. We particularly welcomed research that questioned how emerging technologies are adopted and appropriated in organizations and everyday life and the impact they are having. However, we also remained open and committed to the wider theme of the IFIP 8.6 working group. All papers were double-blind reviewed by at least two expert reviewers. We followed a constructive reviewing process to develop papers and direct authors to other types of submissions when the criteria of full papers were not met. This resulted in 16 full-length papers and two short papers being accepted to be presented at the conference and published in the proceedings, in addition to other poster-style papers to be presented in the conference and that did not appear in the proceedings. The acceptance rate, therefore, was nearly 50%. We are indebted to members of the Program Committee for their help in the reviewing and selection process and providing their comments to us in a timely manner making this event possible.

This book is organized into five parts to reflect the themes of the papers. Part I includes papers that address the adoption of different smart technologies ranging from analytics to smart home devices. Part II presents papers that discuss the adoption and use of social media and different sharing economy models. Part III includes papers that examine the adoption of different Internet-based technologies in government and developing countries. Part IIII includes papers that investigate the general topics of IT project management. The final part includes papers that examine different IS concepts and theories.

Events like these cannot be staged without considerable help and advice from others. Our meeting would not have been possible without the hard work of Peter Bednar as the local organizing chair and Penny Ross as member of the local organizing team. We hope that our meeting and the collection of papers included in these proceedings expand our understanding of the plethora of new technologies that are being offered and adopted in different types of organizations and walks of life and that more work will follow to advance our knowledge in this regard.

September 2018

Amany Elbanna
Yogesh Dwivedi
Deborah Bunker
David Wastell

Organization

Conference Chairs

Amany Elbanna
Yogesh K. Dwivedi
Deborah Bunker
David Wastell

Organizing Chair

Peter Bednar

Program Committee

Carl Adams	University of Portmouth, UK
Jonathan P. Allen	University of San Francisco, USA
Ali Alalwan	Al Balca University, Jordan
Steven Alter	University of San Francisco, USA
Abdullah Baabdullah	King Abdulaziz University, Saudi Arabia
Richard Baskerville	Georgia State University, USA
Peter Bednar	University of Portmouth, UK
Deborah Bunker	University of Sydney, Australia
Donna Champion	Cranfield University, UK
Kieran Conboy	University of Ireland, Galway, Ireland
Jan Damsgaard	Copenhagen Business School, Denmark
Yogesh K. Dwivedi	Swansea University, UK
Andreas Eckhardt	GGS, Germany
Amany Elbanna	Royal Holloway University of London, UK
Brian Fitzgerald	University of Limerick, Ireland
Helle Z. Henriksen	Copenhagen Business School, Denmark
P. Vigneswara Ilavarasan	IIT Delhi, India
Anand Jeyaraj	Wright State University, USA
Karlheinz Kautz	RMIT University, Australia
Arpan Kar	IIT Delhi, India
Banita Lal	University of Bedfordshire, UK
Henrik Lineroth	University of Jonkoping, Sweden
Sven Laumer	University of Bamberg, Germany
Jacob Norbjerg	Copenhagen Business School, Denmark
Jan Pries-Heje	Roskilde University, Denmark
Ravishankar Mayasandra-Nagaraja	Loughborough University, UK

Contents

IT Project Management

Revisiting Concepts and Theories

Being Smart: Adoption Challenges

Establishing an Analytics Capability in a Hospital

Bendik Bygstad[1]([✉]), Egil Øvrelid[1], and Thomas Lie[2]

[1] Department of Informatics, University of Oslo,
Gaustadalléen 23 B, Oslo, Norway
{bendikby,egilov}@ifi.uio.no
[2] Østfold Hospital, Kalnesveien 300, 1714 Grålum, Norway

Abstract. Much of the information produced in hospitals is clinical and stored for the purposes of documentation. In practice, most of it is never used. The potential of analytics is to reuse this information for other purposes. This is easier said than done, because of technical, semantic, legal and organizational hindrances. In particular, hospitals are not organized to leverage the value of big data. In this study we ask, what does it take to establish an analytics capability in a large hospital? Our empirical evidence is a longitudinal study in a high-tech hospital in Norway, where we followed the development an analytics capability, and assessed the organisational benefits. We offer two findings. First, the analytics capability is much more than the technology; it is the network of analytics technology, an analytics team and the medical and administrative decision makers. Second, we identify institutionalization, both organizationally and temporally, of the analytics process as the key success factor.

Keywords: Hospital analytics · Digital infrastructure · Analytics capability

1 Introduction

This study deals with the challenge of establishing an analytics capability at hospitals. The motivation is both practical and theoretical. From a practical point of view, most hospitals produce large amounts of clinical and administrative information every day, but mainly for documentation needs. Most of it is never used for other purposes, such as analytics, in order to support decision-making and improvement processes. From a theoretical perspective, we know much about analytics in general, but much less about analytics in hospitals.

Several challenges have been identified:

- The current portfolios of Health systems are often fragmented and silo oriented, making it difficult to get access to data [1]
- Data are defined and stored in many formats, and the lack of technical and semantic standardisation makes it difficult to combine data from many sources [2]
- Security and privacy concerns are certainly important in the health sector, but also puts serious limitations on the reuse of data [3]

© IFIP International Federation for Information Processing 2019
Published by Springer Nature Switzerland AG 2019.
A. Elbanna et al. (Eds.): TDIT 2018, IFIP AICT 533, pp. 3–14, 2019.
https://doi.org/10.1007/978-3-030-04315-5_1

One issue is clearly under-researched; the organisational aspect of hospital analytics, which deals with the managerial (and to some extent the clinical) use and benefits. Although there is a body of research within strategic management of commercial health organisations [4], the organisation and culture of hospitals are naturally focused on medical treatment. Therefore, we have much less knowledge on how to organise and use analytics, than we have on the technical and application issues. For instance, we know that analytics is more than simply the technology solutions, but what this actually means in a hospital is less clear. We also know little about which governance regime that is effective; should it be centralised or distributed?

Our lens to understand this topic in more depth is analytics capability, which we broadly understand as the ability to produce relevant information, and benefit from analytics [5]. In this explorative study we investigate what is takes to establish an analytics capability in a large hospital, and our research questions are:

- What are the requirements for an analytics capability for a hospital?
- How do we organize an analytics capability for a hospital?

We proceed by reviewing the current research on analytics in general, and the particular challenge of hospital analytics. Then we present our method and empirical evidence, which is a case study in Norway. Our findings highlights that the analytics capability is much more than the technology; it is the network of analytics technology, an analytics team and the medical, administrative and clinical decision makers.

2   Relevant Research

We conduct our research within the information infrastructure perspective [6], which focuses on socio-technical networks, not single systems. This stream of literature have mostly been occupied with evolution of the user base through bootstrapping, network economics and cultivation, and to a lesser degree investigated how re-use of the information contributes to inform patterns of production and performance.

2.1   Analytics

Analytics is defined as "the extensive use of data, statistical and quantitative analysis, explanatory and predictive models, and fact-based management to drive decisions and actions" [7:9–10]. The definition highlights two important aspects; it is *extensive* use of data (i.e. *Big Data*, not simply using quantitative material) and the aim is to *drive decisions and actions* (not simply providing background information for managers).

Both the media and research have provided spectacular examples of how analytics (and "Big Data") have provided new insights and competitive advantage. Global platform firms, such as Google and Facebook, base their multisided business models on analytics, and in the public sector police and tax authorities use analytics to uncover new patterns and insights. In industrial and retail environments, *process analytics* provides a tool for on-going improvement and optimisation [7].

In order to leverage analytics, it is commonly assumed that an organisation needs to develop an *analytics capability*, [5] defined as "the ability to utilize resources to perform a business analytics task, based on the interaction between IT assets and other firm resources" [5:4]. To help practitioners and researchers to assess a particular instance, some analytics maturity frameworks have been introduced [5].

2.2 Hospital Analytics

Several researchers have pointed to the large potential of analytics within health care. Some uses are:

- *Medical research* based on large datasets, such as images, medical signs and genomics data repositories [8, 9]
- *Clinical decision support* including machine learning and AI solutions for IT supported clinical decision making [10] and ambient intelligence solutions [11]
- *Logistics,* for instance flow of patients, and waiting lists [12]
- *Management,* such as financial and process management [13, 14]
- *Quality management,* such as key factors for patient satisfaction [15]

Despite these promises, the status of hospital analytics is generally poor; partly because of fragmented clinical systems and partly because of lack of analytics capacity [2]. In order to understand the issues in more depth we conducted a case study at a high-tech hospital in Norway.

3 Method and Case

The setting for our empirical research is Kalnes general hospital in Østfold County (near Oslo) in Norway. Østfold has about 300.000 inhabitants. The 85.500 square meters high-tech hospital opened in November 2015 and replaced the old Fredrikstad hospital. Kalnes has one of Norway's largest emergency units in addition to general hospital functions such as delivery wards, clinical and surgical departments and psychiatry. Kalnes Hospital serves as an extreme case of our area of concern [16], because of the ambitious efforts to integrate and align clinical work processes and patient records keeping with novel innovative technology to support horizontal process innovation and coordination.

Our case study research approach is based on engaged scholarship [17, 18] inspired by an "insiders ontology" [19] where informants are not only sources of empirical data, but also helpful in constructing narratives and discuss theoretical and practical implications [17]. The approach requires a longitudinal perspective, with strong and trustful relationships between researchers and practitioners.

Our unit of analysis is the whole hospital, i.e. how analytics can exploit the whole digital infrastructure of the hospital. Selected cases are therefore hospitals that have a high degree of digitalisation. Such "extreme cases" are a prerequisite for developing a state-of-the-art analytical capability, and well suited to develop new theory [16].

3.1   Data Collection

From July 2016 to January 2018, we conducted 33 interviews, with CEO, CTO, process manager, analytics experts, clinicians, project leaders, technical experts and cleaning personnel as well as system suppliers. Round one started with interviews where Kalnes management and project leaders presented the main goals as well as the organizing of the IT oriented process innovation initiative. We proceeded by performing observations within the emergency unit and the health wards, where challenges related to process flow were addressed. We followed up with new interviews as well as analyses of documents on patient treatment regulations, political requirements from the regional health authorities and descriptions of the technical solutions. We also participated in local and regional meetings and workshops where findings, including ours, were discussed. Through this bottom-up-investigation, we identified coordinative actors, actors whose central role is to plan and coordinate the movement of patients and information across hospital departments, and were particularly interested in how they use IT to perform and coordinate their work.

In round two, we observed meetings at all levels, particularly the ones related to flow challenges, and where analytics was used in order to shed light on patterns of production and performance. Data was used extensively to inform decisions and solving concrete challenges (Tables 1 and 2).

Table 1. Data collection

Year	Activity and participants	Data
2016–2018	33 Interviews with CEO, CTO, Analytic experts, Process manager, Project managers, clinicians, staff	Goals and purpose of the project, strategic and organizational development and system/analytics implementation
2016–2018	Around 60 h of observation	Views and results of the implementation, the relation between information and decision Use of analytics to identify patterns of performance and production and decision-making
2016–2018	Documentation of process design, system design and technical issues	204 pages on system design, process descriptions, work descriptions

3.2   Data Analysis

We first established a chronology of important events, before we investigated in detail what it takes to establish and maintain analytics activities. In particular, we analysed the interplays between the technologies in use, the analytics team and the various decision makers. From this we constructed a framework of the requirements needed for enabling analytic. Lastly, we analysed and assessed the organisation of the analytics activities.

Table 2. Data analyses

Step	Description	Output
1	Establishing a chronology 2013-16	Case description, Fig. 1
2	Elements in establishing an analytics capability	Sections 4.1 and 4.2
3	Practical and theoretical implications of analytics	Sections 5.1 and 5.2

3.3   Case Chronology

Background 2013–2016

Kalnes Hospital opened in 2015, but work had started already in 2013 to improve horizontal process performance. A work group with organizational workers as well as a number of external consultants modelled 65 work processes. Most of these work processes were sub-processes of 38 different clinical pathways. The Kalnes hospital management signed a contract with a supplier called Imatis. The Imatis solution included three main services:

- A solution for patient self check-in and dealing with queues
- A system for visualisation of patient flow and logistics, with whiteboards
- A message broker for distribution of messages to mobile phones and other units

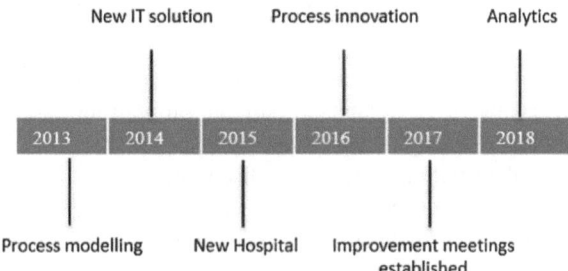

Fig. 1. Chronology

A separate group worked with the details of the Imatis solution and the integration between the package of EPR systems and Imatis to digitalize the processes. The "regional package" consisted of more than 300 applications, maintained and run by the regional IT Centre. The key applications were the electronic patient record (EPR) system, lab system, radiology system and chart and medication system. Because of slow progress, the governance of the start-up package was transferred from the big regional Digital Renewal program, to the Kalnes Hospital project in order to reach the deadline for the opening of the hospital in 2015. The Imatis, or lightweight solution, to support logistics and communication, was strongly supported by the management, and organized as a sub-project.

The solution used self check-in automats, mobile phones, tablets and electronic whiteboards, which were modelled in the processes. The hospital opened November 2015, and the start-up was, although successful, not without challenges. Kalnes was the first hospital in Norway that to this extent used a combination of process innovation technology – to improve patient flow – and the package of EPR systems feeding Imatis through a common interface. At the same time, the combination of these two system regimes enabled the organization to both improve the performance and the communication of the performance, and inspired the organization to strive for continual improvement. The improved transparency of horizontal processes has led to the establishment of collaborative arenas to discuss and find solutions to flow issues. A common aspect of these meetings is that they are short, around 10–15 min, and targeted, and they have become arenas for both identifying challenges and make decisions to deal with them.

The coming of analytics 2017–2018

The main reason for the relatively significant change from being merely occupied with the functional production, to strengthen the focus on horizontal performance, was "a deep feeling of crises related to the patient flow" [process director]. The waiting time at the emergency unit was over 5 h. In 2016, they found that, despite all the work on process innovation, there were few clear improvements in patient flow. Consequently, they had to address the challenges more systematically. They established several interdisciplinary work groups and corresponding arenas to discuss the specific challenges. Examples of such arenas and meetings are improvement teams, capacity meetings, interdisciplinary improvement meeting and weekly status meeting between process director and the teams. The point is to monitor and improve performance on several important areas.

- Improved overview of performance related to interventions
- Improve the overview of lag related to patients on waiting lists
- Identify the amount of postponed interventions
- The time of day when patients are being discharged
- How long it takes to switch between interventions
- Occupancy rate per department

The process director is occupied with underuse and overuse of resources in order to optimize performance. "Our main goal is to ensure even and secure patient flow". But, what does it take to establish an analytic capability in order to reach this goal?

4   Findings

In this part, we will first describe the background for obtaining an analytics capability, that is, what does it take to establish, implement and maintain institutionalization of analytics? Then we describe insights from the particular inform and decision structure Kalnes have established through this work. By institutionalization, we mean that the practice of performing analytics is implemented into the organization as regular activities.

4.1   Analytics Capability

In 2016 when Kalnes acknowledged that the work on process innovation - although successful in changing the digital infrastructure and make more use of information - had made little impact on the flow performance, they decided to establish an analytics capability within the organisation.

The first move was to organise an analytics team, consisting of two data scientists and two clinicians. The team established an ETA structure (Fig. 2) where data from clinical core systems and Imatis was loaded into a file system/transformation system and transformed into analytical data. The task may seem trivial, but neither DIPS nor MetaVision – two of the core clinical systems - had APIs from where structured and 'ready-made' data could be extracted. MetaVision's APIs were inaccessible, and data thus had to be delivered from the supplier to the analytics team. DIPS data sometimes had to be restructured and contextualized to make sense together with Imatis data. The Imatis data were easier to access and extract because of the suppliers interest in making data available across particular sections of the hospital.

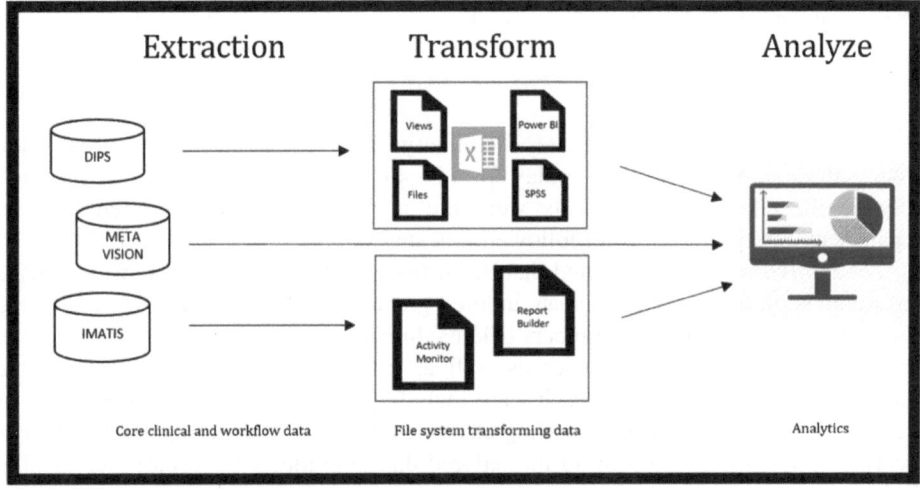

Fig. 2. The ETL process

In addition, this structured ETA system had to be maintained and developed further. The continuous work with data gave qualified insight into how data might be brought together in order to provide a foundation for decision. In this way, the analytics team became a significant expertise on patterns of performance.

The second part of the analytics capability was the establishment of improvement teams, consisting of clinicians and managers. The key task for the improvement teams was to make use of the available analytics to take better decisions. They met regularly to make sense of the data and to take running decisions based on them. At the meetings, important actors from the respective wards participated in the interdisciplinary meetings, provided explanations, and suggested possible solutions to solve a challenge. We offer, below, a more detailed description of how this was organised.

4.2   Organisation of Analytics Process

Five different teams were established as the decision-making part of the analytics capability, as shown in Table 3.

Table 3. Teams in the analytic capability

Meeting	Frequency	Participants	Analytics
Capacity meeting	Every day	Managers at medicine and surgery depts.	Bed capacity
Top management team	Weekly	Top managers	Trends
Cross-disciplinary improvement team	Weekly	Managers	Patient flow and various indicators
Status with process director	Weekly	Analytics team	Patient flow, data
Process improvement patient flow	Bi-weekly	Clinic managers	Patient flow

One of the meetings was the interdisciplinary improvement meeting, chaired by the process director and held every Friday from 08:45. It is a short and intensive meeting, only 15–20 min. The participants were the managers from the different clinical departments. A typical meeting followed this structure:

The analytics expert presented data from both Imatis and EPR systems like Dips and Metavision (see Fig. 2) to create tailored graphs and columns showing trends and fluctuations. The graphs and numbers belonged mainly within three categories of data: time spent on particular processes as well as how long patients are admitted; the number of patients admitted to each ward including corridors, and the performance of the housekeeping department regarding cleaning and dietary services from the order is received to completion. All in all the tailored data provides a good basis for making decisions.

The clinical managers (doctors and nurses) would often interrupt to ask questions: Why is the trend not reflecting the influenza season? Can I have details specified only for my own department? And sometimes protests: This graph shows that our throughput efficiency is lower than the others, but the numbers do not reflect the particulars of our process.

The Process director might take decisions at the table. An example was a decision to admit more than one patient to each patient rooms during the influenza season. Another is to order particular rooms to be cleaned at particular times, for example at 2 pm when the number of tasks may create performance bottlenecks. The ward managers provide contexts for why the numbers is as they are, and what they have done to deal with them. The ward managers might also suggest particular solutions to each challenge, but also request further data to gain more insight. A ward manager said that

I need an overview of the NIV patients (patients with copd, multiple sclerosis or in need of a respirator) and how much each room is used by the particular patient category. To improve the performance i need more data. Facts are very important.

The point with the meeting, then, was cooperation across different sections. As the clinical doctors may "be afraid to lose their beds" [ward manager], some of the data may create tensions. This because logistics might threaten the integrity of medical decisions provided by the clinicians. "I only show numbers, but they must be displayed carefully so that clinicians are not provoked," the analytic expert comments. He continued saying that the meeting has improved the cooperation in that "they understand each other's problems". He also claimed that the "understanding of the mechanisms leading to the trends is increased by repeated focus." "Although it is hard constantly seeking improvement, we know that it takes time to build a culture for doing this." The process director agreed, and claimed that "the meeting has given [the organizational actors] an ability to see the whole that was absent earlier."

5   Discussion

In this part, we return to our research questions. According to Davenport [7: 9-10], analytics is the "extensive use of data, statistical and quantitative analysis, explanatory and predictive models, and fact-based management to drive decisions and actions." Framing this within infrastructure theory [6], we are interested in the relations between the elements described in Sect. 4.1. What does it take to connect the elements in a way that establish an analytic capability? This will be addressed in Sect. 5.1 where we ask: What are the requirements for an analytics capability for a hospital? In the Sect. 5.2 we respond to the question: How do we organize an analytics capability for a hospital?

5.1   What Are the Requirements for an Analytics Capability for a Hospital?

Cosic [5] define analytics capability as "the ability to utilize resources to perform a business analytics task, based on the interaction between IT assets and other firm resources". It is not enough to have all the elements; they have to be connected. Their value as analytic capability rests on the establishment of a network between them, enabling interaction.

In Sect. 4.1, we identified three central elements in establishing an analytic capability at Kalnes hospital. Figure 3 illustrates our overall argument.

The *technology* is important, in that structured and systematic data collection and analyses are at the core of decision-making. A core element is the ETL process, which transforms transaction data into actionable information.

Then, the *analytics team*, in that data has to be carved out, re-structured, and appropriated in order to be comparable. This team really has to understand the detailed context and relationship between detailed clinical data in order to enable a qualified synchronization of these data across wards and sections.

The third element, the *decision makers*, comprises in addition to the medical expertise, also the administrative and strategic management. The administrative

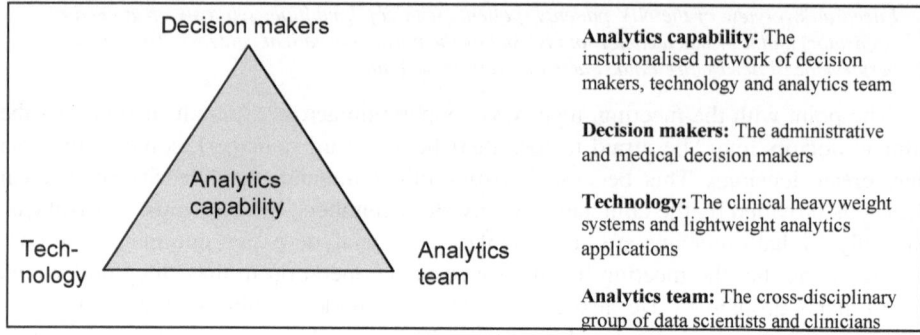

Fig. 3. Elements of the analytics capability

management is distributed within the organization, for example as ward managers, or as workflow coordinator within and between wards. The top management like the process director or research director both take important decision to overarching challenges, and contributes to fulfilling the performance goals set by strategic management.

At Kalnes, these elements, although organized separately, flourished through the interaction. The interdisciplinary improvement meeting where graphs and patterns identified through technology, interpreted and visualized by the analytics team, and displayed in front of decision makers who respond to challenges, demonstrates the advanced capability of Kalnes to use data in the decision-making.

The common team of *improved performance,* aligning medical and logistical interests served by precise and detailed data on performance and production, contributed strongly to bind the elements in the triangle together. This was a foundation for the institutionalization of analytics: the ability to implement, adopt and maintain analytics for a longer time.

Thus, the analytics capability is much more than the technology; it is the on-going network of analytics technology (including the clinical systems), an analytics team and the medical and administrative decision makers. We regard this as an evolving information infrastructure.

5.2   How Do We Organize an Analytics Capability for a Hospital?

Research has shown a significant potential for improvement of patient flow by visual analytics, but creation of shared understandings and shared interpretations are essential for the success of the analytics project [1]. We believe that the key to this is continuous engagement with stakeholders, and in particular we think it is essential to institutionalize the co-operation as a learning process.

How should analytics be formally organised? Davenport [7] recommended a centralised approach, because analytics requires specialised competence. Also, a centralised unit is more likely to prevail over time. Our findings support this, as the success of the analytics group at Kalnes corroborate. However, this point should not be overstated. Our evidence indicates that the most important success factor is the close and regular co-operation between the analytics team and the decision makers. This is because visual analytics is highly contextual [1], and requires continuous interaction and learning. As our case clearly shows, institutionalization of analytics depends on something more than merely the technological extraction of sophisticated data. In the case of Kalnes, we do not believe that the hospital would have been well served by a regional analytics solution, which would have been too far from the decision makers.

At Kalnes hospital the network of technology, analytics team and decision makers worked so closely that they had to be positioned with proximity. This kept the analytics work more intensive, with shorter loops from needed information was requested until it was received, and with more agility in the performance. The elements in the analytics network need to be kept close so that the challenges are taken seriously and solutions may be suggested right away. However, there is a need to maintain a balance between managerial goals and local adaptation. This also because an important overlaying aspect is the importance of management participating in analytics. To motivate for the continuous analytics process, the management has to make sure that institutional performance is actually improved, and that necessary resources are given to the teams and actors. There is consequently a continuous interaction between top management, ward management and clinicians in order to enable and leverage the data-driven organisation.

5.3 Conclusion and Limitations

This study deals with the practical and theoretical challenge of establishing an analytics capability at hospitals. Through a case study at a high-tech hospital in Norway, we offer two contributions. First, the analytics capability is much more than the technology; it is the network of analytics technology, an analytics team and the medical and administrative decision makers. Second, we identify institutionalization, both organizationally and temporally, of the analytics process as the key success factor.

In this study, we have not interviewed patients or relatives, but focuses on the interplay of managers, clinicians and IT staff. The paper is primarily practice-oriented, and we acknowledge that a deeper and more precise investigation into analytics capability will require more quantification and more precise criteria for measuring such capabilities.

References

1. Fitzgerald, J.A., Dadich, A.: Using visual analytics to improve hospital scheduling and patient flow. J. Theor. Appl. Electron. Commer. Res. 4(2), 20–30 (2009)
2. Raghupathi, W., Raghupathi, V.: Big data analytics in healthcare: promise and potential. Health Inf. Sci. Syst. 2, 3 (2014)
3. Bellala, G., Huberman, B.A.: Securing Private Data Sharing in Multi-Party Analytics, 29 July 2016. SSRN: https://ssrn.com/abstract=2816140 or https://doi.org/10.2139/ssrn.2816140
4. Swayne, L.E., Duncan, W.J., Ginter, P.M.: Strategic Management of Health Care Organizations. Wiley, Chichester (2012)

5. Cosic, R., Shanks, G., Maynard, S.: Towards a business analytics capability maturity model. In: Proceeding of 23rd Australasian Conference on Information Systems, Geelon (2012)
6. Hanseth, O., Lyytinen, K.: Design theory for dynamic complexity in information infrastructures: the case of building internet. JIT **25**(1), 1–19 (2010)
7. Davenport, T.H.: Enterprise Analytics. Pearson, Upper Saddle River (2014)
8. Belle, A., Thiagarajan, R., Reza Soroushmehr, S.M., Navidi, F., Beard, D.A., Najarian, K.: Big data analytics in healthcare. Biomed. Res. Int. **2015**, 16 (2015). https://doi.org/10.1155/2015/370194. Article ID 370194
9. Wang, Y., Kung, L., Wang, W.Y.C., Cegielski, C.G.: An integrated big data analytics-enabled transformation model: application to health care. Inf. Manage. **55**(1), 64–79 (2018)
10. Kannampallil, T.G., Franklin, A., Mishra, R., Almoosa, K.F., Cohen, T., Patel, V.L.: Understanding the nature of information seeking behavior in critical care: implications for the design of health information technology. Artif. Intell. Med. **57**(1), 21–29 (2013)
11. Acampora, G, Cook, D.J., Rashidi, P., Vasilakos, A.V.: A survey on ambient intelligence in healthcare. In: Proceedings of the IEEE, vol. 101, no. 12 (2013)
12. Bygstad, B., Bergquist, M.: Horizontal affordances for patient centred care in hospitals. In: Proceedings of the 51st Hawaii International Conference on System Sciences (2018)
13. Agarwal, R., Gao, G., DesRoches, C., Jha, A.K.: Research commentary—the digital transformation of healthcare: current status and the road ahead. Inf. Syst. Res. **21**(4), 796–809 (2010)
14. Fichman, R.G., Kohli, R., Krishnan, R.: The role of information systems in healthcare: current research and future trends. Inf. Syst. Res. **22**(3), 419–428 (2011)
15. Anhang Price, R., et al.: Examining the role of patient experience surveys in measuring health care quality. Med. Care Res. Rev. **71**(5), 522–554 (2014)
16. Gerring, J.: Case Study Research: Principles and Practices. Cambridge University Press, Cambridge (2006)
17. Bygstad, B., Munkvold, B.E.: Exploring the role of informants in interpretive case studies research in IS. J. Inf. Technol. **26**, 32–45 (2011)
18. Mathiassen, L.: Designing engaged scholarship: from real-world problems to research publications. Engaged Manage. Rev. **1**, 2 (2017)
19. Garud, R., Kumaraswamy, A., Karnøe, P.: Path dependence or path creation. J. Manage. Stud. **47**(4), 760–774 (2010)

Why Governing Data Is Difficult: Findings from Danish Local Government

Olivia Benfeldt Nielsen[1]([✉]), John Stouby Persson[2], and Sabine Madsen[1]

[1] Aalborg University, Fibigerstræde 3, 9220 Aalborg, Denmark
{obn, sam}@dps.aau.dk
[2] Aalborg University, Selma Lagerlöfsvej 300, 9220 Aalborg, Denmark
john@cs.aau.dk

Abstract. Data governance has emerged as a promising approach for transforming organizations. While governing data as an organizational asset has clear benefits, no previous studies have reported on the particular challenges faced by practitioners in local government organizations. Against this backdrop, we investigate why it is difficult for local government organizations to explore and exploit their data assets with data governance. Following an engaged scholarship approach, we carried out six group interviews conducted with 34 representatives from 13 different Danish municipalities. From the analysis, we identified nine challenges relating to three overall themes that are critical to governing data in local government: (1) data value and overview, (2) data practices and collaboration and (3) data capabilities and politics. We explain how the three themes extend previous research in data governance and e-government literature. The implications for practice and directions for future research are discussed.

Keywords: Data governance · Public sector · Municipalities · E-government Local government · Engaged scholarship

1 Introduction

Open data, big data and predictive analytics have long promised to transform entire industries and society. Especially public-sector organizations, who routinely store large volumes of data, are keen to pursue new opportunities and create new services, but are frequently restrained by problems with their data [1]. Issues of quality, availability or accuracy appear as distinct barriers, but resolving these only constitute short-term solutions [2]. Harvesting value from data requires mastering the basics of information management, but this is not a job for the IT function alone [3]. Instead, the entire organization needs an overarching direction and here data governance has emerged as a promising approach.

Data governance refers to who holds the decision rights and is held accountable for an organization's decision-making regarding its data assets [4]. It sets the direction for an organization's data management practices. However, data governance literature is still scarce. Scholars in the field construct data governance as frameworks of decision-domains based on theoretical and at times empirical synthesis, but rarely address

© IFIP International Federation for Information Processing 2019
Published by Springer Nature Switzerland AG 2019.
A. Elbanna et al. (Eds.): TDIT 2018, IFIP AICT 533, pp. 15–29, 2019.
https://doi.org/10.1007/978-3-030-04315-5_2

processes of implementation and adoption in practice [5]. While conceptual studies are important, they provide little actionable direction for organizations. Furthermore, no studies report explicitly on the particular challenges of governing data in public organizations [6].

This paper examines data governance challenges faced by local government organizations at the municipal level of the public sector in Denmark. This is a particularly interesting case as Denmark is a world leading country in digitisation according to Europe's Digital Economy and Society Index [7]. Denmark introduced mandatory digital self-service with an 87% adoption rate as of 2016 [8]. This means that storage of digital data about citizens has exploded in the past years, demanding better data management practices. Also, the newest national digital strategy contains three goals that all depend on a number of underlying specific initiatives related to data. This includes better use of data to enable quicker case processing, public sector data as a driver for growth, and increased attention to protect data [9].

For Danish municipalities, who will be responsible for a large part of the implementation, the national initiatives will compel them to undertake structured ways of managing their data with data governance. Doing so, may in some cases seem irrelevant or even at conflict with their primary obligations as a public agency and thus complicate the endeavour to implement data governance. In addition, the creation of value from data requires both exploration of potential opportunities and exploitation of existing assets [10, 11], which in the implementation of strategy may come in many different forms [12]. Exploring data is about generating new insights, while exploiting data about applying these insights [10, 13]. As each have different objectives, it is crucial to recognize the distinction at the outset of any data initiative [13], including data governance. In this context, our paper addresses the research question: *Why is it difficult for local government organizations to explore and exploit their data assets with data governance?*

To elaborate, we focus on the management of large amounts of heterogenous data, from a variety of systems in local government organizations. This is based on the assumption that managing this data requires data governance. We address the research question through engaged scholarship [14]. Following the collaborative variant, we have engaged in joint formulation of problems with municipal practitioners to get an understanding of the challenges that might make it difficult to apply the data governance literature's recommendations in practice [15].

The paper is structured as follows. First, relevant literature is presented. Next, we describe the research approach and detail the data collection and analysis. Subsequently, we present our findings in the form of nine challenges that are central to the municipalities in relation to exploring and exploiting their data assets. The challenges are summarized as three overall themes that provide a succinct answer to the research question. We discuss the findings' contribution to research, implications for practice, and directions for future research. A short conclusion ends the paper.

2   Theoretical Background

Information has been an issue of strategic importance for decades, but recent techno-logical developments have enabled the storage of more information than ever. Data may be considered the building blocks of information [16], and so managing infor-mation as a strategic resource means ensuring responsible treatment of data as orga-nizational assets. Organizations should therefore be aware of their data to use them effectively and ensure their quality; as volume increases, the complexity of managing data will as well [6]. Here, data governance emerges as a structured approach. Scholars frequently discuss data governance in the context of ensuring data quality, presenting this as one of the primary goals of data governance [17–19]. While quality is important, it is only one element of effective data governance, which must be driven by and aligned with business goals [4, 17, 20, 21]. Data governance may then be defined as *companywide processes that specify decision-making rights and responsibilities aligned with organisational goals to encourage desirable behaviour in the treatment of data as an organisational asset* [22, 23]. In other words, data governance sets the principles and direction for an organization's data management practices.

Only few studies within the data governance field focus on implementation and adoption of data governance in practice. Begg and Caira investigate the dilemmas faced by organizations when pursuing data governance, in the context of small to medium enterprises (SMEs) [24]. They identify a series of relevant "quandaries". First, orga-nizations may not recognize the inherent value of their data, nor will they perceive it as existing separate from the IT systems, and some organizations may not even be able to access their data, because it is *"trapped"* with vendors. Secondly, organizations may understand the value data governance can deliver, but may ultimately decide that the effort to achieve this by far exceeds the perceived benefits [24]. These findings indicate that practitioners find it difficult to grasp the value-creating potential of data gover-nance. In another study, Begg and Caira also found that managerial and executive understanding and awareness of data have *major influence* on the organization's ability to conceive a data governance strategy [25]. These studies are relevant to our research because they highlight the importance of understanding value, when implementing data governance, but it is not clear whether this applies to public organizations as well.

Another study has focused explicitly on the public sector, albeit with the per-spective of establishing a master data management function [26]. These findings suggest establishing master data management is difficult due to a series of paradoxes. First, there is a need to identify data owners, but people remain committed to group specific functions, and not to organization-wide development. Second, although there is a recognized need for data governance, tasks and responsibilities are avoided. Third, there is a recognized need for an organization-wide vision of master data, yet individual views remain the order of the day [26]. These findings suggest implementing data-related programs across organizational units is challenging in a public-sector context, but it remains unclear whether this also applies to data governance.

The abovementioned findings suggest that practitioners find it difficult to discover, understand and harness the value-creating potential of data. As such, it provides a starting point for addressing the research question and understanding the challenges of governing data in municipalities. Concepts of exploration and exploitation [10–12] are used to characterize the identified challenges, because distinguishing between these is crucial in data initiatives [13].

3 Research Approach

Our methodology can be described as engaged scholarship [14] with a particular focus on the formulation of problems *with* (*not for*) practitioners [15]. We followed the collaborative form of engaged scholarship to "*co-produce basic knowledge about a complex problem*" [14]. We collaborated with participants in a Danish network for municipal IT practitioners and researchers. The network was founded in 2009 as part of a joint IS research project with a number of municipalities, seeking to increase the degree of public digitalisation and municipalities' ability to innovate with IT. In its current form, the network consists of 13 municipalities and a dozen IS researchers, who collaborate on a set number of workshops and theme days each year. The participating members have previous experiences with engaging in academic IS scholarship, which helped the researchers gain access to the setting, create trust with informants, facilitate cultural understanding and establish rapport [27, 28]. It should be noted that our point of departure for this study is the problem "owners" in practice, namely people working with data in local government. Therefore, we are only concerned with the citizens perspective to the degree, that practitioners bring it up.

3.1 Research Setting

Denmark is a consensual and technologically advanced society. In the Digital Economy and Society Index (2017) that summarises indicators on Europe's digital performance and competitiveness, Denmark holds the first place and is described as a world leader in digitisation [7]. The Danish national digital strategy for 2016–2020 [9] aims to further enhance the use of IT in the public sector in order to deliver good, efficient and coherent services to citizens and businesses. Moreover, the strategy contains three goals that incorporate better use of data to enable quicker case processing, public sector data as a driver for growth, and increased attention to protect data. While interpreting the national digital strategy entails complexities of prioritization, it is highly influential on both central and local government practice [29]. Danish municipalities are somewhat de-centralised and they commission and manage their own data repositories in addition to the central registers. The municipalities are not merely the executive wing of central government. They have a great deal of autonomy in how they organize the delivery of public services and are responsible for a large part of the Danish welfare state, with primary education, day care for children, social welfare, and care of the elderly as important examples. Danish municipalities constitute an interesting case because they already collect and manage vast amounts of data on their citizens. Historically, the governance of IT acquisition and development has been decentralized, focusing mainly on individual and departmental needs, causing a current landscape that is fragmented and consists of hundreds of different systems, across departments within a single municipality. This has resulted in vast amounts of heterogenous, and at times redundant, data across the municipalities, that is in dire need of governance. Ensuring that these data are managed responsibly (exploitation), as well as used to generate new value (exploration) has implications for Danish society as a whole.

3.2   Data Collection

The empirical data was collected by the first author using semi-structured group interviews. The group interview is a qualitative data gathering technique that has the advantages of being inexpensive, data rich, flexible, stimulating to respondents, recall aiding, cumulative and elaborative, over and above individual responses [27]. The participants were members of the abovementioned network and came from several different layers of the municipalities, ranging from managers, to consultants, project managers and technical experts.

As there is a lack of existing empirical studies of data governance in the public sector, group interviews were used in this study to gain empirical data from several hierarchical levels in order to cover a "variety of voices" [30]. Municipalities differ across many characteristics, including size and digital maturity. Group interviews across (and among) practitioners in municipalities therefore allowed for nuances of practice to be brought forth, as the participants could discuss and reflect amongst themselves [27].

The data was collected through six sessions spanning a period of three months (see Table 1). Two sessions were of a general character including participants from different municipalities, and three sessions involved participants from the same municipality. One session only had one participant, and therefore functioned as a classic semi-structured interview [30].

Table 1. Activities for data collection

#	Activity	Participants	Hours
1	General group session	13 representatives from 9 municipalities	3
2	Individual session	1 representative from 1 municipality	1,5
3	Individual group session	4 representatives from 1 municipality	1,5
4	Individual group session	2 representatives from 1 municipality	1
5	Individual group session	2 representatives from 1 municipality	1
6	General group session	20 representatives from 12 municipalities	6
	Total	34 representatives from 13 municipalities	14

The first session introduced data governance as a viable practice and we received feedback from practitioners regarding the necessity for and utility of such an approach in municipal settings. Between session #1 and #6, the first author conducted four interviews, which had the purpose of unfolding specific barriers, challenges, or difficulties related to working with data. As these sessions had fewer participants from the same organization, more time was available for each of the participants to express their views and it was possible to touch upon topics of more sensitive character. The last session focused on presenting, discussing and validating findings, and encouraging further dialogue on how to work with data governance going forward.

3.3   Data Analysis

The data was coded following the conventional approach to qualitative content analysis [31]. First by reading transcripts and field notes, highlighting interesting or relevant parts and collecting them in a separate document. Upon completion, the extracted quotes were arranged as challenges and named. The material was then coded again, using the newly constructed challenges to collapse any duplicates and reduce potential internal contradictions. The process was repeated until challenges could no longer be created, collapsed or split.

In order to reduce potential bias, the last general group session functioned as a site to test the validity of the identified challenges. The last group session had the highest turn out, and thus allowed for valuable refinement of the findings from a variety of perspectives. The analysis resulted in the identification of nine challenges that were further conceptualized at a higher level of abstraction as three main themes (see Table 2).

Table 2. Findings from the analysis

Theme	Challenges	#
Data value and overview	Short-term perspective on data usage	1
	Value from data initiatives are difficult to understand	2
	Lack of overview of existing data	3
Data practices and collaboration	Autonomy within the different departments	4
	Distrust toward data in social fields	5
	Lack of cross-organizational collaboration	6
Data capabilities and politics	Varying levels of data maturity across different departments	7
	Lack of top-level support for data initiatives	8
	Lack of political focus on data usage in municipal context	9

4   Findings

In this section, we present each theme and then detail the challenges it consists of.

4.1   Data Value and Overview

The first three challenges presented above show that efforts to explore and exploit data are complicated by short-term perspectives on usage, lacking overview of existing data sources, and a poor understanding of data value. The three challenges can be summarized under the theme Data value and overview, which emphasizes the municipalities' struggle to understand and express the value-creating potential of data.

Short-term Perspective on Data Usage. A recurring challenge throughout all the sessions revolved around the lack of understanding of what data can be used for, beyond the context of its immediate practice. Currently, data is primarily considered convenient for performing a specific workflow and as a by-product of working in a digital environment: *"Many of those who work with data are not used to thinking of data as an asset [...] It's usually very convenient if [they] can see a citizen in both systems because it's updated... but that's it"* (Development consultant).

Another participant describes municipalities as 'sober', when it comes to collecting and using data. The challenge is framed as a mindset that needs to be changed, rather than specific processes that have to be implemented: *"A municipality is sober: it looks at what we can use data for right now. We have to reverse the approach and acknowledge we have to collect data, even though we do not quite know what we need them for yet, and it's a mental change of dimensions"* (Head of IT).

What needs to happen is a change of the mindset in going from a reactionary to a proactive view on data. However, this will not happen by itself. The employees have to be introduced to the somewhat abstract idea of seeing data as an asset: *"People need to be told this story that you can see data as either something you depend on in being reactive, or where you consider it an asset [and] become a little more proactive"* (Development consultant).

Central points highlighted under this challenge indicate that municipalities find it difficult to start exploring the value-creating opportunities that data might have, because the Danish municipality employees are very focused on their primary obligation, i.e. the day-to-day operations of welfare services. Becoming more data-driven is therefore a major change to the organizational mindset.

Value from Data Initiatives Are Difficult to Understand. Although the participants show enthusiasm and see potential in working more structured with data, they find it challenging to express the potential value to stakeholders in the rest of the organization. Especially framing the value of data initiatives to ensure economic resources for data related projects is difficult: *"Our BI (Business Intelligence) system has been three years on the way, and it has taken us long to convince our management to spend just minimal resources on this. It's hard to sell the idea of infrastructure and data as [infrastructure] upward in the organization"* (IT architect).

While the benefits seem clear to the project members, it is challenging to communicate the value of data initiatives to executive levels. At the same time, other participants question the value, but hear from other municipalities it is 'the best thing' to do: *"We find it hard to spot the value, but we know ... that someone says it's just the best thing you can do. It's also a good foundation [to invest in data governance] and our gut feeling tells us it's a good idea, but we just want this specific use case that illustrates 'this is what we're going to create the foundation for'"* (Financial consultant).

What follows is an amalgamation of issues, where municipal practitioners attempt to secure resources to build an appropriate infrastructure for the future use of data (exploitation). Yet to succeed with this, they need a persuasive, illustrative use case (exploration) to convince the top layers of the organization of the relevance of investing in the use of data as an asset. As such, issues of exploration and exploitation are closely tied together here.

Lack of Overview of Existing Data. Related to challenges of building appropriate infrastructure, most of the municipalities are challenged by fragmented enterprise architecture and legacy systems. In many cases, the municipalities do not even have access to some of their own data, as it is stored on servers placed with the vendors, who delivered the original system, and they demand high costs for providing access. This makes it near impossible to gain an overview of what data actually exists, where it is, who has access to it, and how it may generate value: *"One thing is the complexity of many different solutions, but it is something else to have 40 years of legacy systems that have been implemented at random. There was no consideration of infrastructure at that time [...] we are sitting on a gold mine of data and knowledge that we do not even know about"* (Head of IT).

At the forefront is a very concrete obstacle to exploit data assets, as they are downright difficult to access in legacy systems. Simultaneously, this also makes exploring potential value-generation nearly impossible, as no overview exists.

4.2   Data Practice and Collaboration

The next three challenges show that lack of cross-organizational collaboration and high degrees of autonomy within the departments makes it difficult to start governing data and exploit data assets, while distrust in certain professional domains further complicates data exploration efforts. The challenges can be summarized under the theme Data practices and collaboration, which emphasizes that diverse, local practices make it difficult for municipalities to design and implement shared data governance principles and practices.

Autonomy within the Different Departments. To ensure data treatment in line with the principles set forth by the data governance programme, some degree of standardized processes is necessary. Enforcing this in highly specialized and autonomous departments will be a central challenge according to several participants. The high level of autonomy is pointed to as a distinct feature of the public as opposed to the private sector: *"This is the way you implement decisions, and it is very different [from the private sector], and there is a lot of room for interpretation that makes things not so straightforward"* (Head of IT).

It is highly likely that the different departments will implement a local adaption of a decision, that fits their existing practice, rather than follow the standardized directions. To curb this problem, it is suggested to frame the principles as being of value to the departments, but this would vary too much between the different fields: *"Ideally, it should be of value, but there is a big difference between speaking to a technical department full of engineers, or [speaking to] nurses, pedagogues and teachers, because [then] you should really know your visiting hours and how to communicate"* (Development consultant).

As such, exploiting data assets in departments that are used to and comfortable with working structured and systematically with data will not require the same effort as it will in domains, where exploiting data is not common practice.

Distrust Toward Data in Social Fields. In the same vein as trying to deal with autonomous departments, some professionals remain highly skeptical towards data governance and the role of data in their particular domain. Especially departments within social fields remain distrustful, as their profession is about making individual, subjective judgements regarding sensitive cases: *"Here ..., it is more feeling for the individual case and [they are asking the question] what is it even data is. Here, the anxiety [regarding data] is more pronounced"* (Financial consultant).

In addition, some professionals fear an increase in visibility of data regarding their cases, to other parts of the organization will expose them. They worry it may result in someone higher up making decisions regarding their domain, based on this data, without consulting them. Especially a fear that others might misinterpret data is apparent: *"People fear you interpret the data incorrectly, so just trusting that data is being treated and analysed correctly is a huge change-oriented project in itself"* (Financial consultant).

Overcoming a tradition of suspicion regarding data is perceived as a widespread challenge. Specialists do not trust that data will be exploited appropriately or adequately, and therefore remain skeptical about exploring avenues for new or better use of data.

Lack of Cross-organizational Collaboration. One of the opportunities many municipalities are very keen to pursue, is combining data about a citizen from several systems across departments to gain a full overview of the individual. According to the participants, this will have transformative impact on a wide variety of elements, from the way they monitor the effects of specific initiatives to the way they deliver services to the public. Yet, to do so, the different departments have to establish tight collaboration with each other, but this is difficult: *"You can have a siloed organisation, and then work together across, with good processes. But we don't have that. We try to facilitate data-sharing across with a BI-project, but those are just the terms. The departments simply don't collaborate."* (Financial consultant).

The wider the distance between what purpose a data governance process or principle serves and the person, who has to adhere to it, the less meaningful it might appear: *"The closer you move towards, where we meet the citizens and run everyday operations, the less meaningful [a data governance principle] can be experienced by the employees"* (Head of Digitalization).

As such, cross-organizational collaboration and deconstructing siloes become a pivotal part of the process of exploiting data assets. Yet, the collaborative work required may appear the least meaningful to the employees who are closest to the data.

4.3 Data Capabilities and Politics

The last three challenges suggest that (lack of) capabilities across departments and hierarchal levels makes it difficult to envision a strategic direction for the use of data across a municipality. The varying levels of maturity and a lack of understanding of the value-creating potential of data at both executive and political levels in the munici-palities further complicate the process of exploring and exploiting data assets. There challenges can be grouped under this theme, which emphasizes the need to take varying data capabilities across departments and management functions into account; in general and in particular, if the aim is to develop an organization-wide data gov-ernance programme.

Varying Levels of Data Maturity Across Different Departments. Data governance entails implementing processes and principles that are supposed to be enterprise-wide. However, currently it is not possible to design such a wide-reaching data governance program for a municipality, because the different departments within the municipality have varying levels of data management maturity. Several municipalities point to the employment sector as very experienced in working with data: *"The field of employment is extremely data-driven and guided by managing information, which it has been for many years and I think it's easy to notice how the employees have this experience and focus on data quality and data usage"* (Head of Digitalization).

On the other hand, the elderly sector is in some municipalities not experienced at all, and does not realize how welfare technology may change the foundation of their entire domain. In one case, they are lacking a basic understanding of the role that IT can play in their profession: *"We have just reached out to the elder area, because we have to create a digitization strategy. They do not have it in their consciousness and we would like to help them. The first meeting we had, they thought we were there to discuss which PCs they should have and what phones they should buy. And that was probably the last thing we came to discuss"* (Head of IT).

As such, this challenge is also at the intersection of exploring and exploiting data assets. In order to design and implement data governance for the municipality as a whole, it is necessary to consider the maturity of the individual departments. Depending on the department and their existing data and work practices, it may be more reasonable to focus on either exploration or exploitation of data assets, but the relationship between these remain unclear, thus becoming challenging.

Lack of Top-Level Support for Data Initiatives. Gaining support from the executive levels of the municipalities is framed as a common challenge. According to partici-pants, it is because they need the compelling use case that links working structured and systematically with data to value in the municipal context. They agree that right now, most data initiatives are powered by passionate individuals: *"The passionate cannot drive this alone, because at one point there will be no more passion left. There must be top management support"* (Project manager).

While this challenge relates to the difficulty of understanding and expressing the value that data initiatives (#2) might be able to generate, achieving top-level support also has other objectives and consequences. For example, it may be easier to com-municate the value of data to the rest of the organization, if top-management has understood it and helped frame the goals of data governance as related to the overall goals of the organization. As such, this challenge remains at the intersection of exploration and exploitation; executives cannot comprehend the value creating potential of exploiting data assets, until they have seen successful examples of exploration.

Lack of Political Focus on Data Usage in Municipal Context. Some participants feel digitalization and management of data should be on the political agenda for their municipality. While this may appear to be related to achieving top-level support, getting politicians to see the opportunities for strategic use of data goes beyond improving administrative processes. If data was involved in political discussion, it could shape the future development of the public sector. To engage politicians will be a challenge, as few have capabilities for understanding the value of data: *"No politicians can comment on this meaningfully. It is not a political issue ... in the municipality and when I say that, I mean something like 'data is important because it can make us a better municipality' ... But it's not there, it's only administrative"* (IT architect).

Similar to attaining top-level support, this challenge is also related to the interplay between exploiting and exploring data assets. As suggested by the challenge regarding distrust towards data in social fields (#5), both exploration and exploitation of data assets in a municipal context can become a politically infused endeavour, in that it may disturb some fundamental values. Bringing data usage on the political agenda is thus both an issue of exploring data opportunities to raise awareness regarding its applicability, but also remain an issue of exploitation as powerful interests may influence its strategic direction.

5   Discussion

In this section, we discuss our findings in relation to the theoretical background section and our research question: Why is it difficult for local government organizations to explore and exploit their data assets with data governance? First, we discuss how each theme corroborates previous research on data governance, and how it relates to the broader context of e-government research (summarized in Table 3). Next, we discuss the findings' implications for practice and point to directions for future research.

Table 3.   Related research on data governance and E-government

Challenge theme	Research on data governance	Research on e-government
Data value and overview	SME quandary [24]	Value complexity [37]; Network management [32]
Data practices and collaboration	MDM paradoxes [26]	Situated practices [33]; Mode of collaboration [34]
Data capabilities and politics	SME quandary [25]	Capability maturity [35]; E-government stakeholders [36]

5.1   Contribution to Research

The theme *Data value and overview* extends Begg and Caira's findings from their SME study [24], where they found that the perception of the value-creating potential of data have a major effect on the pursuit of data governance initiatives. From our results, it becomes clear that a basic understanding of data value is also central to challenges with data governance in local government and not only in SMEs. E-government initiatives are often complicated by certain value traditions that are embedded in managers' cultural environments, but rarely explicit and sometimes at conflict with one another (Rose et al. 2015). The managers in Danish local government may hold different value positions that can be both congruent and converging. Thus, when it comes to assigning value to data in local government, many actors bring diverse interests that complicate opportunities for success. This is also highlighted by Guha and Chakrabarti [32] in their conceptualization of e-government networks. They argue e-government projects are prone to failure, if not understood as networks of actors who are forced to co-operate, despite different goals, objectives, and culture. Competing value positions, goals, objectives and actors are thus well-known issues in e-government research, and contribute to understanding challenges within the first theme.

The theme *Data practices and collaboration* extend the findings on establishing master data management in the public sector [26]. Here, they identified a series of paradoxes that point to the difficulty of establishing organization-wide support and responsibility for data initiatives in the public sector. Our findings show that diverse practices across different municipal departments also complicates establishing cross-organizational structures for data governance, and not only master data management. Implementing IT-enabled changes in the public sector requires that processes are incorporated in existing routines, which call for consideration of situated practices and institutionalizing the changes [33]. The friction between existing practices and implementation of e-government initiatives is therefore not new nor unexamined. Additionally, Juell-Skielse et al. [34] examined different modes of collaboration and expectations in inter-organizational e-government initiatives. They found that modes of collaboration do not exist in and of themselves; rather they are inherently related to the benefits they are presumed to produce. Establishing cross-collaboration with data initiatives may therefore require heightened focus on the expected benefits.

Last, the theme *Data capabilities and politics* also extend Begg and Caira's other work on data governance in SMEs [25]. They found that an organization's ability to conceive strategic direction for their data governance is dependent on the top-level's capabilities for understanding data's value creating potential. Our results suggest that perspectives on data in local government remain short-term with a poor understanding of data value at the executive and political levels. In e-government literature, capability maturity implies a focus on the relationship between input areas, such as human, structural, relational, and IT capital and the resulting maturity stages [35]. Practitioners conducting maturity assessments of their local governments can help them prioritize strategies and resources [35] and similarly, consideration of data capability maturity might enable municipal actors to focus their exploration and exploitation efforts. Lastly, Rowley [36] conceptualizes a typology of e-government stakeholder roles related to stakeholder benefits. Understanding e-government stakeholders and mapping the benefits they gain in relation to data governance initiatives may help mobilize support from the appropriate roles.

While the three themes corroborate and extend existing data governance literature, they are not new issues in the e-government literature. This could imply that challenges related to exploration and exploitation of data assets in public organizations require specific attention and examining implementation of data governance in local government should be done with the broader e-government field in mind.

5.2 Implications for Practice and Future Research

The central implication of this study on data governance is how municipal practitioners can understand their challenges with data governance in the context of the three themes. While paradoxes are addressed in other strands of the literature [38], conceiving of challenges constitutes a useful way to be aware of potential pitfalls and developing programs to specifically overcome these. When initiating data governance programs and attempting to implement more structured and systematic practices, it can be useful to consider how challenges might affect initiatives. It may also help managers to identify the most urgent areas and thus prioritize the scarce resources for data initiatives. Moreover, focusing on how challenges relate to issues of exploring and exploiting data assets can assist practitioners in communicating value or getting started with designing and implementing processes.

Our findings and the discussed previous research suggest that data governance in local government is a large-scale change effort that requires a lot more than just the designation of roles and responsibilities. It requires attention to the three themes and broader issues examined in e-government literature. We propose that future research delves into how the three themes of value, practices and capabilities relate or effect each other, in order to conceptualize a relevant theoretical framing of these. While municipal practitioners are keen to pursue data related opportunities, they struggle with issues of exploration and exploitation according to the findings of this study. Studies that explore the three themes' correlation, as well as how to take advantage of the interplay of exploration and exploitation activities are encouraged. Finally, we must emphasize that our investigation of challenges in data governance is limited to the views within local government organizations. Involving the citizens' perspectives and rights pertaining to governing often personal and sensitive data is a very important direction for future research, and a well-known problem in the e-government literature [39–41].

6 Conclusion

Our research shows that it is difficult for local government organizations to explore and exploit their data assets with data governance for three main reasons. Firstly, they struggle to understand and communicate the value that data and data governance might be able to create. Second, diverse, local practices complicate the design and implementation of a shared, standardized approach to data and third, varying data capabilities across departments and among managers and politicians makes it difficult to envision a strategic direction for the use of data across the organization as a whole. These three themes may assist practitioners, who wish to get started with data governance initiatives. Our findings corroborate and extend existing data governance literature for local government organizations and in addition, suggest that the identified themes relate to broader e-government issues.

References

1. Thompson, N., Ravindran, R., Nicosia, S.: Government data does not mean data governance: lessons learned from a public sector application audit. Gov. Inf. Q. **32**, 316–322 (2015)
2. Brous, P.: Paradoxes, conflicts and tensions in establishing master data. In: 24th European Conference on Information Systems, ECIS 2016 (2016)
3. Lee, Y.W., Madnick, S.E., Wang, R.Y., Wang, F.L., Zhang, H.: A cubic framework for the chief data officer: succeeding in a world of big data. MIS Q. Exec. **13**, 1–13 (2014)
4. Khatri, V., Brown, C.V.: Designing data governance. Commun. ACM **53**, 148 (2010)
5. Benfeldt Nielsen, O.: A comprehensive review of data governance literature. In: Selected Papers of the IRIS (2017)
6. Vilminko-Heikkinen, R.: Data, Technology, and People. Tampere University of Technology, Tampere (2017)
7. European Commission: Europe's Digital Progress Report - The Digital Economy and Society Index
8. Spitze & Co: Resultater for overgangen til digital kommunikation 2011–2015 (2016)
9. Danish Ministry of Finance: A Stronger and More Secure Digital Denmark: Digital Strategy 2016–2020 (2016)
10. Benner, M.L., Tushman, M.J.: Exploitation, exploration, and process management: the productivity dilemma revisited. Acad. Manag. Rev. **28**, 238–256 (2003)
11. Gregory, R.W., Keil, M., Muntermann, J., Mähring, M.: Paradoxes and the nature of ambidexterity in IT transformation programs. Inf. Syst. Res. **26**, 57–80 (2015)
12. Peppard, J., Galliers, R.D., Thorogood, A.: Information systems strategy as practice: micro strategy and strategizing for IS. J. Strateg. Inf. Syst. **23**, 1–10 (2014)
13. Peppard, J.: Where do you begin with your (Big) data initiative? Eur. Bus. Rev. (2016)
14. Van de Ven, A.H.: Engaged Scholarship: A Guide for Organizational and Social Research. Oxford University Press on Demand, Oxford (2007)
15. Nielsen, P.A., Persson, J.S.: Engaged problem formulation in IS research. Commun. Assoc. Inf. Syst. **38**, 720–737 (2016)
16. Boisot, M., Canals, A.: Data, information and knowledge: have we got it right? J. Evol. Econ. **14**, 43–67 (2004)
17. Otto, B.: Organizing data governance: findings from the telecommunications industry and consequences for large service providers. Commun. Assoc. Inf. Syst. **29**, 45–66 (2011)
18. Wende, K., Otto, B.: A contingency approach to data governance. In: Proceedings of the 12th International Conference on Information Quality, Cambridge, USA, pp. 1–14 (2007)
19. Weber, K., Otto, B., Österle, H.: One size does not fit all - a contingency approach to data governance. ACM J. Data Inf. Qual. **1**, 1–27 (2009)
20. Alhassan, I., Sammon, D., Daly, M.: Data governance activities: an analysis of the literature. J. Decis. Syst. **25**, 64–75 (2016)
21. Ladley, J.: Data Governance: How to Design, Deploy, and Sustain an Effective Data Governance Program. Newnes (2012)
22. Pierce, E., Dismute, W.S., Yonke, C.L.: The State of Information and Data Governance - Understanding How Organizations Govern Their Information and Data Assets (2008)
23. Otto, B.: Data governance. Bus. Inf. Syst. Eng. **3**, 241–244 (2011)
24. Begg, C., Caira, T.: Data governance in practice: the SME quandary reflections on the reality of data governance in the small to medium enterprise (SME) sector. In: 5th European Conference on Management Information and Evaluation, pp. 75–83 (2011)
25. Begg, C., Caira, T.: Exploring the SME quandary: data governance in practise in the small to medium-sized enterprise sector. Electron. J. Inf. Syst. Eval. **15**, 3–13 (2012)

26. Vilminko-Heikkinen, R., Brous, P., Pekkola, S.: Paradoxes, conflicts and tensions in establishing master data management function. In: 24th European Conference on Information Systems, ECIS 2016 (2016)
27. Fontana, A., Frey, J.H.: Interviewing: the arts of science. In: The Handbook of Qualitative Research, pp. 361–376 (1994)
28. Harvey, L.J., Myers, M.D.: Scholarship and practice: the contribution of ethnographic research methods to bridging the gap. Inf. Technol. People **8**, 13–27 (1995)
29. Persson, J.S., Kaldahl, A., Skorve, E., Nielsen, P.A.: Value positions in E-government strategies: something is (Not) changing in the state of Denmark. In: Proceedings of the 25th European Conference on Information Systems, pp. 904–917 (2017)
30. Myers, M.D., Newman, M.: The qualitative interview in IS research: examining the craft. Inf. Organ. **17**, 2–26 (2007)
31. Hsieh, H.-F., Shannon, S.E.: Three approaches to qualitative content analysis. Qual. Health Res. **15**, 1277–1288 (2005)
32. Guha, J., Chakrabarti, B.: Making e-government work: adopting the network approach. Gov. Inf. Q. **31**, 327–336 (2014)
33. Azad, B., Faraj, S.: E-Government institutionalizing practices of a land registration mapping system. Gov. Inf. Q. **26**, 5–14 (2009)
34. Juell-Skielse, G., Lönn, C.-M., Päivärinta, T.: Modes of collaboration and expected benefits of inter-organizational E-government initiatives: a multi-case study. Gov. Inf. Q. **34**, 578–590 (2017)
35. Kim, D., Grant, G.: E-government maturity model using the capability maturity model integration. J. Syst. Inf. Technol. **12**, 230–244 (2010)
36. Rowley, J.: E-Government stakeholders - who are they and what do they want? Int. J. Inf. Manag. **31**, 53–62 (2011)
37. Rose, J., Persson, J.S., Heeager, L.T., Irani, Z.: Managing e-Government: value positions and relationships. Inf. Syst. J. **25**, 531–571 (2015)
38. Brous, P., Vilminko-Heikkinen, R., Brou, P., Pekkola, S.: Paradoxes, conflicts and tensions in establishing master data. In: Proceedings of ECIS 2016 (2016)
39. Rose, J., Persson, J.S., Heeager, L.T.: How e-Government managers prioritise rival value positions: the efficiency imperative. Inf. Polity **20**, 35–59 (2015)
40. Medaglia, R.: eParticipation research: moving characterization forward (2006–2011). Gov. Inf. Q. **29**, 346–360 (2012)
41. Olphert, W., Damodaran, L.: Citizen participation and engagement in the design of E-government services: the missing link in effective ICT design and delivery. J. Assoc. Inf. Syst. **8**, 491–507 (2007)

A Cognitive Perspective on Consumers' Resistances to Smart Products

Stefan Raff[✉] and Daniel Wentzel

Department of Marketing, TIME Research Area, RWTH Aachen University,
52072 Aachen, Germany
{raff, wentzel}@time.rwth-aachen.de

Abstract. Despite their increasing relevance, research falls short to reveal the key factors hindering the adoption of smart technologies. Therefore, the aim of this exploratory study was to elicit consumers' cognitive representations, i.e. mental models of different smart product concepts based on similarity and dissimilarity judgments, and to label the key dimensions based on which consumers mentally categorize them. This was expected to shed light on drivers of adoption resistance in order to help practitioners in product design and promotion. An innovative mix of two research methods was applied, namely quantitative-descriptive projective mapping and free associations. We found that consumers mentally balance released smart product concepts along with a rationally laden 'useful-useless' dimension and unreleased concepts along with an emotionally laden 'intrusive-useful' dimension. Additionally, this research showcases (1) method diversity in the field of IS and (2) how non-IS scholars who apply new approaches to an IS phenomenon contribute with new perspectives and thus enrich the field as a whole. This is work in progress and part of an overarching mixed-method agenda. The exploratory findings will be used to carve out further research directions for this growing field (e.g. the development of a construct measuring consumers' perceived intrusion of smart products).

Keywords: Smart product · Internet of Things · ICT · Innovation resistance
Adoption barrier · Mental model · Mixed-method research

1   Introduction

In the past decade, the term "smart product" has been buzzing around among politicians, scientists and technology experts [e.g., 66, 68]. For a long time, this terminology appeared to be used mainly for the purpose of philosophizing in technology think tanks and for the marketing of cutting-edge information and communication technology (ICT) at trade fairs. However, driven by advancements in technology, smart products are becoming a tangible reality in the dawn of a new era: the era of the Internet-of-Things (IoT) [2, 14, 57]. Rijsdijk and Hultink [66, 68] define the concept of product smartness as a combination of the dimensions autonomy, adaptability, reactivity, multifunctionality, ability to cooperate, humanlike interaction, and personality, as well as the extent to which a product possesses one or more of these dimensions. Yet, most of the products exhibiting one or more of these characteristics remain a glamorous

© IFIP International Federation for Information Processing 2019
Published by Springer Nature Switzerland AG 2019.
A. Elbanna et al. (Eds.): TDIT 2018, IFIP AICT 533, pp. 30–44, 2019.
https://doi.org/10.1007/978-3-030-04315-5_3

vision of future digitized worlds while, in some areas, they are already hitting our lives. Prime examples are Amazon's Echo or smart watches such as the Apple Watch. Soon, even more sophisticated smart products like autonomous cars will gradually become part of our lives. Digitization is accelerating, and companies across all industries are starting to lift their products to a "smart" level [51].

However, despite its increasing relevance, the market has seen a substantially slower than expected pace of smart product adoption [1]. Currently, the reasons for the slow pace of adoption seem to lie mainly in unknown consumer side factors [1]. A major goal of information systems (IS) research is to predict and to enlighten IS acceptance and usage [88]. For smart product adoption, predicting factors might go beyond the traditional acceptance or resistance evaluations based on perceived usefulness and the perceived ease of use suggested as by the Technology Acceptance Model (TAM) [e.g., 13, 71, 82]. Smart products differentiate in a myriad of ways from traditional computers, thus, due to the radical newness of the products and the application contexts, there might also be new and distinct factors driving consumers' adoption decisions. Therefore, practitioners need to gain in-depth insights into the drivers of resistances that need to be overcome. Hitherto, the field of smart products is lacking such insights. Apart from a considerable amount of technology-focused research in IS literature, only very little research has tackled consumer behavioral issues of smart products [for an exception see: 45 or 73]. Also, there is an apparent lack of initial exploratory research in the field which is reminiscent of the time when e-commerce was a rising phenomenon. Nonetheless, at the time, research on e-commerce benefitted greatly from the combination of inductive, exploratory approaches followed by deductive, confirmatory research [44, 63].

Against this backdrop, exploratory research is needed. Thus, we take a cognition perspective and use projective mapping and free associations as powerful tools in order to explore mental models with regard to smart products. The goal of this research is thus to identify consumers' mental model with regard to different smart product concepts. Increasing the understanding of the existing mental model is expected to be essential in order to obtain further insights into potential sources of adoption barriers and resistances on the consumers' side [43, 64]. Moreover, past research has shown that if for example consumers' existing knowledge structures are applied to promotional messages, consumer understanding is facilitated [23]. Consequently, such increased understanding decreases the perceived complexity and may leverage adoption. From an academic perspective, the emerging insights may as well pave the way for more product-centred research endeavors in a next step. Two overall research questions were developed that should guide the reader through this work: (1) *What is the mental model consumers hold towards different smart product concepts?*, and (2) *What are the dominant mental dimensions based on which consumers differentiate smart product concepts?*

On a broader level, this research aims to add value to IS research through method diversity. This paper showcases how non-IS scholars apply new methodologies to an IS phenomenon in order to introduce new perspectives, disrupt traditional epistemic scripts, and thereby to enrich the field's knowledge ecology as a whole [5, 24, 70]. Moreover, this research is embedded in an overarching mixed-method agenda [37, 83, 84]. It thus follows the repeated calls for methodological pluralism and mixed-method application in IS knowledge generation [83, 84].

The remainder of the paper is organised as follows: Sect. 2 provides a summary of the underlying theory. Section 3 presents the applied research method and the study design. Following, Sect. 4 gives an overview of some of the preliminary results. The Discussion, Contributions and Research Implications are described in Sect. 5. Finally, the paper concludes with Sect. 6.

2 Theoretical Background

2.1 Innovation Resistance

Innovation adoption and acceptance have been the focus of academic literature for some time [e.g., 3, 18, 47, 48, 71, 82]. Most of this research postulates that consumers are open to adopting innovations. However, such pro-innovation bias in current research tends to overshadow the reality of (high-tech) innovation failures with average failure rates of 40–50% [7, 9, 15, 17, 64]. Innovation adoption arises solely if consumer side resistances can be overcome [64]. Therefore, it is essential to investigate these resistances and their nature [19, 64]. Generally, Ram [64] describes them as being dependent on the three factors *perceived innovation characteristics*, *consumer characteristics*, and *characteristics of propagation mechanisms*. In this description, the *consumer characteristics* are defined as a combination of psychological variables and demographics. Moreover, Ram [64] describes the psychological variables as a combination of one's personality, attitudes, value orientation, previous innovative experiences, perceptions and beliefs. In order to understand the psychology of innovation resistance, in this study, the psychological variables of consumers will be specifically targeted [64, 75]. The combined psychological variables such as beliefs or perceptions are held in mental models or cognitive schemas. Bagozzi and Lee [4]. for example introduce mental models as the cognitive representation of the set of ideas a consumer holds about an innovation and that may guide the consumer through the adoption process. Such mental models about product innovation have an important self-regulatory function in the product adoption process [4]. Generally, mental models are an artefact of the overall naïve understandings that humans hold for the world surrounding them and may thus provide clues about sources of resistances.

2.2 The Role of Mental Models and Their Structure

There is broad consensus on the existence of mental models and their appearance as small-scale models of external reality that guide human reasoning and decision-making [9, 11, 38–41, 43, 58–60, 89]. The history of mental models dates back to René Descartes who defines ideas as representations of reality. In this regard, he distinguishes between three kinds of ideas: *ideae innatae*, *ideae adventitiae*, and *ideae factitiae*. Thereby *ideae factitiae* (the fabricated idea) gets most closely to what Ludwig Wittgenstein [89] in his Tractatus Logico-Philosophicus describes by humans developing pictures of facts and define them as models of reality. This idea is in line with Johnson-Laird [40] who supports these notions by defining mental models as the ultimate output of perceptual processes. Later, mental models are further described as small-scale models of reality that are formed through interaction with a target system (e.g., any kind of information regarding the target system 'smart product') which needs to be neither wholly accurate and thorough nor correspond completely with what they model in order to be useful [38, 58]. In this regard, mental models can be cognitively represented in the form of visual images or they can be abstract and non-visual [41]. Moreover, there is no need for humans to understand their surrounding reality up to their fundamental principles in order to form mental models [38]. Furthermore, human mental models should by no means be expected to be neat and elegant but rather messy, sloppy, and incomplete representations of people's perceived environment and sometimes derived from idiosyncratic interpretations [57, 58].

The connection between mental models and (consumer) behavior has been acknowledged for some time in the fields of organization science, system science, marketing, and computer science [e.g., 27, 49, 50, 55, 60, 87, 90, 91]. In consumer research, cognitive structures are investigated mostly in terms of product perceptions, brand attitudes, brand-attribute beliefs or brand personality. As soon as consumers gain new information and connect it with existing knowledge, they are assumed to form cognitive structures in their memory in the form of mental models. Furthermore, in marketing and innovation literature, mental models are described as the interpreted meanings of a product or thing (i.e., a target system) that are formed through experience with a target system (e.g., interacting with the product, reading, online information etc.) and guide consumers' behavior [4, 10, 12, 30, 58, 60, 74, 76, 77, 90, 91]. Zaltman and Coulter [90, 91] postulate that these mental models essentially drive consumers' thoughts and behaviors. However, a major challenge for research is to elicit such mental models and to bring them to life.

Theories of mental model formation are frequently built on similarity judgments (similarity of objects) [25]. In this context, consumers cognitively represent similarities of different product alternatives through the use of comparison attributes [35]. These attributes have either the characteristic of distinct product features or more abstract dimensions [e.g., 79, 80]. In product category choice situations or in choice situations among rather non-comparable product alternatives, consumers use such abstract comparison dimensions (e.g. practicality) [34]. Thereby, the level of abstraction of these dimensions differs based on the consumers' level of experience or expertise with regard to the focal domain. Novices are expected to compare different products on broader and more general, abstract dimensions [85]. In general, the dimensions describe a range of unique attributes or concepts in consumers' knowledge with respect to a specific domain [42].The product category smart product contains a wide range of different products such as autonomous cars or home assistants. These products are rather non-comparable on an attribute or functional level as they, by their inherent nature, satisfy different needs. However, consumers might compare them on the basis of general and abstract dimensions such as 'necessity' or 'frightening' and thus create a generic mental model for the category of smart products [32]. These overall abstract dimensions that are used by consumers to categorize different smart product concepts are expected to provide important indicators about the basic sources of resistances. Johnson et al. [35] find that when studying consumers on a product category level, spatial scaling methods are most appropriate for determining consumers' latent mental dimensions that might drive consumer behavior. Inductively labelling these mental dimensions can be done by analyzing consumers' underlying semantic structures collected by methods such as open-ended interviewing, free associations or pattern notes [9]. These identified dimensions are expected to represent the first and most important parameters whose adjustment may leverage smart product adoption.

Based on a synthesis of the outlined theory, this work's research approach is epitomized by the following exploratory research propositions: (P1) *Smart product resistances are organized in a mental model that crucially guides consumers' adoption process.* (P2) *Unveiling the content of the mental model may shed light on the general nature of factors that induce smart product resistances.* (P3) *Spatial scaling and semantic structures are appropriate for eliciting the key dimensions consumers use to mentally categorize different smart product concepts.*

3   Research Method and Study Design

In academia, there has been a considerable debate on how to model and map cognitive representations and mental models [20, 43], in particular in the field of IS [53]. In general, multidimensional analysis methods (e.g., Multidimensional Scaling – MDS, Multiple Factor Analysis – MFA or Generalized Procrustes Analysis – GPA) are among the most widely used techniques for exploring and modeling cognitive representations or psychological spaces with regard to product categories [26, 33, 35, 60, 61, 78, 86]. Furthermore, the application of such methods is expedient in exploratory settings in which the underlying concepts and dimensions are not developed yet [72]. Projective mapping, particularly well-suited for the inductive set-up of this work's research, will be applied. The quantitative-descriptive method collects data by means of free-choice profiling. Hitherto, it was applied mainly in the field of psychophysics [62, 69]. Originally, it stems from free sorting tasks pursued in experimental psychology to uncover – via statistical analyses – the structure of stimuli in a perceptual space as well as to interpret the underlying categorization dimensions of these spaces [see e.g. 31 or 52]. In projective mapping, participants directly position products or proxies (e.g. tokens) on a sheet of paper based on perceived similarity and dissimilarity judgments as well as provide descriptive free association data for each product [66]. Afterwards, the data can be analyzed using GPA and MFA. This allows for generating a spatial, lower dimensional consensus configuration from a set of individual configurations.

Compared to other scaling methods, this method has a number of advantages. This technique compares all stimuli at once and not by means of pairwise comparisons. This helps to prevent participant fatigue. Also, the projective mapping method is faster because each positioning of a stimulus reflects multiple similarity/dissimilarity judgements. In an initial exploratory setting, it therefore reveals the most important cognitive dimensions faster and easier than other scaling techniques or qualitatively driven mental model elicitation practices such as for example the Zaltman metaphor elicitation technique (ZMET) [56, 90]. Moreover, considering the set of stimuli holistically means that the relationships between multiple pairs are considered in context, as all stimuli are always in view. This appears to be more realistic when it comes to real consumer evaluations of product categories and is thus a major advantage of this technique [46]. It is important to determine the mental model of consumers without deductively encouraging the use of specific evaluative dimensions. Thus, projective mapping suits very well the inductive purpose of this study as it can easily be combined with qualitative data collection methods. Thus, to inductively derive the dimensions, the approach was combined with free associations an established tool in order to efficiently elicit mental models [9]. Participants had to state one free association per product concept. These associations can be plotted into the consensus map in the form of a semantic cloud allowing for inductive interpretation of the axes. Hence, combining projective mapping with the informative quality of free associations allows one to develop the mental dimensions directly from the data.

The participants for the study were recruited on the campus of a large public university ($N = 40$, $M_{age} = 31.6$ years, $50\% =$ women). All participants were offered free refreshments as an incentive. All participants took part voluntarily. The participants were randomly assigned to one of the two study groups (group 1: $N = 20$ and group 2: $N = 20$). The study was conducted in German, the native language of all participants. The stimuli consisted of 16 consumer-oriented smart product concepts, eight of which are not commercially available yet (e.g. autonomous vehicle), while the other eight have already been released on the market (e.g. smart watch). The two groups were derived in order to reveal differences between mental models of released and unreleased products, i.e. differences between established and unestablished products. The participants had to be familiar with all of the released product concepts. The smart product concepts were chosen on the basis of the suggested smartness criteria proposed by Rijsdijk and Hultink [65, 67] and on their ability to possess at least one of them. The study was conducted in a controlled laboratory setting. Participants received a brief introduction regarding the different smart product concepts from the researcher. They were then given 10–15 min to read the concept descriptions again in detail and familiarize themselves with them. For each concept, a token was provided representing a proxy for the mapping task. In a next step, the participants were asked to position the tokens on a large sheet of blank paper; in practice, this sheet is a paper tablecloth measuring 40 cm × 60 cm. Figure 1 shows an example of an individual configuration. The following instructions were given to the participants:

(1) *"You are asked to evaluate the similarities (or dissimilarities) between several smart product concepts. You can do this intuitively, based on your own criteria (except product function), those that you consider substantial. You do not have to specify your criteria. There is no right or wrong."*

(2) *"You have to position the tokens on the tablecloth in such a way that two smart product concepts are positioned close to one another if they appear identical to you and that two smart product concepts are positioned further away from one another if they appear dissimilar to you. Do not hesitate to make use of the entire sheet to strongly express the differences you perceive."*

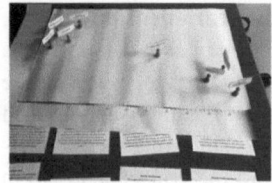 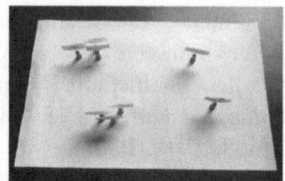 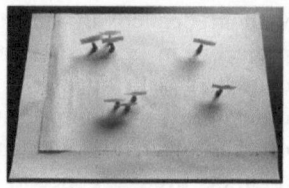

Fig. 1. Individual positioning of the smart product concept tokens from one study participant

In a next step, the participants had to indicate one free association per product concept. In addition, they had to specify whether their association was positively (+), neutrally (/) or negatively (-) connoted. Coordinates were read off and entered into the data matrix.

The derived data matrix consists of N participants in the columns and K product concepts and free associations in the rows, each of them represented by a group consisting of one x and one y coordinate, respectively. The data was analyzed using MFA and GPA [26]. The analysis was pursued in R using the Rcmdr Plugin for the Facto-MineR package. The analysis generated lower dimensional, spatial consensus configurations from the individual participant's configurations. In the derived consensus maps, the rows of the original data matrix are represented as points. The points represent the group average position of the individual's positioning of the product concept. The closer the points are positioned to one another on the map, i.e. the shorter the distance between the points, the more similar they are perceived in the eye of the consumer. Lastly, the derived consensus configurations allow to inductively deducing the central dimensions that were used by the consumers to categorize the different product concepts. The free association data can be superimposed onto the consensus maps, which allowed for the qualitative dimensional interpretation by two independent assessors.

4 Preliminary Results

Although the collected data allows for more in-depth analysis on product and category level, due to limited space, only some of the initial exploratory results of the unreleased group will be outlined very briefly in this paper. Figure 2 represents the consensus configuration from the unreleased group and the semantic cloud that was derived using GPA. The MFA reveals that the two dimensions (Dim 1 and Dim 2) account for more than 53% of the variance in the underlying data. Apparently, there are two very dominant dimensions based on which the participants categorized the different product concepts. Here, dimension 1 describes most of the variance of the participants' categorizations (30, 74%). Besides, the vertical dimension 2 clearly separates the smart product concept '8_AV' from all the other smart product concepts.

Moreover, '2_SH' and '4_SFC' are mentally categorized as being very similar. Interpreting the free association data will help shed light on the qualitative meaning of the mental dimensions. From a dimensional perspective, most of the free associations from the semantic cloud are organized along the horizontal dimension. On the left, they are highly emotional and negatively associated. Products are mostly linked to

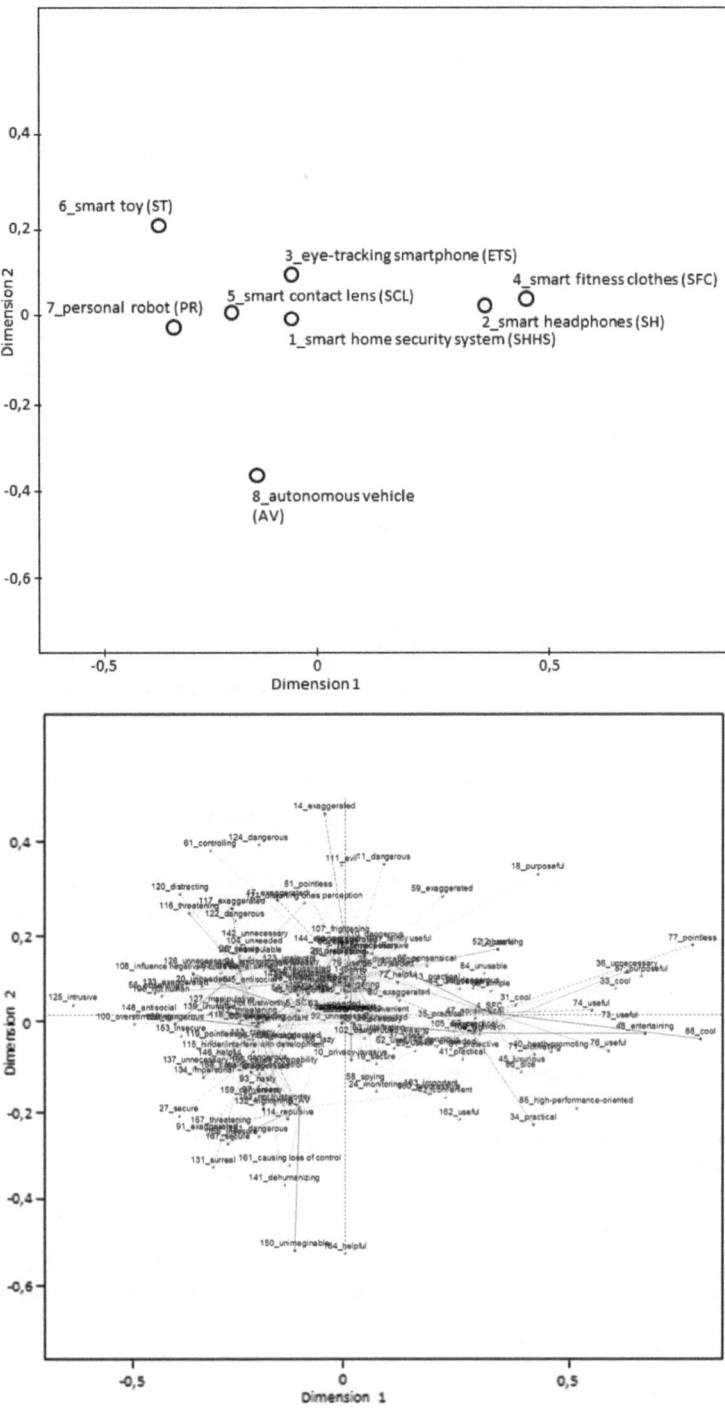

Fig. 2. Consensus configuration (above) and superimposed semantic cloud (below)

associations such as 'intrusive', 'spying on', 'observing' or 'controlling'. On the right, free associations comprise mainly rational, more positive words such as 'useful', 'practical'. In fact, consumers appear to categorize the product concepts mainly along an 'intrusive-useful' dimension. This categorization could reflect some form of consumers' cost-benefit balancing. Regarding the product concepts, it appears that for '2_SH' and '4_SFC', the perceived benefits of usefulness outweigh the perceived costs of intrusion. In contrast, for '6_ST', '7_PR' or '5_SCL' the perceived costs of intrusion seem to prevail. This could imply that for product concepts that involve contact with children, the perceived negative potential of these products is predominant, whereas for more playful and leisure-like applications, the perceived usefulness seems to predominate. Interpretation of the vertical dimension is less clear. However, one could interpret it as an overall dimension of danger. Here, the dimension seems to vary in concreteness. With regard to '8_AV', the associated fear is concrete and mainly due to a perceived loss of control (e.g. free association 'loss of control'). On the other hand, '6_ST' and '3_ETS' are associated with fear on a more general level, which is reflected by terms such as 'dangerous' and 'threatening'. In sum, the two dimensions (accounting for >53% of the variance) appear to consist of an 'intrusive-useful' dimension (Dim 1) and a generic 'fear' dimension (Dim 2). These dimensions seem to be the predominant dimensions based on which consumers mentally categorize and distinguish different unreleased smart product concepts. From a product perspective, the smart product concepts '5_SCL', '7_PR' and '6_ST' in particular appear to have a strong negative connotation in consumers' mental representations. The smart toy was rated negatively by all of the participants, the personal robot by 90% and the smart contact lens by 85%. In general, higher degrees of complexity and radicalism of the smart product concept appear to be aligned with an increase in negative judgments. It could be inferred that increased levels of complexity and radicalism confuse or frighten consumers. In contrast, '4_SFC' and '2_SH' invoke positive connotations and are perceived as useful and cool. Even though only the results from the unreleased smart product group could be outlined briefly here, Table 1 shows the preliminary results of both groups.

Table 1. Mental model summary

Mental dimensions	Study group 1: unreleased	Study group 2: released
Dimension 1	'intrusive – useful'	Usefulness: 'useful – useless'
Dimension 2	Fear: 'abstract (dangerous) – concrete (loss of control)'	Efficiency: 'efficient' – 'inefficient'
Overall mental model	Predominantly negative connotations, emotionally laden	Predominantly positive connotations and highly rational

5   Discussion, Contributions and Research Implications

To date, research providing inductively derived evidence with regard to resistance to smart product concepts is lacking. This research thus contributes to closing this revealed gap by providing initial insights into the psychological drivers that may cause adoption resistances [4, 64]. In light of our preliminary findings, this section will discuss the main contributions of this research paper as well as outline promising avenues for future research.

The preliminary findings seem to provide a clue about a simplifying heuristic or so-called "click" experience that consumers may apply in their evaluation of unreleased smart products [21, 54]. In general, heuristics help to release the complexity from a decision task and thus to reduce cognitive effort and to increase decision making efficiency [81]. Based on our findings, in their initial evaluations of unreleased smart product concepts, consumers seem to put great emphasis on the degree of their intrusive potential. This factor is highly negatively connotated and may therefore represent a significant hindering factor to the adoption of future smart product concepts. Consequently, and due to the technological complexity of smart products, consumers may strive to reduce situational complexity by using the level of perceived intrusion as a heuristic that becomes decisive for adoption or resistance. In this context, our future research will dig deeper and move in the following four directions: (1) consumers evaluations of released versus unreleased smart product concepts; (2) the exact evaluation and decision making styles prior to the adoption of yet unreleased smart products; (3) investigation of the specific product factors that have the most impact on the calculus between the perceived benefit of usefulness and the perceived cost of intrusion [16]. Especially for practice it is of great relevance to increase knowledge about such factors and their psychological impacts as they could represent possible starting points that might be addressed to leverage adoption; (4) the gradual increase of functions in use. Such updates ex-post market release could help to gradually accustom the user to radically new product functions instead of overwhelming the user from the beginning, and thus may avoid resistances.

In addition, having read this work one should bear in mind that it is embedded in an overarching mixed-method agenda whose findings are used to inform a set of confirmatory research endeavors [37, 83, 84]. Following the epistemological idea of the dialectic pluralism, the use of multiple methods and perspectives is expected to add substantial value to research on IS phenomena [36]. The complexity of the focal phenomenon and its interplay with the social environment calls for such a multiple perspective approach in order to be inclusive and to increase the general robustness of the findings [8, 83]. This study contributes with initial, inductively generated knowledge that helps to pave the way for future deductive studies. Going forward, the designs of these studies will be built on the elicited mental models and will deductively develop, complement and validate our initial findings [22]. Further related activities include: (1) a construct development (perceived intrusion of smart products). In relation to Bhattacherjee and Hikmet [6] it seems likely that the revealed aspect of perceived intrusion is unique and specific to the domain of smart technologies and thus needs to be treated as a distinct construct. Thus, we follow the call of Bhattacherjee and Hikmet

[6] to dig deeper into understanding the multifaceted phenomenon of resistance by investing in the development of constructs that may represent significant drivers of resistance to a specific technology; and (2) the development of a research model of smart product adoption that can be tested deductively. In this way, we hope to provide empirical evidence on the exact nomological paths that shape individuals' resistance to smart products [29].

Lastly, we contribute to the current body of knowledge on IS failures [17] as well as to the field of IS in general through method diversity. This paper showcases how non-IS scholars apply new methods to an IS phenomenon towards introducing new perspectives, disrupt traditional epistemic scripts, and thereby enrich the field's knowledge ecology as a whole [5, 70]. In Grover's [24] terms, we think that this research follows the call of pushing IS research to the edges by introducing a new methodological approach. More precisely, it contributes to the 'left edge' through a new form of inductive knowledge production resulting in an innovative dataset.

6 Conclusion

The aim of this paper was to uncover the hitherto unstudied mental models regarding smart product concepts. Building on mental model and innovation resistance theory, a set of exploratory research propositions was developed. Preliminary results of one empirical study revealed that consumers categorize released smart product concepts mainly based on a rationally laden useful-useless dimension and unreleased products along with a very emotionally laden intrusive-useful dimension. Building on our study, we extract knowledge gaps that warrant future investigation, as well as outline implications for practitioners.

The presented findings should be interpreted in light of its limitations. First, our study might be limited due to the overall exploratory research layout. We used a relatively small number of participants, which might not be representative of the whole population. Thus, we would welcome additional rigorous and possibly quantitative studies to specifically confirming our exploratory findings. Given that our data collection was performed in Germany, we are aware that the generalizability of our findings might be also limited due to the cultural setting that may differ from others in terms of cultural beliefs [28]. In conclusion, we hope that IS research benefits from the above findings as well as we hope to fuel future research on the adoption and resistance of smart technologies.

References

1. Accenture: Igniting Growth in Consumer Technology. Customer Survey (2016)
2. Accenture: The Internet of Things: The Future of Consumer Adoption. Market Report (2015)
3. Agarwal, R., Prasad, J.: Are individual differences germane to the acceptance of new information technologies? Decis. Sci. 30(2), 361–391 (1999)

4. Bagozzi, R.P., Lee, K.H.: Consumer resistance to, and acceptance of, innovations. In: Arnould, E.J., Scott, L.M., (Eds.) NA - Advances in Consumer Research. Provo, UT: Association for Consumer Research, pp. 218–225 (1999)
5. Benbasat, I., Zmud, R.W.: The identity crisis within the is discipline: defining and communicating the discipline's core properties. MIS Q. **27**(2), 183–194 (2003)
6. Bhattacherjee, A., Hikmet, N.: Physicians' resistance toward healthcare information technology: a theoretical model and empirical test. Eur. J. Inf. Syst. **16**(6), 725–737 (2007)
7. Castellion, G., Markham, S.K.: Perspective: new product failure rates: influence of argumentum ad populum and self-interest. J. Prod. Innov. Manag. **30**(5), 976–979 (2013)
8. Cao, J., Crews, J.M., Lin, M., Deokar, A., Burgoon, J.K., Nunamaker Jr., J.F.: Interactions between system evaluation and theory testing: a demonstration of the power of a mulitfaceted approach to systems research. J. Manag. Inf. Syst. **22**(4), 207–235 (2006)
9. Carley, K., Palmquist, M.: Extracting, representing, and analyzing mental models. Soc. Forces **70**(3), 601–636 (1992)
10. Christensen, G.L., Olson, J.C.: Mapping consumers' mental models with ZMET. Psychol. Mark. **19**(6), 477–501 (2002)
11. Craik, K.J.W.: The Nature of Explanation. Cambridge University Press, Cambridge (1943)
12. Cuny, C., Opaswongkarn, T.: Why do young thai women desire white skin? understanding conscious and nonconscious motivations of young women in Bangkok. Psychology and Marketing **34**(5), 556–568 (2017)
13. Davis, F.D., Bagozzi, R.P., Warshaw, P.R.: User acceptance of computer technology: a comparison of two theoretical models. Manage. Sci. **35**(8), 982–1003 (1989)
14. Deloitte: Smart Cities report: How rapid advances in technology are reshaping our economy and society. Market Report (2015)
15. Deschamps, J.-P.: Classic root causes of innovation failures—things we all know but sometimes forget. In: Pfeffermann, N., Gould, J. (eds.) Strategy and Communication for Innovation, pp. 41–60. Springer, Cham (2017). https://doi.org/10.1007/978-3-319-49542-2_4
16. Dinev, T., Hart, P.: An extended privacy calculus model for e-commerce transactions. Inf. Syst. Res. **17**(1), 61–80 (2006)
17. Dwivedi, Y.K., et al.: Research on information systems failures and successes: status update and future directions. Inf. Syst. Front. **17**(1), 143–157 (2015)
18. Dwivedi, Y.K., Rana, N.P., Jeyaraj, A., Clement, M., Williams, M.D.: Re-examining the unified theory of acceptance and use of technology (UTAUT): towards a revised theoretical model. Information Systems Frontiers, 1–16 (2017)
19. Ellen, P.S., Bearden, W.O., Sharma, S.: Resistance to technological innovations. an examination of the role of self-efficacy and performance satisfaction. J. Acad. Mark. Sci. **19**(4), 297–307 (1991)
20. Gärdenfors, P.: Conceptual Spaces. MIT Press/Bradford Books, Cambridge (2000)
21. Gigerenzer, G., Goldstein, D.G.: Reasoning the fast and frugal way: Models of bounded rationality. Psychol. Rev. **103**(4), 650–669 (1996)
22. Greene, J., Caracelli, V., Graham, W.: Toward a conceptual framework for mixed-method evaluation design. Educ. Eval. Policy Anal. **11**(3), 255–274 (1989)
23. Gregan-Paxton, J., John, D.R.: Consumer learning by analogy: a model of internal knowledge transfer. J. Consum. Res. **24**(3), 266–284 (1997)
24. Grover, V., Lyytinen, K.: New state of play in information systems research: the push to the edges. MIS Q. **39**(2), 271–296 (2015)
25. Goldstone, R.: An efficient method for obtaining similarity data. Behav. Res. Methods Instrum. Comput. **26**(4), 381–386 (1994)
26. Gower, J.C.: Generalized procrustes analysis. Psychometrika **40**(1), 33–51 (1975)

27. Hill, R.C., Levenhagen, M.: Metaphors and mental models: sensemaking and sensegiving in innovative and entrepreneurial activities. J. Manag. **21**(6), 1057–1074 (1995)
28. Hofstede, G.: Culture's Consequences: Comparing Values, Behaviors, Institutions, and Organizations Across Nations. Sage Publications, Thousand Oaks (2011)
29. Hughes, D.L., Dwivedi, Y.K., Rana, N.P., Simintiras, A.C.: Information systems project failure–analysis of causal links using interpretive structural modelling. Prod. Plan. Control **27**(16), 1313–1333 (2016)
30. Ilyuk, V., Block, L., Faro, D.: Is it still working? task difficulty promotes a rapid wear-off bias in judgments of pharmacological products. J. Consum. Res. **41**(3), 775–793 (2014)
31. Imai, S.: Classification of sets of stimuli with different stimulus characteristics and numerical properties. Percept. Psychophys. **1**, 48–54 (1966)
32. Johnson, M.D.: Consumer choice strategies for comparing noncomparable alternatives. J. Consum. Res. **11**(3), 741–753 (1984)
33. Johnson, M.D., Hudson, E.J.: On the perceived usefulness of scaling techniques in market analysis. Psychol. Mark. **13**(7), 653–675 (1998)
34. Johnson, M.D., Kisielius, J.: Concreteness-Abstract-Ness and the feature-Dimension distinction. Adv. Consum. Res. **12**, 325–328 (1985)
35. Johnson, M.D., Lehmann, D.R., Fornell, C., Horne, D.R.: Attribute abstraction, feature-dimensionality, and the scaling of product similarities. Int. J. Res. Mark. **9**(2), 131–147 (1992)
36. Johnson, R.B.: Dialectical pluralism: a metaparadigm whose time has come. J. of Mix. Methods Res. **11**(2), 156–173 (2017)
37. Johnson, R.B., Onwuegbuzie, A.J.: Mixed methods research: a research paradigm whose time has come. Educ. Res. **33**(7), 14–26 (2004)
38. Johnson-Laird, P.N.: Mental models in cognitive science. Cogn. Sci. **4**(1), 71–115 (1980)
39. Johnson-Laird, P.N.: Mental models and thought. In: Holyoak, K.J., Morrison, R.G., (Eds.) The Cambridge Handbook of Thinking and Reasoning, pp. 185–208 (1983)
40. Johnson-Laird, P.N.: Mental models and deduction. Trends Cogn. Sci. **5**(10), 434–442 (2001)
41. Johnson-Laird, P.N., Byrne, R.M.: Conditionals: a theory of meaning, pragmatics, and inference. Psychol. Rev. **109**(4), 646–678 (2002)
42. Kanwar, R., Olson, J.C., Sims, L.S.: Toward conceptualizing and measuring cognitive structures. In: Monroe, K.B., Arbor, A., (Eds.) Advances in Consumer Research, Association for Consumer Research, MI, pp. 122–127 (1981)
43. Kearney, A.R., Kaplan, S.: Toward a methodology for the measurement of knowledge structures of ordinary people: the Conceptual Content Cognitive Map (3CM). Environ. and Behav. **29**, 579–617 (1997)
44. Keeney, R.L.: The value of internet commerce to the customer. Manage. Sci. **45**(4), 533–542 (1999)
45. Kim, K.J., Shin, D.-H.: An acceptance model for smart watches: implications for the adoption of future wearable technology. Internet Res. **25**(4), 527–541 (2015)
46. Kriegeskorte, N., Mur, M.: Inverse MDS: inferring dissimilarity structure from multiple item arrangements. Front. Psychol. **3**, 245 (2012)
47. Lapointe, L., Rivard, S.: A multilevel model of resistance to information technology implementation. MIS Q. **29**(3), 461–491 (2005)
48. Laumer, S., Eckhardt, A.: Why Do People Reject Technologies: A Review of User Resistance Theories Information Systems Theory, pp. 63–86. Springer, New York (2012). https://doi.org/10.1007/978-1-4419-6108-2_4
49. Love, E., Okada, E.M.: Construal based marketing tactics for high quality versus low price market segments. J. Prod. Brand Manag. **24**(2), 172–181 (2015)

50. Mathieu, J.E., Heffner, T.S., Goodwin, G.F., Salas, E., Cannon-Bowers, J.A.: The influence of shared mental models on team process and performance. J. Appl. Psychol. **85**(2), 273–283 (2000)
51. McKinsey Global Institute: The Internet of Things: Mapping the Value beyond the Hype. Market Report (2015)
52. Miller, G.A.: A psychological method to investigate verbal concepts. J. Math. Psychol. **6**, 169–191 (1969)
53. Montazemi, A.R., Conrath, D.W.: The use of cognitive mapping for Information requirements analysis. MIS Q. **10**(1), 45–56 (1986)
54. Montgomery, H.: Decision rules and the search for a dominance structure: Towards a process model of decision making. Adv. Psychol. **14**, 343–369 (1983)
55. Moran, T.P.: Guest editor's introduction: an applied psychology of the user. ACM Comput. Surv. (CSUR) **13**(1), 1–11 (1981)
56. Nestrud, M.A., Lawless, H.T.: Perceptual mapping of apples and cheeses using projective mapping and sorting. J. Sens. Stud. **25**(3), 390–405 (2010)
57. Ng, I.C.L., Wakenshaw, S.Y.L.: The Internet-of-Things: review and research directions. Int. J. Res. Mark. **34**(1), 3–21 (2017)
58. Norman, D.A.: Some observations on mental models. In: Gentner, D. Stevens, A.L. (Eds.) Mental Models, pp. 7–14. Lawrence Erlbaum Associates, Hillsdale (1983a)
59. Norman, D.A.: Design Rules based on analyses of human error. Commun. ACM, **26**(4), 254–258 (1983b)
60. Norman, D.: The Design of Everyday Things: Revised and, Expanded edn. Basic Books (AZ), New York (2013)
61. Nosofsky, R.M.: Similarity scaling and cognitive process models. Annu. Rev. Psychol. **43**, 25–53 (1992)
62. Pagès, J.: Collection and analysis of perceived product inter-distances using multiple factor analysis: Application to the study of 10 white wines from the Loire Valley. Food Qual. Prefer. **16**(7), 642–649 (2005)
63. Pavlou, P.A., Fygenson, M.: Understanding and predicting electronic commerce adoption: an extension of the theory of planned behavior. MIS Q. 115–143 (2006)
64. Ram, S.: A model of innovation resistance. In: Wallendorf, M., Anderson, P. (Eds.) ACR NA - Advances in Consumer Research, vol. 14, pp. 208–212. Association for Consumer Research, Provo, UT (1987)
65. Rijsdijk, S.A., Hultink, E.J.: The impact of product smartness on consumer satisfaction through product advantage, compatibility, and complexity. In: Proceedings of the 13th PDMA Research Conference, Orlando (2002)
66. Rijsdijk, S.A., Hultink, E.J.: Honey, have you seen our hamster? consumer evaluations of autonomous domestic products. J. Prod. Innov. Manag. **20**(3), 204–216 (2003)
67. Rijsdijk, S.A., Hultink, E.J.: How today's consumers perceive tomorrow's smart products. J. Prod. Innov. Manag. **26**(1), 24–42 (2009)
68. Rijsdijk, S.A., Hultink, E.J., Diamantopoulos, A.: Product intelligence: its conceptualization, measurement and impact on consumer satisfaction. Acad. Mark. Sci. **35**(3), 340–356 (2007)
69. Risvik, E., McEwan, J.A., Colwill, J.S., Rogers, R., Lyon, D.H.: Projective mapping: a tool for sensory analysis and consumer research. Food Qual. Prefer. **5**(4), 263–269 (1994)
70. Robey, D.: Diversity in information systems research: threat, promise, and responsibility. Inf. Syst. Res. **7**(4), 400–408 (1996)
71. Rogers, E.M.: New product adoption and diffusion. J. Consum. Res. **2**(4), 290–301 (1976)
72. Schiffman, S.S., Reynolds, M.L., Young, F.W.: Introduction to Multidimensional Scaling: Theory, Methods. Applications. Academic Press, New York (1981)

73. Schweitzer, F., van den Hende, E.: To be or not to be in thrall to the march of smart products. Psychol. Mark. **33**(10), 830–842 (2016)
74. Schweitzer, F., van den Hende, E.: Drivers and consequences of narrative transportation: understanding the role of stories and domain-specific skills in improving radically new products. J. Prod. Innov. Manag. **34**(1), 101–118 (2017)
75. Sheth, J.N.: Psychology of innovation resistance: the Less Developed Concept (LDC) in diffusion research. Res. Mark. **4**, 273–282 (1981)
76. Strandvik, T., Holmlund, M., Edvardsson, B.: Customer needing: a challenge for the seller offering. J. Bus. Ind. Mark. **27**(2), 132–141 (2012)
77. Sugai, P.: Mapping the mind of the mobile consumer across borders: an application of the Zaltman metaphor elicitation technique. Int. Mark. Rev. **22**(6), 641–657 (2005)
78. Torgerson, W.S.: Multidimensional scaling: I. theory and method. Psychometrika **17**, 401–419 (1952)
79. Tversky, A.: Features of similarity. Psychol. Rev. **84**(4), 327 (1977)
80. Tversky, A., Gati, I.: Studies of similarity. Cogn. Categ. **1**, 79–98 (1978)
81. Tversky, A., Kahneman, D.: Judgment under uncertainty: heuristics and biases. Science **185**, 1124–1131 (1974)
82. Venkatesh, V., Davis, F.D.: A theoretical extension of the technology acceptance model: our longitudinal field studies. Manage. Sci. **46**(2), 186–204 (2000)
83. Venkatesh, V., Brown, S.A., Bala, H.: Bridging the qualitative - quantitative divide: guidelines for conducting mixed methods research in information systems. MIS Q. **37**(1), 21–54 (2013)
84. Venkatesh, V., Brown, S.A., Sullivan, Y.W.: Guidelines for conducting mixed-methods research: an extension and illustration. J. Assoc. Inf. Syst. **17**(7), 435 (2016)
85. Walker, B., Celsi, R., Olson, J.: Exploring the structural characteristics of consumers' knowledge. In: Wallendorf, M., Anderson, P., (Eds.), NA - Advances in Consumer Research, vol. 14, pp. 17–21. Association for Consumer Research. Provo, UT (1987)
86. Wedel, M., Bijmolt, T.H.: Mixed tree and spacial representations of dissimilarity judgments. J. Classif. **17**(2), 243–271 (2000)
87. Woodside, A.G.: Editorial: sense making in marketing organizations and consumer psychology: theory and practice. Psychol. Mark. **18**(5), 415–421 (2001)
88. Williams, M.D., Dwivedi, Y.K., Lal, B., Schwarz, A.: Contemporary trends and issues in IT adoption and diffusion research. J. Inf. Technol. **24**(1), 1–10 (2009)
89. Wittgenstein, L.: Tractatus logico-philosophicus. Wien (1918)
90. Zaltman, G., Coulter, R.H.: Seeing the voice of the customer: metaphor-based advertising research. J. Advert. Res. **35**(4), 35–51 (1995)
91. Zaltman, G.: Rethinking market research: putting people back. J. Mark. Res. **34**(4), 424–437 (1997)

Sharing Economy and Social Media

The Influence of Social Media on Engendering Strategic Organisational Practices – The Case of Two Tanzanian Telecommunications Companies

Shirumisha Kwayu[(⊠)], Banita Lal[(⊠)], and Mumin Abubakre[(⊠)]

Nottingham Trent University, Nottingham, UK
Shirumisha.kwayu2014@my.ntu.ac.uk,
{Banita.lal, Mumin.Abubakre}@ntu.ac.uk

Abstract. The plethora of social media platforms such as Facebook, twitter, Instagram and WhatsApp has enhanced the information systems within organisations while at the same time being a conundrum to executives, who need to develop strategy around this technology. This paper explores the influence of different social media applications on engendering strategic organisational practices using a practice perspective. Through the practice lens and with the guidance of the interpretivist philosophy, this paper collects empirical evidence from two telecom organisations in Tanzania. The findings show that different types of social media applications play different roles in engendering different strategizing methods, such as formal and informal. Depending on the role the application plays. In practice, this will help organisational executives in the selection of social media applications, which is a crucial stage in the development of social media strategy.

Keywords: Social media · Practice perspective · WhatsApp · Strategizing

1 Introduction

The plethora of social media platforms such Facebook, twitter, Instagram, YouTube and WhatsApp create an ecosystem of social media (Hanna et al. 2011) which enhances Information Systems (IS) within organisations through revitalising fundamental processes such as sharing information and receiving feedback from customers and staff (Kwayu et al. 2017). Consequently, this enables organisations to leverage social relationships such as staff relationships as well as customer relationships, which can lead to various benefits such as extending the spheres of marketing (Berthon et al. 2012). On the other hand, the existence of social media platforms within organisations contributes to democratizing organisational communication, thereby reducing organisational control of information while increasing the power of consumers. As a result, most executives are unable and reluctant to develop strategies and resources for engaging effectively with social media (Kietzmann et al. 2011). The reason being that social media platforms can take various forms such as content communities, social networking sites or blogs (Kietzamann et al. 2011), which illuminates different ways in

A. Elbanna et al. (Eds.): TDIT 2018, IFIP AICT 533, pp. 47–59, 2019.
https://doi.org/10.1007/978-3-030-04315-5_4

which social media intertwines with communication practices such as broadcasting, chatting and sharing that occur outside and within the organisation (Treem and Leonardi 2012). Thus, collectively, the co-existence of varying forms of social media platforms in organisations complicates the development of social media strategy within an organisation because of the 'one size fits all' approach (Jarzabkowski 2005). The 'one size fits all' approach is a single strategy for different forms of social media application that exist in an organisation.

Although the use of social media within organisations has advanced in many spheres, the practical application of social media has outpaced the existing empirical studies which examine their use and how social media may change several organisational processes (Leonardi and Vaast 2016). This suggests that organisations are using social media, yet there is a lack of detailed empirical examination of how social media are used and the impact upon organisational practices and strategy. Considering this shortcoming, there is an apparent need for further research to understand these technologies and their effect on different processes, which will help organisations with their strategizing.

Considering the practice of social media in organisations is far beyond the scholarship as aforementioned, this research adopts a practice perspective, which focuses on emergent practices that are enacted from recursive interaction between people and technology (Orlikowski 2000). In addition, the practice perspective encompasses the complexity entwined between people and technology while embedded within a context, making it a suitable approach for studying dynamic technology such as social media without undermining the role of people or technology in contributing to change and stability.

In light of the above, the main question for this research is: *do different social media platforms create different strategic organisational practices*? An interpretivist approach with empirical data from two Tanzanian telecommunications organisations will be used to answer this question. The data is collected through semi-structured interviews with staff and management within the organisations. Thus, this research aims to explore and understand the role of different social media applications in the organisations from the context of the Tanzanian telecommunications industry. Subsequently, it will help us to understand how the type of social media application associates with, and impacts upon, important organisational processes such as customer service and staff welfare (Kietzmann et al. 2011). In theory, this will enhance existing understanding and literature on social media classification, by helping to differentiate and understand different forms and their implications on organisational processes and practices. In practice, this research will help managers to set policies and procedures that will maximise the impact of social media applications on processes within the organisation.

The remainder of this paper is organised as follows: we first discuss the literature review of social media applications and then the practice perspective. This is followed by the methodology, findings, discussion and, finally, the conclusion.

2   Social Media Applications

Social media use is increasingly becoming mainstream within organisations (Pillet and Carillo 2016) affecting firms in a number of ways including reputation, socialisation, knowledge sharing, and power dynamics (Treem and Leonardi 2012). For example, the ranking mechanism on social media applications such as TripAdvisor have shifted power to the consumer, subsequently influencing the reputations of hotels. Thus, considering the effect of social media on organisations and the complexity created by the various forms of social media, several studies have explained how organisations can understand the various forms of social media platforms so that they can develop their respective social media strategy. Kaplan and Haenlein (2010) classified social media into six categories using theories from media and social processes, which are two key elements of social media. They used the 'social presence theory' which suggests that media differ in the degree of social presence allowed to emerge between two communication partners (Short et al. 1976). In addition, they also used the 'media richness theory', which assumes that the goal of any communication is the resolution of ambiguity and reduction of uncertainty (Daft and Lengel 1986). However, with respect to social process, they used self-representation and self-disclosure, whereby self-representation argues that in any social interaction, people have desires to control the impressions that other people have of them, while self-disclosure is the critical step in the development of relationships (Kaplan and Haenlein 2010). Combining these two elements, the media richness theory and social presence theory, Kaplan and Haenlein (2010) established the types of social media that are collaborative projects (i.e. Wikipedia), blogs, content communities (i.e. YouTube), social networking sites (i.e. Facebook), virtual game worlds (i.e. World of Warcraft) and virtual social worlds (i.e. Second Life). The Table 1 below illustrates further.

Table 1. Classification of social media by social presence/media richness and self-representation/self-disclosure

		Social presence /Media richness		
		Low	Medium	High
Self-presentation/self-disclosure	High	Blogs	Social Networking Sites (e.g. Facebook)	Virtual Social Worlds (e.g. Second Life)
	Low	Collaborative Projects (e.g. Wikipedia)	Content Communities (e.g. YouTube)	Virtual Game Worlds (e.g. World of Warcraft)

Source: Kaplan and Haenlein (2010)

Apart from Kaplan and Haenlein's (2010) classification of social media, Kietzmann et al. (2011) presented a framework for analysing social media according to functions. Kietzmann et al. (2011) seven functional blocks are significant in explaining the user experience on the specific features of social media and its implication for organisations. The functional blocks are neither exclusive nor do they all need to be on each social media platform. For instance, twitter facilitates conversation and sharing through tweeting and retweeting, while Facebook embodies the identity function through setting up of profiles. Below is the list of the functions with their meaning and implications for organisations (Table 2).

Table 2. The functional block table of social media

Functional Block	Meaning	Impact
Presence	The extent to which users know if other are available	Creating and managing the reality, intimacy and immediacy of the context
Relationship	The extent to which users relate to each other	Managing the structural and flow properties in a network of relationships
Reputation	The extent to which users know the social standing of others and content	Monitoring the strength, passion, sentiment and reach of users and brands
Groups	The extent to which users are ordered or form communities	Membership rules and protocols
Conversations	The extent to which users communicate with each other	Conversation velocity and the risks of starting and joining
Sharing	The extent to which users' exchange, distribute and receive content	Content management system and social graph
Identity	The extent to which users are ordered or form communities	Data privacy controls and tools for user self-promotion

Source: Kietzmann et al. (2011)

Furthermore, considering the myriad of social media platforms, Piskorski (2014) explains why some social media platforms are more successful than others. He argues that social media applications become successful by providing a single social solution and, once it provides two or more social solutions, it becomes less effective. Given this phenomenon, social media platforms refrain from copying social solutions from other social media platforms to avoid ineffectiveness; hence, this is the reason why different platforms with non-overlapping social solutions can co-exist in an organisation. A social solution is a solution to alleviate social failures and social failures highlight unmet social needs that can occur due to social or economic reasons (Piskorski 2014). For example, LinkedIn offers a social solution of connecting a job seeker with employers whereas Facebook offers a friend solution by connecting friends.

Despite the above explanations of understanding social media applications, any form of classification of social media platforms is still complex due to the multifariousness of social media platforms as well as the continuous updates and developments of social media technology. Consequently, the changing nature of social media applications complicates the classification of social media applications: resultantly, this provides challenges for executives in identifying ways of managing social media in organisations (Culnan et al. 2010). Although the classification process is complex, the above studies have made a considerable effort to classify them through various theories which, in general, have highlighted the importance of examining specific features of social media applications and their implications for organisations. For instance, Locke et al. (2018) suggest that digital activism (i.e. the #MeToo campaign) on twitter is both powerful and unique in its reach because of the way that twitter space is configured. In addition, the above studies have indicated the different attributes of social media applications and their possible impact as well as the existence of multiple platforms within an organisation. Our study intends to go further and add to this existing body of knowledge by deploying the practice theory and using empirical evidence to identify the facets of social media platforms and the specific role they play in organisations.

3 Practice Theory

Scott and Orlikowski (2014) suggest the practice theory as a suitable lens for understanding dynamic technology such as social media since it does not assume stability, predictability or completeness of technology. The practice theory focuses on how people interact with technology in their ongoing activities while enacting structures that influence the emergent and situated use of that technology (Orlikowski 2000). In addition, Orlikowski (2007) conceptualises practice as material since activities are dependent upon material arrangement in which the activities are taking place. For example, information searching through Google depends on Google's page ranking algorithm. Furthermore, the practice theory emphasises the causal relationship that exists between technology, organisational structure and processes, which is located on the interaction of people and technology (Avgerou 2017). Thus, the practice perspective positions us to understand the role of a technology (in this case social media) within the organisation, since it focuses on the activity; hence, enabling us to correlate the facet (materiality) of the technology and its function.

Kwayu et al. (2017) suggest that the practice perspective can help to understand how social media affects strategy, processes and structure as it considers the social context that enables us to gain insight on reality that is dynamic and complex. Also, considering that the social media effect is multiple, dynamic and contemporaneous (Scott and Orlikowski 2012), the focus on practice enables us to capture the reality in the organisation when people interact with social media.

4 Methodology

This research is guided by an interpretivist philosophy that views knowledge as being socially constructed through language, shared meaning and consciousness (Richey et al. 2018). This philosophy is in line with the nature of this research since practices can be regarded as accomplished social activities through the interpretation of practitioners (Orlikowski and Baroudi 1991). In addition, it is qualitative research, where data is collected through semi-structured interviews with staff from two telecom organisations in Tanzania. Pseudo names used for the two organisations are Kurwa and Dotto: both organisations are large with networks across the country and both have adopted social media. The choice of Tanzania, an emerging market, offers a novel context of understanding the impact of Information Technology (IT) on organisations that operate from a different context to the developed world, especially when considering the digital divide that exists between the developed and developing country (Kwayu et al. 2017).

Twenty interviews were conducted with managers and staff from different departments within the respective telecom organisations. The language used was a mix of Swahili and English, depending on the comfort level of the respondent with both languages. The first author, who conducted the interviews, is Tanzanian and fluent in both languages. The interviews were recorded and transcribed, translated and analysed. The analysis process followed an inductive approach, which extracted themes and issues to concentrate upon (Glaser and Strauss 1967). A narrative structuring method was used for analysis: the narrative style is a powerful method of capturing different aspects of our lives without undermining the role of social or material aspects in contributing to stability and change (Golsorkhi et al. 2015). Following the narrative style, our analysis consisted of four main stages that are: summarizing, clustering, displaying and narrating (Pan and Tan 2011). The summarising stage was through unitizing, which is a coding operation where information is extracted from the text. Hence, this produced units of analysis, which are interview segments that range from phrase/sentence to paragraph. Then, the clustering stage where the units were categorised which gave rise to themes such as: WhatsApp group communication, social media marketing, feedback and social media management. Though codes and themes were produced, Saunders et al. (2009) suggest that the narrative style should focus on the originally told form rather than fragmentation, which is done through coding and themes. In addition, Kvale (1996) suggest that narrative structuring should ensure that data is organised temporally while regarding social and organisational context, thus, focusing the story and plots.

5 Findings

In both telecom organisations, social media practice was similar; this section will provide a narrative of social media practice within the two telecom organisations. Different social media applications such as Facebook, twitter, Instagram, YouTube and WhatsApp are common in both organisations. Other examples of social media use within these companies include blogs and social forums such as Jamiiforums, but on a very minimal scale. In general, there are two distinctive ways in which these social media applications are used by the two telecom organisations. These are for external communication, which is associated with marketing, and for internal communication. External communication is communication between the organisation and the customers or the general public. Facebook, Instagram, YouTube, twitter and blogs are used for external communication. The WhatsApp application is used for internal communication. Internal communication is communication taking place inside the organisation between employees within the organisation.

The Human Resources Manager at Kurwa explains the social media practice as follows.

We have not encouraged people to use social media, nevertheless what we have done we said it should be used for marketing. That is what we have accomplished to this point. Although indirectly we use WhatsApp when we have something to share, work. We share in WhatsApp groups with different people for instance finance or other departments. – Human Resources Manager, Kurwa.

As can be deduced from the quote above, social media is intended to be used for marketing specifically. However, informally, WhatsApp is also used internally for work purposes although there is no apparent set procedures or requirements in place to use it for this purpose. The internal and external use shows how a social media application can be identified by the role it plays in an organisation. For example, Facebook, twitter, Instagram can form a category of applications used for external use while WhatsApp application can be categorised as application used for internal use.

Social media applications that are used for external communication help the organisations with functions such as marketing (as abovementioned), public relations and provides a means of getting feedback from customers. These social media platforms used for external communications are carefully selected by the custodians of the organisation communication. Kurwa's Public Relations Manager and Product Development Manager expand on this as follows:

There are many social media but we have selected a few. We chose those, which we can work with them in an easy way. We look at those, which we can do filtering, we can follow up, we can change people ideas, we can get people opinion, and we can ban bad information. –Public Relation Manager, Kurwa.

Customers provide feedback through different social media platforms, the groups and social media pages, which our PR manage. We are on Facebook, twitter YouTube, Instagram and Jamii forums. We on different platforms and we use them to gather feedbacks, complains, and desires of customers. Sometimes we answer all their questions. Therefore, we communicate with customers through these platforms. Hence, we use the platform to help the customers. – Product Development Manager, Kurwa.

The WhatsApp application, which is associated with internal communication, involves staff communicating with other staff either on a one-to-one basis or through groups. The group communication has significantly enhanced collaboration and teamwork within the telecom organisations. In addition, WhatsApp works in parallel with email communication. In some instances, WhatsApp communication substitutes email while at other times WhatsApp communication complements email communication. Although WhatsApp communication is informal and there is no formalised processes in place regarding how and when it should be used, it is a more popular means of communication across departments and organisational levels when compared to formal means such as email communication. This is the case because WhatsApp is faster and easier to use and access than email. Hence, WhatsApp communication facilitates quick solutions which consequently speeds up processes and enhances staff collaboration. Below are some of the explanations that narrate the use of WhatsApp within the telecom organisations in Tanzania:

> *Those are initiative of individual departments. For example, we from regional branches every unit has its own WhatsApp group. Where they can share work related issues, jokes and do whatever. – Regional Manager, Kurwa.*

> *Our office uses WhatsApp. I have a WhatsApp group of eight people we update each other. Not everything you can share through email. Not all the people are using the email. For instance, there are eight customer services but the computers are two. This means some people do not have email system but they are using WhatsApp because it is modern, easy to communicate anything in the office. This is just an example of my office, but in the zone, there are many groups. There is a social group and work group. When I look at my phone I have not less than eight groups and they are all related to work. It simplifies because when you need information in time the phone is nearby. Someone is in Dar es Salaam [headquarters] and is requesting how many agents do you have in your branch. When you send it on WhatsApp group, it becomes easy because everyone shares that information in time. – Branch Manager, Dotto.*

> *Confidential issues go through email. That is the relation. Email is the most formal communication and WhatsApp is more for business updates, direction, asking guidance or way forward. – Zonal Manager, Dotto.*

The distinction between the use of WhatsApp and other social media applications (Facebook, twitter and Instagram) within the telecom organisations is significant. Primarily, the WhatsApp communication is an individual initiative and the organisation has very little control over this form of communication. Thus, it can be rationalised that WhatsApp communication is a practice that emerges from the employees. In addition, although the management has no formal means like policy or procedures to use emerging social media practices like WhatsApp communication, it appears that the organisation is using an interactive way to encourage the positive use of social media, for instance the use of WhatsApp for assisting work processes as indicated above by the Zonal manager of Dotto.

Distinctively, Facebook, twitter and Instagram, which are used for external communication, have a formal recognition within the organisation. The two telecom organisations have official accounts on these platforms and management of these accounts is centralised from the headquarters. The centralisation of social media is a means of controlling practice associated with these applications, consequently enacting a formal status in the following ways. First, individual branches are not allowed to open any account on social media that represents the organisation. Through this restriction, the organisation can maintain a single voice that represents the organisation in respective platforms. Second, centralisation indicates the formal organisation role in the use of social media through backing up with resources such as personnel who manage the social media accounts. The following insights provide an interpretation on the state of social media applications that are used for external communication:

> *I can say that we have officialised social media because we use them for business marketing. Although we need to restrict some comments. Some comments spoil everything and may affect other people's decision. That is the greatest challenge we are facing. It needs to be open but too open is also biased. – Human Resources Manager, Kurwa.*

We have centralised social media, we do not allow our branches to have social media. It is difficult to manage social media from different user and whatever they have needs to represent one Kurwa. – Marketing Manager, Kurwa.

They collect all the feedback and they will come and say that we get this complains about you (branch). Perhaps, there is an incidence has happened in your branch, they will call me or email me and ask me if am aware of that incidence. Therefore, we might be told to change something or do this when that happens. – Double Road Manager, Dotto.

The above findings have highlighted the state of social media in two telecom organisations in Tanzania. It has shown a distinction between social media applications, with the WhatsApp application supporting internal communication while Facebook, Instagram, and twitter support external communication. The next section will discuss the findings in conjunction with the literature and the practice theory.

6 Discussion

This section aims to discuss the findings using a practice perspective to explore the relationship between social media applications and their function within the two organisations. The findings reveal that social media applications are used to accomplish a particular task. For instance, Facebook, Instagram and twitter are used for communication with the customer hence supporting some of the marketing functions such as maintaining customer relationships and receiving feedback. Similarly, the WhatsApp application is used as means for internal communication between staff. From Kaplan and Haenlein's (2010) classification, we observe that applications with high self-disclosure and presentation are used for external purposes such as marketing while WhatsApp, which has low self-disclosure and presentation, is used for internal communication. On the other hand, it can also be argued that the solutions offered by the application determines their role. For example, the WhatsApp groups help collaboration between staff whereas applications such as Facebook, twitter and Instagram that allow posting are used for advertising and marketing – this corresponds with Piskorski's (2014) argument that a social media application becomes popular due to the solution that it brings. Thus, in essence, the social media applications are adopted for functions in which they were designed for, i.e. twitter, Facebook and Instagram are designed with an external outlook to support mass and open communication which orients them as marketing tools. Whereas the WhatsApp application is designed for private communication giving it an internal position within organisation communication. In theory, this suggests that the use of social media is an appropriation of structure inscribed in the application (Orlikowski 2000). In practice, this emphasises the need to understand the structure inscribed within the social media application to understand their role in an organisation. Thus, following Culnan et al. (2010) suggestion that organisations should be mindful when adopting social media, these findings suggest that mindful adoption can be done by examining the structures inscribed within the social media application.

In addition, the findings highlight how social media is extending the scope of IS within the telecom organisations. First, the WhatsApp communication that is done through personal mobile devices substitutes and complements the corporate IT infrastructure. WhatsApp has been used in parallel with the email system in the organisation, it has also enabled the incorporation of staff who had no access to organisational IT infrastructure (i.e. computers) consequently filling that gap. Besides the deficiency of computers (corporate IT infrastructure), the branch manager of Dotto suggests things like mobility design and easiness as reasons for rise of WhatsApp communication in the company. This means that even those with computers tend to substitute or complement their formal/email communication with WhatsApp. This signifies the importance of materiality and the contextual arrangements as reasons for WhatsApp practice in the telecom organisations. Thus, the contextual arrangement of IT infrastructure influences the performance of social media in the organisations. This finding contrasts with Braojos- Gomez et al.'s (2015) argument that organisational IT infrastructure is positively related to social media competence, as the findings in this study suggest that social media conducted through personal devices can be a substitute of organisational IT infrastructure.

Additionally, the findings show that social media models new practices. For example, the zonal manager from Dotto explains thee distinctive ways in which they practice their communication by describing what sort of communication goes through email and what goes through WhatsApp. Likewise, Facebook, twitter and Instagram have shaped how customer service is carried out as the organisations gather feedback, complaints and desires of the customers. These new practices, which are engendered by social media, are significant because they influence the way organisations operate and consequently the way in which value is created. The practice perspective focuses on repetitive activities (Orlikowski 2000) because such activities influence strategic outcomes of the organisation (Jarzabkowski 2005). For example, through practice of gathering and responding to feedback, complains and desires of customer from social media the telecom organisations can attain strategic outcomes such as increasing customer satisfaction.

Furthermore, the cases of the telecom organisations show an 'application role' based strategizing method for social media. From the practice of the organisations, the social media applications which supported external communication had a formal procedural guidance (e.g. Facebook), while for internal WhatsApp communication it was a form of interactive strategizing such as encouraging positive use. Thus, different social media applications are engendering different forms of strategizing such as formal strategizing for applications that have an external role and interactive strategizing for applications with an internal role. In general, this suggests that it is rational for an organisation to develop social media strategies by focusing on the role that social media plays in an organisation, rather than having a collective social media strategy which contains complications of the 'one size fits all' approach.

Lastly, with regards to our research question - *do different social media platforms create different organisational practices?* - the above discussion shows how classification, for instance by Kaplan and Haenlein (2010), can relate a social media application with its role within an organisation. Similarly, Kietzmann et al.'s (2011) classification can help to explain why application functions such as group functionality of WhatsApp is popular within the organisation. Likewise, this can also help to explain why applications such as Facebook, twitter and Instagram - which have the functions of presence, sharing and reputation - are useful for marketing and external communication purposes. Furthermore, the discussion has shown how the contextual arrangement and classification of social media applications are important in understanding the relationship between the application and the role it plays in organisations; thus, contextual arrangement acts as a moderating factor. Therefore, it can be argued that the classification of social media applications and contextual arrangement can help to determine the role that an application plays within the organisation. This has practical implications on social media strategy as it can help executives with the selection of social media applications for the organisation, which is a crucial part of developing social media strategy (Culnan et al. 2010). Also, by understanding the role that each social media application is playing within an organisation, this can help the organisation to decide a form of strategizing; for instance, through a procedural or an interactive way.

7   Conclusion

Social media represents one of the most dynamic forms of information technology in contemporary organisations. The various forms it takes and the functions it performs is a perplexity facing organisations' executives. Efforts to understand the technology are important for helping executives to develop strategy. This research has shown how different social media applications play different roles within organisations engendering different forms strategizing such as formal (procedural) strategizing for applications which had an external role and informal (interactive) strategizing for applications that had an internal role. Thus, this signifies the importance of differentiating social media applications by classifying them to assist in identifying the types of practices that can manifest within organisations. Therefore, this is significant for strategy development as it helps in the selection of social media platforms. Culnan et al. (2010) identifies mindful adoption as an initial and crucial stage in developing social media strategy. Also, this study highlights the importance of the environment in which the selected social media is going to be appropriated. Evidence presented in our research is just an indication; future research can advance this study by exploring the relationship between the different organisational practices, i.e. formal and informal, engendered by different social media types and the development of organisational strategies. Lastly, future research may explore the impact of social media applications such as WhatsApp on creating blurred boundaries between work and play, which is something highlighted in this study.

References

Avgerou, C.: Theoretical framing of ICT4D research. In: Choudrie, J., Islam, M.Sirajul, Wahid, F., Bass, Julian M., Priyatma, J.E. (eds.) ICT4D 2017. IAICT, vol. 504, pp. 10–23. Springer, Cham (2017). https://doi.org/10.1007/978-3-319-59111-7_2

Berthon, P.R., Pitt, L.F., Plangger, K., Shapiro, D.: Marketing meets web 2.0, social media, and creative consumers: implications for international marketing strategy. Bus. Horizons **55**(3), 261–271 (2012). https://doi.org/10.1016/j.bushor.2012.01.007

Braojos-Gomez, J., Benitez-Amado, J. Llorens-Montes, F.J.: How do small firms learn to develop a social media competence? Int. J. Inf. Manage. **35**(4), 443–458 (2015)

Culnan, M., Mchugh, P., Zubillaga, J.: How large U.S. companies can use twitter and other social media to gain business value. MIS Q. Executive **9**(4), 243–259 (2010)

Daft, R.L., Lengel, R.H.: Organizational information requirements, media richness and structural design. Manage. Sci. **32**(5), 554–571 (1986)

Glaser, B., Strauss, A.: The Discovery of Grounded Theory, pp. 1–19. Weidenfeld & Nicolson, London (1967)

Golsorkhi, D., Rouleau, L., Seidl, D., Vaara, E. (eds.): Cambridge Handbook of Strategy as Practice. Cambridge University Press, Cambridge (2015). https://doi.org/10.1017/CBO9781139681032

Hanna, R., Rohm, A., Crittenden, V.L.: We're all connected: the power of the social media ecosystem. Bus. Horizons **54**(3), 265–273 (2011)

Jarzabkowski, P.: Strategy as practice: An activity based approach. Sage (2005)

Kaplan, A.M., Haenlein, M.: Users of the world, unite! The challenges and opportunities of social media. Bus. Horizons **53**(1), 59–68 (2010)

Kietzmann, J.H., Hermkens, K., McCarthy, I.P., Silvestre, B.S.: Social media? Get serious! Understanding the functional building blocks of social media. Bus. Horizons **54**(3), 241–251 (2011). https://doi.org/10.1016/j.bushor.2011.01.005

Kvale, S.: The 1,000-page question. Qualitative inquiry **2**(3), 275–284 (1996)

Kwayu, S., Lal, B., Abubakre, M.: Enhancing organisational competitiveness via social media-a strategy as practice perspective. Inf. Syst. Front. **20**, 1–18 (2017)

Leonardi, P., Vaast, E.: Social media and their affordances for organizing: a review and agenda for research. Acad. Manage. Ann. **11**(1), 150–188 (2016)

Locke, A., Lawthom, R., Lyons, A.: Social media platforms as complex and contradictory spaces for feminisms: visibility, opportunity, power, resistance and activism (2018)

Orlikowski, W.J.: Using technology and constituting structures: a practice lens for studying Technology in Organizations. Organ. Sci. **11**(4), 404–428 (2000). https://doi.org/10.1287/orsc.11.4.404.14600

Orlikowski, W.J.: Sociomaterial practices: exploring technology at work. Organ. Stud. **28**(9), 1435–1448 (2007). https://doi.org/10.1177/0170840607081138

Orlikowski, W.J., Baroudi, J.J.: Studying information technology in organizations: research approaches and assumptions. Inf. Syst. Res. **2**(1), 1–28 (1991). https://doi.org/10.1287/isre.2.1.1

Pan, S.L., Tan, B.: Demystifying case research: a structured– pragmatic–situational (SPS) approach to conducting case studies. Inf. Organ. **21**(3), 161–176 (2011). https://doi.org/10.1016/j.infoandorg.2011.07.001

Pillet, J.C., Carillo, K.D.A.: Email-free collaboration: an exploratory study on the formation of new work habits among knowledge workers. Int. J. Inf. Manage. **36**(1), 113–125 (2016). https://doi.org/10.1016/j.ijinfomgt.2015.11.001

Piskorski, M.J.: A Social Strategy: How We Profit from Social Media. Princeton University Press, Princeton (2014). https://doi.org/10.1515/9781400850020

Richey, M., Gonibeed, A., Ravishankar, M.N.: The perils and promises of self-disclosure on social media. Inf. Syst. Front. (2018). https://doi.org/10.1007/s10796-017-9806-7

Saunders, M., Lewis, P., Thornhill, A.: Research methods for business students. Pearson education (2009)

Scott, S.V., Orlikowski, W.J.: Reconfiguring relations of accountability: materialization of social media in the travel sector. Accounting, Organ. Soc. **37**(1), 26–40 (2012). https://doi.org/10.1016/j.aos.2011.11.005

Scott, S., Orlikowski, W.: Entanglements in practice: performing anonymity through social media. MIS Q. **38**(3), 873–893 (2014). https://doi.org/10.25300/misq/2014/38.3.11

Short, J., Williams, E., Christie, B.: The social psychology of telecommunications (1976)

Treem, J.W., Leonardi, P.M.: Social media use in organizations: exploring the affordances of visibility, editability, persistence, and association. Commun. Yearb. **36**, 143–189 (2012)

Examining Convergence Behaviour During Crisis Situations in Social Media - A Case Study on the Manchester Bombing 2017

Milad Mirbabaie[1(✉)], Deborah Bunker[2], Annika Deubel[1],
and Stefan Stieglitz[1]

[1] University of Duisburg-Essen, Duisburg, Germany
{milad.mirbabaie,annika.deubel,
stefan.stieglitz}@uni-due.de
[2] The University of Sydney, Sydney, Australia
deborah.bunker@sydney.edu.au

Abstract. Convergence Behaviour Archetypes (CBA) describe the many different ways that individuals spontaneously and collectively move towards an emergency situation. If this movement is not managed effectively, crisis management issues and problems can emerge and lead to an exacerbation of the crisis situation e.g. panic, convergence of people and resources towards danger, convergence of excess and unrequired people and resources etc. Users of social media platforms express different motivations and behaviours while converging on a crisis. While this behaviour has been analysed in previous research, an understanding of convergence behaviour facilitated by social media platforms to an effective level of control, is yet to be achieved. This paper examines how Twitter users, converged on the Manchester Bombing 2017. We identified the most impactful convergence behaviour archetypes, including those with the highest perceived legitimacy of convergence i.e. those deemed by the Twitter network, to have a necessary and meaningful role in the crisis. Manual content and social network analyses were conducted on our data by identifying three roles that determine the Twitter users with the highest impact regarding their retweet behaviour. We determined that Helpers, Mourners and Detectives had the highest impact on crisis communication in this event.

Keywords: Convergence Behaviour · Crisis communication · Social media
Social network analysis · Information systems

1 Introduction

Nowadays, man-made disasters caused by acts of terrorism are occurring with an increasing prevalence [11, 41]. With the development of Web 2.0, the use of *Information and Communication Technologies* (ICT), such as social media like Twitter or Facebook, have emerged as an important technological trend [18, 39]. These easily accessible Internet-based applications enable users to create and share content-based information and opinions while seemingly having unlimited reach within a communications network in real-time with no cost [14]. Recent studies consider social media

© IFIP International Federation for Information Processing 2019
Published by Springer Nature Switzerland AG 2019.
A. Elbanna et al. (Eds.): TDIT 2018, IFIP AICT 533, pp. 60–75, 2019.
https://doi.org/10.1007/978-3-030-04315-5_5

to be one of the most popular sources of receiving and collecting essential crisis information [22, 25] so, therefore, these social networks have various benefits for crisis communication and crisis management.

On the one hand, people can use social media to make sense of what has happened and gather information more quickly while responding collectively [35, 40]. On the other hand, these social networks are not only used for collecting critical news, but also for delivering emotional support to people affected by the crisis [26].

In addition, research has revealed that social media users exhibit different intended behaviours to converge on a crisis, that is reflected in their crisis communication on social networking sites. This specific behaviour is called *Convergence Behaviour (CB)*. It describes the movement of individuals or resources towards the crisis event [10] and can be categorised into a specific *Convergence Behaviour Archetype (CBA)*. While these CBA and their legitimacy in crisis situations, have been examined in crisis behaviour research, there is a substantial gap in our knowledge of how CBA are facilitated and legitimized by social media use during crises.

For instance, the legitimacy of Convergence Behaviour has been questioned by various researchers, as "Convergence, at its heart, presents a conflict of legitimacy" [21, p. 103]. People have different intentions when converging on a crisis claiming that their reasons are valid, and their requirement to participate in crisis communications is necessary. As all CBA present certain difficulties and challenges to emergency officials, the legitimacy of these different behaviour types is hard to determine. Researchers have specified that in social media, CBA assume a certain kind of legitimacy through a "wider sphere of influence" [45, p. 4]. Thus, if users deem a social media post to be legitimate and trustworthy, its influence increases and the author might emerge as an opinion leader [48] and a reliable information source during a crisis. Opinion leadership is mainly characterised as the social media users' influence on others' behaviours and even their attitudes. Until now, we have yet to understand which CBA exert the biggest influence on crisis communication in social media. In developing this understanding, further knowledge on which CBA have the highest potential for perceived legitimacy on social networks during a crisis, can be developed.

In this paper, we will therefore aim to answer the following research question:

RQ: What Convergence Behaviour Archetypes have the biggest impact (influence and legitimacy) on social media crisis communication?

In order to answer the question, we analysed the communication network on the social media platform Twitter, during the terror attack in Manchester on 22 May 2017. This study provides a new approach to filtering and analysing Twitter data to highlight and identify CBA on social media by conducting a social network analysis (SNA). Distinctive roles were initially identified that were introduced in previous research studies [38]. Through this analysis, we were able to determine the top users and influencers of the platform that lead the Twitter communication (retweetability) during the Manchester Bombing. This gave us a different perspective on this crisis incident when compared to previous crisis incident research, which has mainly relied on text mining analysis approaches. We were then able to identify the CBA for every tweet through applying a manual content analysis (MCA) to the dataset.

Thereafter, the role measures of each Twitter user were added to a total value for the CBA in order to determine the Impact Measure (IM) of the archetype and therefore identify the most impactful CBA that emerged during the Manchester Bombing.

The remainder of this paper is structured as follows. In Sect. 2 we describe the status quo of the literature. In Sect. 3 we introduce our applied research methods. We then describe the results and develop our discussion. Lastly, we summarise our findings, point out the study limitations and highlight possible future directions.

2   Literature Review

2.1   Crisis Communication on Social Media

Crisis communication represents a domain that describes the "process of creating a shared meaning" [9, p. 2] among all individuals that are involved or affected by a crisis. Effective crisis communication is a fundamental principal to successful crisis management and disaster relief [15, 18]. In recent years, the use of social media for crisis communication has increased substantially and emerged as a rapidly growing trend [1, 23]. As a new source of information for the general public, social networking sites are used for information exchange about emergency situations on both a global and local level and have actually changed how crisis information is created and distributed to individuals both directly impacted by a crisis and those merely observing [7, 9, 46].

Understanding this rapid widespread diffusion of social media adoption, and assessing what and how information is spreading, as well as identifying emerging crisis communication problems and issues, is critical for crisis management so as to initiate an effective crisis response by professionals [12]. As a result, research in crisis communication on social media has gained momentum in recent times. For example, research has emerged during the last few years that helps explain the process of *Sensemaking* during crises. Researchers [29] investigated what kinds of information were communicated through social media in order for users to make sense of the situation. They used a relatively new approach of identifying different roles that represent the users with the highest *Information Diffusion Impact (IDI)* regarding their retweetability [38]. In fact, identifying social media users with the highest impact, has been a large field in many disciplines researching social media, such as politics or social media marketing, but has only occasionally been applied in crisis communication.

Previous research indicates that three influence measures exist to understand what different roles users play in social media. Firstly, the indegree, a metric that describes all incoming relations of a user in a Social Network Graph, represents the *Popularity* of an individual. Secondly, the number of retweets serve as the *Perceived Content Value* of a users' post. Lastly, the mentions represent the *Name Value* of a person [8].

Previous researchers based their study of IDI on the act of retweeting, indicating it to be "the principal factor" [38, p. 2] of *Information Diffusion (ID)*. They applied a self-introduced user classification to three roles on the Twitter datasets of the Great Eastern Japan Earthquake in 2011 and the Boston Marathon Bombing in 2013. Identifying emerging leaders or impactful users in crisis communication might also be an effective way of identifying posts that ensure a higher probability of reliability and truthfulness [27, 28], although this is not guaranteed. In the last few years, there has been an increasing concern about false information propagation on social media. As stated earlier, the sheer mass of information on social networking platforms provides valuable insight and news for officials, emergency managers and first responders, as well as traditional media sources [7, 33]. Social media platforms, however, also enable false and unreliable information to be spread throughout the network [2, 15]. Since social media platforms generate massive amounts of information that is already hard to manage, the monitoring, identification and analysis of reliable and truthful social media data continue to be one of the main challenges for crisis and emergency managers.

2.2 Convergence Behaviour

It would seem that the overall belief of emergency managers is that people who are affected by a crisis respond in a socially disorganised and disoriented manner [4, 37]. However, research highlights that people actually form a collective intelligence and act in a rational way instead of exhibiting disorganised behaviour [4, 47].

In general, *convergence* means *"the movement or inclination and approach towards a particular point"* [10, p. 3]. Contrary to the general image of behaviour in emergency situations, people, resources and information spontaneously converge *toward* a disaster area instead of moving away [6, 10, 21]. This behaviour causes many officials and emergency managers to grapple with the impact of *Convergence Behaviour (CB)* [4]. Instead of losing control and fleeing the crisis area in fear, people try to gather as much information as possible about the situation and, based on this information, make quick decisions in order to save their lives and often to aid others in need of help [19]. Thus, in many instances, officials can be caught "off guard" when an unanticipated number of people turn up to an event, or a large amount of information is generated by reaction to an event, which can, if uncontrolled and unmanaged, complicate crisis management. Understanding the different motives people may have while converging on a crisis, must be better understood to control mass movement of people towards a crisis [45].

With the increased use of digital media as well as ICT, CB can be exhibited not only in the physical but also virtual environment. The use of social networking platforms enables CB to adopt new forms of interaction between actors responding to a crisis [20, 30]. CB in the era of social media is therefore no longer limited by geographical or physical boundaries, but creates a possibility of event participation and convergence for people all over the world through social networks [34, 45]. Through the forming of a collective intelligence during disaster situations, many people start to volunteer in order to support officials or help those affected by the crisis [21]. CB encompasses major negative aspects as well, indicating that it should be controlled to some degree [4, 45]. In general, digital *Convergence Behaviour Archetypes (CBA)* might flood social networks with messages, making it hard to find important and required information, causing poor crisis response or misuse of resources [45]. This especially concerns crisis volunteers, who digitally converge on a crisis to support and aid official emergency managers [42].

In order to control and predict CB, it is inevitable that we must also increase our overall understanding and knowledge of it. Depending on the individual or group's intention and the reason behind converging on a crisis situation, each individual reveals a prominent behaviour [5] through their actions. Based on this range of behaviour, researchers [10] identified five different CBA, which are: *the Returnees, the Anxious, the Helpers, the Curious* and *the Exploiters* [10]. Additionally, other researchers [21] were able to find two new types of Convergence Behaviour which were *the Fans* or *Supporters* and *the Mourners*. The transformation of CB in social media enabled the emergence of new types such as *the Detectives* [45] or *the Manipulators* [6]. Another recent analysis of bystanders CB, [5] uncovered the emergence of *the Furious* and *the Impassive*.

Each CBA attributes to itself a high degree of legitimacy in participation in crisis communication [21], however, not every CBA has a useful role to play in crisis management. This issue has been explored [21, 45] but is yet to be examined in detail.

The CBA reveal the motivation of individuals who converge on a crisis and can also provide an answer as to why CB occurs in crisis situations. Table 1 presents all CBA in evidence so far.

3   Method

3.1   Case Study

In order to address the research question, we conducted an analysis of a Twitter communication dataset centred on the terror attack that occurred in Manchester, United Kingdom, on 22 May 2017 21:31 (UTC). The attacker detonated a bomb after a concert by the American singer Ariana Grande. Twenty-three people were killed by the bombing, including the attacker and 250 more were injured. The Manchester Bombing was examined due to the nature of the event (terrorist attack) as well its international impact.

We focussed on Twitter, which is currently the most popular microblogging service with over 313 million users [5, 38], because of its 140-character communication structure which has recently been expanded to 280 characters, Twitter allows users to make short and public statements [49] with fast and spontaneous information diffusion while reaching a large group of users [17, 32, 47]. These characteristics have been found to be very useful in crisis response.

3.2   Data Collection

For our purpose, we considered a social media analytics framework proposed by researchers [43], which acts as a guideline for social media analytics tools and methods. While originally based on the analysis of political communication on social media, it has been previously extended and the possibility of applying it in other research fields, such as crisis communication, was recently noted [44].

Table 1. Convergence Behaviour Archetypes.

Behaviour	Characteristics of social media communications activities	Examples
The Returnees [10]	Enquire about properties they left behind and status updates about crises	*'Back at my house. Whole area looks devastated.'*
The Anxious [10]	Information seeking about missing persons, shelter and medical aid or general expression of fear	*'Please, if anyone has seen my friend let me know. We need to know she's okay!'*
The Helpers [10]	Help in identifying false crisis information, create and share posts about possible shelters	*'If anybody needs a place to stay, message me. I live nearby.'*
The Curious [10]	Ask questions about what happened and crisis conditions	*'What happened? Anybody know?'*
The Exploiters [10]	Scamming or spreading of false information, use crisis to promote own organisation/products	Misuse of the crisis hashtag for own products, e.g. *'#ManchesterBombing try out our new product!'*
The Fans or Supporters [21]	Supportive and grateful social media posts regarding disaster relief and official rescuers	*Staff underpaid and overworked, but there when we truly need them. Thank you.'*
The Mourners [21]	Paying tribute to victims or people affected by the crisis	*'Simply heartbroken by the news. Rest in peace.'*
The Detectives [45]	Surveillance activities, sharing news and information to increase information management	*'Police operation after **unconfirmed** gunshots and explosion.'*
The Manipulators [6]	Attention seeking and manipulative behaviour	*'That proves I was right all along. They should all be banned!*
The Furious [5]	Expression of anger and resentment about the crisis situation	*'What a cowardly act of terror. This is unbelievable!'*
The Impassive [5]	Don't actively take part in crisis communication, "reportage" function	e.g. passively sharing their own location

For data selection purposes, we chose a keyword-based tracking approach by focusing on the hashtags #Manchester and #ManchesterBombing, as these were the most prominent hashtags that were used on Twitter during the terror attack. Moreover, only English tweets were examined due to the crisis location, which is an English-speaking city. The nature of the event (terrorist attack) also ensures the internationality applicability of and interest in, this research project. The tracking method targeted the Twitter API[1], which is an interface, enabling us to receive data from Twitter. For analysis, a self-developed Java crawler was used to collect the data through the

---

[1] https://developer.twitter.com/en.html, last access 2018/02/05.

Search API, by using the library Twitter4J[2]. Subsequently, we saved the data in a MySQL database. In total, 3,265,007 tweets were collected from 22 May 21:31:00 to 24 May 23:59:59 (UTC). We chose to examine this specific timeframe to not only analyse the actual crisis, but also consider the post-crisis communication.

3.3 Data Analysis

In order to answer our research question, we firstly filtered the dataset by identifying the top central users that participated in the crisis communication on Twitter during the event. This was done by identifying the social network roles using a previous framework [38], which contains the roles of *Information starters*, *Amplifiers* and *Transmitters* [38]. The top 300 users of each role were identified to highlight the occurrence of influential users in every stage of the event. To meet this objective, we conducted a *Social Network Analysis (SNA)* using the tool *Gephi*[3], which is an open-source software tool for analysis as well as visualisation of networks and complex datasets [31]. In conducting a SNA, the data was visualised by a network consisting of nodes and edges, in which the nodes represent the users and the edges represent the different relations between the users [29]. A SNA allowed us to study the structures of the relationships between the users during a certain time span through different techniques and measures.

The *degree centrality (DC)* measures the influence of the different actors on the network by the number of relationships that are established with other members, or in other words, it describes the total number of edges connected to the users [13, 24]. In direct graphs, there exists two kinds of DC. While the *in-degree* represents the number of edges coming into a node and therefore portrays all incoming relations (here: being retweeted), the *out-degree* describes the edges going out of a node, thus representing all outcoming relations (here: retweeting other users). The *betweenness centrality (BC)* represents the importance of a node to the shortest path lengths through the network. Users with a high betweenness centrality enable the flow of information from one network cluster to another [13], as they represent the nodes with the shortest path length.

- *Information Starters*: Information Starters are the most frequently retweeted users and are measured by the in-degree centrality. By being retweeted the most, the Information Starters contain the highest perceived content value.
- *Amplifiers*: The Amplifiers are identified by the amount of retweeting. While they do not tweet interesting content by themselves, they have the potential to diffuse information. The Amplifiers are measured by the out-degree centrality.
- *Transmitters*: Transmitters act as bridges between several Twitter communities that are built in a network through the interaction of the users with each other. They are necessary to reach other communities, which results in a broader information transmission. The community clusters can be detected by conducting a Modularity calculation in Gephi. Transmitters are measured the by betweenness centrality.

---

[2] http://twitter4j.org, last access 2018/02/05.
[3] https://gephi.org/, last access 2018/02/05.

Next, we coded the 900 filtered tweets of all three role categories with a *Manual Content Analysis* using the characteristics of the CBA definitions given in Table 1 as a coding scheme. Thus, the number of occurrences of each Convergence Behaviour type was identified. Subsequently to reviewing this analysis, an additional method needed to be applied to the dataset. As the assignment of roles represents an approach for identifying the most impactful users but not whole user groups, this method alone is not sufficient in determining the most impactful CBA, since they vary in how frequently they occur. For example, one CBA might have the highest average in-degree, but only 5 tweets of this type might have appeared in the dataset. In contrast, another CBA might have a slightly smaller average in-degree, however, over 100 tweets of this type might have appeared in the dataset and therefore their impact might actually be higher, since the average measure does not contain any information frequencies. To identify the CBA with the most impact in crisis communication during the Manchester Bombing, the measures of each CBA of the respective roles were tallied to an overall measure of each CBA. Hence, this case study proposes an extended method to identify the most impactful user groups, by CBA. Figure 1 represents this formula to determine the measure, which we labelled as *Impact Measure*.

This formula was applied to every CBA occurring in the three roles (Information Starters (I), Amplifiers (O) and Transmitters (B)). The CBA that contains the highest value of the calculated Impact Measure (*IM*), is considered to have the highest impact.

4   Findings

4.1   Manual Content Analysis

The Manual Content Analysis revealed the number of CBA in each role, which are displayed in Fig. 2.

4.2   Social Network Analysis

When importing the data in Gephi, the unfiltered Network consists of 1,358,404 nodes and 2,838,008 edges. By filtering the data for the top 300 of each of the roles (Information Starters, Amplifiers and Transmitters), we identified the most influential users in terms of retweet behaviour, so the network then consists of 847 nodes and 8,286 edges. In addition, a Modularity calculation with a Resolution of 1.0 resulted in 3 main community clusters.

Some intersections between roles were also detected. While the Information Starters shared 9 users with the Amplifiers and 98 users with the Transmitters, the Amplifiers and the Transmitters intersected with 21 users. Thus, a total number of 228 intersections occurred in this dataset. Figure 3 visualises the social network graph that was analysed in this study, whereby the medium grey nodes represent the Information Starters, the light grey nodes the Amplifiers and the dark grey nodes the Transmitters.

Information Starters
The Information Starters alone consisted of 276 nodes and 394 edges. Their in-degree value ranged from 1,669 (lowest) to 7,6564 (highest) whereby their network analysis

$$\sum IM(I,O,B) = m(I,O,B)_1 + \cdots + m(I,O,B)_n$$

Fig. 1. Formula to determine the Impact Measure.

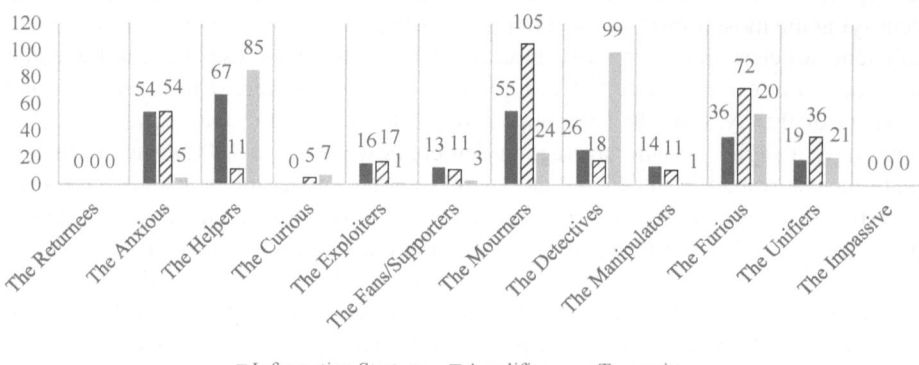

■ Information Starters   ▨ Amplifiers   ■ Transmitters

Fig. 2. The occurrence of CBA in each role.

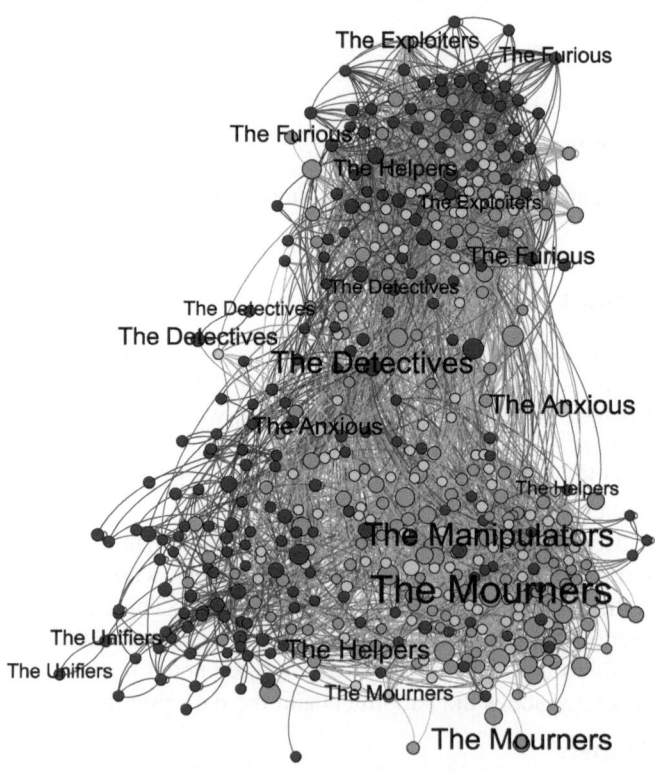

Fig. 3. Social network graph.

shows that nodes with a higher in-degree have more relations with each other, while nodes with a lower in-degree did not have any interaction with the other nodes. The Information Starters had an average follower count of 936,026.38 and were averagely retweeted 51,384 times, while they retweeted other posts 3 times on average. Along with the Amplifiers, the Information Starters consist of 3,958 edges, while with the Transmitters have 959 edges. Hence, their network consists of 5,311 edges in total.

Amplifiers
The network of the Amplifiers consists of 279 nodes and 34 edges. Their out-degree value ranges from 39 (lowest) and 475 (highest). The users have an average follower count of 9,600.79 and are retweeted 89 posts on average, whereas their own tweets were averagely retweeted 8 times. While they barely have edges with themselves, the Amplifiers contain of 3,958 edges with the Information Starters and 3,336 edges with the Transmitters. In total, their network comprises of 7,328 edges.

Transmitters
The network of the Transmitters contains 292 nodes and 1,027 edges. The betweenness centrality ranges from 301,013,002 (lowest) to 278,139,622,76 (highest) with an average of 3,717,157,952. In contrast to the average path length of 5.162 of the whole dataset, the Transmitters comprise an average path length of 7.017 and an average follower count of 137,706.53. Their tweets were averagely shared 1629 times, while the Transmitters themselves retweeted posts 18 times on an average basis. The Transmitter consist of 959 edges with the Information Starters and of 2,209 edges with the Amplifiers. Thus, their network contains 4,195 edges in total.

4.3 Computational Analysis

The Impact Measure, i.e. the sum of all the measures for each CBA has been determined using the proposed formula from Fig. 1. As the numbers are in some cases high and hard to grasp, the percentage of the Impact Measure (p (I, O, B)) was additionally calculated. The results are displayed in the Table 2 below.

Table 2. Results of the Impact Measure calculation.

CBA	ΣIM(I)	$p(I)$	ΣIM(O)	$p(O)$	ΣIM(B)	$p(B)$
Returnees	–	–	–	–	–	–
Anxious	234,574	15.27	927	3.44	27,444,902,321	2.57
Helpers	426,045	27.73	1,965	7.29	274,745,984,251	25.75
Curious	–	–	585	2.17	37,389,355	0.00
Exploiters	44,992	2.92	1,720	6.38	2,366,080,254	0.22
Supporters	56,259	3.66	952	3.54	4,067,205,681	0.38
Mourners	309,209	20.13	9,222	34.26	311,761,760,731	29.22
Detectives	182,625	11.89	1,384	5.14	358,407,938,140	33.59
Manipulators	41,606	2.71	1,338	4.97	1,979,825,464	0.19
Furious	174,774	11.38	6,123	22.74	58,703,065,797	5.50
Unifiers	66,260	4.31	2,713	10.07	27,552,920,068	2.58
Impassive	–	–	–	–	–	–

5 Discussion

By conducting a manual content analysis, we were able to reveal a new Convergence Behaviour type that manifests in crisis communication. *The Unifiers* developed a strong motivation of social cohesion by bringing people in the Twitter network together as well as showing strength and solidarity in times of crises. The emergence of *the Unifiers* also matches with current research findings, as it has been indicated that users who provide emotional support and express solidarity by tweeting posts with a positive sentiment, are noted as having a central role on social media communication networks like Twitter, during crisis situations [3, 16]. An emerging sense of community can, therefore, help social media users to feel better about what is occurring in the crisis situation and also better cope with their emotions. As these characteristics do not fit with current knowledge and characteristics of existing CBA, this study therefore proposes to introduce the new and distinctive CBA category of *the Unifiers*. In contrast to other CBA, *the Unifiers* use the crisis to express positive thoughts and attempt to bring the people together.

The Unifiers   Expression of solidarity, emotional support and the motivation to strengthen the cohesion of social media users in times of crises and to create a sense of community among the social network.
We will not give in to this cowardice. I stand in solidarity with the brave people of #Manchester. (@khalid4 PB, 2017). [Tweet, Content Analysis].

The goal of this study was to identify the most impactful CBA based on three roles, by conducting a Social Network Analysis. In contrast to [29], which determined large intersections between the roles, i.e. mainly between the Information Starters and the Amplifiers, almost no intersections of these two roles could be detected in our study. It is therefore suggested that, in contrast to their previous assumption, these two roles need to be better differentiated. Also, larger intersections between the Information Starters and the Transmitters were identified, suggesting that in this case study, many users who were retweeted the most, could also disseminate their tweets into different communities of the network. Furthermore, we revealed that, the Information Starters have, in contrast to the Amplifiers and the Transmitters, the most followers with an average follower count of 936,026.38.

As opposed to [5], who identified a high occurrence of *the Impassive*, this study could not detect this CBA. We conclude that, while many users assume the role of this type, it does not have an overall high impact on crisis communication.

The results have shown that, based on the three roles that determine the most impactful users based on their retweet behaviour, different CBA can be considered as the most impactful depending on the assigned role.

As for the Information Starters, our analysis has revealed that, based on the developed Impact Measure (IM), *the Helpers* represent the CBA with the highest impact. This means that, overall, the tweets of *the Helpers* were retweeted the most. We were therefore able to confirm previous research that highlights the problematic abundance of volunteers on social media, which can cause unwanted noise of this CBA

[42, 45] during a crisis event. As previously stated, the Information Starters can be accredited with high perceived legitimacy, since these users are the most frequently retweeted by other individuals. Thus, our results suggest that social media users accredit *the Helpers* for being the most legitimate CBA. Next to *the Helpers*, *the Mourners* are also evaluated as having a high IM. Additionally, *the Anxious* have the third highest IM(I), proving that social media users assign individuals who search for missing loved ones and seek help on Twitter, as having a high legitimacy.

Regarding the Amplifiers, *the Mourners* emerged to have the highest IM(O) and therefore can be considered to have the highest overall impact by retweeting posts the most. Consequently, *the Mourners* contain not only a high perceived content value as they represent the second most impactful Information Starters, but they also have an important role in amplifying content on Twitter. The second most impactful Amplifier was *the Furious*. The results show that the retweet function was therefore mostly used by the CBA who express their emotions through their tweets, as grief and anger are considered to have a high sentiment [11, 36].

Focussing on Transmitters, the results of the IM(B) calculation implies *the Detectives* to be the most impactful CBA thus being the users who transform and disseminate tweets and knowledge into different communities the most. The *Mourners,* however, only had a slightly lower IM(B). Further, *the Helpers* represent the CBA with the third highest impact. Besides these three archetypes, all others had a surprisingly low measure, indicating that *the Detectives*, *the Mourners* and *the Helpers* are the main CBA who disseminate content through different communities. This strengthens the occurrence of their own content and we can assume that this ensures that many users from different networks are informed about the latest news and possibilities to get help.

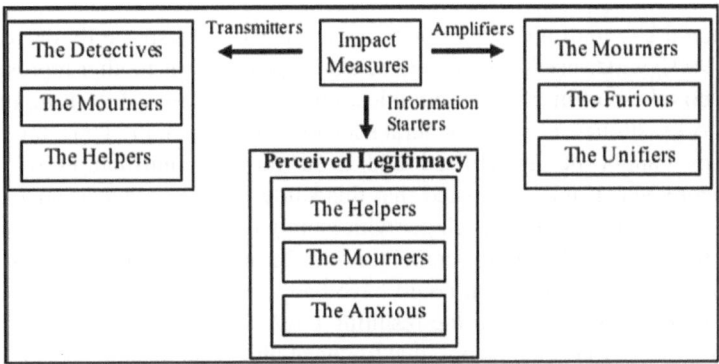

Fig. 4. The top three most impactful CBA of each role.

The fact that *the Mourners* are at least the second most impactful CBA in all three roles is rather unforeseen, since previous research has never isolated or discovered a high occurrence or impact of this CBA. Their high impact on crisis communication can therefore be perceived as problematic, as it is to be assumed that their tweets create a high level of noise which can aggravate crisis management efforts.

Figure 4 outlines the three CBA with the highest impact on crisis communication of each role, whereas the Information Starters simultaneously represent the CBA with the highest perceived legitimacy.

6   Conclusion

Our study extends existing literature on Convergence Behaviour (CB) on social media during crisis situations. It serves as a very first step in the identification of the Convergence Behaviour Archetypes (CBA) that have the biggest impact on crisis communication and thereby the highest perceived legitimacy. This work was able to identify *the Helpers* to be the CBA that was most retweeted throughout the crisis and therefore consisting of the highest perceived legitimacy. Moreover, *the Mourners* had the highest impact by retweeting the most. This would seem to indicate that those social media users who create content based on their emotional state tend to retweet the most. Lastly, *the Detectives* were able to disseminate information into different communities the most. With *the Unifiers*, the study was able to detect a new CBA. We were thus not only able to extend the knowledge on how users converge on social networks during crisis situations, our results can also help crisis managers to gain more insight into users' behaviour. Knowing which behaviour on social media has the biggest impact, might aid them in controlling the sheer mass of information that is generated during a crisis event.

One should be mindful of the limitations of this work. Firstly, only one crisis event looking at 900 Twitter users was analysed. Consequently, it is neither representative of all users who take part in crisis communication on Twitter, nor does it represent other social networks, studies, crises or general social media behaviour. Thus, the results and contributions cannot be generalised and need further confirmation by additional research. Moreover, it must be noted that this study analyses a terror attack that took place at a concert of an American singer with mainly under-aged fans and listeners. The possibility that the social media users might have been significantly younger than users in other case studies of this kind, could have had a big influence on the overall crisis communication and therefore on the resulting CBA that were detected.

By applying the roles, it was possible to reveal the social media users and CBA that had the most impact regarding their retweet behaviour. One question that could additionally be answered in further research, is if these CBA change their role during the crisis communication *do they get affected or impacted by communication with other users*? Further, other approaches (than the application of the three roles) could be used in an analysis to identify CBA impact, such as the follower count.

This work has detected a strong emotional impact during the Manchester Bombing. While this might not be surprising due to the crisis type, it can further be assumed that CBA not only differ in their intent on converging on a crisis, but also in their emotional states. Further research could therefore explore this finding in more detail and examine the emotional impact of CBA with a sentiment analysis.

To enhance our findings, which focus on the issue of legitimacy, the approach applied by this work could be extended by comparing the perceived legitimacy of the social media users with those CBA that emergency management agencies see as having legitimate roles to play in a crisis. What archetypes are the most useful for emergency services agencies to enlist for crisis communications purposes on social media? Qualitative surveys in cooperation with emergency organisations might serve to shed light on these questions.

References

1. Acar, A., Muraki, Y.: Twitter for crisis communication: lessons learned from Japan's tsunami disaster. Int. J. Web Based Communities **7**, 392 (2011)
2. Akhgar, B., Fortune, D., Hayes, R.E., Manso, M., Guerra, B.: Social media in crisis events. In: Proceedings of the IEEE International Conference on Technologies for Homeland Security, pp. 760–765 (2013)
3. Albris, K.: The switchboard mechanism: how social media connected citizens during the 2013 floods in Dresden. J. Contingencies Cris. Manag. **4**, 1–8 (2017)
4. Auf der Heide, E.: Convergence behavior in disasters. Ann. Emerg. Med. **41**, 463–466 (2003)
5. Bunker, D., Mirbabaie, M., Stieglitz, S.: Convergence behaviour of bystanders: an analysis of 2016 Munich shooting Twitter crisis communication. In: Proceedings of the Australasian Conference on Information Systems (2017)
6. Bunker, D., Sleigh, A.: Social media use and convergence behaviours during disasters: a cloud with a silver lining or a fog of manipulation? In: Proceedings of the Information Systems Research Conference Scandinavia (2016)
7. Cameron, M.A., Power, R., Robinson, B., Yin, J.: Emergency situation awareness from Twitter for crisis management. In: Proceedings of the 21st International Conference Companion on World Wide Web - WWW 2012 Companion, p. 695 (2012)
8. Cha, M., Haddai, H., Benevenuto, F., Gummadi, K.P.: Measuring user influence in Twitter: the million follower fallacy. In: International AAAI Conference on Weblogs and Social Media, pp. 10–17 (2010)
9. Fischer, D., Posegga, O., Fischbach, K.: Communication barriers in crisis management: a literature review. In: Proceedings of the 2016 European Conference of Information Systems (2016)
10. Fritz, C.E., Mathewson, J.H.: Convergence Behavior in Disasters: A Problem in Social Control (1957)
11. Giner-Sorolla, R., Maitner, A.T.: Angry at the unjust, scared of the powerful: emotional responses to terrorist threat. Pers. Soc. Psychol. Bull. **39**, 1069–1082 (2013)
12. Girtelschmid, S., Salfinger, A., Pröll, B., Retschitzegger, W., Schwinger, W.: Near real-time detection of crisis situations. In: The 39th International ICT Convention MIPRO 2016, pp. 247–252 (2016)
13. Golbeck, J.: Analyzing the Social Web, 1st edn. Morgen Kaufmann, Burlington (2013)

14. Gupta, A., Joshi, A., Kumaraguru, P.: Identifying and characterizing user communities on Twitter during crisis events. In: Proceedings of the 2012 Workshop on Data-Driven User Behavioral Modelling and Mining from Social Media - DUBMMSM 2012 (2012)

15. Hagen, L., Keller, T., Neely, S., DePaula, N., Robert-Cooperman, C.: Crisis communications in the age of social media: a network analysis of Zika-related tweets. Soc. Sci. Comput. Rev. **35**, 1–19 (2017)

16. He, X., Lu, D., Margolin, D., Wang, M., Idrissi, S.E., Lin, Y.-R.: The signals and noise: actionable information in improvised social media channels during a disaster. In: Proceedings of the 2017 ACM on Web Science Conference - WebSci 2017, pp. 33–42 (2017)

17. Hong, L., Torrens, P., Fu, C., Frias-Martinez, V.: Understanding citizens' and local governments' digital communications during natural disasters: the case of snowstorms. In: Proceedings of the ACM Web Science Conference, pp. 141–150 (2017)

18. Houston, J.B., et al.: Social media and disasters: a functional framework for social media use in disaster planning, response, and research. Disasters **39**, 1–22 (2015)

19. Imran, M., Castillo, C., Diaz, F., Vieweg, S.: Processing social media messages in mass emergency: a survey. ACM Comput. Surv. **47**, 67 (2015)

20. Jenkins, H.: Convergence Culture: Where Old and New Media Collide, 1st edn. New York University Press, New York (2006)

21. Kendra, J.M., Wachtendorf, T.: Reconsidering convergence and converger legitimacy in response to the world trade center disaster. In: Research in Social Problems and Public Policy, vol. 11, pp. 97–122 (2003)

22. Knuth, D., Szymczak, H., Kuecuekbalaban, P., Schmidt, S.: Social media in emergencies - how useful can they be. In: Information and Communication Technologies for Disaster Management (ICT-DM) (2016)

23. Laudy, C., Ruini, F., Zanasi, A., Przybyszewski, M., Stachowicz, A.: Using social media in crisis management. SOTERIA fusion center for managing information gaps. In: Proceedings of FUSION 2017, 20th International Conference on Information Fusion, pp. 1855–1862 (2017)

24. Leon, R.D., Rodríguez-Rodríguez, R., Gómez-Gasquet, P., Mula, J.: Social network analysis: a tool for evaluating and predicting future knowledge flows from an insurance organization. Technol. Forecast. Soc. Change **114**, 103–118 (2016)

25. Lindsay, B.R.: Social Media and Disasters: Current Uses, Future Options and Policy Considerations (2011)

26. Liu, B.F., Austin, L., Jin, Y.: How publics respond to crisis communication strategies: the interplay of information form and source. Public Relat. Rev. **37**, 345–353 (2011)

27. Lozano, E., Vaca, C.: Crisis management on Twitter: detecting emerging leaders. In: Proceedings of the International Conference on eDemocracy and eGovernment, pp. 140–147 (2017)

28. Mendoza, M., Poblete, B., Castillo, C.: Twitter under crisis: can we trust what we RT? In: Proceedings of the First Workshop on Social Media Analytics, pp. 71–79 (2010)

29. Mirbabaie, M., Zapatka, E.: Sensemaking in social media crisis communication - a case study on the Brussels bombings in 2016. In: Proceedings of the 25th European Conference on Information Systems, pp. 2169–2186 (2017)

30. Morris, C., Rubin, S.: Backpacking, social media, and crises: a discussion of online social convergence. Inf. Commun. Technol. Tour. **2013**, 207–217 (2013)

31. Muhongya, K.V., Maharaj, M.S.: Visualising and analysing online social networks. In: Proceedings of the International Conference on Computing, Communication and Security (2015)

32. Mukkamala, A., Beck, R.: Presence of social presence during disasters. In: Proceedings of the Pacific Asia Conference on Information Systems (2017)
33. Nazer, T.H., Xue, G., Ji, Y., Liu, H.: Intelligent disaster response via social media analysis - a survey. ACM SIGKDD Explor. **19**, 46–59 (2017)
34. Palen, L.: Online social media in crisis events. Educ. Q **31**, 76–78 (2008)
35. Palen, L., Liu, S.B.: Citizen communications in crisis: anticipating a future of ICT-supported public participation. In: Proceedings of the Human Factors in Computing Systems (2007)
36. Kanavos, A., Perikos, I., Vikatos, P., Hatzilygeroudis, I., Makris, C., Tsakalidis, A.: Modeling ReTweet diffusion using emotional content. In: Iliadis, L., Maglogiannis, I., Papadopoulos, H. (eds.) AIAI 2014. IAICT, vol. 436, pp. 101–110. Springer, Heidelberg (2014). https://doi.org/10.1007/978-3-662-44654-6_10
37. Perry, R.W., Lindell, M.K.: Understanding citizen response to disasters with implications for terrorism. J. Contingencies Cris. Manag. **11**, 49–60 (2003)
38. Pervin, N., Takeda, H., Toriumi, F.: Factors affecting retweetability: an event-centric analysis on Twitter. In: International Conference of Information Systems, pp. 1–10 (2014)
39. Ramluckan, T.: Factors affecting the use of social media as a crisis communication tool in South Africa. In: Proceedings of the IST-Africa 2016 Conference, pp. 1–11 (2016)
40. Shaw, F., Burgess, J., Crawford, K., Bruns, A.: Sharing news, making sense, saying thanks: patterns of talk on Twitter during the Queensland floods. Aust. J. Commun. **40**, 23–40 (2013)
41. von Sikorski, C., Schmuck, D., Matthes, J., Binder, A.: "Muslims are not Terrorists": Islamic state coverage, journalistic differentiation between terrorism and Islam, fear reactions, and attitudes toward Muslims. Mass Commun. Soc. **20**, 825–848 (2017)
42. Starbird, K., Palen, L.: "Voluntweeters": self-organizing by digital volunteers in times of crisis. In: Proceedings of the Conference on Human Factors in Computing Systems (2011)
43. Stieglitz, S., Dang-Xuan, L.: Social media and political communication: a social media analytics framework. Soc. Netw. Anal. Min. **3**, 1277–1291 (2013)
44. Stieglitz, S., Mirbabaie, M., Ross, B., Neuberger, C.: Social media analytics – challenges in topic discovery, data collection, and data preparation. Int. J. Inf. Manag. **39**, 156–168 (2018)
45. Subba, R., Bui, T.: An exploration of physical-virtual convergence behaviors in crisis situations. In: Proceedings of the Annual Hawaii International Conference on System Sciences, pp. 1–10 (2010)
46. Tim, Y., Yang, L., Pan, S.L., Kaewkitipong, L., Ractham, P.: The emergence of social media as boundary objects in crisis response: a collective action perspective. In: Proceedings of the Thirty Fourth International Conference on Information Systems (ICIS), pp. 196–215 (2013)
47. Vieweg, S., Palen, L., Liu, S.B., Hughes, A.L., Sutton, J.: Collective intelligence in disaster : examination of the phenomenon in the aftermath of the 2007 Virginia tech shooting. In: Proceedings of the International Association for Information Systems for Crisis Management, pp. 44–54 (2008)
48. Xu, W.W., Sang, Y., Blasiola, S., Park, H.W.: Predicting opinion leaders in Twitter activism networks. Am. Behav. Sci. **58**, 1278–1293 (2014)
49. Zhao, D., Rosson, M.B.: How and why people Twitter: the role that micro-blogging plays in informal communication at work. In: Proceedings of the ACM International Conference on Supporting Group Work, pp. 243–252 (2009)

Online Group Buying (OGB) in Agricultural Food Businesses: An Exploratory Study

Mohammad Hossain[1]([⊠]), Abu-Noman Ahmmed[2], Shams Rahman[1], and Caroline Chan[1]

[1] School of Business IT and Logistics, RMIT University, Melbourne, Australia
{mohammad.hossain, shams.rahman,
caroline.chan}@rmit.edu.au
[2] Faculty of Agriculture, Sher-e-Bangla Agricultural University,
Dhaka, Bangladesh
nomanfarook@yahoo.com

Abstract. Although agricultural produces occupy a reasonable portion of OGB businesses, glaringly, a limited research has been reported investigating the issues related to OGB businesses for agricultural commodity. To understand the enablers and inhibitors of OGB adoption in agricultural businesses, we conducted an exploratory research in a developing country i.e., Bangladesh which is unique in many contexts. Based on the data obtained from two focus group discussions and two interviews, we reported a unique OGB business model, particularly form the context of a developing country. This model also explains how OGB can operate in this specific industry. Moreover, we developed a framework to explain adoption of OGB in agricultural businesses. To the best of our knowledge, this is a unique effort employed to explain OGB dynamics from the perspective of supply-side stakeholders, and specifically in agricultural food sector. We briefly reported some practical implications of this study and offered future research directions.

Keywords: Online group buying (OGB) · Diffusion · Framework
Agriculture · Exploratory

1 Introduction

Over the two decades, many industries took advantage of Internet and telecommunication networks to reach to customers and sell products and services through different channels. Following the significant success of *e*-commerce in the 1990s, a number of innovative companies restructured their business model and launched group-buying websites (e.g., Mercata.com, Mobshop.com) where consumers with similar product-interests can congregate to obtain significant discounts from sellers for buying bulk quantity [11]. *Online group buying (OGB)* refers to collective buying and extends traditional *e*-commerce shopping model where consumers obtain volume discounts on the products or services from various businesses that are offered in OGB websites. In OGB, interested customers get deal when the number of customers exceeds a minimum required number. OGB vendor websites charge merchants a fee upon a successful deal [12]. The outcome of OGB is win-win, where the consumers receive

A. Elbanna et al. (Eds.): TDIT 2018, IFIP AICT 533, pp. 76–89, 2019.
https://doi.org/10.1007/978-3-030-04315-5_6

high discounts and the sellers attract bulk selling in a relatively short period of time. The OGB websites play a central intermediary role by facilitating the exchange of information, products, and payments, and arrange the delivery of goods (in most cases OGB vendor website generates an electronic coupon, send to customer email, which to be redeemed on the seller's premises) – hence removing a number of intermediaries from the supply chain.

In developing countries the role of intermediaries in food supply chain is very much questionable [5]. For example in Bangladesh, in general, farmers bring their produce to rural markets and sell the same to intermediaries, who then resell the produce to wholesalers or retailers in urban markets. In this process, the rural farmers become deprived of the fair price for their produce. Every year over 12000 farmers commit suicide for not had been successful to recover the productions costs whereas the end-customers pay as much as ten times the growers get [13]. Fortunately, OGB can assist the farmers for quick disposal of their harvest directly to the consumers and thus reduce transaction costs and farmers' dependence on intermediaries, while improving collective bargaining power of the consumers.

Since its inception OGB has attracted reasonable attention in academic literature where most of the studies examined it from customers' perspectives [e.g., 4, 9]. However, literature does not say much about the supplier-side of OGB. Hence, the core objective of this study is to explore the factors related to OGB adoption from the perspective of the suppliers-side of OGB, in the context of agricultural food businesses. To address the research objective, we conducted a field study in Bangladesh through focus group discussions and interviews. Data have been analysed using content analysis techniques. From data analysis we developed a revised OGB business model that could be operationalized in the agriculture industry in a developing country. Moreover, we developed a framework to explain adoption of OGB in agricultural businesses, which is a unique effort employed to explain OGB dynamics from the perspective of supply-side stakeholders, and specifically in agricultural food industry.

The reminder of this paper is organized as follows. The next section presents a background of the context followed by explaining the research method we applied. Then, the findings of the interviews have been discussed that lead to develop a framework. In the final sections, we discuss the implications of our research and acknowledge the limitations.

2   Background

In Bangladesh, agricultural landholdings are relatively small and scattered where small and marginal farmers represent 80% of all farmers [15]. Where the average farm size in Australia, for example, is 4331 ha [1], the same is less than a hectare (0.24 ha) in Bangladesh [16]. Moreover, the farmers have either no or negligible access to information or data about the actual market mechanism including the customer demand, price structure and market competition. Given that most of the growers are small-to-medium sized farmers, they lack the capacity to transport their commodities to bigger metropolitan markets, leaving no other option for them but to sell their harvests to local intermediaries. As the intermediaries take the major share of profit, a large number of farmers become unable to recover the production cost itself.

In recent times, Bangladesh is experiencing a huge growth of mobile telecommunications and mobile-based Internet – about 80% of rural farmers own mobile phones. It provides farmers with enormous potential to converse with the traders. Although a few isolated attempts have been made by telecommunication providers in Bangladesh to provide farmers with some market information, including the indicative selling price of agricultural commodities, there is hardly any noteworthy technological tool to help farmers reaching the actual buyers and receive competitive price for their produce. In this regard, OGB (using mobile Internet platform) holds potential for the farmers to have the opportunity of having a greater access to consumers and secure better price.

3   Research Method

OGB is relatively a recent phenomenon and is still in an early stage of development [4]. More precisely, OGB research from business perspective is scarce. Extant literature [e.g., 19] suggests that a qualitative approach is particularly suitable for a situation where the extant theories and constructs are inadequate to explain the phenomenon of interest. In order to gain insights into the OGB particularly from the business perspectives, this research therefore applied an explorative qualitative approach by conducting interviews.

3.1   Sample and Data Collection

During 2016–17 we conducted two focus group discussion (FGD) sessions (with 6 and 4 participants respectively) and two interviews among different OGB stakeholders in Bangladesh (government official, business entity, academician, journalist, and technical expert). Given that OGB is a new phenomenon and thus individual expertise has not developed yet, we used FGD because it is useful for dealing with new, complex, and unstructured problems. Also, opinions from multiple backgrounds is more productive than single interviews because participants can react to each other and, in this way, generate more ideas than on their own. However, the interviews have been conducted because some interviewees could not attend the FCD sessions because of keeping anonymity.

We identified the participants by applying convenient and purposeful sampling. To ensure a variety of responses and to cover as many aspects as possible, participants have been recruited representing different stakeholder-groups (see Table 1). For the discussions, we used a semi-structured interviewing approach, with six standard questions (shown in Appendix A). In some cases, we asked additional questions based on the answers to the initial questions and probed when required. With the written permission of the interviewees, we (audio) recorded the interviews. Interviews were conducted in the local language i.e., Bengali (with a mixture of English). A professional transcription agency transcribed them as the interview was recorded. Then, a bilingual native Bengali professional translator translated it into English, and finally retranslated back to Bengali. This back-translation provided us the opportunity to compare the translation perfection and equivalency; and we made minimal adjustments [11].

3.2   Data Analysis

We conducted an exploratory analysis to identify important factors from the qualitative data. The interview transcripts were read by one of the authors who used a data reduction and presentation technique for analyzing, triangulating, and documenting the contents of the transcripts to identify and group similar quotes [12]. First, we identified the first-order concepts directly from the interviews. While doing this, by analyzing and understanding the context we developed common themes; for example, "traffic", "traffic jam", "[road] congestion", "slow movement [of traffic], etc. have been identi-fied as a single theme (i.e., traffic). Then, a group of similar first-order concepts (e.g., storage facilities, payment gateway, or access to technology) were categorized to develop a second-order theme i.e., "infrastructural challenge". Accordingly, the themes were convened into the dimensions (e.g., challenges) of the framework. Two authors of this study repeated the entire coding process and compared their codes. Minor dis-agreements were discussed and resolved with the help of the other author. While discussing the data (in the following section) we presented some excerpts (we provided the code of the respondent in subscript e.g., R_A refers to the respondent A).

4   Findings

4.1   Redesigning OGB Business Models in Agriculture

Based on the discussions of the respondents, a unique OGB models has been evolved, which can be called as *online group buying-group selling* (OGB-GS) where not only the buyers but also the producers (i.e., farmers) would form groups to participate in the OGB marketplace. This model is believed to be better for a country like Bangladesh where the farmers produce relatively small quantity, which is more than what they can consume but too less to transport to the market. Here, the small farmers can meet in a virtual *e*-marketplace of OGB-GS and form groups to consolidate their produces. Then, they can take the produce to market as a single consignment. This concept is consistent with 'co-operative farming', used to be practiced in Bangladesh couple of years ago [14, 17]. However, because of a number of scams, cooperative farming is now ceased, but R_A and R_E believe that it will be essential for Bangladesh and for OGB-GS.

The 'group selling' component of the devised model makes the micro farmers carrying the costs collectively and get the benefit of selling bulk amount which pre-viously was enjoyed by only the 'fat resellers'. This OGB-GS model can be further institutionalized and operationalized by involving non-government-organizations (NGOs) in at least two processes. First, an NGO in each locality will facilitate con-solidation of information by providing an online platform where farmers can upload the products' quality, quantity, price, availability, etc. Initially, a dedicated person from the NGO will manage the website; that person will receive pictures and associated infor-mation from the farmers to upload. The NGO will provide training to the farmers so that eventually they can manage the contents themselves.

Table 1. The profile of the respondents

Respondent	Code	The respondents
FG1	R_A	Department of Agricultural Marketing
FG1	R_B	Operations and Marketing Managers to one of the three largest agro farms
FG1	R_C	Four academician from two agricultural university
FG2	R_D	Managing Director of a business venture with agro-based foods
FG2	R_E	Ex-Director, Department of Agricultural Extension
FG2	R_F	(Information) System Analyst, Software Developer – 2 persons
Interview1	R_G	Owner-manager of a medium farm (>200, <500 employees)
Interview2	R_H	Journalist active in food adulteration reports

Second, the physical facility of the NGO will be used as the consolidation point of the produce from where they will be transported further. Meanwhile, the NGOs will acquire warehouses in the urban areas from where: (i) the OGB initiator or the individual customers can collect the produces, or (ii) the produces will be distributed to the retail shops. However, when the demand of a specific order from a retail business coincides with the supply of produces, the delivery can be direct (bypassing the storage in warehouse). The NGO will manage the transportation too.

The OGB-GS model is much plausible in Bangladesh because there are number of NGOs working in the grass-root level and are very close to the farmers. Also, it is likely that a number of small farmers have borrowed money from the NGO and this will be a good opportunity for both of the parties to maximize the return from effective trading of the agricultural produces and facilitating the repayment of the debt. Also "… NGO would offer credit for that and adjust the cost from sales". "They can also engage contract growers (who produce organic foods) in OGB. … The growers pay a commission to the NGO, while the customers [who appreciate organic food] get them effectively. The field-workers [of NGOs] can be engaged in this process who would visit the contract-farms randomly to check authenticity of farming techniques" (RC).

4.2 The Dimensions of OGB-GS Framework

The framework consists the drivers, barriers, challenges, and benefits of OGB adoption in the agricultural sector in a developing country. First we present a brief discussion of these factors and then introduce the framework.

4.2.1 Drivers

OGB-GS is driven by technological, social, and entrepreneurial drivers. These are frequently related to ubiquity and rapid change in the business environment.

Technological drivers: The main technological driver for OGB-GS business in Bangladesh is the unprecedented development in the telecommunication networks and Internet. In 2011 the country experienced the phenomenal growth of over 900% of Internet users [7]. Still, the growth rate is 15–16% a year [7]. Agreeing with prior cases [e.g., 3], R_D suggests that emergence of new technologies affect performance of existing business: *"The farmers can easily send us [SMS] text and inform about their produces, which could not be believable five years ago. They now get better access to market performance"* (R_E). While ISP-based Internet is still an urban privilege, mobile telecommunication operators are providing substantial services in and outside urban areas, which can be utilized in OGB-GS businesses.

"We see a number of agri businesses [mainly in Dhaka city] who run their business mainly via Facebook" (R_D). *"As Bangladesh is a significant user of online social media, OGB merchants can view networking sites as a tool to reach to the customers. They could use the social networking sites as a means to manage customer relationships, build community, discuss business issues among the businesses and create business networks, and create feedback loops regarding their products and services"* (R_G).

Another technological improvement that enhanced Bangladeshi people's use of Internet and social networks is the facility of typing in their mother language. This advancement could be capitalized by OGB-GS where the stakeholders do not need to deal with language barrier anymore (e.g., overall use, English name of the produces).

Social drivers: The huge consumer-base (170 million people living in just 147,570 km^2) is considered as a driver for OGB-GS. Because of the size of the population as well as of the area, and a society with collectivism culture, developing a group among the people with similar interests from vicinity is not a problem.

"In fact, collective buying is an inherent culture of the Bangladeshi society. Children buy expensive sports gears collectively; the vast majority people (i.e., Muslims) buy and sacrifice cattle collectively... Applying this collective practice, buying bulk quantity of produces [by a group of people] at significant reduced price should not be an issue in Bangladesh" (R_H).

Furthermore, consumers in Bangladesh are getting more serious than before about the food they consume. *"The print and electronic media, and now-a-days social media, in Bangladesh have been playing a significant investigatory-and-watchdog role revealing the mechanisms of food adulteration, and thus increase people's health consciousness"* (R_H). The respondents, particularly R_D and R_G, believe that OGB-GS can provide a successful market structure in Bangladesh where authentic farmers will not need to rely on intermediaries but can the consumers more directly, and consumers inspire them by buying in bulk.

Entrepreneurial drivers: The entrepreneurial culture of the country may drive OGB-GS while this business model can contribute to unemployment. *"But the success of such a new business model needs strong [entrepreneurial] leadership and innovativeness"* (R_B). For example, one of the acute challenges of OGB-GS in Bangladesh would be the delivery and distribution of the perishable products. The respondents urge that the stakeholders need to be innovative; they simply cannot copy and paste a practice from somewhere else. They need to show leadership skills and *"realize the potentials of OGB and then set effective strategy and roadmap"*.

"The social and business structures of the country inspire people to be entrepreneur. You will see thousands of entrepreneurs in every sector. Because of the huge population and less availability of jobs, people tend to be entrepreneur – OGB could grab this opportunity. Young entrepreneurs can take part in every stage of the OGB-GS business – from consolidating the produce to coordinating to transportation and ending with distributing/delivering the products" (R_C).

"We may think about a couple of options: tagging with the established retail chain stores where customers will come and redeem the electronic coupon, establish a number of outlets in the areas where the most orders come from (e.g., commercial districts where working colleagues will buy the produces and pick them up on the way to go home), and establishing a number of warehouses in the city and distribute the produces to a local agent who will home deliver the products" (R_G).

Category	Drivers
Technological drivers	Telecommunication and Internet technology
	Online social networking
	Typing in mother language
Social drivers	Huge consumer-base
	Health consciousness
Entrepreneurial drivers	Leadership
	Innovativeness

4.2.2   The Barriers

Despite the benefits and opportunities offered by OGB-GS, there are several barriers that would delay the development of an operational marketplace, and slow and low OGB adoption in Bangladesh. Here, we defined perceived barriers as the extent to which the factors that would reject or delay the implementation of OGB in terms of the customer and business participation. Based on the field study results, two main barriers are identified: economic and technical.

Economic barriers: The first economic challenge is that the participation in OGB-GS markets will incur costs to the supply-side stakeholders; it is a real challenge for them to recover the costs and gain positive return on investment.

"Any requirement of an extra investment [for OGB business] for a farmer will not be appreciated. If the cost components are taken care of by the third parties who will recover the costs in the long run, could be the solution in the context. Before asking the farmers to invest, the third party vendors needs to provide the proof of concept; otherwise the individual farmers will not trust the model" (R_E).

Cost issue is even more critical because of the relatively small size of online customers in Bangladesh – that restricts the businesses from reaching economy of scale. Also, an acceptable critical mass consisting online sellers and buyers, which is needed for profitable OGB operation, is insufficient in food businesses.

"Although Internet has been used by a good number of people, they are mainly Facebook users. Only a very few percentage of them do shopping from online markets, let alone the food commodities. Physical stores are still the preferred place to shop - people still love to feel the tomato than order them online" (R$_D$).

Technical barriers: The OGB market expects all or most of the technical impediments of e-commerce. The technical barriers not only hinder them to adopt e-commerce business models, but are also a source of frustration. The main technical barrier is the unreliable electric power (i.e., power outage). It impacts use of computers and electronic devices. Also, Internet connection (both telecom based as well as ADSL) is not consistent. *"It is not unlikely that in the middle of a transaction, you lose Internet connection! Also, the Internet speed limits users to download a page with lots of graphics and/or flash. [The quality of Internet] definitely is an impediment for OGB in Bangladesh"* (R$_F$). In order to drive OGB, Bangladesh government may provide hotspots and/or computer kiosks in the rural markets for free.

Another barrier for OGB marketplace to start in Bangladesh is related to lack of technical people available with sufficient expertise in technical, legal, and marketing issues; or prohibitively expensive. The respondents did worry that if the technical issues are not addressed seriously, farm businesses will not be able to utilize the digitalization initiatives and thus mass people will not get the benefits from OGB. Here, government may appoint technical persons in rural areas who would assist the farmers to run the OGB-GS businesses – this provision is common in developing countries [18].

Category	Drivers
Economic	Size of the online consumers – economy of scale & critical-mass
	Cost of doing business
	Return on investment
	Taking a shared responsibility of ongoing costs
Technical	Power outage
	Internet drop out/speed
	Lack of IT/technical competencies (workforce)
	Lack of infrastructure (e.g., Web server) & IT sophistication

4.2.3 The Challenges

First we identify the difference between 'barriers' and 'challenges'. *Barriers* are the obstacles that prevent or slow down the movement; in order to succeed, a firm must get through the barriers the face. On the contrary, *challenges* are the demanding tasks that firms try to overcome; a firm not necessarily have to take on the challenges but will make it better if accomplished. There are a number of challenges for OGB business in Bangladesh, which we grouped into three categories: infrastructural, legal, and operational.

Infrastructural challenges: Generally speaking, developing countries struggle with various challenges with respect to infrastructural facilities. OGB associates the inherent challenges of e-commerce including delivery [2]. In addition, product distribution with limited and inefficient transport infrastructure is huge challenge. *"Taking orders online is easy but delivering the products on-time is not, especially for a country with huge traffic* (R_D). In order to expedite deliveries, R_D suggests for having distributed warehouses (than centralized) in various locations. He also suggests using bicycle or motorbike for delivery, depending on the order size, to mitigate the delivery issue because of traffic jam

Another key infrastructural barrier to OGB is electronic payment systems. "Only less than 5% [bank] cards can be used in online shopping". Moreover, the payment gateways are yet to be settled (for instance, PayPal is not available in Bangladesh, till this article is produced)[1]. RB suggested that virtual credit cards with micro-payment facilities could be issued so that mass people could shop online. The concept is similar to the gift cards to redeem in online shopping. There will be no physical card but the numbers (like a credit card) will be issued against the balance the customer has in associated bank account. Also, as people in Bangladesh are highly using mobile money transfer services of the banks (e.g., Rocket, BKash), OGB customers could be given the opportunity to transfer funds.

Legal challenges: There are at least three different legal or regulatory issues associated with OGB[2]. The fundamental legal challenge is to identify a person uniquely in Bangladesh. For example, in spite of implementing biometric mobile SIM registration system, still hundreds of scams and blackmailing are made over the mobile phone everyday but many criminals are left unidentified [6]. Hence, this is a big challenge for the businesses to make sure if the current law and law enforcement agencies could protect businesses from financial irregularities. Safeguarding both the businesses and the customers, updating the relevant laws to address the online platform and their proper application are challenging. Also, government can develop a professional third party that would work on quality assurance and compliance monitoring of the products. At the business side, in order to reduce disputes, OGB businesses should document their pricing, privacy policies, shipping restrictions, contact information, and business practices on the Websites.

Cultural challenges: The cultural issues are important for OGB because they determine how people interact with the vendors, merchants, and within the groups. Along with the e-commerce issues, OGB includes additional challenges such as trust on the group-leader or initiator [8] and discount mechanism [10]. Lack of trust and reputation especially to unknown merchants is a serious challenge.

"Given all the potential benefits of OGB, still I think a major cultural change will be needed to make people to buy groceries from online markets. Still customers prefer to shop from markets or hawkers although they cannot assure quality etc. [Hence], customers need to change their behavior. In order to get healthy food, they should not compromise with the look and price with quality" (R_G).

---

[1] Yet there are some 3rd party service providers for gateway management; they manage transactions particularly within the country.

[2] Most legal challenges related to e-commerce are also valid for OGB e.g., cybercrime. We do not redundantly discuss the legal issues of OGB which are common for e-commerce models.

"Altogether, we need to create a culture of mutual trust, which I believe will take shape with one good reputed business. Online markets in Bangladesh have passed a decade but unfortunately not a single business could become a giant and establish unquestionable trustworthiness among the customers. The reputation of the existing players is not universal. This is frustrating. In general, people want to trust a vendor in online shopping channel, but the eventual dealings [by the businesses] do not respect such trust" (R_D)". Moreover, *"in a developed country food adulteration using pesticides is unthinkable, but almost every agricultural food in Bangladesh is poisoned. ... We have to come out from such ill practice and develop trust and reputation among the consumers. OBG has a great future in this regard because the reputation of a farm can be disseminated quickly and easily through Internet and from groups of customers"* ($R_{H)}$.

Category	Challenges
Infrastructural	Product delivery and return
	Payment gateway
	Order fulfilment of large orders – multiple warehouses & automation
	Limited access to technology (e.g., computer, Internet)
	Technology know-how
	Political instability
Legal	Cybercrime
	Privacy and security of data
	Quality assurance – standardization and compliance monitoring
Cultural	Trust – reputation dyad
	Individualist within collectivist culture
	Risk-averse
	Developing trust and reputation especially to unknown OGB merchants and vendor (as the shopping channel)
	Knowledge culture

4.2.4   The Benefits

All interviewees recognized a high potential of OGB in Bangladesh for agricultural commodities. Overall, they considered OGB-GS as 'an opportunity with extreme potential'. The benefits are clustered in: (1) economic, (2) operational, and (3) social.

Economic benefits: "Although the farmers have changed the [economic] outlook of the agriculture industry and the country, their own socioeconomic condition remains same. They have been deceived by the traditional market systems where don't have a formal access to the wholesale or retail markets and thus they can't sell their products without the interference of the middlemen. ... Now, we strongly believe that this is the time when the actual people will get the most benefits [through OGB-GS] – the farmers would market their own products collectively to collective customers" (R_C).

All respondents believe that OGB can increase economic outlook of the farmers through bulk sale. They put 'create increased economic value for the farming community' as the main objective/expected benefit of OGB strategies in Bangladesh. They advocate that OGB-GS can provide the small farms the opportunity to handle large volume of work associated in online platform against a small customer-base per each individual farm. The revised model (i.e., OGB-GS) accommodates the businesses to work collaboratively (and share the costs of doing business) and thus the ability to participate in online platform and take the advantage of digital businesses. Consequently, small farms get a unique opportunity to compete with large ones. Additionally, farms can take the advantage of inexpensive advertising and marketing. Thus, the farms can use it as an additional channel for selling products economically. Additionally, businesses can understand the customer behavior directly and better – what they want, in what quantity, and what time, etc.

Operational benefits: In general, farmers in Bangladesh bring their produce to rural markets and sell the same to intermediaries such as 'dalals' (go-betweens) or 'arot-daars' (resellers), who then resell the produce to wholesalers or retailers in urban markets. In this process, with some exceptions, the rural farmers become deprived of the fair price for their produce. Unfortunately, state agencies hardly play any role to regulate this market mechanism. Lack of having an open, transparent, direct and competitive market where farmers could access the right buyers is the main reason for such irregularities.

OGB has the potential to reduce involvements of the intermediaries and thus will contribute to the marginal producers. It can reduce information asymmetry and enhance transparency along the supply chain because the producers will have direct access to the customers. They can dispose a large quantity of products with dynamic pricing strategy; in particular, with lower prices but selling in bulk. This market system would empower them to set the dynamic pricing of the produces according their longevity conditions. Hence, OGB will provide greater choices to small farmers and allow them with better and timely access to the market. In essence, it would improve their bargaining position relative to prospective buyers which, in turn, would help negotiating better prices through a competitive e-market process. In summary, OGB would ensure quicker disposal of the harvest, reduce waste and eliminate unnecessary transaction costs including the cost for searching the right buyers or sellers, inventory holding-cost and negotiation cost.

Social benefits: OGB offers various social benefits. First, it has the potential to develop a 'good for all' culture – the actual players of the economy i.e., farmers will get appropriate price for their produces while the customers will get them at cheaper price than in the retail markets. When an OGB market operates, it creates jobs (transport, warehouse, delivery, payment agencies, etc.). Also, OGB may enhance food quality where farmers will share the production process with rich information (text, image, and video); some group of customers may even go for contact farming with a group of farmers.

Second, it is a common perception that OGB business model will increase social value through direct and indirect group building and interaction. It can contribute to the collectivistic society of Bangladesh particularly in the urban areas where people are losing the bonding day by day. It also motivates altruistic behavior of the citizens – "you included me in a group to buy rice, I shall add you in buying meat". "OGB also will improve quality of decision-making through collective opinions. A bunch of people cannot make a wrong choice (RA)."

Category	Benefits
Economic	Increased revenue from bulk sale
	Reduce intermediary commissions
	Reducing operational and marketing costs
	Opportunity to bargain instead of selling at a fixed price (optimal price setting)
	Development of innovative product/service
Operational	Disintermediation of the middlemen
	Can liquidate large quantities in a short period of time
	Reduce information asymmetry through direct access to consumers & more visibility of product information (e.g. price, quality) to consumers
Social	Social interaction
	'Good for all' culture
	Improved decision-making through confidence on others
	Altruism

From the content analysis, we found that the OGB-GS adoption in Bangladesh's agricultural sector represents a novel situation because of some unique features of the country and the industry. The respondents discussed about a number of associated factors to consider explaining OGB adoption in agricultural industry, which we utilized to develop a framework, mostly from the business perspectives (see Fig. 1). The proposed framework consists of four higher-level dimensions: drivers, barriers, challenges, and benefits.

5 Conclusions

5.1 Implications of the Study

Although OGB has been used in developed countries for some years, it is still at infancy stage in developing countries. Some characteristics of developing countries make huge difference for OGB success. The current study intends to shed light on these issues. We summarize that, as experience accumulates and technology improves, the cost-benefit ratio of OGB will increase, resulting in greater rates of OGB adoption by businesses. It also urges for educated people to be engaged in OGB business, especially so that they can contribute to policy making and other areas where the typical illiterate farmers cannot. In Bangladesh it is glaringly observed that agriculture businesses lack of agriculture graduates; this study suggests that OGB stakeholders should assess the need and scope of participating, by examining the need and preferences of the customers. They also should assess the effectiveness of participation in terms of the business's objectives and customer behavior. The analysis would assist them analyzing, for example, if the products are offered as bulk as opposed to individual items, and if then the visitors can be converted to a customer. Businesses should carefully consider the target customers and the products, based on their preferences. Eventually, the associated factors (some of them explored in the current study) would be confirmed and thus the industry will take a workable shape.

5.2   Limitations

This study has a few limitations that may be addressed by future research. This study focuses on reporting the elements of the OGB adoption framework (e.g., drivers, barriers, challenges, and benefits); however, it is possible that these factors affect each other. Future research will investigate such inter-affects. In addition, future study will investigate the relative effect of the elements and their associated variables by applying an analytical hierarchical model. Also, future analysis is required to understand the adoption-diffusion process – how a farm moves from pilot testing to implementation to extension. Finally, the developed model should be validated with empirical data.

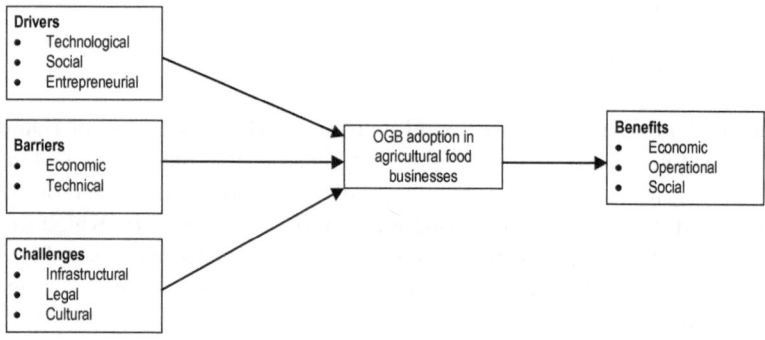

Fig. 1.   OGB adoption framework in agriculture businesses

5.3   Conclusion

Prior studies consider OGB as a sustainable business model for many businesses; our study extends the OGB model, in developing countries, to group-selling (by the farmers) and group-buying (for customers). It also found that, the farms in developing countries found OGB models difficult to understand, formulate, and implement; and also as challenging to operate because of existing financial (payment method, risk of transaction, dispute resolution) and physical infrastructure (delivery, return), and culture of the market and customers. In addition, this study developed a framework to understand the OGB business, however, with a little effort offering solutions to the challenges and barriers.

References

1. ABS. Agricultural Commodities, Australia, 2015–16 (2017). http://www.abs.gov.au/ausstats/abs@.nsf/mf/7121.0. Accessed 15 Mar 2018
2. Agwu, E., Murray, P.J.: Empirical Study of barriers to electronic commerce adoption by small and medium scale businesses in Nigeria. Int. J. Innov. Digit. Econ. **6**(2), 1–19 (2018)
3. Anjum, R.: Design of mobile phone services to support farmers in developing countries, School of Computing. University of Eastern Finland, Finland (2015)

4. Che, T., et al.: Antecedents for consumers' intention to revisit an online group-buying website: a transaction cost perspective. Inf. Manag. **52**, 588–598 (2015)
5. Ferreira, K.J., Goh, J., Valavi, E.: Intermediation in the supply of agricultural products in developing economies. Harvard Business School, pp. 1–33 (2017)
6. Hasnat, M.A., RAB detains 8 over SMS lottery scam, in Dhaka Tribune, Dhaka (2016)
7. Hasnayen, E., Sultana, S.: Internet use in Bangladesh: problems and prospects. Int. J. Comput. Sci. Inf. Technol. Res. **4**(3), 251–260 (2016)
8. Hsu, M.-H., et al.: Determinants of repurchase intention in online group-buying: the perspectives of DeLone & McLean IS success model and trust. Comput. Hum. Behav. **36**, 234–245 (2014)
9. Hung, S.-W., Cheng, M.-J., Hsieh, S.-C.: Consumers' satisfaction with online group buying – an incentive strategy. Int. J. Retail. Distrib. Manag. **43**(2), 167–182 (2015)
10. Kauffman, R.J., Wang, B.: New buyers' arrival under dynamic pricing market microstructure: the case of group-buying discounts on the Internet. J. Manag. Inf. Syst. **18**(2), 157–188 (2001)
11. Liu, Y., Sutanto, J.: Online group-buying: literature review and directions for future research. ACM SIGMIS Database **46**(1), 39–59 (2015)
12. Liu, Y., Sutanto, J.: Buyers' purchasing time and herd behavior on deal-of-the-day group-buying websites. Electron. Mark. **22**(2), 83–93 (2012)
13. Mahapatra, D.: Over 12,000 farmer suicides per year, Centre tells Supreme Court. The Times of India, Delhi, India (2017)
14. O'Connor, J.: Issues in establishing agricultural cooperatives. In: Trewin, R. (ed.) Cooperatives: Issues and trends in developing countries. ACIAR Technical Reports, Australian Centre for International Agricultural Research, Canberra, Australia. pp. 3–9 (2003)
15. Quasem, M.A.: Conversion of agricultural land to non-agricultural uses in Bangladesh: extent and determinants. Bangladesh Dev. Stud. **34**(1), 59–85 (2011)
16. Rapsomanikis, G.: The economic lives of smallholder farmers: an analysis based on household data from nine countries. In: Food and Agriculture Organization of the United Nations (2015)
17. Saadullah, M.: Smallholder dairy production and marketing in Bangladesh. Smallholder dairy production and marketing-Opportunities and constraints. NDDB (National Dairy Development Board) and ILRI (International Livestock Research Institute), Nairobi, Kenya, pp. 7–21 (2002)
18. Venkatesh, V., Bala, H., Sykes, T.A.: Impacts of information and communication technology implementations on employees' jobs in service organizations in India: a multi-method longitudinal field study. Prod. Oper. Manag. **19**(5), 591–613 (2010)
19. Yin, R.K.: Qualitative research from start to finish. Guilford Publications, New York (2015)

Adoption of Sharing Economies of Communitive Consumption Providing an Exchange of Services: A Conceptual Frame Work

Zainah Qasem[1]([⊠]), Raed Algharabat[1], and Ali Abdallah Alalwan[2]

[1] The School of Business Department of Marketing,
The University of Jordan, Amman, Jordan
{z.qasem, r.gharabat}@ju.edu.jo
[2] Amman College of Banking and Finance,
Al-Balqa' Applied University, Amman, Jordan
alwan.a.a.ali@gmail.com

Abstract. Over the past decade many successful and fast-growing businesses, such as Airbnb, Uber, DogVacy, RelayRides, TaskRabbit, have developed. What these businesses have in common were their underlying business models which are the sharing economies of communitive consumption. Consequently, under-standing what kind of communitive consumption services are customers willing to participate in, and examining factors that shape customers attitude towards CC and eventually intention to engage with communitive consumption in an online context is very important for practitioners, customers, and policymakers alike. Our intention in this paper is to present a conceptual framework that offers an understanding of factors affecting consumers' attitudes and intentions towards adopting communitive consumption platforms. However, our focus will be directed towards communitive consumption platforms which provide services with direct relationship and effect on property and individuals with sentimental value to communitive consumption user such as pets. To achieve our goal of understanding consumer adoption of communitive consumption we provided a theoretical foundation for discussion and future research about these new, alternative consumption modes by proposing a series of testable research propositions; which we intend developing into empirical studies.

Keywords: Social commerce
Sharing economies of collaborative consumption (CC) · Social exchange theory

1 Introduction

Over the past decade, many successful and fast-growing businesses, such as Airbnb, and Uber, have developed. What these businesses have in common were their underlying business models which are based on the sharing economies of collaborative con-sumption (CC) and "collective exchange", by which many customers access goods and services that are provided by a peer (Botsman and Rogers 2010; Benoita et al. 2017).

© IFIP International Federation for Information Processing 2019
Published by Springer Nature Switzerland AG 2019.
A. Elbanna et al. (Eds.): TDIT 2018, IFIP AICT 533, pp. 90–101, 2019.
https://doi.org/10.1007/978-3-030-04315-5_7

PwC research estimates that the total transactions for the four sectors dominated by CC (accommodation, transport, crowdfunding and lending, skilled or unskilled labour) in Europe, is valued at €28 billion in 2016, will see a 20-fold increase to €570 billion by 2025 (PwC 2017). Having this said, there is probably a span of taking a ride by Uber, via renting out our apartment via Airbnb, to let someone unknown be a babysitter for our kids. The sentimental value of object involved in the relationship between service provider and receiver is expected to play a significant role in shaping this relationship. Consequently, understanding what kind of communitive consumption services are customers willing to participate in, and examining factors that shape customers attitude towards CC and eventually intention to engage with CC in an online context is very important for practitioners, customers, and policymakers alike (Hamari et al. 2015).

Further, the shift towards favouring product ownership, the increasing interest in understanding the societal impact of consumption (Schor and Fitzmaurice 2015), and the burgeoning digital platform and consumer eagerness to use mobile applications facilitated peer-to-peer business models and introduced CC as an alternative for consumers (Yaraghi and Ravi 2017). Thus, CC is expected to have a significant societal impact and results in a potential alteration in e-commerce patterns and impact on online sales.

Our intention in this paper is to present a conceptual framework that offers an understanding of factors affecting consumers' attitudes and intentions towards adopting CC platforms. However, our focus will be directed towards CC platforms which provide services with direct relationship and effect on property and individuals with sentimental value to CC user such as pets.

2   Literature Review

2.1   Social Commerce

Social commerce is a form of Internet-based activities that depend on peer-to-peer interaction, and it utilises social media to "support social interactions and user contributions to assist activities in the buying and selling of products and services online and offline" (Wang and Zhang 2012, p. 2). Similarly, Yadav et al. (2013) defined social commerce as an "exchange-related activities that occur in, or are influenced by, an individual's social network in computer-mediated social environments, where the activities correspond to the need recognition, pre-purchase, purchase, and post-purchase stages of a focal exchange" (Yadav et al. 2013, p. 312).

In view of this, social commerce is associated with exchange-related activities which include, but not limited to, transaction, and computer-mediated social environment that encompass activities related to both consumer and companies contained under social commerce domain (Huang and Benyoucef 2017).

Taking into consideration social commerce definition and main associations, CC, — "an economic system in which assets or services are shared between private individuals, either free or for a fee, typically by means of the Internet" (Oxford 2017), is categorised a form of social commerce.

2.2   Sharing Economies of Collaborative Consumption (CC)

CC is acknowledged as an emerging trend that is altering consumer behaviour in the twenty-first century (Economist 2013). Hamari et al. (2015) formed a holistic definition to CC by combining previous knowledge about CC and the mapping of 254 CC websites. Their definition suggested that CC is "a peer-to-peer-based activity of obtaining, giving, or sharing the access to goods and services, coordinated through community-based online service" (Hamari et al. 2015, p. 1).

Based on Hamari et al. (2015) definition, CC practices are sharing two commonalities. First, is their dependence on the internet, and second is their reliance on non-ownership models using consumer goods and services (Botsman and Rogers 2010; Kaplan and Haenlein 2010; Wang and Zhang 2012; Belk 2014). The latter argument suggests that CC will result in a shift in consuming culture from a culture of owning towards a culture of sharing. It also indicates that this shift is motivated and driven by peer-to-peer internet platforms which link consumers and allow them to make more efficient use of underutilised assets (Martin 2016). However, there has been much less research examining variable affecting people decision to adopt CC.

Never the less, CC is considered an umbrella concept that includes many information and communication technology developments which endorses sharing the consumption of goods and services through online platforms (Botsman and Rogers 2010). Schor and Fitzmaurice (2015) suggested that the there are four main categories that CC consumption goes under—re-circulation of goods, optimising the use of assets, building social connections and exchange of services. This paper's primary focus is on understanding consumer adoption of CC providing an exchange of services.

2.3   Sharing Economies of Collaborative Consumption Providing an Exchange of Services

Sharing economies which focus on providing an exchange of services is not a new concept to the market of services (e.g. Time-banks). However, the growing desire for communal consumption, and the widespread of collaborative web communities; led to the reintroducing of the concept (Schor and Fitzmaurice 2015). The market has many peer-to-peer platforms that are serving as CC providing an exchange of services in different domains, including but not limited to, hospitality service, delivery of passengers, and pet fostering. These platforms are considered a C2C sharing platforms that are often being facilitated by an external provider like an online platform. The market has many successful companies and platforms that are providing access to CC that provides services (e.g. CouchSurfing, Uber, and Dogvacay).

When observing platforms separately, each platform provides a service that targets products and individuals with different level of sentimental value to CC users.

2.4   Products and Property Perceived Value

Product perceived value is a subjective construct that varies between customers, cultures, and times (Sanchez et al. 2006). People tend to evaluate product perceived value based on their functionality; emotional functionality and utilitarian functionality

(Burns and Evans 2000). Emotional functionality refers to "the experience of an emotional bond with a product, which implies that a strong relationship or tie exists between an individual and an object" (Muggea et al. 2009, p. 467).

Perceived emotional values are a matter of degree. For example, jewellery is expected to have a higher sentimental value than a kitchen tool (McDonagh et al. 2002). When a person perceives an object as high in emotional value, the person will develop an emotional attachment to the product—an emotional target-specific bond between a person and a specific object (Bowlby 1979). As a result, the object will acquire a meaning beyond functional meaning and becomes an extraordinary object.

Overall, being attached to a specific product will generate positive emotions such as happiness, love, warmth, and pride towards the object (Schultz et al. 1989). Hence, people will start to cherish their relationship with the product and show protective behaviour towards it (Muggea et al. 2009).

Previous studies suggests that people can form emotional attachments to a variety of objects including (pets, places, and celebrities) (Shimp and Madden 1988; Adams-Price and Greene 1990; Alperstein 1991; Rubinstein and Parmelee 1992; Hirschman 1994; Sable 1995; as cited by Thomson et al. 2005).

CC emerged from many technological developments that have facilitated the sharing of tangible and intangible products using different Internet-based IT systems (Hamari et al. 2015). Therefore, this paper will look at CC as an information and communications technology. As a result, the literature on technology acceptance will provide a theoretical background for this paper.

3   Theoretical Background

The theoretical foundations for the acceptance models encompass many models that are related to information systems. For example, the original technology acceptance model (TAM) (Davis 1986; Davis et al. 1989) and its models derived from TAM such as UTAUT and UTAUT2 (Venkatesh et al. 2003; Venkatesh et al. 2012). It also includes theories that are borrowed from other disciplines and adapted to information system disciplines such as the Innovation Diffusion Theory (Matzner et al. 2015) and Social exchange theory (SET) (Emerson 1976). The model we propose is based on the SET as a theoretical foundation and will incorporate constructs from UTAUT2.

3.1   The Unified Theory of Acceptance and Use of Technology (UTAUT)

UTAUT was developed by Venkatesh et al. (2003) as a holistic model that incorporates constructs from eight different theories and proposes an understanding of new technology adoption. UTAUT consists of four fundamental variable—performance expectancy, effort expectancy, social influence, and facilitating conditions and four moderating variables gender, age, experience, and voluntariness of use (Venkatesh et al. 2003). UTAUT was extended to accommodate for consumer use setting by integrating hedonic motivation, price, and habit. The extended UTAUT (UTAUT2) suggest that in the context of consumer use of information technology, both utilitarian benefits and hedonic benefits are considered vital factors of technology use Venkatesh et al. (Venkatesh et al. 2012)

3.2 Social Exchange Theory (SET)

SET postulates that human relationships are formed by the use of a subjective cost-benefit analysis and the comparison of alternatives (Emerson 1976). Thus, SETs central proposition is that individuals intend to choose the relationship that maximises their benefits. SET has been extensively adopted as one of the most significant theories to explain social interaction information systems and served as a theoretical framework which can sufficiently reflect the characteristics of CC such as peer-to-peer relationships (Stafford 2008; Chen 2013 as cited by Kim et al. 2015).

Consumers' assessment of benefit and cost indicates a proactive cost-benefit analysis. In this paper, we suggest that consumer benefit comprise constructs that were examined by previous studies and reported to motivate consumers to engage in CC these are: enjoyment of using the system, social benefit, and cost-benefit (Hamari et al. 2015). On the other hand, the cost of the consumer is the perceived risk related to trust.

4 Research Model and Hypothesis Development

4.1 Attitude

Attitude is "an individual's positive or negative feelings (evaluative affect) about performing the target behaviour" (Fishben and Ajzen 1975, p. 216). Attitudes definition suggests a relationship between attitude and behaviour. Thus we hypothesise that

H1: there is a positive relationship between attitude and behaviour in CC that provides a service involved with the product with sentimental value.

However, in CC, there is an assumption that these two constructs are not necessarily related. Therefore, there is a need to study consumer relationship with them separately (Hamari et al. 2015). This discrepancy is attributed to consumer analysis of benefit and cost relationship which might lead to a different behaviour than the one expected to match with the attitude.

4.2 Enjoyment of Using the System

Perceived enjoyment is an important dimension of intrinsic motivator defined as "the extent to which the activity of using the computer is perceived to be enjoyable in its own right" (Davis et al. 1992, p. 1113). Enjoyment has been the focus of many studies interpreting Internet and Communication Technologies acceptance and sharing related activates (Van der Heijden 2004).

Hwang and Griffiths (2017) reported a positive relationship between hedonic factors (e.g. enjoyment) and attitude towards online shopping. In the CC context, Hamari et al. (2015) have also reported a positive relationship between enjoyment and attitude and behaviour.

Similarly to previous studies, we are proposing that in the context of CC providing an exchange of service to property and individuals with sentimental meaning, people will engage in this activity for what is beyond utilitarian value, such as meeting people who share the same hobby (e.g. collectors and pet owners). Therefore, we propose incorporating enjoyment into our model as an intrinsic factor.

H2a: Perceived enjoyment from participating in CC platforms positively influences attitude towards CC that provides a service involved with the product with sentimental value.

H2b: Perceived enjoyment from participating in CC platforms positively influences attitude towards CC that provides a service involved with the product with sentimental value.

4.3   Economic Benefits

A previous study by Hennig-Thurau et al. (2007) endorsed that consumers are significantly attracted by CC when they recognise earning more benefits when using it in comparison to the cost. Tussyadiah (2015) stated that CC is an attractive substitute for consumers due to its economic benefits (i.e. low cost), which was considered necessary after the global financial crisis. Hence we are proposing to incorporate economic benefit as an influencer of attitude.

H3a: Perceived economic benefits from participating in CC positively influences attitude towards CC that provides a service involved with the product with sentimental value.

H3b: Perceived economic benefits from participating in CC positively influences behaviour towards CC that provides a service involved with the product with sentimental value.

4.4   Social Benefit

The context of CC is characterised as a philanthropic context. Batson (1998) defines philanthropy as "actions intended to benefit one or more people other than oneself" (Batson 1998, p. 282). Bullard and Penner (2017) argued that making an impact in the lives of others by giving up one's own personal resources (e.g., money, time) is a fundamental part of philanthropic behaviour. However, economic theory of maximising behaviour and rational choice suggests that people do not view giving up resources as a desired behaviour (Crocker and Linden 1998). Relatedly, the perceived impact has been recognised as a psychological instrument that endorses philanthropic giving (Erlandsson et al. 2015; Bullard and Penner 2017). Accordingly, individuals are more willing to engage in an activity if they perceive that they can make a significant impact with their actions. Thus, social benefit - as an outcome of philanthropic behaviour - is assumed to have a role in shaping consumer attitude and behaviour towards CC.

People are reported to participate in activities that involve sharing, and helping others driven by an obligation to do good for other people (Prothero et al. 2011). Therefore, believing in the importance of getting involved in online platforms as a mean to support the community is expected to influence people attitude and behaviour towards adopting the use of CC that provide a service involved with the product with sentimental value.

H4a: Social benefit positively influences attitude towards CC that provides a service involved with the product with sentimental value.

H4b: Social benefit positively influences behaviour towards CC that provides a service involved with the product with sentimental value.

4.5   Trust

Trust has always been an important factor in online communication and usage. Mayer et al. (1995) defined trust as "the willingness of a party to be vulnerable to the actions of another party based on the expectations that the other party will perform a particular action important to the trustor, irrespective of the ability to monitor or control that other party" Mayer et al. (1995, p. 172)

Owyang et al. (2013) proposes numerous challenges related to CC concept. Lack of trust between peer-to-peer users and lack of reputation and standard are some of these challenges. Mistrust among strangers and concerns for privacy were suggested as trust related issues that form barriers and affect CC (Olson 2013).

A very recent study by Mittendor (2018) found evidence that trust in the intermediary' and 'Trust in providers' are decisive for the obtainers' intentions on the online platform. Using and adopting CC implies a certain level of trust (Botsman and Rogers 2010), for example, giving a product with sentimental value like your pet contains high risk. Thus, we propose that.

H5a: Trust has a positive relationship towards attitude in CC that provides a service involved with the product with sentimental value.

H5b: Trust has a positive relationship towards behaviour in CC that provides a service involved with the product with sentimental value.

4.6   Technology

Finally, the CC is an Internet and Communication Technology. Therefore, it can be influenced by the characteristics of the technology. For example, Chong et al. (2009) suggested that ease of use, complexity and trainability of the technology systems has a vital role in predicting adoption of online platforms that allow multiple users to interact, collaborate, and transact with each.

Comparably, consumers are believed to adopt CC if they perceive the technology systems effortless and easy to use. Therefore, we propose that

H6a: effort expectancy positively influences attitude towards CC that provides a service involved with the product with sentimental value.

H6b: effort expectancy positively influences behaviour towards CC that provides a service involved with the product with sentimental value.

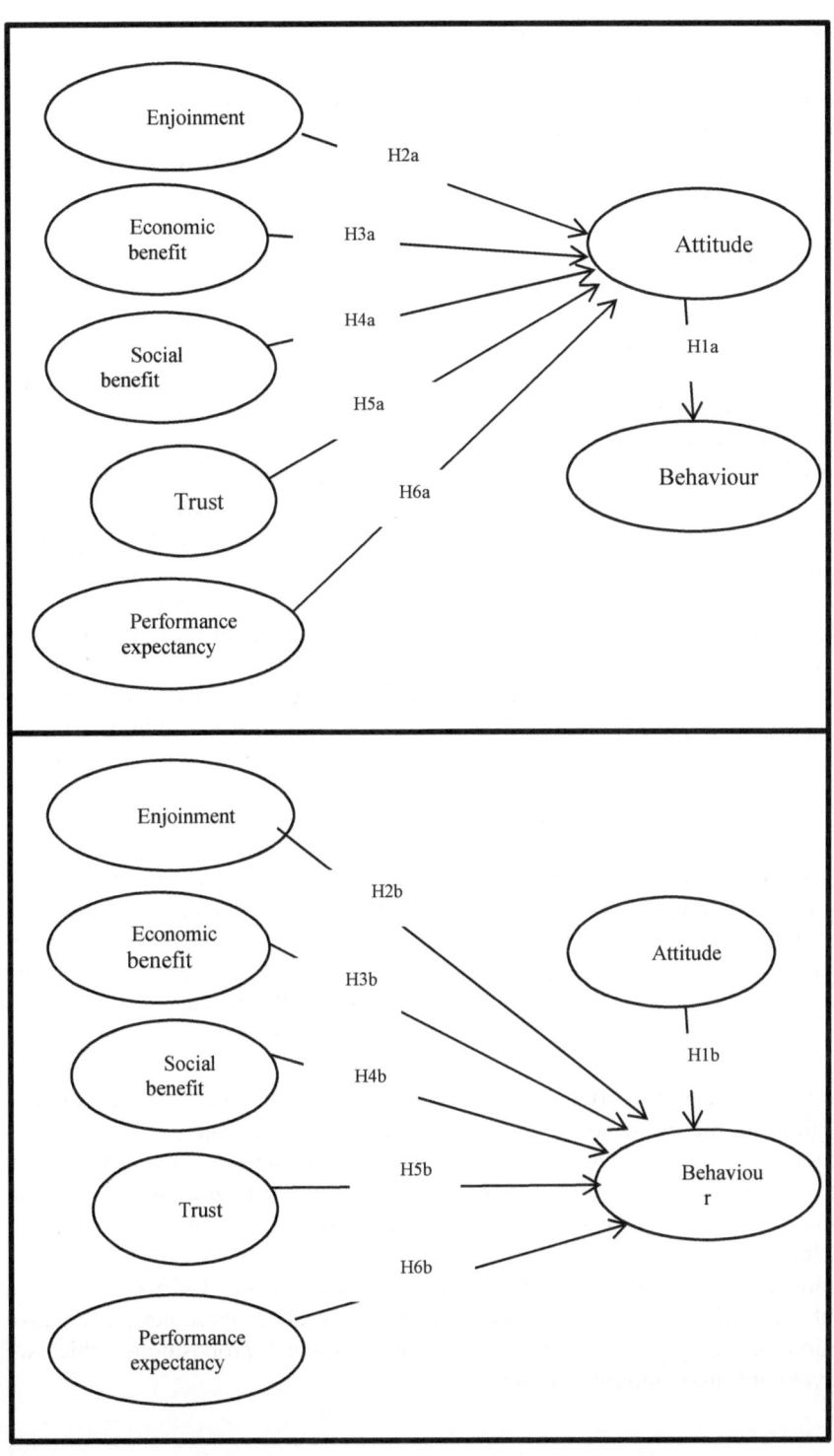

5 Proposed Research Methodology

As discussed above, the current study model and research hypotheses were proposed based on two models that explain consumer adoption behaviours of new technology (UTAUT and SET). The targeted context of this study will be people who use CC to receive services that are concerned with properties and individual with sentimental value. Consumer research suggests that people can form emotional attachments to a variety of objects, including pets (Thomson et al. 2005). Therefore, we are proposing developing a survey based quantitative research which will be allocated to actual users of DogVacy as an example of CC platforms that are providing service involved with a product with sentimental value, and pet owner as potential users of such as platforms.

Factors will be measured using scale items adopted and adapted when necessary from previous studies that have measured proposed items in online context. To measure attitude we will use a five-item scale adapted from Ajzen (1991). To measure behaviour, we will use a four-item scale adapted from Bhattacherjee (2001). To measure enjoyment we are using a five-item scale adapted from van der Heijden (2004). To measure economic benefit we are using a four-item scale adapted from Bock et al. (2005). To measure performance expectancy, we are using a five-item scale adapted from Venkatesh et al. (2003). To measure trust, we are using a four-item scale adapted from Corritore et al. (2003). To measure we are using a four-item scale adapted from social benefit Barnes and Mattsson (2017).

Once the data is collected, a structural equation modelling analysis will be conducted to validate the conceptual model and verify the significance of the hypothesis.

6 Conclusion and Future Work

The rapid change in consumer attitudes towards product ownership and the societal impact of consumption (Schor and Fitzmaurice 2015), technology progression (Botsman and Rogers 2010), and a desire for communal consumption have created a shift of attitudes towards consumption in general, and put more importance on sharing economies as an alternative for consumers (Hamari et al. 2015; Cheng 2016). Altogether, has brought great importance to understanding what influences consumers to adopt CC.

There are different categories that CC consumption goes under—re-circulation of goods, optimising the use of assets, building social connections and exchange of services (Schor and Fitzmaurice 2015). However, our primary concern is CC providing an exchange of services. Specifically, services that target products and individuals with sentimental value to consumers (e.g. pet caring and fostering, babysitting, and jewellery exchange).

To achieve our goal of understanding consumer adoption of CC we provided a theoretical foundation for discussion and future research about these new, alternative consumption modes by proposing a series of testable research propositions; which we intend developing into empirical studies.

References

Adams-Price, C., Greene, A.L.: Secondary attachments and adolescent self-concept. Sex Roles **22**, 187–198 (1990)

Ajzen, I.: The theory of planned behavior. Organ. Behav. Hum. Decis. Process. **50**(2), 179–211 (1991)

Alperstein, N.M.: Imaginary social relationships with celebrities appearing in television commercials. J. Broadcasting Electron. Media **35**, 43–58 (1991)

Barnes, S., Mattsson, J.: Understanding collaborative consumption: test of a theoretical model. Technol. Forecast. Soc. Chang. **118**, 281–292 (2017)

Batson, C.D.: Altruism and prosocial behavior. In: Gilbert, D.T., Fiske, S.T., Lindzey, G. (eds.) Handbook of social psychology. McGraw-Hill, Boston (1998)

Belk, R.: You are what you can access: sharing and collaborative consumption online. J. Bus. Res. **67**(8), 1595–1600 (2014)

Benoita, S., Bakerb, T., Boltonc, R., Gruberd, T., Kandampully, J.: A triadic framework for collaborative consumption (CC): motives, activities and resources and capabilities of actors. J. Bus. Res. **79**, 219–227 (2017)

Bhattacherjee, A.: Understanding information systems continuance: an expectation-confirmation model. MIS Q. **25**, 351–370 (2001)

Bock, G.W., Zmud, R.W., Kim, Y.G. Lee, J.N.: Behavioral intention formation in knowledge sharing: Examining the roles of extrinsic motivators, social-psychological forces, and organizational climate. MIS Q. 87–111 (2005)

Botsman, R., Rogers, R.: What's Mine is Yours: The Rise of Collaborative Consumption. Collins, New York (2010)

Bowlby, J.: The Making and Breaking of Affectional Bonds. Tavistock, London (1979)

Bullard, O., Penner, S.: A regulatory-focused perspective on philanthropy: promotion focus motivates giving to prevention-framed causes. J. Bus. Res. **79**, 173–180 (2017)

Burns, A.D., Evans, S.: Insights into customer delight. In: Scrivener, S.A.R., Ball, L.J., Woodcock, A. (eds.) Collaborative Design, pp. 195–203. Springer, London (2000). https://doi.org/10.1007/978-1-4471-0779-8_19. ISBN 1-85233-341-3

Chen, R.: Member use of social networking sites - an empirical examination. Decis. Support Syst. **54**(3), 1219–1227 (2013)

Cheng, M.: Sharing economy: a review and agenda for future research. Int. J. Hosp. Manag. **57**, 60–70 (2016)

Chong, A.Y.-L., Ooi, K.-B., Sohal, A.: The relationship between supply chain factors and adoption of E-collaboration tools: an empirical examination. Int. J. Prod. Econ. **122**(1), 150–160 (2009)

Corritore, C.L., Kracher, B., Wiedenbeck, S.: On-line trust: concepts, evolving themes, a model. Int. J. Hum Comput Stud. **58**(6), 737–758 (2003)

Crocker, D., Linden, T.: Ethics of consumption. The Good Life, Justice and Global Stewardship (1998)

Davis, F.D., Bagozzi, P., Warshaw, R.: Extrinsic and intrinsic motivation to use computers in the workplace. J. Appl. Soc. Psychol. **22**(14), 1111–1132 (1992)

Davis, F., Bagozzi, R., Warshaw, P.: User acceptance of computer technology: a comparison of two theoretical models. Manag. Sci. **35**(8), 982–1003 (1989)

Davis, F.: A technology acceptance model for empirically testing new end-user information systems: theory and results. Ph.D. thesis. Massachusetts Institute of Technology (1986)

Emerson, R., Theory, E.: Social exchange theory. Ann. Rev. Sociol. **2**, 335–362 (1976)

Erlandsson, A., Björklund, F., Backström, M.: Emotional reactions, perceived impact and perceived responsibility mediate the identifiable victim effect, proportion dominance effect and in-group effect, respectively. Organ. Behav. Hum. Decis. Process. **127**(1), 1–14 (2015)

Fishbein, M., Ajzen, I.: Belief, attitude, intention, and behaviour: an introduction to theory and research. Addison-Wesley, Reading (1975)

Hamari, J., Sjöklint, M., Ukkonen, A.: The sharing economy: why people participate in collaborative consumption. J. Assoc. Inf. Sci. Technol. **67**(9), 2047–2059 (2015)

Hennig-Thurau, T., Henning, V., Sattler, H.: Consumer file sharing of motion pictures. J. Mark. **71**(4), 1–18 (2007)

Hirschman, E.C.: Consumers and their animal companions. J. Consum. Res. **20**, 616–633 (1994)

Huang, Z., Benyoucef, M.: The effects of social commerce design on consumer purchase decision-making: an empirical study. Electron. Commer. Res. Appl. **25**, 40–58 (2017)

Hwang, J., Griffiths, M.A.: Share more, drive less: Millennials value perception and behavioral intent in using collaborative consumption services. J.Consum. Mark. **34**(2), 132–146 (2017)

Kaplan, A.M., Haenlein, M.: Users of the world, unite! The challenges and opportunities of social media. Bus. Horiz. **53**(1), 59–68 (2010)

Kim, J., Yoon, Y., Zo, H.: Why people participate in the sharing economy: a social exchange perspective. In: Pacific Asia Conference on Information Systems (PACIS) (2015)

Matzner, M., Chasin, F., Todenhöfer, L.: To share or not to share: towards understanding the antecedents of participation in IT-enabled sharing services. In: Proceedings of Twenty-Third European Conference (2015)

Martin, C.J.: The sharing economy: a pathway to sustainability or a nightmarish form of neoliberal capitalism. Ecol. Econ. **121**, 149–159 (2016)

Mayer, R.C., Davis, J.H., Schoorman, F.D.: An integrative model of organizational trust. Acad. Manag. Rev. **20**(3), 709–734 (1995)

McDonagha, D., Brusebergb, A., Haslamc, C.: Visual product evaluation: exploring users' emotional relationships with products. Appl. Ergon. **33**, 231–240 (2002)

Mittendorf, C.: Collaborative consumption: the role of familiarity and trust among millennials. J. Consum. Mark. (2018). (just-accepted)

Muggea, R., Schoormansa, J.P., Schiffersteinb, H.N.: Emotional bonding with personalised products. J. Eng. Des. **20**(5), 467–476 (2009)

Olson, K.: National study quantifies reality of the "Sharing Economy" movement (2013). http://www.campbell-mithun.com/678_national-study-quantifiesreality-of-the-sharing-economy-movement. Accessed 18 Feb 2018

Owyang, J., et al.: The collaborative economy. Technical report. Altimeter Group, San Maeto (2013)

Oxford: Sharing economy (2017). https://en.oxforddictionaries.com/definition/sharing_economy. Accessed 7 Feb 2018

Prothero, A., et al.: Sustainable consumption: opportunities for consumer research and public policy. J. Public Policy Mark. **30**(1), 31–38 (2011)

PwC: Infographic: the popularity of the collaborative economy (2017). https://www.digitalpulse.pwc.com.au/infographic-popularity-collaborative-economy/. Accessed 08 May 2018

Rubinstein, R.L., Parmelee, P.A.: Attachment to place and the representation of the life course by the elderly. In: Altman, I., Low, S.M. (eds.) Place attachment, pp. 139–163. Plenum, New York (1992)

Sable, P.: Pets, attachments, and well-being across the life cycle. Soc. Work **40**, 334–341 (1995)

Sanchez, J., Callarisa, L., Rosa, M., Rodriguez, R., Moliner, M.: Perceived value of the purchase of a tourism product. Tour. Manag. **27**, 394–409 (2006)

Schor, J.B., Fitzmaurice, C.J.: Collaborating and connecting: the emergence of the sharing economy. In: Reisch, L., Thogersen, J. (eds.) Handbook on Research on Sustainable Consumption. Edward Elgar, Cheltenham (2015)

Schultz, S.E., Kleine, R.E., Kernan, J.B.: These are a few of my favorite things: Toward an explication of attachment as a consumer behavior construct. Adv. Consum. Res. **16**, 359–366 (1989)

Shimp, T.A., Madden, T.J.: Consumer-object relations: a conceptual framework based analogously on Sternberg's triangular theory of love. Adv. Consum. Res. **15**, 163–168 (1988)

Stafford, L.: Social exchange theories. In: Engaging Theories in Interpersonal Communication: Multiple Perspectives, pp. 377–389. Sage Publications (2008)

The Economist: Peer-to-peer rental, the rise of the sharing economy on the internet, everything is for hire (2013). https://www.economist.com/news/leaders/21573104-internet-everything-hire-rise-sharing-economy. Accessed 7 Feb 2018

Thomson, M., MacInnis, D., Park, W.: The ties that bind: measuring the strength of consumers' emotional attachments to brands. J. Consum. Psychol. **15**(1), 77–91 (2005)

Tussyadiah, Iis P.: An Exploratory Study on Drivers and Deterrents of Collaborative Consumption in Travel. In: Tussyadiah, I., Inversini, A. (eds.) Information and Communication Technologies in Tourism 2015, pp. 817–830. Springer, Cham (2015). https://doi.org/10.1007/978-3-319-14343-9_59

Yadav, M.S., de Valck, K., Hennig-Thurau, T., Hoffman, D.L., Spann, M.: Social commerce: a contingency framework for assessing marketing potential. Journal of Interactive Market. **27**, 311–323 (2013)

Yaraghi, N., Ravi, S.: The current and future state of the sharing economy. Brookings India IMPACT Series No. 032017, March 2017. http://large.stanford.edu/courses/2017/ph240/carlton1/docs/032017.pdf. Accessed at 08 May 2018

Van Der Heijden, H.: User acceptance of hedonic information systems. MIS Q. **28**(4), 697–704 (2004)

Venkatesh, V., Thong, Y., Xu, X.: Consumer acceptance and use of information technology: extending the unified theory of acceptance and use of technology. MIS Q. **36**(1), 157–178 (2012)

Venkatesh, V., Morris, M., Davis, G., Davis, F.: User acceptance of information technology: toward a unified view. MIS Q. **27**(3), 425–478 (2003)

Wang, C., Zhang, P.: The evolution of social commerce: the people, management, technology, and information dimensions. Commun. Assoc. Inf. Syst. **31**(1), 105–127 (2012)

Toward a Conceptual Model for Examining the Role of Social Media on Social Customer Relationship Management (SCRM) System

Abdullah M. Baabdullah[1]([⊠]), Nripendra P. Rana[2],
Ali Abdallah Alalwan[3], Raed Algharabat[4], Hatice Kizgin[2],
and Ghazi A. Al-Weshah[5]

[1] Department of Management Information Systems,
Faculty of Economics and Administration, King Abdulaziz University,
Jeddah, Kingdom of Saudi Arabia
baabdullah@kau.edu.sa
[2] School of Management, Swansea University, Bay Campus,
Fabian Way, Swansea SA1 8EN, UK
nrananp@gmail.com, hatice.kizgin@swansea.ac.uk
[3] Amman College of Banking and Finance,
Al-Balqa Applied University, Amman, Jordan
Alwan_jo@bau.edu.jo
[4] The School of Business Department of Marketing,
The University of Jordan, Amman, Jordan
r.gharabat@ju.edu.jo
[5] Faculty of Business Al-Balqa Applied University, Salt, Jordan
weshahl20@yahoo.com

Abstract. Organizations worldwide are becoming more interested in utilizing social media applications to enhance their marketing capabilities. One of the main fruits of integrating social media applications into the marketing, information technology and information systems areas is social customer relationship management (SCRM). SCRM has been the focus of attention for both marketing academics and practitioners. However, as this area is quite new, there is a need to propose a theoretical foundation explaining how using social media platforms for SCRM systems could predict customer engagement and customer relationship performance. Three main factors, i.e. social media use, a customer-centric management system, and relationship marketing orientation, are considered as key predictors of SCRM. SCRM is proposed as a key determinant of customer engagement, which in turn affects customer relationship performance. The proposed research methodology suggests conducting a quantitative study to validate the current study model. Further discussion regarding the research contribution and main limitations are provided in the last sections.

Keywords: SCRM · Social media · Customer engagement · Jordan

© IFIP International Federation for Information Processing 2019
Published by Springer Nature Switzerland AG 2019.
A. Elbanna et al. (Eds.): TDIT 2018, IFIP AICT 533, pp. 102–109, 2019.
https://doi.org/10.1007/978-3-030-04315-5_8

1 Introduction

Recently, organizations worldwide seem to have become more interested in utilizing different information technology and digital marketing tools to sustain their relationships with their customers as well as to maintain their market share [5, 9, 11, 26, 36]. Web 2.0 and social media applications (i.e. Facebook, Twitter, Instagram, YouTube, and Snapchat) therefore have been the focus of attention for modern organizations [4]. This is due to the innovative nature of such applications, which attract millions of customers and allow a high degree of interactivity either between customers themselves or between customers and organizations. Noticeably, customer relationship management (CRM) systems are progressively considering social media platforms as new mechanisms to conduct their activities [29]. A CRM system is one of the most important enterprise systems in addition to supply chain management (SCM) and enterprise resource planning (ERP).

As a result of integrating social media applications into the area of CRM systems, a new trend called social CRM (SCRM) has evolved [5]. Conceptually, SCRM was defined by [30, p. 319] as "the integration of customer-facing activities, including processes, systems, and technologies, with emergent social media applications to engage customers in collaborative conversations and enhance customer relationships" [30, p. 319]. In fact, SCRM could not exist without such revaluation of expanding the uses of social media and Web 2.0 applications over the CRM area [14]. Such integration has emerged with the intention of providing firms and companies with more capabilities to contribute to customer satisfaction and experience [1, 4, 27, 29]. SCRM also expands the horizon of CRM activities with a sufficient level of customer participation and engagement, which, in turn, significantly reflects on the overall marketing performance [20, 21, 28, 36].

However, there is always a critical question regarding the feasibility and applicability of using social media tools for SCRM activities [3]. This calls for further examination and explanation of the related issues of SCRM and its feasibility and applicability as a new system considered by marketers [4, 29]. More importantly, there are a limited number of studies that have tested how using social media platforms for SCRM systems could add value to organization performance [3]. As this area is quite new, the current study realizes the necessity of proposing a theoretical foundation which could provide a clear picture explaining how using social media platforms for SCRM systems could predict customer performance.

2 Literature Review

SCRM issues have been the focus of a number of recent studies (i.e. [5, 15, 25, 29, 40]. Some of these studies (i.e. [13, 15, 22, 35]) reported that SCRM could contribute many values and utilities for marketers. For example, marketers are currently more able to efficiently produce a large amount of data with a certain degree of customization, interactivity, and informativeness [6]. Further, due to the interactive nature of Web 2.0 applications that empowers customers to actively communicate and interact with other customers and organizations, there are more opportunities to build online community and strong brands [23]. This, in turn, leads to more customer involvement and engagement [29]. In this regard, customers are more active and engaged with marketing activities conducted in social media such as creating their own content, publishing their experience, encouraging other customers, and so on [4, 29]. In the light of such advantages of SCRM, a large amount of time, effort, and money has been projected in the area of SCRM systems [27].

However, [5] argued that if the adoption of SCRM systems is very low, organizations would not be able to reach the related values of SCRM effectively. [10] recently assured the importance of the contribution of SCRM to the marketing services activities in the hotel context such as enhancing customer associations, customer performance, and financial performance. [31] emphasized the role of social media tools in the area of SCRM via enhancing the role of value co-creation as well as arguing how the integrated mechanism of SCRM could be accelerated by engaging the social capabilities that are available in the social media platforms, which, in turn, reflects in both financial and non-financial performance. As reported by [3], modern organizations are looking forward to applying SCRM systems to have an effective means of contact with their customers as well as to sustain their associations with them. This is in addition to the ability of SCRM to facilitate accessing the big data available in social media platforms about customers.

Even though these studies have attempted to examine either the adoption of SCRM or the impact of SCRM systems, there is still a need to clarify the main dimensions of SCRM over the social media platforms and how such dimensions could contribute to financial and customer performance. Therefore, this study attempts to fill this gap by proposing a conceptual model which could cover the fundamental aspects of SCRM over the social media area.

3   Conceptual Model and Research Hypotheses

Based on a critical review of the main models and studies (i.e. [8, 15, 16, 18, 19, 31]) that have tested SCRM, this study formulates the current model presented in Fig. 1. In detail, a Capabilities-Based Perspective was considered in the current study as a theoretical foundation [30]. As seen in Fig. 1, the most important antecedences and consequences are considered in one single model. As this study considers the implementation of SCRM over the social media platforms, it was important to consider the impact of social media on SCRM. Indeed, this impact of social media has been addressed by [16, 29, 31]. Relationship marketing orientation was argued by [16] as an important requirement for SCRM. [2, 30] approved the critical role of customer-centric management. It was also important that the impact of SCRM on customer engagement has been validated by different studies such as [15, 16, 29]. Finally, customer

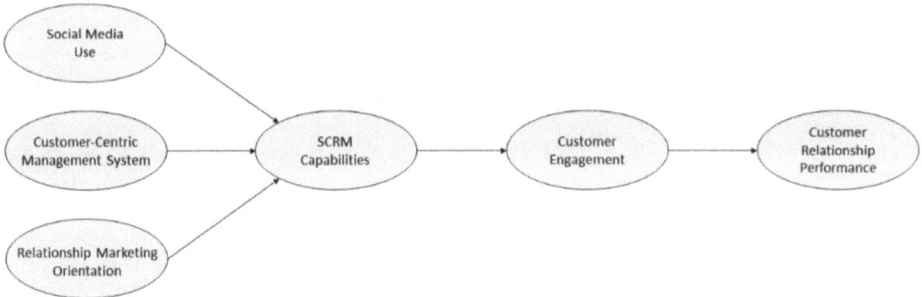

Fig. 1. Conceptual model (Adapted from [8, 15, 16, 18, 31])

relationship performance (financial and non-financial) was proposed to be the main consequences of SCRM and engagement. Accordingly, this study proposes the following research hypotheses:

H1: Social media use will positively influence SCRM capabilities.

H2: A customer-centric management system will positively influence SCRM capabilities.

H3: Relationship marketing orientation will positively influence SCRM capabilities.

H4: SCRM capabilities will positively influence customer engagement.

H5: Customer engagement will positively influence customer relationship performance.

It is also worth indicating that SCRM is addressed as a multidimensional construct in the current study. This is in line with what has been proposed and supported [17, 18, 31]. These dimensions are presented in Fig. 2. By the same token, three main dimensions, i.e. behavioural, cognitive, and emotional, are all adapted to reflect customer engagement. (See Fig. 3. These aspects of customer engagement were adopted from [15]).

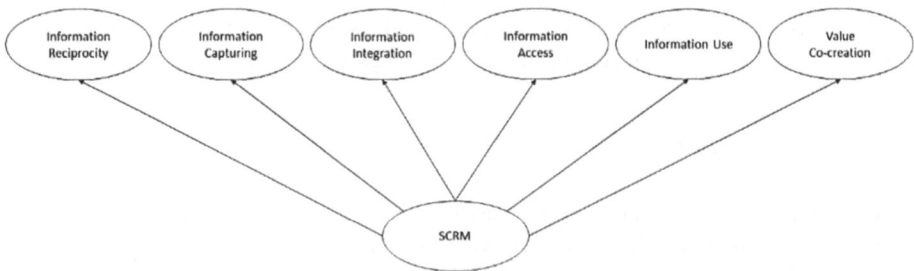

Fig. 2. SCRM capabilities (Adapted from [17, 18, 31])

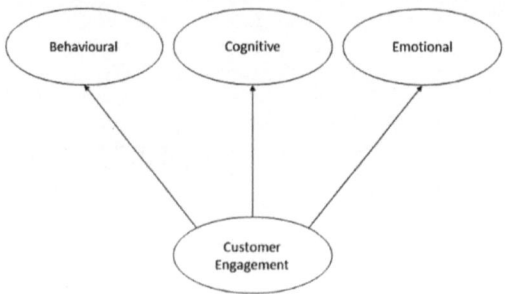

Fig. 3. Customer engagement dimensions (Adapted from [15, 16])

4   Proposed Research Methodology

As discussed above, the current study model and research hypotheses has been proposed based on what has been tested and supported in prior studies. Thus, the nature of this study seems to be more positivist deductive, and accordingly, the quantitative method has been adopted to capture adequate statistical evidences [7, 12, 24]. The targeted context of this study will be different firms from the service context in Jordan: mobile communication firms, banks, and travel and tourism agencies in Jordan. This is due to the fact that these firms have extensively adopted and apply social media tools for SCRM activities. Moreover, these organizations have their place in different social media platforms (Facebook, Instagram, Twitter, and YouTube) along with the fact that millions of customers follow these firms on social media platforms. In detail, a field survey questionnaire will be allocated to marketing managers, staff in the marketing department, social media managers, and admins at these organizations. Factors will be measured using scale items adapted from previous studies. For instance, the main aspects of SCRM, i.e. information reciprocity, information capturing, information integration, value co-creation, and information use, will be adapted from [18]. These items have also been validated and tested by [27, 31, 37–39]. Items from [16, 18, 32] will be adapted to test the customer relationship orientation construct. The customer-centric management system will be tested using scale items from [27]. The scale adapted from [15, 16, 35] will be considered to evaluate customer engagement. Once the data has been collected, it will be processed using structural equation modeling analyses to validate the conceptual model and research hypotheses.

5   Research Contribution

Even though there is considerable interest in the applications of social media tools for marketing aims, there is still a strong need to explain and examine how SCRM could be accelerated by such applications. This is in addition to the fact that a comprehensive theoretical model is much needed to see which aspects in SCRM systems could be affected by social media use. This model should also clarify how SCRM activities in social media could contribute to customer engagement and customer relationship performance. Therefore, this study would hopefully provide further understanding regarding the related issues of SCRM over the social media platforms especially in the light of the limited number of studies that have tested SCRM over the social media platforms. Further, the targeted context of this study as mentioned in the proposed research methodology is different service organizations in Jordan. Indeed, such issues have yet to be examined in Jordan or even in the Arab countries. This in turn confirms the importance of conducting this study. While the prior SCRM studies have considered an individual context like banking, i.e. [33, 37]; tourism, i.e. [33]; and hotels, i.e. [34], this study considers different kinds of organizations over the service context. Thus, rich results could be attained once this model has been empirically tested which could provide more clues to help firms in how they can effectively apply SCRM activities over the social media area.

6   Limitations and Future Research Directions

In spite of the considerable contribution that could be attained in the current study, there is a number of limitations that really restrict this study. For example, this study is more conceptual and theoretical, and it has not been tested yet. Therefore, there is a need to collect adequate statistical evidences by collecting data from the targeted organizations who are interested in SCRM activities in social media. The current study model was built based on what has been discussed and approved over the prior literature. This could affect the applicability of the current model over the Jordanian context especially in the fact that most of the prior studies have been conducted in the developed countries. Therefore, conducting an exploratory study using a number of interviews with those who are experts in CRM and social media marketing could be more useful.

References

1. Abed, S.S., Dwivedi, Y.K., Williams, M.D.: Social media as a bridge to e-commerce adoption in SMEs: a systematic literature review. Mark. Rev. **15**(1), 39–57 (2015)
2. Abeza, G., O'Reilly, N., Reid, I.: Relationship marketing and social media in sport. Int. J. Sport Commun. **6**(2), 120–142 (2013)
3. Ahani, A., Rahim, N.Z.A., Nilashi, M.: Forecasting social CRM adoption in SMEs: a combined SEM-neural network method. Comput. Hum. Behav. **75**, 560–578 (2017)
4. Alalwan, A.A., Rana, N.P., Dwivedi, Y.K., Algharabat, R.: Social media in marketing: a review and analysis of the existing literature. Telematics Inform. **34**, 1177–1190 (2017)
5. Askool, S., Nakata, K.: A conceptual model for acceptance of social CRM systems based on a scoping study. Ai Soc. **26**(3), 205–220 (2011)
6. Berthon, P.R., Pitt, L.F., Plangger, K., Shapiro, D.: Marketing meets Web 2.0, social media, and creative consumers: implications for international marketing strategy. Bus. Horiz. **55**(3), 261–271 (2012)
7. Bhattacherjee, A.: Social Science Research: Principles, Methods, and Practices, 2nd edn. University of South Florida, Tampa, Florida, USA (2012)

8. Choudhury, M.M., Harrigan, P.: CRM to social CRM: the integration of new technologies into customer relationship management. J. Strateg. Mark. **22**(2), 149–176 (2014)
9. Coulter, K.S., Roggeveen, A.: "Like it or not" consumer responses to word-of-mouth communication in on-line social networks. Manage. Res. Rev. **35**(9), 878–899 (2012)
10. Diffley, S., McCole, P., Carvajal-Trujillo, E.: Examining social customer relationship management among Irish hotels. Int. J. Contemp. Hosp. Manage. **30**, 1072–1091 (2018)
11. Dwivedi, Y.K., Rana, N.P., Tajvidi, M., Lal, B., Sahu, G.P., Gupta, A.: Exploring the role of social media in e-government: an analysis of emerging literature. In: Proceedings of the 10th International Conference on Theory and Practice of Electronic Governance, pp. 97–106. ACM, March 2017
12. Dwivedi, Y., Irani, Z.: Understanding the adopters and non-adopters of broadband. Commun. ACM **52**(1), 122–125 (2009)
13. Hajli, N., Shanmugam, M., Papagiannidis, S., Zahay, D., Richard, M.O.: Branding co-creation with members of online brand communities. J. Bus. Res. **70**, 136–144 (2017)
14. Harrigan, P., Miles, M.: From e-CRM to s-CRM. Critical factors underpinning the social CRM activities of SMEs. Small Enterp. Res. **21**(1), 99–116 (2014)
15. Harrigan, P., Evers, U., Miles, M., Daly, T.: Customer engagement with tourism social media brands. Tour. Manage. **59**, 597–609 (2017)
16. Harrigan, P., Soutar, G., Choudhury, M.M., Lowe, M.: Modelling CRM in a social media age. Australas. Mark. J. (AMJ) **23**(1), 27–37 (2015)
17. Jaakkola, E., Helkkula, A., Aarikka-Stenroos, L.: Service experience co-creation: conceptualization, implications, and future research directions. J. Serv. Manage. **26**(2), 182–205 (2015)
18. Jayachandran, S., Sharma, S., Kaufman, P., Raman, P.: The role of relational information processes and technology use in customer relationship management. J. Mark. **69**(4), 177–192 (2005)
19. Kapoor, K.K., Tamilmani, K., Rana, N.P., Patil, P., Dwivedi, Y.K., Nerur, S.: Advances in social media research: past, present and future. Inf. Syst. Front. **20**(3), 531–558 (2018)
20. Leeflang, P.S., Verhoef, P.C., Dahlström, P., Freundt, T.: Challenges and solutions for marketing in a digital era. Eur. Manage. J. **32**(1), 1–12 (2014)
21. Leung, X.Y., Bai, B., Stahura, K.A.: The marketing effectiveness of social media in the hotel industry: a comparison of Facebook and Twitter. J. Hosp. Tour. Res. **39**(2), 147–169 (2015)
22. McCarthy, J., Rowley, J., Jane Ashworth, C., Pioch, E.: Managing brand presence through social media: the case of UK football clubs. Internet Res. **24**(2), 181–204 (2014)
23. McCole, D.: Seasonal employees: the link between sense of community and retention. J. Travel Res. **54**(2), 193–205 (2015)
24. Orlikowski, W.J., Baroudi, J.J.: Studying information technology in organizations: research approaches and assumptions. Inf. Syst. Res. **2**(1), 1–28 (1991)
25. Shareef, M.A., Mukerji, B., Dwivedi, Y.K., Rana, N.P., Islam, R.: Social media marketing: comparative effect of advertisement sources. J. Retail. Consum. Serv. (2017). https://doi.org/10.1016/j.jretconser.2017.11.001
26. Lewis, P.J.S., et al.: Circulating microRNAs as potential markers of human drug-induced liver injury. Hepatology **54**(5), 1767–1776 (2011)
27. Trainor, K.J., Andzulis, J.M., Rapp, A., Agnihotri, R.: Social media technology usage and customer relationship performance: a capabilities-based examination of social CRM. J. Bus. Res. **67**(6), 1201–1208 (2014)
28. Tuten, T., Solomon, M.: Social Media Marketing. 2. Painos. Sage Publication, Thousand Oaks (2015)

29. Wang, Z., Kim, H.G.: Can social media marketing improve customer relationship capabilities and firm performance? dynamic capability perspective. J. Interact. Mark. **39**, 15–26 (2017)
30. Trainor, K.J.: Relating social media technologies to performance: a capabilities-based perspective. J. Pers. Selling Sales Manage. **32**(3), 317–331 (2012)
31. Diffley, S., McCole, P.: Extending customer relationship management into a social context. Serv. Ind. J. **35**(11–12), 591–610 (2015)
32. Sin, L.Y.M., Tse, A.C.B., Yim, F.H.K.: CRM: conceptualization and scale development. Eur. J. Mark. **39**(11–12), 1264–1290 (2005)
33. Giannakis-Bompolis, C., Boutsouki, C.: Customer relationship management in the era of social web and social customer: an investigation of customer engagement in the Greek retail banking sector. Procedia Soc. Behav. Sci. **148**, 67–78 (2014)
34. Alalwan, A.A., Dwivedi, Y.K., Rana, N.P., Williams, M.D.: Consumer adoption of mobile banking in Jordan: examining the role of usefulness, ease of use, perceived risk and self-efficacy. J. Enterp. Inf. Manage. **29**(1), 118–139 (2016)
35. Algharabat, R., Alalwan, A.A., Rana, N.P., Dwivedi, Y.K.: Three dimensional product presentation quality antecedents and their consequences for online retailers: the moderating role of virtual product experience. J. Retail. Consum. Serv. **36**, 203–217 (2017)
36. Algharabat, R., Rana, N.P., Dwivedi, Y.K., Alalwan, A.A., Qasem, Z.: The effect of telepresence, social presence and involvement on consumer brand engagement: an empirical study of non-profit organizations. J. Retail. Consum. Serv. **40**, 139–149 (2018)
37. Alalwan, A.A., Dwivedi, Y.K., Rana, N.P., Algharabat, R.: Examining factors influencing Jordanian customers' intentions and adoption of internet banking: extending UTAUT2 with risk. J. Retail. Consum. Serv. **40**, 125–138 (2018)
38. Dwivedi, Y.K., Rana, N.P., Janssen, M., Lal, B., Williams, M.D., Clement, M.: An empirical validation of a unified model of electronic government adoption (UMEGA). Gov. Inf. Q. **34**(2), 211–230 (2017)
39. Dwivedi, Y.K., Rana, N.P., Jeyaraj, A., Clement, M., Williams, M.D.: Re-examining the unified theory of acceptance and use of technology (UTAUT): towards a revised theoretical model. Inf. Syst. Front. (2017). https://doi.org/10.1007/s10796-017-9774-y
40. Shareef, M.A., Mukerji, B., Alryalat, M.A.A., Wright, A., Dwivedi, Y.K.: Advertisements on Facebook: identifying the persuasive elements in the development of positive attitudes in consumers. J. Retail. Consum. Serv. **43**, 258–268 (2018). https://doi.org/10.1016/j.jretconser.2018.04.006

Government and Infrastructure

Critical Success Factors of the Digital Payment Infrastructure for Developing Economies

Naveen Kumar Singh[1]([✉]), G. P. Sahu[1], Nripendra P. Rana[2]([✉]),
Pushp P. Patil[2]([✉]), and Babita Gupta[3]([✉])

[1] Motilal Nehru National Institute of Technology Allahabad, Allahabad, India
rajput.naveen07@gmail.com, gsahu@mnnit.ac.in
[2] Emerging Markets Research Centre (EMaRC), School of Management,
Swansea University Bay Campus, Swansea SA1 8EN, UK
{n.p.rana,919286}@swansea.ac.uk
[3] College of Business, California State University, Monterey Bay, USA
bgupta@csumb.edu

Abstract. This paper studies the Critical Success Factors' (CSFs) for the adoption of Digital Payment System in India. There are few studies about the literature on CSFs for the adoption of the digital payment system in the Indian context. This study is an attempt to cover this gap. In this study, we reviewed the theories for adoption model at the individual level used in Information System (IS) and discussed four technology model including "Technology Acceptance Model" (TAM). Ten factors have been identified with extensive literature review and review of selected models namely; Perceived Ease of Use, Perceived functional benefits, Awareness, Availability of Resources, Government as a policy maker, Performance Expectancy, Social Influence, Price Value, Experience & Habit, and Risk-taking ability. An expert from academic industry has been taken as a reviewer or consultant of the selected variables. The CSFs may ensure that they are the predictors and the important factors for adoption of digital payments system in India. The study mainly uses the deductive approach to consider the primary and secondary sources of data. The analyses of these models take into account through Interpretive Structural Modeling (ISM) methodology and develop a model for effective adoption of Digital Payment System in India. The paper also makes future recommendations for further research studies.

Keywords: Technology Acceptance Model (TAM)
Interpretive Structural Modeling (ISM) · Digital Payment System
Critical Success Factor (CSF)

1 Introduction

"Digital Payment will acquire around 15% of the total GDP", estimated by the Boston Consulting Group (BCG) in their report Digital Payment 2020. The report also estimated that around 90% of the customer will acquire digital payment for their daily (online and offline both) transactions. Payment plays an important part in country's major decisions like; monetary policy, fiscal policy, financial sector and economic

© IFIP International Federation for Information Processing 2019
Published by Springer Nature Switzerland AG 2019.
A. Elbanna et al. (Eds.): TDIT 2018, IFIP AICT 533, pp. 113–125, 2019.
https://doi.org/10.1007/978-3-030-04315-5_9

development [20, 42]. It is one of the important issues and having substantial changes policies in across the world. In traditional stage, barter system was used to fulfil the need [1] through the exchange of one good with other required goods, like livestock, crop, food etc. But in the modern era of the digital payment system, which is totally different from the traditional way of exchange of goods; here the transactions are made by using digital currencies with the help of an electronic medium. Digital Payment refers to the set of rules & regulations, procedures, method, medium (i.e. mobile phones, computers, laptops etc.), processes and interbank funds transfer systems which accelerate the circulation of money in the country or currency area [22]. The study conducted to fulfill the objective of research, the objectives are:

- To carry-out a comprehensive literature review on adoption of Digital Payment.
- To identify the Critical Success Factors (CSFs) for effective adoption of Digital Payment System in India.
- To develop a model for effective adoption of Digital Payment System using Interpretive Structural Modeling (ISM) Methodology.
- To develop a set of recommendations for effective adoption of Digital Payment System in the developing economies like India.

The structure of this paper is as shown – Sect. 2 is literature review of the related study including identification of CSFs on the basis of adopted theories and related literature, it also provides the background, history of digital payment system; Sect. 3 is the explanation of related theories and methodology of the study; Sect. 4 discussed the identification of variable affecting adoption of digital payment system and research model development; Sect. 5 presented the study's finding and result with the help of Interpretive Structural Modeling (ISM) methods. Section 6 discusses the findings and brief conclusion of the study; Sect. 7 is the last section of the study provides the future recommendation and its limitation and probably potential direction for future studies on adoption of Digital Payment System.

2   Review of Literature

Cashless transactions were introduced in the early 1950s and become "ready money" to the users, which reduce the risk of an individual like, handling of cash, theft by pickpocket etc. and national risk like, corruption, black money, stockiest etc. During the 1990s' cashless transactions become more popular with the popularity of e-Banking in developed countries. Late 2010, digital methods of payment became more popular in across the world. At the earlier stage, online modes of payment like Paypal, Plastic cards, Mobile wallet systems, e-Banking etc. helped the users to make a digital transaction. Different types of payment system existed before the emergence of digital payment system in India. People deposited money manually at the bank branch, sahukar, jewelers, etc. and the banking system operations were done on paper/files manually, which lead to a slow transaction, more chance of errors, maintenance and keeping of register. The process of maintaining, ledger posting, and keeping of register without using any single machine called "Book Keeping". Hardly one computer present at one whole branch which helps to cover some sort of manual work in the branch, more the one computer are like "triton among the minnows".

The worldwide propagation of the Internet led to the birth of e-Commerce, which further allows the electronic transfer in a technological environment. The growth of e-Commerce depends on its speed, digitalisation, accessibility, and availability. The internet provides the facility to make quick decision making in business activities, like advertising, auction, negotiation, ordering, paying for merchandise and sourcing [43]. E-Commerce allows the companies to reach potential customers from one corner to another corner of the world. But the problem in global transaction system is the lack of standard finance system in an open electronic market. E-Commerce requires authentication, non-repudiation, trust, and security for successful implementation of technology [17] and for this purpose Digital signature is one of the best examples of Internet authentication and non-repudiation [11]. Moving against the drawback of digital payment like overflow of currency, black money, corruption, terror funding etc. provides the transparency in the flow of currency and an easy way to track money anywhere and anytime. There are various methods to make digital transaction in India (Cashless India) including, Internet Banking, Banking Cards, Unified Payments Interface (UPI), Unstructured Supplementary Service Data (USSD), Aadhar Enabled Payment System (AEPS), Mobile Wallets, Bank Pre-Paid Cards, Point of Sale (POS), Mobile Banking, and Micro ATMs. The government of India started Digital India Program to promote digital transaction, digital literacy, awareness, use of internet etc. which transforms India into a digitally empowered society and digital friendly economy. A program like "Digital India" provides an intensified impetus for future progress for electronic governance and would promote not only growth but also provides e-Services, e-Product, e-Devices, digital manufacturing, and job creation. E-Governance and Service on Demand is an important component in Digital India Program of Government of India. It offers seamlessly integrated, real-time online services, to Indian citizen with a platform for the digital mode of financial transactions. The program "Digital India" started by the government of India (GOI), encouraged and supported by the other private as well as public organisations of the country and contributing their effort to make India cashless.

Ministry of Electronic and Information Technology (MeitY), Government of India envisages internet and mobile-enabled information and services access anytime, anywhere in the whole country, especially in the semi-urban, rural and remote part of India (GOI). MeitY further envisages common e-Government infrastructure that offers end-to-end online transfer experience for the Indian citizen, business and other governmental functions like, accessing various government information to Indian citizens, Payment gateway interface etc. After the implementation of e-payment methods, people can use digital payment methods for numerous purposes such as, online shopping, bill payment, fund transfer, etc. According to a local study, the level of technology continues to rise; fears continue to rise as well. According to Johnson [19], Fear of commercial failure or loss of competitive advantages is "driving high levels of innovation among commercial firms, information systems suppliers and financial institutions".

3 Research Methodology

The use of Information Technology (IT) in the workplace remains a core concern of Information Systems (IS) research and practice of the Government. The troubling problem of information technology is underutilized systems, in place of impressive advances in hardware and software capabilities [38]. Less use of installed systems has become major factor underlying the "productivity paradox" surrounding uninspiring returns from organisational investments in IT [32]. Adoption is a primary decision made by a user to interact with the technology [40]. A number of studies have been investigated for the adoption of new technology in developed countries [36] but very few in developing countries [5]. In this study, we studied various theories for IT adoption models at the individual level used in IS literature and discuss in prominent models used in this study. The models used for the study are: Technology Acceptance Model (TAM) [13], Unified Theory of Acceptance and Use of Technology (UTAUT) [39], The Theory of Reasoned Action (TRA) [16], and The Theory of Planned Behaviour (TPB) [2] because these models are the only ones that are at the individual level. The Diffusion of Innovation (DOI) [30] and Technology–Organization–Environment framework (TOE) [6] are at the firm level. The DOI and TOE are not discussed further because these are not the part of our study, rest of the theories are discussed in the following sub-sections.

3.1 Technology Acceptance Model (TAM)

According to Davis [13, 14], this model develops the intention to use the IS, which influences the individuals' decision of actual usage of the technology. This model derived two beliefs Perceives Usefulness (PU) & Perceived Ease of Use (PEU), which intended use of a technology. This is broadly studied and accepted model in technology adoption [35] and according to this model ease of use has also been found to be an important constraint of intention to use new technology [25].

Perceived Ease of Use (PEU). It is the degree to which user believes that it would be free of efforts by using a particular system [13]. There is lots of research which provides evidence of the significant effect of ease of use on intention to use [13, 21, 23, 26, 34]. Among the potential adopters of software, PEU has a positive effect on intention to adopt [21]. Similarly, according to Guriting and Ndubisi [18], bank customers are likely to use online banking and other banking services when the technology easy to use; and [23], for online trading system PEU was correlated with intention toward the use of the online trading system. PEU has a significant effect the development of initial willingness to use of Internet Banking [27]. Thus PEU predicts the acceptance of technology with end users' beliefs on technology [14, 38].

Perceived Usefulness (PU). It is the degree to which user believes that with the help of the technological system, it would help to enhance performance and productivity in the workplace.

3.2   Unified Theory of Acceptance and Use of Technology (UTAUT)

There are five behavioral intentions in this model [39]:

Performance Expectancy. It is a degree to which user believes that the system will help to gain his/her performance.

Effort Expectancy. It is a degree in which user believes the ease of use of the technology.

Social Influence. It is the reaction, impact, of the society for the use of new technology by the individual.

Facilitating Condition. It is the belief of the individual that the organization and technical infrastructure exist to support the individual.

Behavioral Intention. It is the individuals' subjective probability of performance. There are four moderate determinants of the individual in this model: gender, age, experience, and voluntariness of use.

3.3   The Theory of Reasoned Action (TRA)

TRA derived from the study of human attitude and behavior. TRA posits the antecedents of behavior are users' intention and the strength of the persons' intention to carry out that certain behavior corresponds with the likelihood of the behavior taking place. The following three antecedents are derived from this model are:

Attitude. It means the intention to use the technology.

Subjective Norms. It is the perception that the persons who are important to the individual perform the questionable behavior, and

Behavioral Intention. It is a belief that performing behavior lead to a specific outcome. TRA finds its origin in the field of social psychology. It defines the link between intentions, behavioral beliefs, social norms, personal attitude, and behavior of an individual. According to Ajzen & Fishbein [4], an individuals' behavior is identified by its behavioral intention to performance. This intention is further identified by the individuals' behavioral attitudes, traits, and subjective norms towards the behavior. [16] also claims that there are some other factors which are known as external variables, influence the behavior only in an indirect way by influencing the attitude or subjective norms. The variables like; characteristics of the task, types of development implementation, political influences, organizational structure etc. [14].

3.4   The Theory of Planned Behavior (TPB)

TPB expands the area of pure volitional control identified by TRA [2]. It is a social-psychological model which is extensively in the domain of IS for predicting, examining and explaining the human behavior [15]. According to this model, the actual behavior is driven by users' intentions that are influenced by factors related to personal, social and environmental. TPB examines and predicts users' intention and behavior in situations where the individual user might lack control over their own behavior [2, 6, 37]. TPB supply more information to explain human behavior, so it can be said that it is more powerful and superior than the other technology adoption models predicting and explaining human behavior [24, 33, 34].

4   Variable Which Affects the Adoption of Digital Payment System

On the basis on above models adopted for the study and extensive review of literature in the area of technology adoption, there are following Critical Success Factors' were identified to develop a model for effective adoption of digital payment in India. There are a number of studies that have investigated adoption of technology in developed countries [36] but very few or no studies that have been focused in developing countries [5] and also no standard model has been given by any of them for use in developing countries. For instance, there is no dominating method for digital payment system in India. To develop a model for effective adoption of digital payment system a few factors are identified, such as:

Perceived Ease of Use. It refers to the degree of effort required to adopt the digital payment methods in place of traditional methods. The more complex process needed the more efforts to adopt the technology and vice versa [13, 14].

Perceived Functional Benefits. Functional benefits provide the advantages of adoption of new technology to the user and the society [29].

Availability of Resources. It includes medium or device, methods, availability of the Internet, software, ICT with additional features like access of use, speed, and cost of internet [29].

Performance Expectancy. User adopts any new technology with this belief that the new technology will help him/her to gain in the performance and productivity, reduce cost, and save time providing overall growth to the individual as well as the society [39, 41].

Government as Policy Maker. Policy makers should be context specific, sensitive, and have the strongest impact on the user. It requires coordination with the other private or public institutions to make a strategy for implementation of innovative technology system.

Awareness. It consists the users' knowledge, education, and consciousness of digital payment system including its characteristics, functionality, advantages and disadvantages [29].

Social Influence. This consists of mouth to mouth publicity of the individual to use digital payment adoption methods. In this factor, users insist and help others to use the technology [39, 41].

Price Value. Price refers to the charges or commission of the services avail by the user to use the technology. So the charge taken by the government to the user should be low [41].

Experience & Habit. Past experience provides the platform to adopt new technology. It reflects the learning and past behaviors of the technology [41].

Risk Taking Ability. Risk plays an important role in the adoption of any new technology. Hence, the government should provide belief to the user that organizational and technological infrastructure exists to help the user.

A research model (Fig. 1) is proposed to validate the hypotheses. The model will be validated in a future study with the help of effective statistical tools and methods.

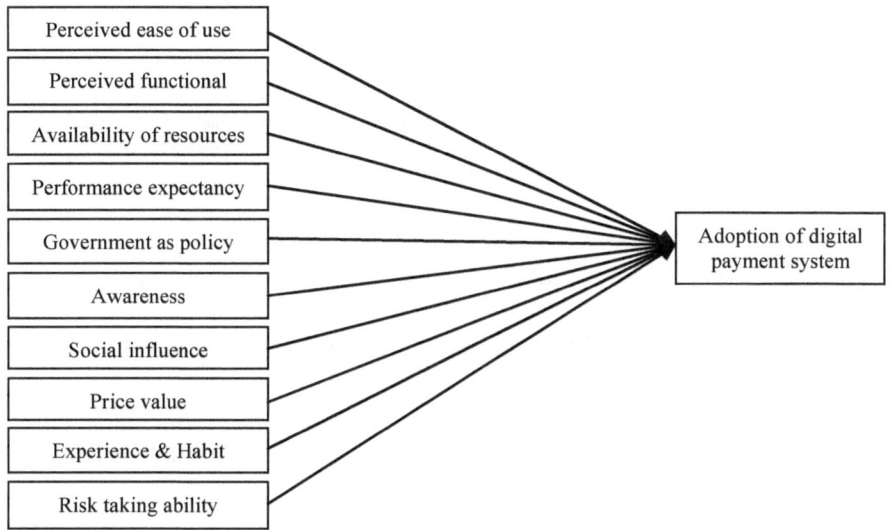

Fig. 1. Research model of the study

The proposed research model provided ten effective critical factors based on the existing theories and literature review. We will implement these CSFs in our further studies which will be related to consumer perception of adoption of the digital payment system. Structural Equation Modeling (SEM) will be used as a technique of analysis which provides a comprehensive model (Fig. 2) indication the hierarchy of variables and linkage of variables from each other. SEM-based analysis generally having two stages, first; Measurement Model and second; Structural Model. Measurement Model aims to identify constructs variables that fit to analyse the further studies. In getting fit variables Confirmatory test Factor Analysis (CFA) will be used. While on the other hand, Structural Model aims to identify a model which is feasible with the help of Goodness of Fit (GoF) test. To test the suitability of the model the statistical method will be used, namely; Goodness of Fit Index (GFI), Adjusted Goodness of Fit Index (AGFI), Root Mean Squares error of Approximation (RMSEA), Chi-Square test (X^2), and Root Mean Squares Residual (RMSR). To test the reliability, AMOS application will be used in SEM as a composite measure of reliability. If the value of Construct Reliability (CR) will be ≥ 0.70, then the construct will be deemed as good reliability.

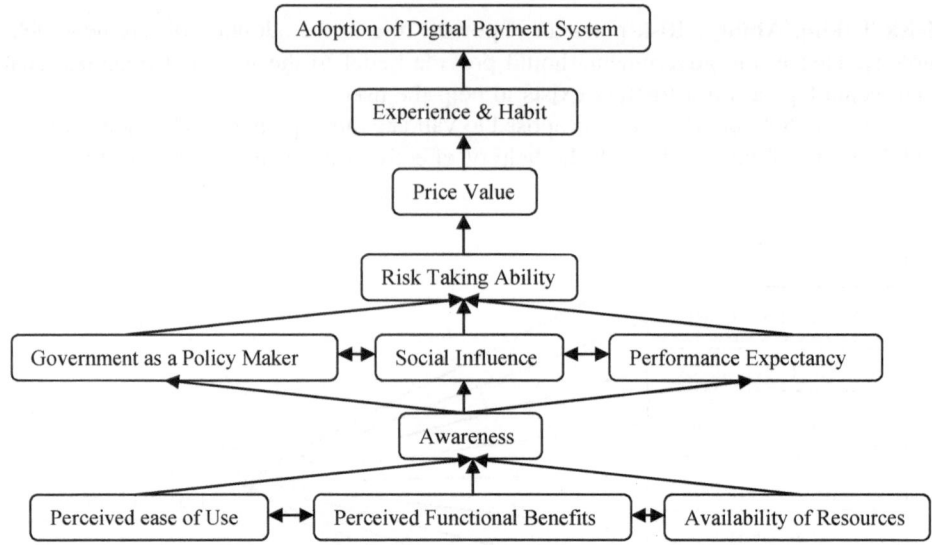

Fig. 2. Model for adoption of digital payment system

For this purpose, data will be collected through online as well as offline survey method with the help of a questionnaire. The target respondent will be individual customers who are directly related to procurement procedure.

5   Model Development Through Interpretive Structural Modeling (ISM)

ISM model enables the researchers to establish a relationship among the identified critical success factors with the help of a formal structure [10]. It is an interactive learning process which determines an interdisciplinary direction and provides level which shows the priority among the CSFs. With the help of literature review and a formal interview with academic experts of the related domain, a model has been developed using ISM methodology. This model is used to interpret the relationship and direction between the variables, to a better understanding of interdependency [31]. Hence, ISM modeling is used to develop an effective model for adoption of the digital payment system. There are several steps followed to develop the model [12]:

- Identified CSFs with the help of extensive literature review and expert opinion (Fig. 1).
- For pair-wise relationship, Structural Self-Interaction Matrix (SSIM) has been developed through expert advice and interviews.
- Reachability Matrix has been developed with the help of SSIM to check the transitive matrix (Table 1).

- To check the relationship from another axis, Antecend Set has been developed with the help of SSIM (Table 2*).

Table 1. Reachability matrix

Factors (j) (i)	11	10	9	8	7	6	5	4	3	2	1
1	1	0	1	1	0	1	0	1	0	1	1
2	1	1	1	1	0	1	0	1	1	1	1
3	1	1	0	1	1	0	0	0	1	0	1
4	1	0	0	0	0	1	1	1	0	1	1
5	1	0	0	1	1	0	1	0	1	0	0
6	0	1	1	1	1	1	0	0	0	1	1
7	1	0	1	1	1	1	1	0	0	1	1
8	0	1	1	1	0	1	1	0	0	0	0
9	1	1	1	0	0	0	1	0	0	0	0
10	1	1	0	1	0	1	1	0	0	1	0
11	1	0	0	0	0	0	0	0	0	0	0

- Development of Intersecting set from the factors which are intersecting between Reachability matrix and Antecend Set (Table 2*).

Table 2. Reachability, antecend, and intersection set and level of factors

Sl no	Reachability set	Antecend set	Intersection set	Level
1	1, 2, 4, 6, 8, 9, 11	1, 2, 3, 4, 6, 7	1, 2, 4, 6	VII
2	1, 2, 3, 4, 6, 8, 9, 10, 11	1, 2, 4, 6, 7, 10	1, 2, 4, 6, 10	VII
3	1, 3, 7, 8, 10, 11	2, 3, 5	3	VI
4	1, 2, 4, 5, 6, 11	1, 2, 4	1, 2, 4	VII
5	3, 5, 7, 8, 11	4, 5, 7, 8, 9, 10	5, 7, 8	V
6	1, 2, 6, 7, 8, 9, 10	1, 2, 4, 6, 7, 8, 10	1, 2, 6, 7, 8, 10	V
7	1, 2, 5, 6, 7, 8, 9, 11	3, 5, 6, 7	5, 6, 7	V
8	5, 6, 8, 9, 10	1, 2, 3, 5, 6, 7, 8, 10	5, 6, 8, 10	III
9	5, 9, 10, 11	1, 2, 6, 7, 8, 9	9	II
10	2, 5, 6, 8, 10, 11	2, 3, 6, 8, 9, 10	2, 6, 8, 10	IV
11	11	1, 2, 3, 4, 5, 7, 9, 10, 11	11	I

- Based on the Intersecting set a hierarchal graph has been drawn by removing transitive relationship (Fig. 2).
*Table 2 included both the sets.

We followed these following steps to prepare the SSIM as well as Reachability Matrix (Table 2) to construct the ISM model (Fig. 2):

1. If (i) is the predictor of (j) then (i, j) cell entry in the SSIM is A, then the equivalent (i, j) entry in the Reachability Matrix becomes 1 and the (j, i) cell entry become 0;
2. If (j) is a predictor of (i) then (i, j) cell entry in the SSIM is B, then the equivalent (i, j) entry in the Reachability Matrix becomes 0 and the (j, i) cell entry become 1;
3. If (i) and (j) are both predictors of each other then (i, j) cell entry in the SSIM is C, then the equivalent (i, j) and (j, i) both entries in the Reachability Matrix becomes 1;
4. If (i) and (j) both are not a predictor of each other then (i, j) cell entry in the SSIM is D, then the equivalent (i, j) and (j, i) both entry in the Reachability Matrix becomes 0;

Table 1 highlights the completed matrix when all the cell references have been converted to the binary format (i.e., 0 and 1) as the rules of ISM followed by Reachability Set, Antecend Set, and Intersection Set.

Table 2 identifies all ten critical success factors influencing the adoption of digital payment system. Table 2 also shows the Reachability Set and Antecend Set which help the researcher to categories the factor into different levels (i.e. from I to VII). These levels help the researcher to develop a model (Fig. 2) for a better understanding of interdependency on each other.

Developed ISM model represents the relationship between the selected CSFs in both direct and indirect way. All the factors are divided into seven different levels starting from bottom to top. Hence, the Model (Fig. 2) shows bottom-up approach where the factors at the bottom are the predicators of its upper factor/s. Like, Perceived ease of use, Perceived functional benefits & Availability of Resources (Level VII) are interdependent on each other and, are directly predictor of Awareness. These three factors (Perceived ease of use, Perceived functional benefits & Availability of Resources) are also indirectly predictor of rest of the other factors. Similarly, Awareness (Level VI) is directly predictor of factors; Government as a policy-maker, Social Influence, and Performance Expectancy (Level V) and so on. At the end of the hierarchy Adoption of Digital Payment System (Level I) is the immediate predictor of Experience and Habit (Level II). Therefore, this model provides an easy and clear hierarchal direction among the selected CSFs of Digital Payment System.

6   Discussion and Conclusion

With the help of TAM, UTAUT, TRA and TBP model including extensive literature review, there are ten CSFs were defined, which are responsible for the effective adoption of Digital Payment System. ISM provides the category-wise level from the identified CSFs, which shows the degree of importance of factors among all the CSFs. The objective of the study is to identify the CSFs for effective adoption of a digital payment system in India and the findings confirm that all the CSFs are related to Digital Payment System in India. The government of India and online transactions facility provider such as Banks, Non-Banking Financial Corporation (NBFC), Mobile Wallets, Payment Banks etc. should continually enhance their financial services with attractive offers, discounts, digital literacy, and awareness. It is observed that there are factors which are also responsible for digital payment system [8, 28] like lack of trust, internet connectivity, awareness, and training etc. According to Böhle [9], digital payment methods should prove themselves to be convenient, secure and effective to cover the greater market in comparison with physical cash. In the rapidly growing economy where Perceived ease of use, Perceived functional benefits, and availability of resources have high impact on the digital payment system, similarly on the other side, Experience and Habit have a low impact on the adoption of Digital Payment System in India. The main contribution of this study includes an attempt to identify the significant variable using TAM, UTAUT, TRA, and TPB for successful adoption of the digital payment system in India.

7 Recommendations and Limitations

Finally, it would be useful to suggest the direction of the future research in the area of Digital Payment System. The technology adoption in the other sectors may slightly differ from the Digital Payment sector. This study used limited literature. This problem could be resolved in the next phase of the study where larger data will be utilised by the researchers. This study serves as a pre-cursor for the current digital payment system in India. In future, this study can incorporate more research and experts. The result may vary from country to country, at different location, environment etc. The present model has neither been approved by any governing body nor statistically, tested and validated. Thus, the model is required to be statistically tested and verified using different approaches like SEM, Confirmatory Factor Analysis (CAF) etc. Researchers can continue this study using analysis like MICMAC analysis. Very little research is available that focuses on the platform of adoption of digital payment and no research is available on the interaction among the factors using ISM. The present ISM based model help the managers and policy makers to understand the relationship between the variables.

References

1. Achor, P.N., Robert, A.: Shifting policy paradigm from cash-based economy to cashless economy: The Nigeria experience. Afro-Asian J. Soc. Sci. **4**(4) (2013)
2. Ajzen, I.: The theory of planned behavior. Organ. Behav. Hum. Decis. Process. **50**(2), 179–211 (1991)
3. Ajzen, I.: Perceived behavioural control, self-efficacy, locus of control, and the theory of planned behaviour. J. Appl. Soc. Psychol. **32**(4), 665–683 (2002)
4. Ajzen, I., Fishbein, M.: Understanding attitudes and predicting social behavior (1980)
5. AlShihi, H.: E-government development and adoption dilemma: Oman case study. In: 6th International We-B (Working for e-Business) Conference (2005)
6. Baker, J.: The technology–organization–environment framework. In: Information Systems Theory, pp. 231–245. Springer, New York (2012)
7. Bandura, A.: Self-efficacy: toward a unifying theory of behavioural change. Psychol. Rev. **84**, 191–215 (1977)

8. Bihari, S.C.: Green banking-towards socially responsible banking in India. Int. J. Bus. Insights Transform. **4**(1) (2010)
9. Böhle, K., Krueger, M., Herrmann, C., Carat, G., Maghiros, I.: Electronic payment system: strategic and technical issues (2000)
10. Bolanos, R., Fontela, E., Nenclares, A., Pastor, P.: Using interpretive structural modelling in strategic decision-making groups. Manag. Decis. **43**(6), 877–895 (2005)
11. Coffey, T., Saidha, P.: Non-repudiation with mandatory proof of receipt. ACM SIGCOMM Comput. Commun. Rev. **26**(1), 6–17 (1996)
12. Laurie Hughes, D., Dwivedi, Y.K., Rana, N.P., Simintiras, A.C.: Information systems project failure – analysis of causal links using interpretive structural modelling. Prod. Plan. Control. **27**(16), 1313–1333 (2016)
13. Davis, F.D.: Perceived usefulness, perceived ease of use, and user acceptance of information technology. MIS Q. **13**, 319–340 (1989)
14. Davis, F.D., Bagozzi, R.P., Warshaw, P.R.: User acceptance of computer technology: a comparison of two theoretical models. Manage. Sci. **35**(8), 982–1003 (1989)
15. Dwivedi, Y.K., Wade, M.R., Schneberger, S.L.: Information Systems Theory: Explaining and Predicting Our Digital Society. Springer Science & Business Media, vol. 1 (2011)
16. Fishbein, M., Ajzen, I.: Belief, Attitude, Intention and Behavior: An Introduction to Theory and Research Reading. Addison-Wesley, MA (1975)
17. Garrett, S., Skevington, P.: An introduction to e-commerce. BT Technol. J. **17**(3), 11–16 (1999)
18. Guriting, P., Oly Ndubisi, N.: Borneo online banking: evaluating customer perceptions and behavioural intention. Manag. Res. News **29**(1/2), 6–15 (2006)
19. Johnson, O.: e-Payment Options in Electronic Marketplaces, MSc Information Systems Dissertation, Leeds University (1999)
20. Johnson, O.E.: Payment Systems. Monetary Policy and the Role of the Central Bank, International monetary fund (1998)
21. Karahanna, E., Straub, D.W.: The psychological origins of perceived usefulness and ease-of-use. Inf. Manag. **35**(4), 237–250 (1999)
22. Kokkola, T.: The payment system. Payments, Securities and Derivatives, and the role of the eurosystem. Frankfurt am Main: ecB (2010)
23. Lau, S.M.: Strategies to motivate brokers adopting on-line trading in Hong Kong financial market. Rev. Pac. Basin Financ. Mark. Policies **5**(4), 471–489 (2002)
24. Mathieson, K.: Predicting user intentions: comparing the technology acceptance model with the theory of planned behaviour. Inf. Syst. Res. **2**(3), 173–191 (1991)
25. Moon, J.W., Kim, Y.G.: Extending the TAM for a World-Wide-Web context. Inf. Manag. **38**(4), 217–230 (2001)
26. Norzaidi, M.D., Salwani, I.M.: Evaluating technology resistance and technology satisfaction on students' performance. Campus Wide Inf. Syst. **26**(4), 298–312 (2009)
27. Ramayah, T., Jantan, M., Mohd Noor, M.N., Razak, R.C., Koay, P.L.: Receptiveness of internet banking by Malaysian consumers: the case of Penang. Asian Acad. Manag. J. **8**(2), 1–29 (2003)
28. Rockart, J.F.: Chief executives define their own data needs. Harvard Bus. Rev. **57**(2), 81–93 (1978)
29. Rogers, E.M.: Diffusion of Innovation. The Free Press of Glencoe, New York (1962)
30. Rogers, E.M.: Diffusion of innovations (1995)
31. Sahu, G.P., Singh, M.: Green information system adoption and sustainability: a case study of select Indian Banks. In: Conference on e-Business, e-Services and e-Society, pp. 292–304. Springer International Publishing (2016)

32. Sichel, D.E.: The productivity Slowdown: is a growing un-measurable sector the culprit? Rev. Econ. Stat. **79**(3), 367–370 (1997)
33. Taylor, S., Todd, P.: Assessing IT usage: the role of prior experience. MIS Q. **19**(4), 561–570 (1995)
34. Taylor, S., Todd, P.: Understanding information technology usage: a test of competing models. Inf. Syst. Res. **6**(2), 144–176 (1995)
35. Teo, T.S., Lim, V.K., Lai, R.Y.: Intrinsic and extrinsic motivation in Internet usage. Omega **27**(1), 25–37 (1999)
36. Titah, R., Barki, H.: E-government adoption and acceptance: a literature review. Int. J. Electron. Gov. Res. (IJEGR) **2**(3), 23–57 (2006)
37. Triandis, H.C.: Interpersonal behaviour. Brooks/Cole, Monterey (1977)
38. Venkatesh, V., Davis, F.D.: A theoretical extension of the technology acceptance model: four longitudinal field studies. Manage. Sci. **46**(2), 186–204 (2000)
39. Venkatesh, V., Morris, M.G., Davis, G.B., Davis, F.D.: User acceptance of information technology: Toward a unified view. MIS Q. **27**, 425–478 (2003)
40. Venkatesh, V., Morris, M.G., Sykes, T.A., Ackerman, P.L.: Individual reactions to new technologies in the workplace: the role of gender as a psychological constructs. J. Appl. Soc. Psychol. **34**(3), 445–467 (2004)
41. Venkatesh, V., Thong, J.Y., Xu, X.: Consumer acceptance and use of information technology: extending the unified theory of acceptance and use of technology (2012)
42. World Bank: Financial systems and development. World Bank Policy and Research Series No. 15., Washington, DC (1990)
43. Yu, H.C., His, K.H., Kou, P.J.: Electronic Payment Systems: an analysis and comparison of types. Technol. Soc. **24**, 331–334 (2002)

New Infrastructure Technology and Smart Institutional Interventions: The Case of Implementing Government Cloud Computing in Oman

Khalid Alzadjali[1,2]([✉]) and Amany Elbanna[1]([✉])

[1] School of Management, Royal Holloway University of London, Egham,
Surrey TE200EX, UK
khalid.alzadjali.2013@live.rhul.ac.uk,
Amany.Elbanna@rhul.ac.uk
[2] Muscat Municipality, P.O.Box 79, PC 100 Muscat, Sultanate of Oman

Abstract. Cloud computing technology presents a case of centralized technology that requires adherence to standard and planned approach for its adoption and implementation. There is little knowledge on how institutions could influence the successful migration to the cloud considering the challenges of adopting technology infrastructure. This research questions: How do institutions influence the implementation of cloud computing and to what effect? It examines the institutional intervention practices that influence the migration of the IT services of the Ministry of Health to a national government cloud platform in Oman. The study adopts concepts from institutional theory. The findings reveal that isomorphic pressures play an important role in the successful migration to cloud services. It also shows that mimetic pressure plays a propelling role that supports finding and accepting solutions and pushes the migration forward.

Keywords: Information infrastructure · Cloud computing · Implementation
Institutional theory · Isomorphic mechanisms

1 Introduction

Cloud Computing (CC) presents one of the growing new infrastructure technology. It refers to the delivery of computing capabilities as a service to organisations to use over the Internet on a utility-like payment model (Armbrust et al. 2010; Mell et al. 2011b; Wang et al. 2016). Cloud Computing provides an alternative hosting of information technology (IT) services outside organisational boundaries and offers standard uniform services for the entire organisation. The adoption of cloud computing services is rising as organisations seek ways to acquire IT services faster, cheaper and with a shorter implementation time (Gratner 2014; Meulen 2017).

Indeed, the organisational spend on cloud computing adoption continues to soar (Wilczek 2018). Interestingly, reports show that governments interest and spend on cloud computing is similar to other industries. For example, Gartner's recent survey shows that companies spend an average of 20.4% of their IT budgets on cloud while

© IFIP International Federation for Information Processing 2019
Published by Springer Nature Switzerland AG 2019.
A. Elbanna et al. (Eds.): TDIT 2018, IFIP AICT 533, pp. 126–142, 2019.
https://doi.org/10.1007/978-3-030-04315-5_10

Local governments spend 20.6% of their IT budgets on cloud, and national governments spend 22% (Meulen 2017). With this high level of spend, it is important to understand how governments adopt and migrate to the cloud and how different institutional interventions could be devised to improve the chances of success.

Research suggests that cloud computing adoption by organisations disrupts many of our accumulated knowledge on typical systems implementation and infrastructure complexity (Bhat 2013; Choudhary et al. 2013; Wang et al. 2016). The reported successful stories of cloud adoption and migration contrast the accumulated knowledge regarding IS infrastructure implementation (Star et al. 1994); Hanseth and Moneteiro, 1997; Hanseth et al. 1996; Hanseth and Lyytinen 2006). It also goes against the knowledge that IT implementation in government is typically surrounded by complexity and failure (Avgerou 2000; Currie et al. 2007; Iannacci 2010). Research on Cloud Computing is still in its infancy. There is a need to understand the different adoption dimensions of this new technological infrastructure (Tilson et al. 2010b).

This study aims to understand the nature of institutional interventions that could influence government's agencies adoption and migration to the cloud. It aims to answer the question of: How do institutions influence the implementation of cloud computing and to what effect? To answer the research question, the study examines the migration to government cloud computing services in the context of Sultanate Oman. The specific type of cloud computing examined is Infrastructure as a Service (IaaS). The study adopts an institutional perspective considering the important role that institutional context and forces play in systems adoption and implementation (Avgerou 2000; Currie and Guah 2007). This perspective offers a macro view of the institutional action and context that has been largely absent from IS infrastructure research (Iannacci 2010). In doing so, this study contributes to IS infrastructure research as much as it contributes to cloud computing research. It provides an in-depth understanding of the institutional actions and practices involved in the interventions to encourage the adoption and migration to cloud services.

Following the introduction, the paper proceeds as follows. The second section presents a brief literature review of CC and IS infrastructure implementation in government. The third section presents the theoretical foundation of the research. The fourth section presents the research methods and describes the case study. The fifth section presents an analysis of the case study and the last section provides further discussion and presents the research's conclusion and contribution.

2 Literature Review

This section presents a brief literature review of CC, Information Systems implementation in Government, and IS Infrastructure research in government.

2.1 Cloud Computing

The National Institute of Standards and Technologies defines cloud computing as "a model for enabling convenient, on-demand network access to a shared pool of configurable computing resources (e.g., networks, servers, storage, applications, and services) that can be rapidly provisioned and released with minimal management effort or service provider interaction" (NIST 2009). There are three types of services offered through CC. These types are Software as a Service (SaaS), Platform as a Service (PaaS) and Infrastructure as a Service (IaaS) (Armbrust 2010; Creeger 2009; Durkee 2010). Software as a Service (SaaS) refers to business systems that are delivered as a service using the Internet (Armbrust 2010). Platform as a Service (PaaS) means that the users have a cloud environment in which they can develop their environment and use software that they have developed (Armbrust 2010). Infrastructure as a Service (IaaS) is the most basic model of CC services, where the client simply leases the infrastructure that is needed for the application or business continuity requirements (Armbrust 2010). Moreover, cloud computing could be categorised according to its ownership to three main types: public, private and hybrid. Certain types of cloud emerge according to the interest of particular groups, for example, community cloud or government cloud.

Studies of CC focused on the technical aspects particularly in the area of grid computing and virtualisation (Güner et al. 2014; Mahmood et al. 2014; Oliveira et al. 2014; Sabi et al. 2016). Studies that considered the organisational and social aspects are either definitional, factor-based or occupied by proofing the concept by identifying its business benefits. Previous research describes the type of services, offerings and the business benefits of the cloud (Buyya et al. 2010; Creeger 2009; Youseff et al. 2008). Studies have investigated the business values of CC and viewing it from various perspectives. For example, from the vendor's perspective, some studies identified the key players in the cloud business and future cloud strategies (Bhat 2013; Hoberg et al. 2012). Others studies describe the business values from the client's perspective, organisations as well as individuals (Hoberg et al. 2012; Leimeister et al. 2010; Marston et al. 2011). In this regard, specific areas of business have also been studied, such as healthcare (Giniat 2011; Sultan 2014) and CRM implementation (Petkovic 2010). Studies have also investigated the issues of security (Chang et al. 2016; Goode et al. 2015), regulation (Schneider et al. 2014), policies (Armbrust 2010) of cloud computing and the role of government as a policymaker and regulator (Marston et al. 2011). Other studies examined the determinant of CC adoption and produced lists of factors that affect the adoption including relative advantage, complexity, top management support, firm size, competitive pressure among others (Low et al. 2011; Oliveira et al. 2014)

Although this research is valuable in finding different factors that contribute to the success of CC, it misses in-depth views on its adoption and implementation. A recent survey of CC literature highlights the lack of case studies in the area and also the lack of research that goes beyond the adoption decision of CC to examine the implementation and migration issues (Wang et al. 2016).

2.2   Technology Infrastructure

Technology infrastructure; also identified as digital infrastructure and information infrastructure, has been defined as a group of technologies and human elements, networks, systems and process that contribute to the functioning of an information system Tilson et al. (2010b). Hanseth et al. (2010) define Information Infrastructure as: "a shared, open (and unbounded), heterogeneous and evolving socio-technical system (which we call installed base) consisting of a set of IT capabilities and their user, operations and design communities".

Technology infrastructure research has been conducted in information systems from the 1990s with the advent and ubiquitous use of the Internet (Ciborra et al. 1998; Hanseth et al. 1997; Hanseth et al. 1996). However, it continues to present a thin strand of research in IS despite the widespread adoption and diffusion of large technological infrastructure. IS field has focused, in general, on IT governance, system development, and in studying IS effects on individuals, groups, organizations, market and limited research on Information Infrastructure (II) have been introduced when compared with overall IS research (Sidorova et al. 2008). Tilson et al. (2010b)) showed that there is a dearth of IS research on technology infrastructure. They reviewed articles published in ISR and MISQ during the past 20 years reveals that only around 2% of articles have focused on infrastructural issues (Tilson et al. 2010b). Tilson et al. (2010a)) have also highlighted the existence of weak theoretical grounding and understanding of Information Infrastructure as a new form of IT.

Studies of Information Infrastructure tend to focus on how to conceptualize IT infrastructure (Monteiro et al. 2014). These studies have mainly focused on design (Pipek et al. 2009; Star et al. 1996) and standards making (Hanseth et al. 2006; Hanseth et al. 1997). In this regard, studies examined the tension between the local and global contexts in IT infrastructure design (Braa et al. 2007; Ribes et al. 2009; Ure et al. 2009). Research into the process of implementing IT infrastructure had identified many issues that should be considered when contemplating on introducing information infrastructure. For example, tension between standardisation and flexibilities (Hanseth et al. 2006), tension between top-down and button up governance (Constantinides and Barrett 2014), local and global standardization (Silsand and Ellingsen 2014; Star and Ruhleder 1996), paradox of control (Nielsen and Aanestad 2006), paradox of change (Braa et al. 2007), bootstrapping issues (Hanseth and Aanestad 2003), legitimation (Constantinides and Barrett 2014), and interpretation.

IS infrastructure research has been dominated by a micro perspective that focuses on the development of standards and diverse use of IS infrastructure Pipek et al. (2009)). However valuable and insightful, this micro-level perspective on IS infrastructure has largely overlooked the important role played by institutions in the adoption of IS infrastructure and its large-scale projects (Iannacci 2010). It has not considered the nature of institutional interventions and deliberate actions that influence IS infrastructure adoption. This is despite scholars' longstanding calls arguing for the inevitable role of institutions (King et al. 1994) and invitations for IS researchers to incorporate institutional view in their research (Baptista et al. 2010; Currie 2009; Currie et al. 2009).

IS infrastructure research has largely overlooked the new generation of technology such as cloud computing that requires the migration of IT services to a third party and the model of providing it as a service over the Internet. The adoption and migration to cloud services present a new type of infrastructure that demand uniform implementation and use and hence the top-down approach to the implementation. This new IT infrastructure model questions the relevance of many of the valuable research on standard making, bottom-up approach of implementation and tensions of control and flexibility. It invites research to examine the migration issues and the top-down approach of its implementation.

3   Theoretical Foundation

This study adopts the concepts of isomorphic mechanisms from institutional theory as a theoretical lens. Institutional theory (Meyer 1979; Tolbert and Zucker 1994; Teo et al. 2003; Scott 2008:37) provides a powerful explanation to account for the role and influence of external institutions on organisations and outcomes (Liang et al. 2007). Institution is defined as 'a social order or pattern that has attained a particular state or property' Jepperson (1991). Institutional theory argues that change in organisations are driven by an inevitable push towards what is known as homogenisation (DiMaggio et al. 1991). This homogeneity of organisations is known as isomorphism and is argued to be infused by the desire for legitimacy and yielding to institutional forces (DiMaggio and Powell 1983). Isomorphism can be identified as a process that forces one unit in a population to be similar to other units that face the same set of environmental condition (Currie 2012). There are three types of institutional isomorphic forces, coercive, mimetic, and normative.

Coercive isomorphism occurs when organization comply to the "formal and external pressures exerted upon them by other organizations upon which they are dependent, and the cultural expectations in the society within which the organization's function" (DiMaggio and Powell 1983, p. 150). Coercive pressures can be collections of rules, policies, procedures or collective agreements where the behaviour of every member of an institution is affected by the decisions of those who shape the institution's structure (Kondra et al. 2009). In this regard, government regulations, law and policies are examples of coercive pressure.

Mimetic isomorphism presents tendency of organisations to imitate other organisations perceived to be legitimate. Mimetic isomorphism occurs as a result of organisations attending to uncertainty responding to new problems, unclear goals, poorly understood technology or unclear solutions which invite them to search for a viable solution that has been already implemented or tested by others (DiMaggio et al. 1983).

Normative isomorphism occurs as a result of 'the collective struggle of members of an occupation to define the conditions and methods of their work, to control the production of future member professionals, and to establish a cognitive base and legitimisation for their occupational autonomy' (DiMaggio and Powell 1983, p. 152). This normative pressure considers particular types of behaviours that define goals and objectives as legitimate and designate appropriate ways to achieve them (Scott 2001). Normative isomorphism significantly influences social actions by imposing constraints on social behaviours. These behaviours take the form of political signposting what people are routinely expected to do (Scott 2008) (Table 1).

Institutional theory has been widely adopted in organisation studies and management literature (Kostova et al. 2008). In Information Systems, the adoption of institutional theory has been advocated (Mignerat et al. 2009). IS studies adopted it to examine government policies and national level adoption of technology (Grimshaw et al. 2006; King et al. 1994), a particular sector, industry (Chiasson et al. 2005) or a single organisation (Davidson et al. 2007; Gosain 2004). The institutional isomorphic pressures has also been used in IS research (Gosain 2004) to examine the adoption of technology such as website (Flanagin 2000), EDI (Teo et al. 2003), ERP (Benders et al. 2006; Liang et al. 2007) and for supply chain (Lai et al. 2006) and outsourcing (Ang et al. 1997), compliance to security behaviour and policies (Herath et al. 2009; Hu et al. 2007).

Table 1. Institutional isomorphic pressures

Institutional pressures	Description
Coercive	The result of both formal and informal pressure posed by one organisation on the other organisation upon which they are dependent and by cultural expectations in the society within which organisations function (DiMaggio et al. 1983)
Normative	The normal social action that considers particular types of processes or behaviours as legitimate (Scott 2001)
Mimetic	Occur when new organisation technologies are poorly understood and when goals are not clear, and their environment creates uncertainty; the organisation then tend to model themselves on other organisations (DiMaggio et al. 1983)

Previous research on IT infrastructure has paid insufficient attention to the institutional perspective in favour of examining micro-level practices and scholars argue for the importance and value of adopting an institutional lens and considering the role of institutions (Iannacci 2010). Recently, Monteiro et al. (2014)) argue that studying IT Infrastructure from institutional theory perspective "can be a major enhancement to examine what scope exists for proactive Information Infrastructure interventions, policy, and governance—and how these may vary under different Information Infrastructure forms and settings" (Monteiro et al. 2014).

4 Research Methodology

4.1 Research Setting

The case study explores the implementation of the national government cloud computing project in Oman (Oman G-Cloud). Sultanate of Oman is a country located in the Arabian Peninsula bordered by United Arab Emirates, Saudi Arabia, and Yemen. Oman is part of the Gulf Cooperation Council (GCC) which also includes the following countries; Saudi Arabia, UAE, Qatar, Bahrain, and Kuwait (GCC 2015). GCC countries are unique in their stage of development. The United Nations Development Programme in Human Development Index considered GCC countries in 2015 as "very highly ranked" in human development placed right below developed countries and well above other developing countries and Oman is ranked 52nd in this index (UNDP 2015). This unique status of GCC allows them to be studied independently. Also, they share similar cultural, economic, social and political characters which can be different from other developing countries. Moreover, the last United Nation's E-government Survey in 2014 ranked Oman 48th in the E-government development index increasing 18 ranks from the 2010 survey.

Oman G-Cloud is one of the e-government initiatives where the implementation started in 2014. The initiative is intended to provide services to the government agencies in Oman and to set up a shared infrastructure including servers, network, storages and applications to all government agencies to meet all their IT infrastructure requirements. The rationale of the project is that having G-Cloud in place, government agencies can focus on their core business, reducing the IT budget, increasing their agility and providing the public e-Services at higher efficiency (ITA 2015). The project is owned by the Information Technology Authority of Oman (ITA). ITA has proposed to all government agencies a government CC services to achieve its e-government objectives and integration. ITA decided to implement the private cloud model. The private cloud is a model where the cloud infrastructure is operated exclusively for an organization. This model can be managed by the organization or a third party, and it is can be within the organization premises or outside (Mell et al. 2011a). With this model, the ITA has decided to build G-Cloud using Open Source (OpenStack). Using Open source was a strategic decision to avoid the lock-in challenges of the off-the-shelf package along with many other typical benefits of open source. On December 19, 2013, ITA signed an agreement with Nortal; an international software development company, for the supply, design, delivery, implementation and operation of the G-Cloud for three years. During the time when the data collection was conducted for this research, there were several projects which were hosted through the G-Cloud. One of these projects is the Ministry of Health (MoH) e-portal (MoH e-portal) which is the focus of this paper.

4.2 Research Methods

This research adopts a qualitative interpretive approach which allows in-depth explo-ration of social and cultural phenomena (Myers 2010). It views people as social actors capable of creating and interpreting their own independent and inter-dependent meanings as they interact with the world around them (Orlikowski et al. 1991; Saunders et al. 2007). The use of theory in this research paradigm offers an initial framework and sensitising device that help researchers to make sense of the collected data (Gregor 2006; Miles et al. 1994; Walsham 1995). It adopts a case study approach to gain a rich understanding of the phenomenon (Myers 1997; Walsham 1995) in its natural setting (Benbasat et al. 1987; Yin 2014). This approach is well suited to the research questions that require a detailed understanding of institutional influences.

The level of analysis of this research is on the national level as the government CC project in Oman is being implemented for the whole government of the country. Different government agencies are utilizing or are in the process of utilizing the gov-ernment cloud. The research reported here is part of a wider project to examine the implementation of government cloud in Sultanate of Oman. It focuses on the national project of CC led by the Information Technology Authority of Oman (ITA) and the Ministry of Health adoption. This type of case study is considered as an embedded (*Multiple units of analysis*) single case (Yin 2014).

Multiple sources of data collection were employed. They include 30 face-to-face interviews with senior managers, managers, technical staff and vendors of Information Technology Authority of Oman (ITA) and the Ministry of Health (MoH). Interviews were conducted in the period between 29/07/2015 and 27/12/2015. All interviews were recorded and transcribed verbatim. Interviews lasted between 40 min and two hours with an average of one hour. Interviewees were chosen from management and technical levels on the basis of their involvement in G-cloud. Documents were also reviewed including government reports, vendors' reports and presentation slides, websites in addition to technical manuals and reports. Data collection continued until saturation was reached and no further information was emerging from data sources (Marshall et al. 2013) Fossey et al. (2002) Saunders et al. (2007). The first author has also utilized by invitation only chat groups on WhatsApp (the online chat application) of professionals working on the project. This group discussed IS and government issues freely and anonymously in some cases, which presented an excellent opportunity for the researcher to observe these conversations. It was also an opportunity to ask questions and get feedback from many professionals.

All transcriptions and documents have been carefully read and were subject to open coding. The data were not forced into categories but allowed emerge through creating new categories. For example, coercive and mimetic mechanisms were much prominent in the data than normative mechanisms reflecting that they had a stronger influence in the implementation.

5 Research Findings

The research findings highlight that the MoH cloud implementation project has faced different institutional pressures. These pressures have pushed the implementation forward and encouraged MoH to adopt and migrate to the cloud. The following sections present the different institutional pressures and interventions that influenced the adoption and implementation of cloud computing in the Ministry of Health (MoH).

5.1 Coercive Institutional Pressure

MoH has been subjected to different practices that exerted coercive pressure on it to adopt the G-cloud. These practices are categorized as political power, centralized policies, financial resources, rules and regulations, compliance and standardizations.

The political power of ITA made it possible for it to give priorities to projects that are consistent with the G-cloud. One of the senior managers at the ITA explains:

'we are giving priorities to the e-transformation projects, many of the e-transformation projects are under development or on planning phase, so it makes it easy for the organizations and for ITA to build their application on the G-cloud-enabled environment from the start'.

In addition, ITA is mandated by the cabinet's office to achieve e-government, which granted further power to ITA over government agencies and ministries where MoH is one.

In addition, the ITA senior executives had a good relationship with the MoH senior managers, which helped the implementation of G-Cloud. One of the IT management team in MoH states that:

> 'The decision was made by a senior manager in Ministry of Health and a senior manager in ITA to join the G-Cloud and the G-cloud team in ITA, and the member of the evaluation team in e-tender have evaluated which company who will do the implementation of e-health portal along with hosting it in the G-Cloud'.

The political power of ITA together with the established relationship with senior management of MoH has influenced the decision of MoH to join and influenced MoH staff to accept this decision.

The financial incentives that ITA offered have also played an important role in making MoH migration to the G-cloud favourable. Staff agree that the zero charge policy that ITA offered was an incentive to join the cloud. While ITA has offered MoH to the join the G-cloud amidst the latter involvement in tendering and contractual arrangement with the supplier of the e-health portal, the financial incentives ITA offered made joining the G-cloud a cheaper option that gave it the necessary incentive to change its contractual and tendering arrangement. A senior IT manager in the MoH stated:

> 'Well after we had distributed the tender of e-Health project, the G-Cloud was not in the picture at all. After that, we knew that the ITA started to build the G-Cloud. We again asked the vendors to provide us with the financial cost if we move to G-Cloud and how much will it cost us. We found out that the G-Cloud is much better financially' MOH01, 29/07/2015.

Another MoH IT manager also added that:

> 'Joining the G-Cloud was mainly to save cost on the hardware. It was the time we were finalising the tender, and then the ITA was offering this solution, and it was offered for free' MOH02, 29/07/2015.

However, financial resources were not the only leverage suited to apply pressure into joining the G-Cloud. Human resources that were provided as *Management Control* with the G-Cloud were also another important factor in influencing how the e-Health portal would be implemented in the G-Cloud. Accepting to join the G-Cloud meant that the MoH information infrastructure would be managed and controlled by a professional government agency that had the human resources capable of managing different information infrastructure areas such as network and security. One of the ITA's Project managers clarified this by saying:

> 'If I am in the G-Cloud, I am free of my responsibility... It will be the responsibility of the G-Cloud team to set the G-Cloud environment to set up for the ministry; then the vendor was given access. So for me, as a Ministry, I do not have to worry about it. The second scenario, which is hosting in the Ministry. I have to deploy a Ministry IT team, which I think does not have the capabilities to do that. So, we are freeing the MOH from HR requirements also' ITA07, 30/11/2015.

During the implementation of the e-Health project, the standards set by the ITA for all government agencies to join the G-Cloud faced challenges. These standards could be considered the *rules and regulations* to which any government agencies that wanted to join the G-Cloud would have to comply. The e-Health project was the first one for the G-Cloud to host an application from an external government agency. As such, it was a learning curve for both the ITA and MoH teams, as they faced many new and unexpected challenges. From the early implementation period, the e-Health's vendor used an agile methodology approach. This meant that some e-Health modules could be activated as soon as they were completed, with no need to wait for the whole portal to be ready. The e-Health team's *requirements* pressured the G-Cloud team to have the G-Cloud ready for the e-Health portal which has resulted in a temporary stage solution. A vendor staff member stated:

> 'To achieve our requirement; the ITA came up with the concept called the mini-cloud. So, while the ITA was doing the proper cloud project on the side, they did a mini-cloud for the MoH to cater for our requirement' MOH08, 23/08/2015.

As the implementation stages progressed, the ITA team started introducing more standards to be applied to the e-Health portal. Some of these had been clearly communicated to the MoH team through different means—such as documents—while others, such as *security standards*, were introduced later.

Moreover, the MoH was the first who implemented several security standards. The ITA's project manager for the MoH added:

> 'All the policies that were prescribed by the ITA were put there. It was first as to have everything to be as per Public Key Infrastructure (PKI), and Mobile PKI for users who wanted to get access the username and password. We were the first who implemented the integration with MOC (Ministry of Commerce) and integration with ROP (Royal Oman Police) for all the G-to-B services through the ITA integration platform. We were also the first who used the cyber sources e-payment and so many things we used to do for the first time' ITA07, 30/11/2015.

Although some of these standards, such as the PKI, were hard to implement, the MoH agreed to them because of *top-down* pressure from the ITA, and because it believed it would benefit from them in the long run.

Moreover, the MoH had to comply with the ITA's *rules and regulations* when it came to where to host its application. Another IT manager of the MoH explained:

> 'I think there are instructions from the ITA that any portal has to be hosted inside Oman, not outside the country. It has to be hosted in the G-Cloud, or it must be hosted internally. I consider it to be dangerous if it is not hosted internally inside Oman. I cannot imagine seeing my data to be managed or hosted by a cloud company outside Oman or by a private corporation. So it is fine as it is now, hosted by the ITA G-Cloud, as they have secured MPLS' MOH04, 09/08/2015.

5.2   Normative Institutional Pressure

Normative institutional force also influenced the implementation of standards for the e-Health portal in the G-Cloud. One of these stemmed from ITA building *general knowledge* base for MoH team of the team who managed and implemented the e-Health portal. One of the MoH's IT managers stated:

> 'I know the G-Cloud can provide you with high availability and can have an endless amount of space' MOH02, 29/07/2015. 'The ITA held several seminars, and they invited us. We understand it, and we encourage it' MOH05, 11/08/2015.

During the implementation, the normative pressure derived from the MoH's team resulted in contesting some standards introduced by the ITA. The MoH staff and vendor's general knowledge enabled them to contest the implementation process, request a Mini-cloud, and overcome some security standard issues in the initial stages of the implementation. Departments such as networking and security had their concerns over the G-Cloud's implementation and had requested to ease the way of verifying requests. The MoH is a large government agency with over 240 sites all over Oman, and many of its IT staff members held the privileges needed to make changes to their application. Once the e-Health portal was hosted in the G-Cloud, making local changes was no longer possible. One of the MoH's managers stated that:

> 'The ITA wanted to impose their standards on our system, especially the security standards. For example, they had many concerns, and we asked them to give us many exceptions.. almost every action we took, nearly every click returned an error from the ITA, because they had to analyse all the traffic to make sure it was not an attack, so they had to make an exception on their system to make it pass' MOH02, 29/07/2015.

A project specialist also raised his concerns for the usability of the PKI system, which is an embedded standard throughout the G-Cloud in the MoH portal, by saying:

> 'We understand this has to be a hard effort and it might affect the usability of the portal, but then we had a long discussion, me and the DG of IT, so we thought about it, and we preferred to start from the beginning and mitigate that risk as a PKI team' ITA07, 30/11/2015.

5.3   Mimetic Institutional Pressure

Mimetic practices played a major part in the implementation of the e-health. Participants were convinced that the implementation of this standard infrastructure, however, might not suit their immediate needs, cannot be escaped as they perceived it as presenting an international standard that other countries and organisations adopt. They believed that since others implemented it, then they had to implement it as well. This view has surfaced in most interviews. For example, one of the managers of the e-health portal describes the G-cloud as *"a new trend in hosting government network"*. The e-health portal management also adds:

> 'If you look at other countries experience you will find that they have one portal for the whole government and G-Cloud would help in this one portal" and the network manager adds "I believe the whole world is going to the cloud". Staff believed that "it is the latest trend and that "the whole world is going to the cloud' MOH04, 09/08/2015. They looked at other *countries*

that had implemented cloud computing and considered this to be a legitimate reason to be part of the G-Cloud. The e-Health portal management team elaborated on that by saying:
'If you look at other countries' experience, you will find that they have one portal for the whole government, and the G-Cloud would help in this one portal' MOH03, 09/08/2015.

The view that it has been successfully implemented by other countries such as Estonia has played an important role in pushing the implementation forward and overcoming disagreements and issues raised.

6 Discussion

This research questioned: How do institutions influence the implementation of cloud computing and to what effect? It examined the case of national government CC in Oman and in particular the implementation case of Ministry of Health e-Health portal. The research findings showed institutional pressures play an important role in information infrastructure solutions such as the G-Cloud. The G-Cloud is a form of information infrastructure in which resources are centralised and work in the virtual setting. Applying standardisation to the different government agencies became one of the leading challenges of implementing the G-Cloud. It is argued in this research that coercive, mimetic, and normative institutional forces play an important role in implementing the G-Cloud.

The study shows that the coercive and mimetic forces play a significant role in establishing the standards which allowed successful implementation of the G-Cloud in MoH. The normative pressures led professionals to resist some of the standards of G-Cloud. However, propelled by the mimetic pressure, these professional were fast in finding solutions and compromises. This was particularly exhibited in the finding of temporary stage solution of the mini-cloud to overcome the existence of different requirements and timetables.

The finding differs from Currie (2012) work where institutional isomorphic forces became conflicted with efforts to impose organizational change. While IT professionals in MoH negotiated the standards, which were enforced from the G-cloud team over the e-health portal, this has not resulted in resistance and implementation failures as the National Health program in Currie (2012) study. The zero-charge policy was a motive to join the G-Cloud alongside other financial incentives. The research shows that MoH was encouraged to adopt CC as a way of solving the complexities and saving cost when implementing large Information Infrastructure in a government organization. This was further enforced by the mimetic pressure of CC as a new trend that has been successfully implemented in other countries and large organisations. These findings contrast what previous research emphasised regarding the negative results of negotiation, contesting and resistance of standards implementations in infrastructure adoption (Hanseth et al. 2010; Sahay et al. 2009). Evidence of the problems and failures of centralized control in public sector infrastructure development from top-down are clear in the literature (Adler-Milstein et al. 2008; Currie et al. 2007). The case study shows that the G-cloud implementation that comes with standards from a national government can be achieved. This contrasting finding could be due to the nature of the cloud computing as a centralised technology that requires standard approach to the migration.

7   Conclusion

While technology infrastructure research has maintained a micro organisational focus and has not paid attention to the possibility of intervention, this study shows that successful CC implementation requires institutional intervention. This responds to Monteiro et al. (2014)) call for research on IT Infrastructure "to examine what scope exists for proactive Information Infrastructure interventions".

This paper makes several contributions to the IS field in general and, more specifically, to the study of information infrastructure, cloud computing, and institutional theory in IS. The paper contributes to existing theory in the area of information infrastructure by investigating the implementation of cloud computing through the lens of institutional theory. There are few previous studies of information infrastructure implementation at the macro level (Brown et al. 2011; Hanseth et al. 1998; Iannacci 2010). Adopting the institutional perspective is important in view of the role that institutional forces play in information infrastructure implementation (Avgerou 2000; Currie et al. 2007). Moreover, this paper contributes to the area of cloud computing by investigating the adoption and implementation of cloud computing in government. It describes qualitative, interpretive, and empirical research into cloud computing, an area in which there is a dearth of previous research. The study contributes to institutional theory in IS by providing a comprehensive understanding of how various institutional forces impact information infrastructure. It identifies three institutional forces that play different roles in the implementation process.

The findings of this paper and their implications also make important contributions to practice. Although government organisations and particularly health sector have previously invested in IT infrastructure projects, many of these failed to achieve their objectives or were only delivered after long delays. This study provides government decision makers with useful insights into how institutional forces can help to achieve the implementation of new forms of information infrastructure solutions, such as cloud computing.

This paper lays the ground for several future studies. It focused only on the IaaS type of cloud computing. Future research could explore other types of services, such as PaaS and SaaS, and explore government agencies' implementation issues using these services. Future research could also study the effect of the institutional forces on cloud computing implementation in developed countries. Another and possibly related area that needs study is the influence of national culture on the acceptance of information infrastructure standards.

References

Adler-Milstein, J., McAfee, A.P., Bates, D.W., Jha, A.K.: The state of regional health information organizations: current activities and financing. Health Aff. **27**(1), 60–69 (2008)

Ang, S., Cummings, L.L.: Strategic response to institutional influences on information systems outsourcing. Organ. Sci. **8**(3), 235–256 (1997)

Armbrust, M., et al.: A view of cloud computing. Commun. ACM **53**(4), 50-58 (2010)

Avgerou, C.: IT and organizational change: an institutionalist perspective. Inf. Technol. People **13**(4), 234–262 (2000)

Baptista, J., Newell, S., Currie, W.: Paradoxical effects of institutionalisation on the strategic awareness of technology in organisations. J. Strateg. Inf. Syst. **19**(3), 171–183 (2010)

Benbasat, I., Goldstein, D.K., Mead, M.: The case research strategy in studies of information systems. MIS Q. **11**(3), 369–386 (1987)

Benders, J., Batenburg, R., Van der Blonk, H.: Sticking to standards; technical and other isomorphic pressures in deploying ERP-systems. Inf. Manag. **43**(2), 194–203 (2006)

Bhat, J.M.: Adoption of cloud computing by SMEs in India: a study of the institutional factors. In: Proceedings of the Nineteenth Americas Conference on Information Systems (2013)

Braa, J., Hanseth, O., Heywood, A., Mohammed, W., Shaw, V.: Developing health information systems in developing countries: the flexible standards strategy. MIS Q. **31**(2), 381–402 (2007)

Brown, D.H., Thompson, S.: Priorities, policies and practice of e-government in a developing country context: ICT infrastructure and diffusion in Jamaica. Eur. J. Inf. Syst. **20**(3), 329–342 (2011)

Buyya, R., Broberg, J., Goscinski, A.M.: Cloud Computing: Principles and Paradigms. Wiley, New York (2010)

Chang, V., Ramachandran, M.: Towards achieving data security with the cloud computing adoption framework. IEEE Trans. Serv. Comput. **9**(1), 138–151 (2016)

Chiasson, M.W., Davidson, E.: Taking industry seriously in information systems research. MIS Q., 591–605 (2005)

Choudhary, V., Vithayathil, J.: The impact of cloud computing: should the IT department be organized as a cost center or a profit center? J. Manage. Inf. Syst. **30**(2), 67–100 (2013)

Ciborra, C.U., Hanseth, O.: From tool to Gestell: agendas for managing the information infrastructure. Inf. Technol. People **11**(4), 305–327 (1998)

Creeger, M.: Cloud computing: an overview. ACM Queue **7**(5), 626–631 (2009)

Currie, W.: Contextualising the IT artefact: towards a wider research agenda for IS using institutional theory. Inf. Technol. People **22**(1), 63–77 (2009)

Currie, W.L.: Institutional isomorphism and change: the national programme for IT–10 years on. J. Inf. Technol. **27**(3), 236–248 (2012)

Currie, W.L., Guah, M.W.: Conflicting institutional logics: a national programme for IT in the organisational field of healthcare. Journal of Information Technology **22**(3), 235–247 (2007)

Currie, W.L., Swanson, E.B.: Special issue on institutional theory in information systems research: contextualizing the IT artefact (2009)

Davidson, E.J., Chismar, W.G.: The interaction of institutionally triggered and technology-triggered social structure change: an investigation of computerized physician order entry. MIS Q. **31**(4), 739–758 (2007)

DiMaggio, P.J., Powell, W.W.: The iron cage revisited: institutional isomorphism and collective rationality in organizational fields. Am. Sociol. Rev., 147–160 (1983)

DiMaggio, P.J., Powell, W.W.: The new institutionalism in organizational analysis, Chicago University, Chicago, USA (1991)

Durkee, D.: Why cloud computing will never be free. ACM Queue, 01–10 (2010)

Flanagin, A.J.: Social pressures on organizational website adoption. Hum. Commun. Res. **26**(4), 618–646 (2000)

GCC 2015. Foundations and Objectives of GCC

Giniat, E.J.: Cloud computing: innovating the business of health care. Healthc. Financ. Manag. **65**(5), 130–131 (2011)

Goode, S., Lin, C., Tsai, J.C., Jiang, J.J.: Rethinking the role of security in client satisfaction with Software-as-a-Service (SaaS) providers. Decis. Support Syst. **70**, 73–85 (2015)

Gosain, S.: Enterprise information systems as objects and carriers of institutional forces: the new iron cage? J. Assoc. Inf. Syst. **5**(4), 6 (2004)

Gratner 2014. Predicts 2014: Cloud Computing Affects All Aspects of IT

Gregor, S.: The nature of theory in information systems. MIS Q. **30**(3), 611–642 (2006)

Grimshaw, D., Miozzo, M.: Institutional effects on the IT outsourcing market: analysing clients, suppliers and staff transfer in Germany and the UK. Organ. Stud. **27**(9), 1229–1259 (2006)

Güner, E.O., Sneiders, E.: Cloud Computing Adoption Factors In Turkish Large Scale Enterprises, PACIS, AISeL, Chendu, China, pp. 353–361 (2014)

Hanseth, O., Jacucci, E., Grisot, M., Aanestad, M.: Reflexive standardization: side effects and complexity in standard making. MIS Q. **30**, 563–581 (2006). Special Issue

Hanseth, O., Lyytinen, K.: Design theory for dynamic complexity in information infrastructures: the case of building internet. J. Inf. Technol. **25**(1), 1–19 (2010)

Hanseth, O., Monteiro, E.: Inscribing behaviour in information infrastructure standards. Account. Manage. Inf. Technol. **7**(4), 183–211 (1997)

Hanseth, O., Monteiro, E.: Changing irreversible networks. ECIS, pp. 1123–1139. http://www. idi.ntnu.no/~ericm/ecis.html1998

Hanseth, O., Monteiro, E., Hatling, M.: Developing information infrastructure: the tension between standardization and flexibility. Sci. Technol. Hum. Values **21**(4), 407–426 (1996)

Herath, T., Rao, H.R.: Encouraging information security behaviors in organizations: role of penalties, pressures and perceived effectiveness. Decis. Support Syst. **47**(2), 154–165 (2009)

Hoberg, P., Wollersheim, J., Krcmar, H.: The business perspective on cloud computing-a literature review of research on cloud computing. In: AMCIS, AISeL (2012)

Hu, Q., Hart, P., Cooke, D.: The role of external and internal influences on information systems security–a neo-institutional perspective. J. Strateg. Inf. Syst. **16**(2), 153–172 (2007)

Iannacci, F.: When is an information infrastructure? Investigating the emergence of public sector information infrastructures. Eur. J. Inf. Syst. **19**(1), 35–48 (2010)

ITA. 2015: ITA G-Cloud overview, ITA

Jepperson, R.L.: Institutions, institutional effects, and institutionalism. In: Powell, W.W., DiMaggio, P. (eds.) The New Institutionalism in Organizational Analysis, pp. 143–163. University of Chicago Press, Chicago (1991)

King, J.L., Gurbaxani, V., Kraemer, K.L., McFarlan, F.W., Raman, K., Yap, C.-S.: Institutional factors in information technology innovation. Inf. Syst. Res. **5**(2), 139–169 (1994)

Kondra, A.Z., Hurst, D.C.: Institutional processes of organizational culture. Cult. Organ. **15**(1), 39–58 (2009)

Kostova, T., Roth, K., Dacin, M.T.: Institutional theory in the study of multinational corporations: a critique and new directions. Acad. Manag. Rev. **33**(4), 994–1006 (2008)

Lai, K.-H., Wong, C.W., Cheng, T.E.: Institutional isomorphism and the adoption of information technology for supply chain management. Comput. Ind. **57**(1), 93–98 (2006)

Leimeister, S., Böhm, M., Riedl, C., Krcmar, H.: The business perspective of cloud computing: actors, roles and value networks. In: ECIS Proceedings, AISeL, pp. 1–12 (2010)

Liang, H., Saraf, N., Hu, Q., Xue, Y.: Assimilation of enterprise systems: the effect of institutional pressures and the mediating role of top management. MIS Q., 59–87 (2007)

Low, C., Chen, Y., Wu, M.: Understanding the determinants of cloud computing adoption. Ind. Manage. Data Syst. **111**(7), 1006–1023 (2011)

Mahmood, M.A., Arslan, F., Dandu, J., Udo, G.: Impact of cloud computing adoption on firm stock price–an empirical research. In: AMCIS (2014)

Marston, S., Li, Z., Bandyopadhyay, S., Zhang, J., Ghalsasi, A.: Cloud computing—the business perspective. Decis. Support Syst. **51**(1), 176–189 (2011)

Mell, P., Grance, T.: The NIST definition of cloud computing (draft). NIST special publication 800(145), 7 (2011a)

Mell, P., Grance, T.: The NIST definition of cloud computing: recommendations of the national institute of standards and technology. The National Institute of Standards and Technology - The US Department of Commerce (2011b)

Meulen, R.V.D.: Understanding cloud adoption in government. Gartner (2017). https://www.gartner.com/smarterwithgartner/understanding-cloud-adoption-in-government/

Mignerat, M., Rivard, S.: Positioning the institutional perspective in information systems research. J. Inf. Technol. **24**(4), 369–391 (2009)

Miles, M.B., Huberman, A.M.: Qualitative Data Analysis: An Expanded Sourcebook, 2nd edn. London, England: California, USA (1994)

Monteiro, E., Pollock, N., Williams, R.: Innovation in information infrastructures: introduction to the special issue. J. Assoc. Inf. Syst. **15**(4), 4 (2014)

Myers, M.: Qualitative research in information systems. Association for Information Systems. http://www.qual.auckland.ac.nz/

Myers, M.D.: Qualitative research in information systems. Manage. Inf. Syst. Q. **21**(2), 241–242 (1997)

NIST 2009. Working definition of cloud computing, in US government

Oliveira, T., Thomas, M., Espadanal, M.: Assessing the determinants of cloud computing adoption: an analysis of the manufacturing and services sectors. Inf. Manag. **51**(5), 497–510 (2014)

Orlikowski, W.J., Baroudi, J.J.: Studying information technology in organizations: Research approaches and assumptions. Inf. Syst. Res. **2**(1), 1–28 (1991)

Petkovic, I.: CRM in the cloud, pp. 365–370. IEEE, Subotica, Serbia (2010)

Pipek, V., Wulf, V.: Infrastructuring: toward an integrated perspective on the design and use of information technology. J. Assoc. Inf. Syst. **10**(5), 447–473 (2009)

Ribes, D., Finholt, T.A.: The long now of technology infrastructure: articulating tensions in development. J. Assoc. Inf. Syst. **10**(5), 375–398 (2009)

Sabi, H.M., Uzoka, F.-M.E., Langmia, K., Njeh, F.N.: Conceptualizing a model for adoption of cloud computing in education. Int. J. Inf. Manage. **36**(2), 183–191 (2016)

Sahay, S., Monteiro, E., Aanestad, M.: Configurable politics and asymmetric integration: health e-infrastructures in India. J. Assoc. Inf. Syst. **10**(5), 4 (2009)

Saunders, M.N., Saunders, M., Lewis, P., Thornhill, A.: Research methods for business students, 4/e. Pearson Education Iimited, Essex (2007)

Schneider, S., Sunyaev, A.: Determinant factors of cloud-sourcing decisions: reflecting on the IT outsourcing literature in the era of cloud computing. J. Inf. Technol. **31**(1), 1–31 (2014)

Scott, R.W.: Institutions and Organizations. Sage Publication, Thousand Oaks (2001)

Scott, W.R.: Approaching adulthood: the maturing of institutional theory. Theor. Soc. **37**(5), 427–442 (2008)

Sidorova, A., Evangelopoulos, N., Valacich, J.S., Ramakrishnan, T.: Uncovering the intellectual core of the information systems discipline. MIS Q. **31**(3), 467–482 (2008)

Star, S.L., Ruhleder, K.: Steps towards an ecology of infrastructure: complex problems in design and access for large-scale collaborative systems. In: Proceedings of the 1994 ACM Conference on Computer Supported Cooperative Work, ACM 1994, pp. 253–264 (1994)

Star, S.L., Ruhleder, K.: Steps toward an ecology of infrastructure: design and access for large information spaces. Inf. Syst. Res. **7**(1), 111–134 (1996)

Sultan, N.: Making use of cloud computing for healthcare provision: opportunities and challenges. Int. J. Inf. Manage. **34**(2), 177–184 (2014)

Teo, H.H., Wei, K.K., Benbasat, I.: Predicting intention to adopt interorganizational linkages: an institutional perspective. MIS Q. **27**(1), 19–49 (2003)

Tilson, D., Lyytinen, K., Sorensen, C.: Desperately seeking the infrastructure in IS research: conceptualization of "digital convergence" as co-evolution of social and technical infrastructures. In: 2010 43rd Hawaii International Conference on System Sciences (HICSS), IEEE 2010a, pp. 1–10 (2010a)

Tilson, D., Lyytinen, K., Sørensen, C.: Digital infrastructures: the missing IS research agenda 20th anniversary special issue of emerging challenges. Inf. Syst. Res. **21**(5), 748–759 (2010b)

UNDP 2015: Human Development Report 2015, United Nations Development Programme, New York, USA (2015)

Ure, J., et al.: The development of data infrastructures for Ehealth: a socio-technical perspective. J. Assoc. Inf. Syst. **10**(5), 3 (2009)

Walsham, G.: Interpretive case studies in IS research: nature and method. Eur. J. Inf. Syst. **4**(2), 74–81 (1995)

Wang, N., Liang, H., Jia, Y., Ge, S., Xue, Y., Wang, Z.: Cloud computing research in the IS discipline: a citation/co-citation analysis. Decis. Support Syst. **86**, 35–47 (2016)

Wilczek, M.: IT governance critical as cloud adoption soars to 96 percent in 2018. In: CIO (2018)

Yin, R.K.: Case Study Research: Design and Methods, 5th edn. Sage Publications, Washington (2014)

Youseff, L., Butrico, M., Da Silva, D.: Toward a unified ontology of cloud computing. In: Grid Computing Environments Workshop, GCE 2008, IEEE 2008, pp. 1–10 (2008)

Intelligent Monitoring and Controlling of Public Policies Using Social Media and Cloud Computing

Prabhsimran Singh[1(✉)], Yogesh K. Dwivedi[4],
Karanjeet Singh Kahlon[2], and Ravinder Singh Sawhney[3]

[1] Department of Computer Engineering & Technology,
Guru Nanak Dev University, Amritsar, India
prabh_singh32@yahoo.com
[2] Department of Computer Science, Guru Nanak Dev University,
Amritsar, India
karankahlon@gndu.ac.in
[3] Department of Electronics Technology, Guru Nanak Dev University,
Amritsar, India
sawhney.ece@gndu.ac.in
[4] School of Management, Emerging Market Research Center (EMaRC),
Swansea University, Swansea, UK
y.k.dwivedi@swansea.ac.uk

Abstract. Lack of public participation in various policy making decision has always been a major cause of concern for government all around the world while formulating as well as evaluating such policies. With availability of latest IT infrastructure and the migration of government think-tank towards realizing more efficient cloud based e-government, this problem has been partially answered, but this predicament still persists. However, the exponential rise in usage of social media platforms by general public has given the government a wider insight to overcome this long pending dilemma. This paper presents a pragmatic approach that combines the capabilities of cloud computing and social media analytics towards efficient monitoring and controlling of public policies. The proposed arrangement has provided us some encouraging results, when tested for the policy of the century i.e. GST implementation by Indian government and established that proposed system can be successfully implemented for efficient policy making and implementation.

Keywords: Cloud computing · E-Government · GST · Sentiment analysis
Social media analytics · Twitter

1 Introduction

Traditionally, the public policy making decisions have always involved only the government agencies and bureaucrats, with general public been never allowed to become a party to it [1]. This led to a sharp decline in conviction as well as reliance of public towards the government [2, 3]. The gap between the government & the public

© IFIP International Federation for Information Processing 2019
Published by Springer Nature Switzerland AG 2019.
A. Elbanna et al. (Eds.): TDIT 2018, IFIP AICT 533, pp. 143–154, 2019.
https://doi.org/10.1007/978-3-030-04315-5_11

dramatically increased and currently both are struggling to maintain harmony with their relationship [4]. E-Government is one such powerful tool that holds all the essentials to improve the relationship between the general public and the government [5] as it strongly put emphasis on maintaining transparency, enhancing public participation and upgrading the quality of service [6]. However, the required ICT (Information and Communication Technology) infrastructure, implementation and operational cost have become a major bottleneck towards the implementation of e-government. Cloud computing is one such popular as well as reliable technology that can provide solution of this delinquent issue [7]. With several inbuilt advantages such as on-demand scalability and pay-as-use have motivated many countries to adapt cloud computing based e-government [8]. However, the important point of public participation in policy making still remains a distant dream. To overcome this severe problem, governments all around world have started making use of social media to acquire appropriate feedback from the various realms of society regarding various public policies [9].

This paper proposes an innovative and smart approach which unitizes the capabilities of cloud computing and social media analytics for efficient monitoring and controlling of public policies. The main objective of this research is to increase public participation in policy making decisions. We have applied our proposed system to GST (Goods and Services Tax) implemented by Indian Government which was an attempt to unify all the taxes in the country [10, 11]. The results have been observed to be quite encouraging, showing that the proposed approach can be instrumental in efficient policy making decisions.

2   Review of Literature

The literature review is classified into two sections. The first section highlights the use of cloud computing in e-government. While the second section highlights the use of social media for policy making.

2.1   Use of Cloud Computing in E-Government

E-Government is the use of ICT and other web technologies to provide more effective, efficient and transparent service to its citizens & employees [12]. Although ICT provides lot of advantages, yet the required technical infrastructure, implementation cost and requirement of skilled staff becomes major obstacles towards e-government implantation [13]. With the emergence of cloud computing, these challenges can be addressed up to the fair degree of satisfaction for all the stake holders [7]. Cloud computing consists of large shared pool of computer resources which provide features like on-demand scalability and pay-as-use [14]. These advantages have played a decisive factor in motivating the governments of many countries to migrate from traditional costly e-government model to more cost efficient and scalable cloud based e-government model [8]. Not only this, but cloud based e-government model is also building a strong foundation for smart cities [15].

2.2 Use of Social Media for Policy Making

Nowadays, social media have become an integral part of everyday life, irrespective of the status of any individual [16]. This virtual world provides a perfect platform for people from all around the world to discuss topics of common interest such as sports, entertainment and even politics. Talking about politics, at least 33% of social media users comments, discusses or post about politics on these platforms [17]. Even government have realized the potential of social media and because of this various government agencies are extensively started using these social media to connect with general public [18]. Since social media is increasing the interaction between public and government, hence this indeed is providing a solution to problem of public participation [19]. Generally, people post something regarding government, politics or policies which might be intentional or unintentional [17] and government can utilize this content for providing better services to its citizens [19].

Both the above sections show that considerable work has been done in field of cloud computing based e-government and use of social media for policy making having their own advantages and benefits. But till date no effort has been made to combine both these services. This paper aims to unitize the capabilities of cloud computing and social media analytics for efficient monitoring and controlling of public policies.

3 Research Methodology

The primary objective of this paper is to unitize the capabilities of cloud computing and social media analytics for efficient monitoring and controlling of public policies. For this cloud based system is proposed. Figure 1 shows the architecture of the proposed system. The proposed system has three main components: (a) Data acquisition component (b) monitoring component and (c) Controlling component.

(a) **Data acquisition component:** Data acquisition component is responsible for data collection from various social media platforms like Facebook, Twitter, Instagram etc. This data collection task is performed on continuous basis in a time specific manner. After collection this data from various sources this user content is stored in cloud database so that the computations can be effectively made.

(b) **Monitoring Component:** This component is responsible for performing the monitoring activities. These monitoring activities are performed using various social media analytics techniques, where different operations are performed on the user content for extracting important decision making information [20]. Table 1 shows the various social media analytics techniques. The results of these different analytics are again stored in cloud database.

(c) **Controlling Component:** This component is responsible for providing alerts and sends calculated information to the government so that appropriate control measures can be taken based upon these results generated by the monitoring component.

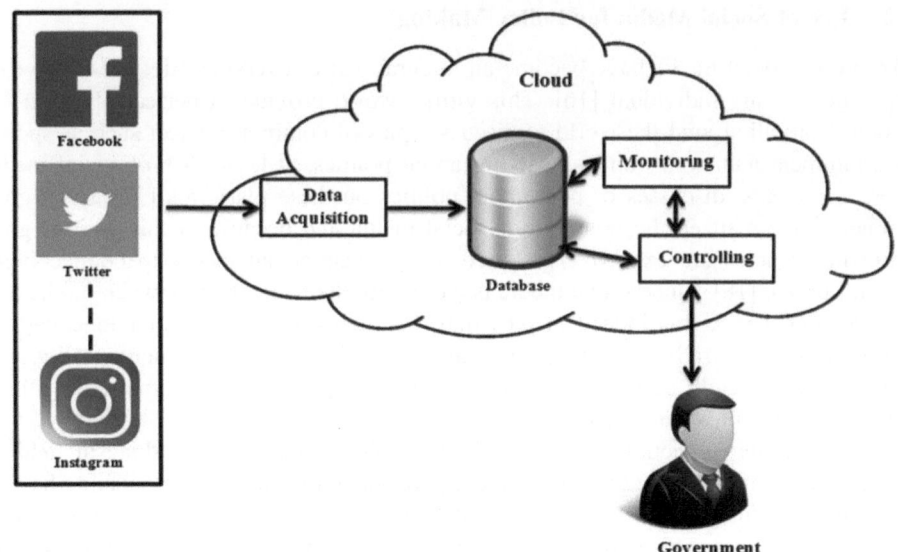

Fig. 1. Architecture of proposed model

Table 1. Various social media analytics techniques

Descriptive analysis	Content analysis	Network analysis	Space-time analysis
Tweet statistics [21]	Sentiment analysis [25]	Friend follower networks [28]	Time series analysis [31]
#Hashtags analysis [22]	Topic modeling [25]	Network layout [29]	Geo-location analysis [32]
@Mentions analysis [23]	Lexical diversity [27]	Cluster analysis [30]	
Word cloud [24]		Centrality analysis [22]	

4   Implementation and Results

For implementation on cloud we have used Amazon EC2 [33]. For computation we have used RStudio server. Data for experimentation has been collected from Twitter. Data was fetched based upon specific #hashtag (#GST). In total 41,823 tweets were collected from June 23, 2017 to July 16, 2017. For better interpretation of the results tweet collection period was broken into 3-phases (Pre-GST, In-GST and Post-GST). The detail of tweet collection is shown in Fig. 2.

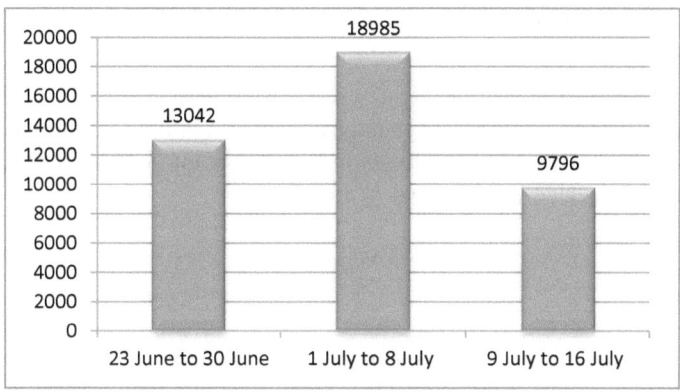

Fig. 2. Tweet collection details

4.1   Tweet Statistics and Data Preprocessing

In total 41,823 tweets were collected from 35,400 different users from India. In total 2,873 users were detected who tweeted more than one tweet, accounting a total of 6,423 tweets. The details of tweet statistics are given in Table 2.

Table 2. Tweet statistics

	Phase-1	Phase-2	Phase-3
Total tweets	13042	18985	9796
Max tweets in a day	3026	4622	1552
Min tweets in a day	526	440	671
Total unique senders	11711	15187	8502
Average tweets per sender	1.11	1.25	1.15
Average tweet per phase	1630.25	2373.12	1224.5

Data preprocessing is an important task, which aims to prepare data for various data mining task [34]. Since Twitter data contained lot of noise and unwanted stuff, task of data preprocessing was performed [35]. First and foremost thing we did in preprocessing was to remove multiple tweets from same user. A total of 6,423 such multiple tweets from same users were removed using same technique as used by Singh et al. [36]. These tweets were removed in order to maintain normality; otherwise this would have led to biased results. On remaining 35,400 tweets various preprocessing tasks were performed such as conversion to lower case, removing punctuations, removing special characters and finally removing web links.

4.2   Sentiment Analysis

Sentiment analysis is often regarded as most effective tool to map public response towards an entity [19]. Sentiment analysis is defined as a text analytic technique which deals with extraction of sentiment from given piece of text. Sentiment analysis consists of two sub-operations: (a) E-Motion Analysis [37] and (b) Polarity Analysis [38].

(a) **Polarity Analysis:** Polarity analysis deals with polarity identification i.e. positive or negative. The result of polarity analysis is shown in Fig. 3, while the treemap of positive and negative words is shown in Fig. 4. For interpretation of the results we use a threshold value (μ) as given in Eq. 1.

$$\mu = \frac{\sum NegativeTweets}{\sum Tweets} \tag{1}$$

For our calculations we have taken μ = 50% (Threshold Value) i.e. whenever μ > 50%, this will be alarming signal for the government that citizens are not happy with the policy and some appropriate measure are required to overcome this unrest.

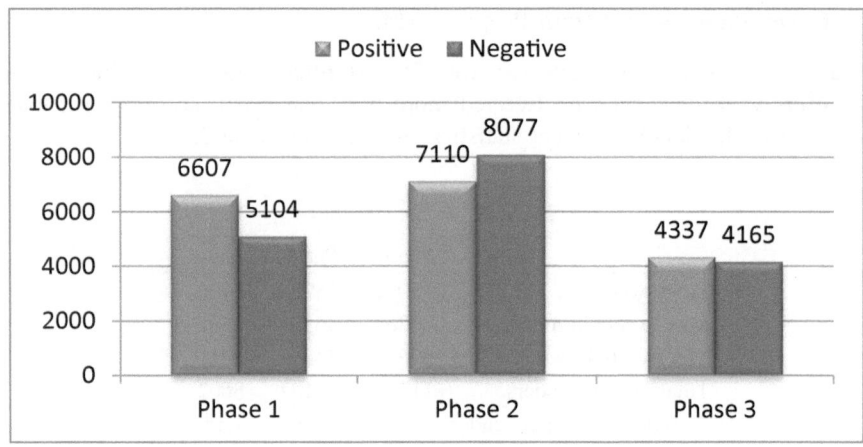

Fig. 3. Results of polarity analysis

Inference: During phase-1 (Pre-GST Period) the overall threshold value μ < 50%, this shows that citizens were in favor of GST as it ended multi tax system and hence giving a hope that prices of fast moving consumer goods (FMCG) [39] will go down. However, as soon as GST was actually implemented on July 1, 2017 (In-GST Period) the threshold value μ > 50%, showing unrest among citizens. This unrest was due to various problems encountered by public as soon as GST was implemented. From consumer's perspective negative sentiment was due to the fact that traders were charging GST over and above maximum retail price (MRP). Similarly, the traders were unhappy because of the confusion about GST rates on various goods plus they needed to update their current inventory system which led to increased expenses. Since we discussed that as soon as threshold value μ > 50%, it is an alarming signal for the government to take appropriate steps. So acting upon this, government soon issued warnings to traders that they cannot charge over MRP for any good [40, 41].In addition

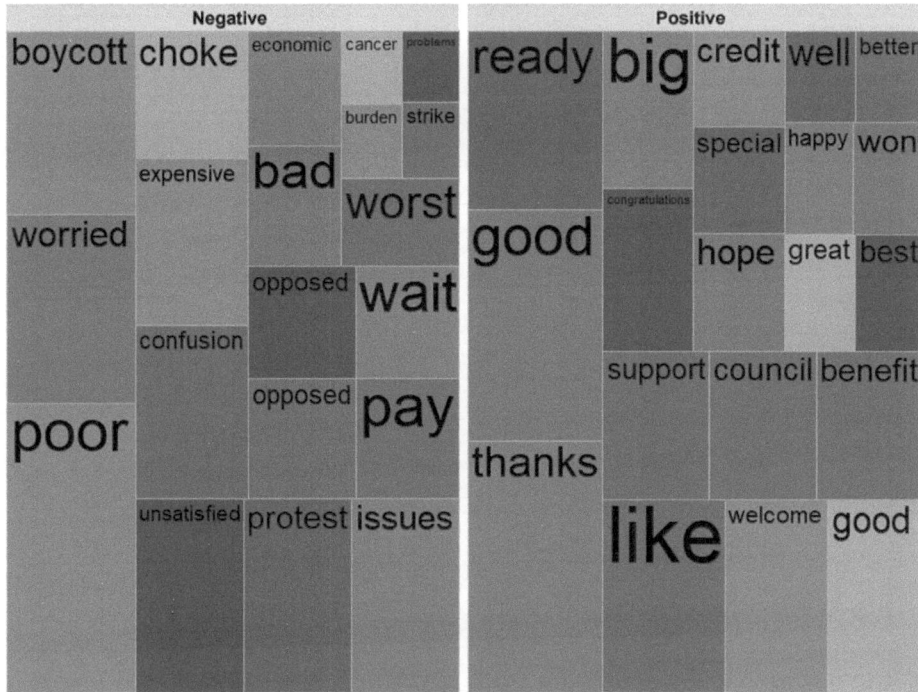

Fig. 4. Treemap of positive and negative words

to this government also introduced various courses to train traders and make them familiar with GST filling and other related processes [42]. As a result of these measures by the government the threshold value again became $\mu < 50\%$ during phase-3 (Post-GST). This provided a concrete proof that the actions taken by government after phase-2 did helped to win the trust of citizens.

(b) **E-Motion Analysis:** It is a sentiment analysis operation, in which given data is classified according to emotion lexicon comprising of words having association with eight emotions (Trust, Surprise, Sadness, Joy, Fear, Disgust, Anticipation and Anger). The result of e-motion analysis is shown in Fig. 5.

Inference: Phase-1 (Pre-GST Period) dominates emotions such as trust, anticipation and joy indicating support of people for GST. These results totally got reversed during phase-2 (In-GST Period) as emotions like fear & sadness dominated, showing unrest among citizens and alerting government to take appropriate steps. As soon as appropriate steps have been taken by government results of phase-3(Post-GST Period) started to fall in line with phase-1 (Pre-GST Period), indicating support for GST once again (Fig. 5).

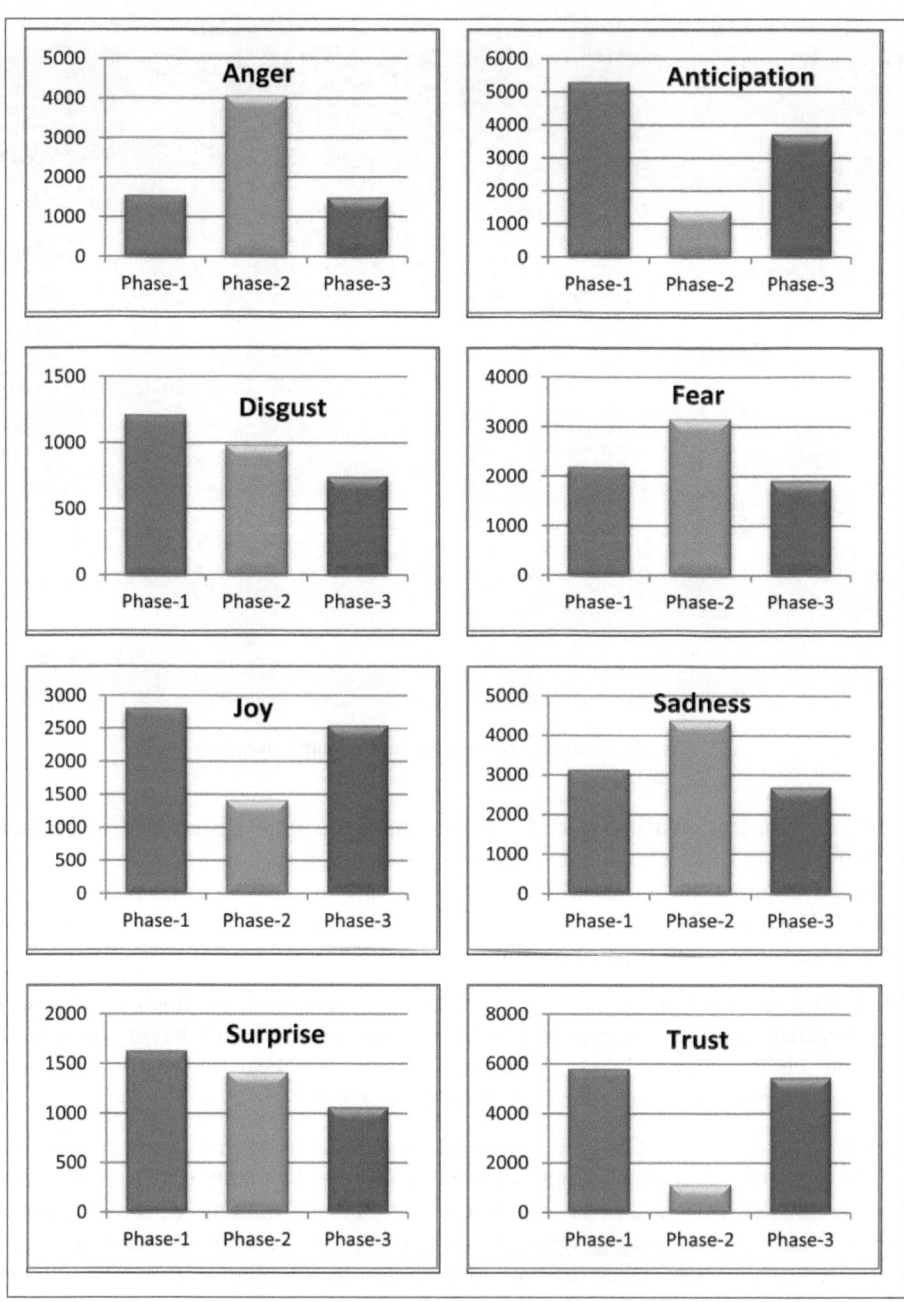

Fig. 5. Results of E-motion analysis

4.3 Geo-location Analysis

Location based analysis is a very crucial tool for gathering information, while mapping public response towards an entity [43]. Although all tweets do not contain location from where they were tweeted, yet we can't ignore them as they provide important information about the actual location, hence helping policy makers to target the audience while finding solution to their problem. Since in the previous section we detected that during phase-2 (In-GST Period) the overall sentiment was on negative side, it is essential to see which states and cities are worst affected so that appropriate solution can be found. Figure 6 shows location wise analysis of two markets of Mumbai city from where negative tweets were sent.

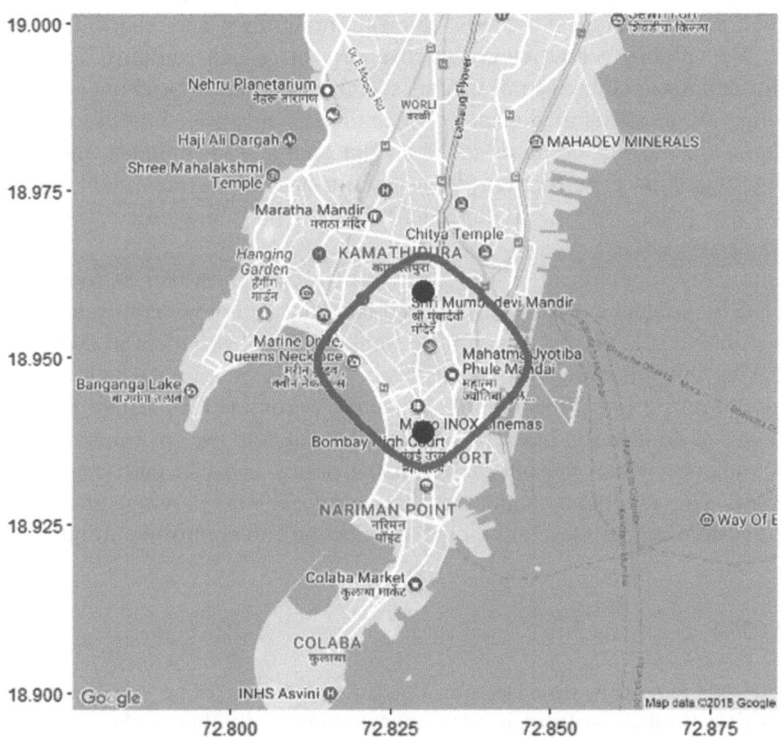

Fig. 6. Results of location based analysis

Inference: This location based analysis is extremely important; as it gives us the targeted audience which is unhappy with the policy and hence government can take appropriate steps keeping in mind the demands or problems of this targeted group. Since these two points indicates markets of Mumbai city, hence it shows that traders of these markets are not happy and government needs to take appropriate steps accordingly.

5   Conclusions

Technology is changing at tremendous pace and all the national governments are continuously adopting newer technologies for providing enhanced services to its citizens. Multiple efforts are being done to bridge down the gap between the policy makers and the general public, for whom these policies are designed & implemented. Cloud computing and social media platforms have emerged as two significantly powerful tools for the central governments all around the world to communicate and provide quality services to its citizens. However, all the studies done till date to the best of our knowledge have utilized the advantages of these tools independently and no fruitful effort has ever been made towards combined implementation of these powerful tools. We started our research work to combine the selective capabilities of cloud computing and social media analytics towards efficient monitoring and controlling of public policies. We propose a new cloud based approach, which captures the response of public through data gathered from various social media platforms about any policy. For monitoring various social media analytics techniques are applied on this captured data. Based upon the results of these social media analytics techniques, the appropriate controlling operation is performed. We tested our proposed system with data collected towards "the policy of the Independent India" GST implementation by Indian government.

The initial results indicate a strong support for GST, however as soon as the GST became reality, traders and consumers faced hardship and the overall sentiment dipped towards negative side giving an alarming signal to the government to take appropriate actions. After this government took various controlling measures which again resulted in increase of positive sentiment among citizens. A prominent contribution made in this research was to do location based analysis which can help the government to select the targeted audience which are affected with the policy and can take control measures accordingly. These implementation results were quite encouraging, insisting that the proposed system can be used for efficient monitoring and controlling of public policies.

References

1. Severo, M., Feredj, A., Romele, A.: Soft data and public policy: can social media offer alternatives to official statistics in urban policymaking? Policy Internet **8**(3), 354–372 (2016)
2. Hibbing, J.R., Theiss-Morse, E.: Introduction: studying the American people's attitudes toward government. In: What is it About Government that Americans Dislike, pp. 1–7 (2001)
3. Rosenstone, S.J., Hansen, J.: Mobilization, Participation, and Democracy in America. Macmillan Publishing Company, New York (1993)
4. Janssen, M., Rana, N.P., Slade, E.L., Dwivedi, Y.K.: Trustworthiness of digital government services: deriving a comprehensive theory through interpretive structural modelling. Public Manage. Rev. **20**(5), 647–671 (2018)
5. Shareef, M.A., Dwivedi, Y.K., Kumar, V., Kumar, U.: Reformation of public service to meet citizens' needs as customers: evaluating SMS as an alternative service delivery channel. Comput. Hum. Behav. **61**, 255–270 (2016)

6. Dwivedi, Y.K., Akhter Shareef, M., Simintiras, A.C., Lal, B., Weerakkody, V.: A generalised adoption model for services: a cross-country comparison of mobile health (m-health). Gov. Inf. Q. **33**(1), 174–187 (2016)

7. Mohammed, F., Ibrahim, O., Ithnin, N.: Factors influencing cloud computing adoption for e-government implementation in developing countries: instrument development. J. Syst. Inf. Technol. **18**(3), 297–327 (2016)

8. Sharma, R., Sharma, A., Singh, R.R.: E-governance & cloud computing: technology oriented government policies. Int. J. Res. IT Manag. **2**(2), 584–593 (2012)

9. Grubmüller, V., Götsch, K., Krieger, B.: Social media analytics for future oriented policy making. Eur. J. Futures Res. **1**(1), 20 (2013)

10. Ahmad, E., S. Poddar: GST reforms and intergovernmental considerations in India (2009)

11. Joseph, N., Grover, P., Rao, P.K., Ilavarasan, P.V.: Deep analyzing public conversations: insights from Twitter analytics for policy makers. In: Kar, A.K., et al. (eds.) I3E 2017. LNCS, vol. 10595, pp. 239–250. Springer, Cham (2017). https://doi.org/10.1007/978-3-319-68557-1_22

12. Jeong, K.-H.: E-Government, the Road to Innovation; Principles and Experiences in Korea. Gil-Job-E Media (2006)

13. Rana, N.P., Dwivedi, Y.K., Williams, M.D.: Analysing challenges, barriers and CSF of egov adoption. Transf. Gov. People Process Policy **7**(2), 177–198 (2013)

14. Sadiku, M.N., Musa, S.M., Momoh, O.D.: Cloud computing: opportunities and challenges. IEEE Potentials **33**(1), 34–36 (2014)

15. Clohessy, T., Acton, T., Morgan, L.: Smart City as a Service (SCaaS): a future roadmap for e-government smart city cloud computing initiatives. In: Proceedings of the 2014 IEEE/ACM 7th International Conference on Utility and Cloud Computing, pp. 836–841. IEEE Computer Society (2014)

16. Kapoor, K.K., Tamilmani, K., Rana, N.P., Patil, P., Dwivedi, Y.K., Nerur, S.: Advances in social media research: past, present and future. Inf. Syst. Front. **20**(3), 531–558 (2018)

17. Hossain, M.A., Dwivedi, Y.K., Chan, C., Standing, C., Olanrewaju, A.S.: Sharing political content in online social media: A planned and unplanned behaviour approach. Inf. Syst. Front. **20**(3), 485–501 (2018)

18. Bertot, J.C., Jaeger, P.T., Hansen, D.: The impact of polices on government social media usage: issues, challenges, and recommendations. Gov. Inf. Q. **29**(1), 30–40 (2012)

19. Ceron, A., Fedra, N.: The "Social Side" of public policy: monitoring online public opinion and its mobilization during the policy cycle. Policy Internet **8**(2), 131–147 (2016)

20. Stieglitz, S., Dang-Xuan, L.: Social media and political communication: a social media analytics framework. Soc. Netw. Anal. Min. **3**(4), 1277–1291 (2013)

21. Purohit, H., Hampton, A., Shalin, V.L., Sheth, A.P., Flach, J., Bhatt, S.: What kind of# conversation is Twitter? Mining# psycholinguistic cues for emergency coordination. Comput. Hum. Behav. **29**(6), 2438–2447 (2013)

22. Chae, B.K.: Insights from hashtag# supplychain and Twitter analytics: considering Twitter and Twitter data for supply chain practice and research. Int. J. Prod. Econ. **165**, 247–259 (2015)

23. Shuai, X., Pepe, A., Bollen, J.: How the scientific community reacts to newly submitted preprints: article downloads, Twitter mentions, and citations. PLoS ONE **7**(11), e47523 (2012)

24. McNaught, C., Lam, P.: Using Wordle as a supplementary research tool. Qual. Rep. **15**(3), 630 (2010)

25. Liu, B.: Sentiment analysis and opinion mining. Synthesis lectures on human language technologies **5**(1), 1–167 (2012)

26. Llewellyn, C., Grover, C., Alex, B., Oberlander, J., Tobin, R.: Extracting a topic specific dataset from a Twitter archive. In: Kapidakis, S., Mazurek, C., Werla, M. (eds.) TPDL 2015. LNCS, vol. 9316, pp. 364–367. Springer, Cham (2015). https://doi.org/10.1007/978-3-319-24592-8_36

27. Cohen, R., Ruths, D.: Classifying political orientation on Twitter: it's not easy! In: ICWSM (2013)

28. Hale, S.A.: Global connectivity and multilinguals in the Twitter network. In: Proceedings of the SIGCHI Conference on Human Factors in Computing Systems, pp. 833–842. ACM (2014)

29. HerdaĞdelen, A., Zuo, W., Gard-Murray, A., Bar-Yam, Y.: An exploration of social identity: the geography and politics of news-sharing communities in twitter. Complexity 19(2), 10–20 (2013)

30. Walther, M., Kaisser, M.: Geo-spatial event detection in the Twitter stream. In: Serdyukov, P., et al. (eds.) ECIR 2013. LNCS, vol. 7814, pp. 356–367. Springer, Heidelberg (2013). https://doi.org/10.1007/978-3-642-36973-5_30

31. Mathioudakis, M., Koudas, N.: Twittermonitor: trend detection over the twitter stream. In: Proceedings of the 2010 ACM SIGMOD International Conference on Management of Data, pp. 1155–1158. ACM (2010)

32. Singh, P., Sawhney, R.S., Kahlon, K.S.: Sentiment analysis of demonetization of 500 & 1000 rupee banknotes by Indian government. ICT Express (2017). http://dx.doi.org/10.1016/j.icte.2017.03.001

33. AWS - Amazon EC2. https://aws.amazon.com/ec2/

34. Van den Broeck, J., Cunningham, S.A., Eeckels, R., Herbst, K.: Data cleaning: detecting, diagnosing, and editing data abnormalities. PLoS Med. 2(10), 267 (2005)

35. Haddi, E., Liu, X., Shi, Y.: The role of text pre-processing in sentiment analysis. Procedia Comput. Sci. 17, 26–32 (2013)

36. Singh, P., Sawhney, R.S., Kahlon, K.S.: Forecasting the 2016 US presidential elections using sentiment analysis. In: Kar, A.K., et al. (eds.) I3E 2017. LNCS, vol. 10595, pp. 412–423. Springer, Cham (2017). https://doi.org/10.1007/978-3-319-68557-1_36

37. Mohammad, S.M., Turney, P.D.: Emotions evoked by common words and phrases: using mechanical turk to create an emotion lexicon. In: Proceedings of the NAACL HLT 2010 Workshop on Computational Approaches to Analysis and Generation of Emotion in Text, pp. 26–34. Association for Computational Linguistics (2010)

38. Ou, G., et al.: Exploiting community emotion for microblog event detection. In: Proceedings of the 2014 Conference on Empirical Methods in Natural Language Processing (EMNLP), pp. 1159–1168 (2014)

39. Economic Times. https://economictimes.indiatimes.com/news/economy/policy/gst-rate-guide-know-all-the-things-that-will-get-cheaper-after-midnight/articleshow/59386840.cms

40. Business Standard News (a). http://www.business-standard.com/article/economy-policy/mrp-retailers-can-sell-gst-inventory-with-new-price-stickers-till-30-sep-117070500333_1.html

41. Business Standard News (b). http://www.business-standard.com/article/economy-policy/gst-rollout-govt-to-penalise-manufacturers-for-not-reprinting-revised-mrp-117070400756_1.html

42. NDTV News. https://www.ndtv.com/education/100-hour-certificate-course-in-gst-launched-1719199

43. Amirkhanyan, A., Meinel, C.: Density and intensity-based spatiotemporal clustering with fixed distance and time radius. In: Kar, A.K., et al. (eds.) I3E 2017. LNCS, vol. 10595, pp. 313–324. Springer, Cham (2017). https://doi.org/10.1007/978-3-319-68557-1_28

E-Government Project Design in Developing Countries

Diana Frost[(✉)] and Banita Lal

Nottingham Business School, Nottingham Trent University, Nottingham, UK
{diana.frost,banita.lal}@ntu.ac.uk

Abstract. The purpose of this paper is to develop a conceptual framework as an integrated approach to Electronic Government project design and evaluation in developing countries. Innovations In information and Communication Technologies (ICT) have resulted in a radical transformation of business models, opening new channels of communication and offering cost-effective methods for business processes. Research in e-Government underscores the adoption of these technologies by Governments for the provision of more effective and efficient service delivery. Yet failures of e-Government projects in developing countries are well-documented and a review of the literature suggests that there remains, to an extent, disconnects between e-Government research and actual policy formulation processes or professional practices in developing countries. This paper asserts that for these smaller economies, e-Government project design and evaluation necessitates a more integrated approach which draws from research in the e-Government and ICT4D domains; thus, encompassing a multiple stakeholder perspective including Government (as primary stakeholder) and citizens/businesses. Such an approach that encapsulates the unique characteristics of smaller economies offers a practical analytical tool in their design of e-Government projects, highlighting core components for consideration and identifying where misalignment between stakeholder needs and systems objectives may occur.

Keywords: Electronic government · e-Government · ICT for development
ICT4D · Information and communication technologies · Information systems

1 Introduction

The convergence of Information and Communication Technologies (ICTs) is widely considered as a key underlying attribute of advanced economic systems [1–4] and thus promoted as a solution for overcoming some of the issues pertaining to under-development in emerging economies [5]. Accordingly, these countries attempt to leverage new and rapidly diffusing digital media to become effective participants in an increasingly competitive global environment [6]. However, in a continually evolving knowledge-based era, technology diffusion has been uneven, with many economies facing often insurmountable challenges to the effective exploitation of opportunities that digital technologies offer as a new source of wealth. Such obstacles may include an inadequate physical infrastructure, insufficient technological capabilities, and ineffective

© IFIP International Federation for Information Processing 2019
Published by Springer Nature Switzerland AG 2019.
A. Elbanna et al. (Eds.): TDIT 2018, IFIP AICT 533, pp. 155–176, 2019.
https://doi.org/10.1007/978-3-030-04315-5_12

ICT policies [1, 7, 8]. These challenges are particularly endemic in the implementation and sustainability of e-Government initiatives in developing countries [9–12] and contribute to high rates of failure post-project implementation [12]. Thus, development and long-term sustainability of e-Government projects in developing countries are often derailed not only by institutional procedures, policies and capabilities, but also by extraneous factors such as the technological capabilities of end-users and misalignment between project outcomes and stakeholder expectations [11–15].

Research suggests that, as in the design of any information system, successful outcomes of an e-Government project are dependent on continued assessment of the project during its entire life-cycle, from the initial analysis (pre-design) phase to any post-implementation activities [16–18]. Any such process should necessarily be rooted in "a stakeholder-centric process which makes explicit both the desired and the current outcomes, and which supports the managed alignment of these throughout the project life-cycle" [16, p. 177]. However, the validity of extending traditional models of information systems evaluation to the design processes of e-Government projects is brought into question [18] as assumptions concerning decision-making processes, project management structures, financial sources, design processes and policy/regulatory procedures may not be appropriate in the context of e-Government. Furthermore, the design of any e-Government project may necessitate coordination among a broad range of stakeholders including disparate Government ministries and departments, organisations, businesses and citizens. By the same token, evaluation of misalignment in stakeholder expectations [19, 20] should consider wide variations in stakeholder interests depending on the type of implemented e-Government service, be it a Government-to-Government (G2G), Government-to-Citizen (G2C), Government-to-Businesses (G2B) or Government-to-Employee (G2E) service. Indeed, the evaluation of multiple stakeholder interests in e-Government initiatives invariably represents a significant challenge as "the goals of national government, local government, public service providers (both profit-driven and not-for-profit), voluntary and community organisations and individual members of the public are rarely congruent" [16, p. 175].

Thus, in exploring existing evaluative processes for e-Government projects, a cursory examination of past literature on e-Government research in developing countries highlighted a focus on the supply-side issues in project implementation such as inadequate policy/regulatory frameworks, ineffective political support and an inefficient physical infrastructure [11, 13, 21–24]. In the same vein, the ICT for Development (ICT4D) literature on technology adoption and diffusion in developing countries highlights the demand-side challenges such as lack of broadband connectivity, lack of access to adequate technologies and low levels of ICT literacy [25–27]. However, the literature yielded limited evidence of an integrated or consistent approach to evaluative design processes for e-Government projects that combines a multi-dimensional approach in the examination of supply-side issues, with added focus on multiple stakeholder perspectives in project design [16, 28]. Such an integrated approach which overlaps defined boundaries in the ICT4D and e-Government literature is more feasible to an exploration of the perceived barriers to the success of e-Government projects [29, 30], though past research continues to identify "noticeable gaps between academic theories, commercially available methodologies and actual evaluation practice" [18, p. 252]. Thus, in contemplating the demand-side and supply-side factors for consideration in e-Government, two key questions emerge:

- *What are the core underlying components for success in the design of an e-Government project?* and
- *How are the inter-relationships among these identified components described?*

Motivated by the desire to understand these inter-dependencies and their impact on the success of e-Government projects in developing countries, this led to the formulation of a conceptual framework that defines an integrated approach to design and evaluation of e-Government projects. The framework advances a multifaceted exploration of key issues from the perspective of multiple stakeholders including Government as primary stakeholder, and other intended beneficiaries such as citizens, organisations, and businesses. The framework subsequently evolved from an examination of demand-side and supply-side issues in e-Government project implementation from the ICT4D and e-Government literature. It is therefore anticipated that the results of this research will contribute to the continued e-Government dialogue on project design and assessment processes and further the debate in the ICT4D literature on technology adoption and diffusion within developing countries.

The remainder of the paper is organised as follows. Section 2 provides a brief description of the approach to the methodology in the development of the conceptual framework. Section 3 discusses the process in the development of the conceptual framework which includes a review of the literature on information systems evaluation processes, with a narrowed focus on approaches to e-Government assessment. The section also examines literature in the e-Government and ICT4D domains with the overall aim to highlight any overlapping areas of research and identify the key components in the design and evaluation of e-Government projects in developing countries. Section 4 describes the conceptual framework, based on a review of the literature from Sect. 3. The framework highlights the interdependencies and interrelationships among the identified components and proposed approaches to analysing misalignment among these components. Section 5 discusses proposed future research for testing, and enhancing, the conceptual framework and discusses any perceived research limitations.

2   Research Methodology

A structured-case approach is adopted in the development of the conceptual framework. Such an approach based on:

"…the use of a formal process model comprising three structural components: a conceptual framework, a pre-defined research cycle and a literature-based scrutiny of the research findings, to assist the researcher in theory building. The conceptual framework represents the researcher's aims, understanding and theoretical foundations and the research cycle guides data collection, analysis and interpretation; together, these structures make the research process visible, record its dynamics and document the process by which theory is induced from field data. The literature based scrutiny compares and contrasts the outcomes of the research process with a broad range of literature to support or challenge the theory built" [31, p. 236].

An interpretivist research paradigm rooted in qualitative data analyses offers a "process of describing, interpreting and seeking understanding and possibilities in order to reach a shared meaning" [32, p. S3]. The initial conceptual framework is therefore developed from a critical review of the literature which assists in identifying the key research themes. The structured-case approach then follows an iterative non-sequential cycle in the refinement of the model through: (a) planning of the research to be undertaken; (b) data collection; (c) data analysis; and (d) reflection on the outcomes [31].

The literature is therefore first examined to gain an understanding of the primary components in e-Government design. These components are used in the development of the conceptual framework. Future research findings of e-Government projects in developing countries, and a continued critical review of the literature, will contribute to successive iterations and refinement of the framework. "Therefore, the conceptual framework is a series of evolving models that are reviewed and refined over the life of the research project." [31, p. 235].

3   Components in E-Government Design and Evaluation

The literature highlights the critical importance of the effective measurement and evaluation processes to determine the added value of implemented information systems [16, 17]. Evaluation in this context is defined as "the process of analyzing the functioning and/or usage of a system so that decisions can be made concerning the effectiveness of the system in satisfying its design objectives [33, pp. 17–18]. Such evaluation "happens in many ways (e.g. formally and informally), uses diverse criteria (e.g. financial, technical, social), follows rigorous methodologies or 'gut feelings' [18, p. 1]. Central to effective evaluation processes is an early identification of any potential misalignment between stakeholder needs and the applied information technology which may ultimately lead to *correspondence failure,* defined in the information systems literature as the lack of correspondence between objectives and evaluation [34]. One potential result of such misalignment "is that IS evaluation practice tends to become separated from business needs and plans on the one hand, and from organizational realities that can influence IS implementation and subsequent effectiveness on the other" [33, p. 6]. Thus, in the information systems (IS) literature, different approaches to evaluation are proposed: Beynon-Davies [34] discusses the adoption of evaluation techniques at different stages of the life-cycle – *Strategic evaluation* that occurs pre-design with the objective of determining the feasibility of the proposed system; *Formative evaluation* which involves a continuous assessment of the system against its objectives during the development phase; *Summative evaluation* during post-implementation to determine cost/benefits of the system; and *Post-mortem evaluation* conducted if a system is abandoned prior to implementation. However, such traditional information system evaluation models typically focus on business performance and financial measures of success post-project implementation, with the host organisation serving as the primary, or invariably, the sole stakeholder in project development.

More recent models encompass stakeholder perspectives in evaluation, using techniques such as measurement of user satisfaction with the information system. These models, however, may not be appropriate within the e-Government realm where:

> "there might be several decision makers or stakeholders involved, with different opinions and possibly conflicting objectives and definitions of the problematic nature of the situation; there may be difficulties in quantification of many important factors; transparency and accessibility of the model will be very important, thus often ruling out mathematical models; the [operation research] person's role will often be one of facilitator with a group of participants; and uncertainties will not simply be reduced to probabilities". [35, p. 368]

Thus, in proposing models for evaluation of e-Government projects, a soft systems approach has been suggested, where the focus is on organisational and social aspects that are typically not accommodated within traditional approaches to IS evaluation [36]. Other more recent e-Government evaluation models suggest a multi-dimensional approach to eliciting information about system usage which may be generated from user feedback or technical measures of system performance [37, 38]. Thus, e-Government evaluation is broadly categorised into two groups: "The first group focuses on measuring e-government success in terms of the "readiness" of a country's infrastructure, technological capacity, and resources....The second group of e-government evaluation studies focuses on evaluating the project in terms of how successful information technology has been on the ground' [39, p. 329]. However, as highlighted in the e-Government literature, "there is still widespread and continuing disagreement as to the factors and metrics to include in any formal ICT evaluation approach" [36, p. 160] and, therefore, little consensus in the literature on precisely what those primary components in e-Government evaluation should be. This may in part be due to the differences in stakeholder interests and levels of capabilities required that is defined by the type of implemented e-Government project. Moreover, with recent advances in information and communication technologies, the application of ICT in developing countries tends to a discussion of how the technologies can more effectively contribute to socio-economic development specifically in the achievement of outlined sustainable development goals [41] in sectors such as education and healthcare. This adds a layer of complexity in the evaluation of e-Government projects where, traditionally, the majority of e-Government projects had "clearly identifiable socioeconomic costs and benefits, for example, gains in time or money to pay government bills, or to comply with taxes and other dues, or to obtain a registration certificate." [39, p. 330], projects such as health information systems are more human development focused [39]. In addressing these challenges to e-Government evaluation, some researchers suggest a capabilities approach [39] to assess how the project meets development criteria where evaluation indicators include the ability of a community to "access information, process and evaluate information technology, and use it in the community members' own lives" [39, p. 330]. This cursory review of the e-Government and ICT4D literature suggests that any approach to evaluation should not only focus on the interrelationships among core components in project design but also encompass multiple stakeholder perspectives. Thus, in reflecting upon the different e-Government evaluation approaches proposed in the literature two key questions emerge:

- *What are the core underlying components for success in the design of an e-Government project?* and
- *How are the inter-relationships among these identified components described?*

The answer to these two questions are explored through a review of the e-Government and ICT4D literature, and thus contribute to the development of the conceptual framework. This paper asserts by exploring these inter-relationships through the conceptual framework at every stage of the life cycle, potential misalignments between the core components can be identified. In exploring the literature to identify the underlying components that are viewed as key to e-Government success, several key themes emerged. The following sections discuss the six identified themes emerging from e-Government research (and tangentially the information systems literature) and the ICT4D literature on core components underlying e-Government project design and implementation. Table 1 summarises the key themes and sources from the literature.

Table 1. Key themes from e-Government literature

Key theme	Source
Information infrastructure: information sharing; information networks	[42–47]
Policy and regulatory frameworks: ICT policy, education policy, telecommunications policy	[1, 39, 46, 48]
Technological capabilities: Staffing and skills; IT literacy	[34, 42, 49–52]
Physical capital: ICT infrastructure; technologies	[34, 42, 45, 48, 53, 54]
Human capital: skills, individual capabilities	[43, 54, 55]
Social capital: social networks, relationships, community networks	[47, 53, 56–59]

3.1   Information Infrastructure

The important role of information and knowledge in determining the pace of technological advancement is highlighted throughout the e-Government literature [43]. These information networks facilitate capacity development among developing countries and also assist economies in their awareness of, and adaptation to, changes in the global environment; thus, playing a positive role in socio-economic development [44]. These networks underlie the information infrastructure, defined as "a set of interlocking institutions that together guide or constrain the behaviour of consumers, suppliers, public officials and citizens" [60, p. 19] and that which encompasses "the technologies, organizations and capabilities that facilitate production and use of ICTs" [61, p. 13]. Hence, the concept of an *information infrastructure* by definition, moves focus away from the underlying telecommunications infrastructure and information systems to also include the role of individuals in facilitating effective information and knowledge exchange networks. Moreover, the information infrastructure is viewed as a key contributor to socio-economic development and to improving governance in developing countries through a number of mechanisms including: greater access to government services; facilitating participation in governance processes; rapid dissemination of news to the population; enhancing transparency and accountability of government and minimising barriers to participation in economic markets [44].

Of note in the development literature is the concept of *regional resource aggregation* defined as a form of interdependent relations between states that share common experiences and interests for the purpose of working together to achieve commonly set goals [51, 58]. An in-depth discussion of the topic is not presented at this stage of our research; however, it is worth noting emphasis on the importance of shared values or characteristics for developing effective information exchange networks, what [62] appropriately calls the 'preconditions of success' or 'factors that enhance the chances of success', and that these factors range from the economic [63] and cultural [64] to the political [62].

3.2   Policy and Regulatory Frameworks

The creation of an effective telecommunications policy and regulatory framework within developing countries is viewed as particularly crucial for promoting competition in markets that have traditionally been dominated by monopoly providers. "As legal frameworks and laws provide a range of civil and criminal penalties and enforcement procedures, they are particularly essential to advance the e-government development agenda of a country" [46 p. 1935]. As such, the policy and regulatory framework contributes to a reduction in the perceived risk of investment in regions such as Africa that have long been described as regions of high investment risk [65]. However, the telecommunications sector presents a particular challenge as it is a "moving target…it not only moves constantly ahead but it also shifts direction about every half century" [66, p. 19]. Thus, in responding to the dynamic ICT sector, an effective policy framework should focus not only on areas such as telecommunications policies and regulation, but also on improving technological capabilities through education, incentives for ICT usage, and other policies concerning access such as security and privacy policies [1]. Moreover, the underlying policy and regulatory framework, viewed as a key component in the success of an implemented e-Government project, should at a minimum: facilitate information-sharing across Government agencies [47], promote competition in the sector [67, 68], provide access to tools and education to enhance ICT literacy [69], improve access [70, 71] and support ICT integration in sector-specific areas such as healthcare [72, 73].

3.3   Technological Capabilities

Woods [74] asserts that the "Information Revolution is more than the technology itself…integrated digital technologies (informatics) introduces a single tool with which to address a broad range of human and institutional development functions…it calls for allocation of resources to realize the potential of the technology and concepts" (p. 11). Accordingly, within the e-Government and ICT4D literature, a country's level of "technological capability" is another component used to evaluate the ability of the country to promote and sustain technological advancement [57]. The concept of technological capability therefore encompasses a broad range of definitions such as that which determines a country's overall capacity to innovate using modern technologies or the capacity of the country to exploit the advantages of ICT and internet-based opportunities [75, 76]. The ICT4D literature typically considers technological capability under broad headings such as "capacity development", "capacity building" or "capacity enhancement" thus emphasising the ability of actors such as individuals, groups, organizations, institutions and countries to perform specified functions, solve problems and set and achieve objectives, by acquiring the requisite skills and developing the capability to use those skills [77, 78]. Therefore, assessments of technological capabilities encompass the technological absorptive capacities of end-users, such that "individuals need to be aware of the e-Government solutions and/or applications available and be able to adopt and use them" [84, p. 23]. Nonetheless, many developing countries exhibit low levels of requisite technological capabilities and a perceived slow pace of technological innovation which may be attributed to many domestic factors including the cultural value systems, neglect of formal education, apathy towards research and development, slow socio-economic development, inadequate policies, lack of resources, improper allocation of resources, poor economic performance, lack of political will and a general disregard for innovation [51, 52]. Therefore, for the technological benefits of e-Government projects to be realised, the literature emphasises the need for developing countries to build capacities for exploiting potential technological advantages by increasing their level of *technological capabilities*, viewed as a scarce resource in many developing countries [61, 76].

3.4   Physical Capital

Central to the development of a knowledge-based economy are the underlying technologies that are crucial "not only for the rapid dissemination of information and knowledge but also for the creation of a Web of relationships that transcend national borders and bureaucratic barriers" [45, p. 4]. We use the term physical capital in this context to encompass the information and communication technologies that are viewed as essential to the development of e-Government [54]. However in the context of e-Government in developing countries the choice of adopted technologies is critical as these technologies should provide the most effective solution taking financial considerations (cost of the technology), environmental considerations (for example the terrain) or other infrastructural considerations (for example access to electricity). The ICT4D literature therefore emphasises that the selection of *appropriate* technologies is apt in developing countries that may face access challenges to the fixed physical infrastructure and that more appropriate technologies such as wireless and mobile technologies serve as viable alternatives for expanding the fixed line network [25, 79].

3.5   Human Capital

Human capital, that encompasses the skills and knowledge possessed by an individual, plays a critical role in capacity development through its "availability as a collective resource and through specific, individual contributions" [55, p. 19]. Inferentially, this suggests an increased need for higher levels of human capital as an economy becomes more knowledge-intensive [74]. "Just as physical capital is created by changes in materials to form tools that facilitate production, human capital is created by changes in persons that bring about skills and capabilities that make them able to act in new ways" [80, p. S100]. The human capital factor, or specifically the accumulation of knowledge and skills of each individual which can be acquired through formal education, on-the-job learning and training [58, 81, 82], is highlighted in the ICT4D literature and viewed as a key contributor to collective technological progress within a society [43]. Moreover, human capital is viewed as one of the important determinants of e-Government development [54, 83] as "e-government services, to the extent that they use mainly text-based communication, assume a high level of literacy." [83, p. 637] and further asserts that though the physical infrastructure facilitates the supply of e-Government, it is the level of human capital that determines its demand [83].

3.6 Social Capital

More recent information systems literature places greater emphasis on a socio-technical approach to systems design and development that encompasses not only the technical factors, but also the human and social factors that may impact system design [54]. It is this social capital that is more apparent in developing countries [56], as it encapsulates traditional forms of knowledge transfer and is defined as "the ability of individuals within a group to form relationships of trust, cooperation and common purpose." [58, p. 103]. Though authors remain divided about the exact perception of social capital or social cohesion within a society, few dispute its integral role in building capacity [53]. Authors such as Fukuda-Parr and Hill [77], Rodrigo [75] and Fountain [85] assert that this social capital is the foundational element for capacity development within a country and argue that small economies in particular are at a distinct advantage in establishing strong informal social networks, whether based on religion, cultural values, political affiliation, or economic status. Lundvall [57] further emphasises that small economies are at a comparative advantage since they are better able to develop closeness in social relationships. This argument is corroborated by Fukuda Parr and Hill [77] who state that "non-industrial societies have few formal institutions but they do have highly developed skills and complex webs of social and cultural relationships" (p. 9) that they can tap into.

It would be remiss not to mention that a key theme underlying the ICT4D literature is a lack of consensus on exact measures of social capital (alternatively called social cohesion). Woolcock [86] explicates three types of social capital - (1) 'bonding' social capital which refers to the relations between family members and close friends; (2) 'bridging' social capital which refers to the relationships forged between more distant acquaintances and colleagues such as in the diaspora; and (3) 'linking' social capital which emphasizes vertical linkages with external formal institutions – and attempts to highlight the necessity of each type in the development of human capital, and knowledge creation and transfer [80]. Yet, no single measure of social capital exists. Unlike other forms of capital that use financial measures, social capital is defined by the type and extent of relationships among individuals. Coleman [80] further emphasises the challenges in applying social capital measures - "If physical capital is wholly tangible, being embodied in observable material form, and human capital is less tangible, being embodied in the skills and knowledge acquired by an individual, social capital is less tangible yet, for it exists in the relations among persons" (p. S100). Thus, in a review of the development literature, authors including Grootaert [56], Field [59], Fukuyama [87], Knack and Keefer [88], Narayan and Pritchett [89], Putnam [90] suggest that *social capital* can be measured by factors such as levels of trust in government and in communities, membership of organizations or different social groups, types of networks, network density and the characteristics of groups to which people belong.

3.7 Summary

In answer to the question - *What are the core underlying components for success in the design of an e-Government project?* – a preliminary literature review highlighted that six primary themes dominate the literature on exploring the success factors for e-government in developing countries. The identified themes are: (a) Information Infrastructure; (b) Policy and Regulatory frameworks; (c) Technological capabilities; (d) Physical capital, (e) Human capital and (f) Social capital. We therefore view these as the six components in e-Government design. In the development literature, a combination of the latter three factors - human, social, and physical capital – are viewed as significant contributors to a country's level of economic growth [56]. These forms of capital contribute to the overall investment in e-Government project development, and are as critical to its success as the level of financial capital. Therefore in answering the second question - *How are the inter-relationships among these identified components described?* – an understanding of the roles of human, social, and physical capital in contributing or supporting the development of the other components (that is Information Infrastructure, Policy and Regulatory Framework, and Technological capabilities) is sought. The following section discusses these inter-dependencies that emerged from an exploration of the ICT4D and e-Government literature.

4 Interdependencies Among Components

A clear distinction is made in the ICT4D and e-Government literature on the crucial role of social and human aspects in the development of information networks, policy and regulatory frameworks, and technological capabilities [53, 54, 75, 77, 85]. Furthermore, the literature emphasises the underlying role of information and communication technologies (physical capital) in the development of these components [45, 91, 92]. The Information Infrastructure, Policy and Regulatory Framework, and Technological Capabilities are therefore viewed as the core components in e-Government; that is, the overall *enablers,* as their presence creates an enabling environment for e-Government project development. To summarise the discussion from the previous section:

- **Information infrastructure** – characterizes the underlying information systems and the impact of institutions, social networks, and policies on its development;
- **Policy and Regulatory Frameworks** – encompasses an understanding of the policies (including ICT, education, and other policies), legal framework, international standards and the policy implementation process, and
- **Technological capabilities** – describes the capacity of the society to exploit the advantages of information and communication technologies and/or Internet-based opportunities.

In a similar vein human capital, physical capital, and social capital are regarded as *facilitators*, or the building blocks for each component:

- **Physical capital** – in the context of e-Government, physical capital refers to the underlying telecommunication networks or information and communication technologies for access;
- **Human capital** – this describes the capacities of an individual such as the level of education, and
- **Social capital** – this refers to the capacities developed through interactions within a community or society.

However, what is evident from the literature is the uneven contribution of the different forms of capital – for example, the initial review of the literature asserts the crucial roles of social capital and human capital in the development of technological capabilities, and physical capital is viewed on the periphery; that is, it facilitates or enhances the roles of the other forms of capital. In the development of technological capabilities for e-Government, it is the physical capital (information and communication technologies) that make it easier to develop capacities through information and knowledge exchange. We discuss these dependencies in more detail in the following subsections, highlighting the main components in e-Government project design and distinguish between the forms of capital that are the building blocks to each component.

4.1   Technological Capabilities: Social Capital and Human Capital

There is a shift in focus in the literature, moving human capital from the periphery to the centre of economic growth theory; thus, increasing attention on the methods by which individuals in a society can accumulate knowledge and develop the requisite skills to sustain growth [8]. One of the primary contributors to capacity development is the presence of social networks as these networks facilitate the relationships that make it easier for people to collaborate [57, 58]. Likewise, the important role of *social capital,* the degree to which individuals in a community have cooperated for collective problem solving, is also asserted by Fukuda-Parr [77]: "capacity development is a larger concept [than human resource development].… it refers not merely to the acquisition of skills, but also to the capability to use them… this in turn is not only about employment structures, but also about social capital." (p. 10). Thus, the pivotal role of social relations in acquiring information, building capacities and improving the quality of education in a society is underscored throughout the development literature [56, 80]. Moreover, social capital is viewed as a direct contributor to the creation of human capital [80], where social relations may promote interest in, and access to, information. Hence, the level of technological capabilities is not only dependent on the abilities of human capital to exploit the advantages of ICT, but also on relevant information networks for capacity building. Social capital contributes to the development of technological capabilities by facilitating the creation of effective networks for information and knowledge exchange.

Thus, requisite levels of technological capabilities are crucially dependent on the skills embodied by the individual, that is, the human capital and by social capital, the collective capabilities of a society or community. Past research suggests that development of these capacities can be enhanced by the presence of information and communication technologies (physical capital) making it easier for individuals and societies to collaborate for information and knowledge exchange. We therefore propose that:

The level of technological capabilities in a society is dependent on the human capital that may be acquired through the creation of relevant social networks.

Figure 1 offers a visual representation of the inter-dependencies between the three factors, highlighting the underlying roles of human capital and social capital in the development of technological capabilities.

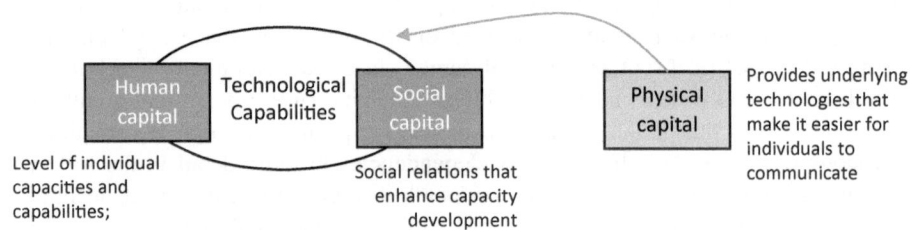

Fig. 1. Interdependencies – Technological capabilities (adapted from [96])

4.2   Information Infrastructure: Physical Capital, Social Capital

The rapid innovations in information and communication technologies has underpinned the expansion of the knowledge economy, providing more convenient and ready access to information. Expansion and long-term sustainability of the information infrastructure is therefore dependent on the underlying *physical infrastructure* [91, 92], that is, the technologies utilized in the creation of the underlying information and communication networks [61].

> "The development of the NII [National Information Infrastructure] in practice has encompassed technologies as diverse as POTS (Plain old telephone service), digital broadcasting, the Internet and other multimedia, in both the private and public sectors" [44, p. 54].

However, the information infrastructure is not defined solely by the technologies; the importance of social networks among individuals for facilitating knowledge exchange cannot be underestimated [59, 81, 93]. An examination of these networks in the context of e-Government therefore seeks to understand the role of community (and other support networks) in facilitating and enhancing information and knowledge exchange among individuals. As Bowles and Gintis [94] assert, that "communities can sometimes do what governments and markets fail to do because their members, but not outsiders, have crucial information about other members' behaviours, capacities, and needs" (p. F423).

The underlying assumption is the pivotal role of community relationships in enhancing information and knowledge networks and thus, by extension, the role that such relationships play in supporting e-Government activities. Thus, we propose that:

The underlying physical infrastructure and the level of social capital influences the creation and sustainability of effective information networks to support e-Government.

Figure 2 offers a visual representation of the inter-dependencies highlighting the underlying roles of human capital and social capital in the information infrastructure and the supporting role of human capital.

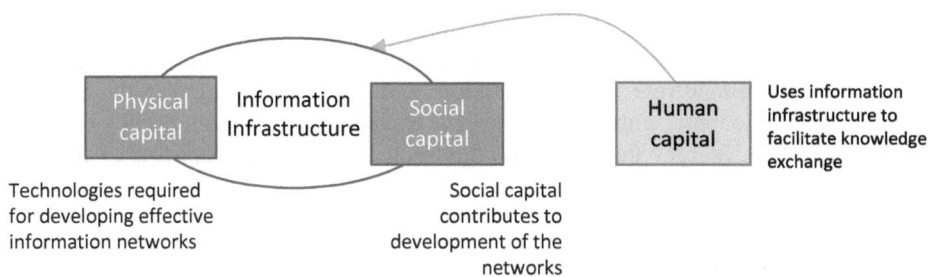

Fig. 2. Interdependencies – Information Infrastructure (adapted from [96])

4.3   Policy/Regulatory Framework: Human Capital, and Physical Capital

The importance of an effective policy and regulatory framework is well-documented [1, 46]; however, the benefits of such a framework can be severely undermined if regulators lack the training, resources, or motivation to implement it [95]. Furthermore, developing countries may be slow in perceiving or reacting to events within the international system because of their lack of resources, especially of individuals who have the capabilities to navigate complex regulatory processes [95]. Thus, human capital plays a critical role in ensuring that effective policy and regulatory frameworks to support e-Government are developed. What is evident is that the design of any policies is determined and shaped by the type of adopted technologies. Such policies may be general information and communications policies that facilitate access to and use of the information, or sector-specific such as policies in healthcare and education that may offer safeguards for security and privacy of data. Thus, we propose that:

The adoption of ICT is facilitated by the policy and regulatory framework, and the types of implemented policies are influenced by the available level of human capital for policy design and implementation (Fig. 3).

4.4   Summary

This section reviewed the literature to gain an understanding of the interdependencies and interrelationships among the core components in e-Government. The literature highlighted the primary components of technological capabilities, information infrastructure, and policy/regulatory frameworks. Development of each of the components are dependent on a combination of forms of capital, identified as: human capital,

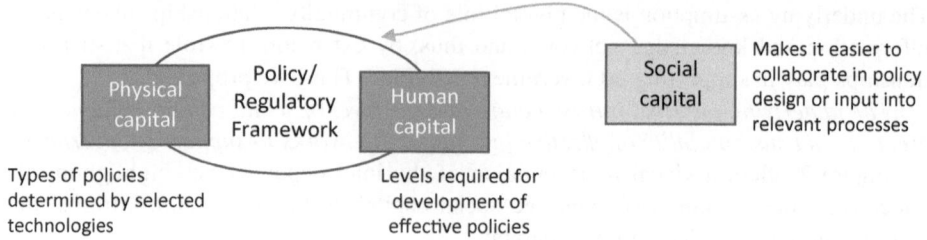

Fig. 3. Interdependencies – Policy/Regulatory Frameworks (adapted from [96])

social capital and physical capital. A review of the e-Government and ICT4D literature emphasised the crucial role of a combination of two forms of capital to the development of the components, with the third form of capital serving in a supporting role. The following section merges the results of this section in the development of the conceptual model.

5   Conceptual Framework

The review of the e-Government and ICT4D literature identified the core components that are influential in e-Government project design and highlighted the interdependencies among the factors that support the development of these core components. These relationships are shown in the developed conceptual framework that highlights the interdependencies and interrelationships among these components. Conceptually, the framework aims to draw focus upon those interrelationships among core defining components that are influential in project design and, thus, helps to identify where misalignment may occur that can ultimately lead to project failure. The conceptual framework, visualised in Fig. 4, highlights the dynamic, multi-dimensional nature of research into e-Government project design and benefits from theoretical foundations in the ICT for Development and e-Government literature. To understand these interdependencies within a wider context, the authors intend to analyse this framework using data from an existing e-Government project in order to obtain conclusions leading to the development of the conceptual framework. Thus, initial research will focus on an in-depth case study that will lead to drawing relevant conclusions that can further refine the conceptual model and extend the research to an examination of the framework within the context of a developing country.

The conceptual framework underscores the multi-dimensional approach to e-Government design and evaluation, highlighting the core components – namely: technological capabilities, information infrastructure and policy frameworks – and the combination of supporting factors that are required for their development. Thus, technological capabilities lie at the intersection of human capital and social capital as, without the development of either, sustainability of adequate levels of technological capabilities is unlikely. Conversely, the framework helps to identify those components that are most influenced by changes in the underlying factors of physical capital, social capital and human capital. Therefore, any approach to e-Government requires a

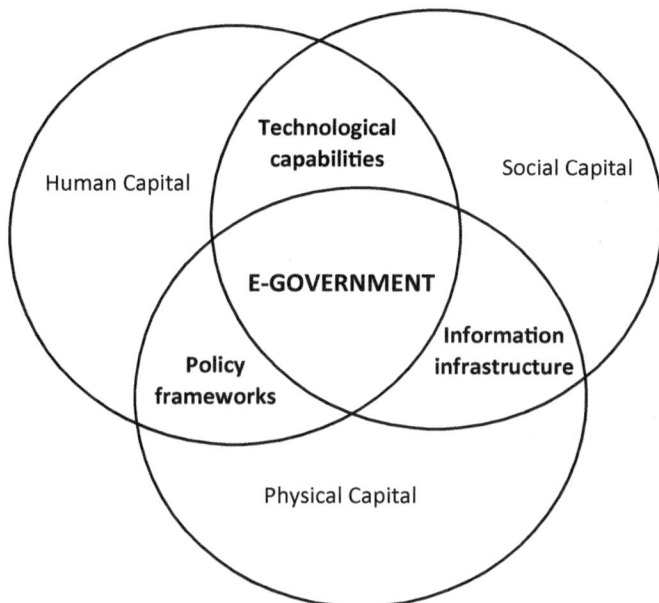

Fig. 4. Conceptual Framework for e-Government design (adapted from [96])

systemic approach in examination of these factors and address any imbalances in requisite levels for e-Government success as the framework brings focus to those areas where misalignment may occur; for example, where levels of human capital do not sufficiently satisfy the technological capabilities required for the e-Government project or, conversely, where the project does not adequately help to achieve desired goals in increasing human capital. Moreover, any such analysis of these components should proceed in parallel as the components exhibit close inter-dependent relationships.

Therefore, in examining each component, several questions need to be addressed; thus, the following paragraphs briefly discuss some questions that may arise when examining its role in e-Government. By no means exhaustive, the questions highlight the interdependencies in the relationships between the respective components:

1. Information infrastructure:

   What is the existing underlying physical infrastructure?
   What information networks have been created to support information/knowledge exchange?
   Has social capital played a role in the development of these networks?
   What is the role of these networks in developing technological capabilities?

2. Policy/Regulatory framework

   What policies have been developed to support the implemented project? (and tangentially, *how have the implemented policies facilitated, or hindered, the sustainability of the project?*)

What are the capacities for policy design?
Who are the key policy decision-makers?
What is the policy design process?
Who are the primary stakeholders and what are their roles in the process?
How does the process affect or impact on the adoption of technologies?

3. Technological capabilities

What is the existing level of technological capabilities (including access to requisite technologies)?
What is the existing level of social capital?
How are capacities and stakeholder expectations determined prior to project design?
What initiatives have been promoted to support the development of capabilities?
What are the initial stakeholder requirements?
Do stakeholder expectations align to project outcomes?

The initial research will examine the design and implementation of a single e-Government project within a developed economy. Though there are inherent differences in institutional structures, culture, policy and regulatory frameworks, socio-economic characteristics and technology capabilities, examination of the central components within the context of a developed economy provides a constructive platform for further refinement of the conceptual framework. However this research will then be extended to developing countries, to focus on the inherent characteristics these countries leverage to take advantage of the opportunities offered by the introduced technologies.

6   Implications, Limitations and Future Research Directions

This paper developed a conceptual framework to examine the interdependencies among factors in the design and development of e-Government projects by exploring the e-Government and ICT4D literature. The complexities of this multidimensional approach to e-Government are apparent but, as this paper asserts, adopting such an approach helps in identifying any misalignment between stakeholder needs and the implemented technology. As Baxter and Sommerville [40] assert "the failure of large complex systems to meet their deadline, costs, and stakeholder expectations are not, by and large, failures of technology. Rather, these projects fail because they do not recognise the social and organisational complexity of the environment in which the systems are deployed" [p. 10]. Thus, complexities and questions in the design and evaluation of e-Government using this framework are evident. For example, complexities arise in deciding approaches to stakeholder identification. Qualitative techniques such as interviews (including focus group discussions) may be required to effectively collect data from stakeholder groups; however, once those stakeholder groups have been identified, how will users be selected to participate? Or, in examining the processes for policy design and implementation where multiple disparate Government ministries and departments are involved and/or require a protracted ratification through a central ministry, how can capacities for policy development be effectively determined? Further, as the literature showed, social capital poses a significant challenge as there is little consensus on structured approaches to its measurement. Moreover "if the dominant definition of social capital is in terms of networks and norms, the question of how to strengthen these is an open one" [97, p. 24]

In adopting the structured-case method approach, continued research in the area will include the collection, analysis and interpretation of data from research conducted on e-Government projects in developing countries to help further refine and redefine the framework. Application of the framework using qualitative and quantitative data gathered from the case studies will require an examination of each of the components and include further exploration of the literature for in-depth analyses of the existing theoretical models and approaches to measures for each of the components. As the framework is intended to examine these issues through the entire systems life cycle, and further to post-implementation activities, continued and future research will examine longitudinal studies of e-Government projects. To further refine the model, future research will be conducted using projects across multiple sectors and encompassing multiple stakeholder groups.

However, the application of the framework is not without its limitations. The framework omits extraneous factors that though discussed in the e-Government literature as influential in success or failure, are not only difficult to define or measure but also difficult to encapsulate within the formal framework. These factors include the pervasiveness of political corruption [24] or end-user trust and confidence in Government agencies [26]. In refining the framework, these extraneous factors may need to be included in future successive iterations. Grimsley et al. [16], for example, emphasise that levels of social capital help to build end-user trust in e-Government and contrariwise. The conceptual framework, however, is a broad starting point to a discussion and exploration of these issues and we posit helps bring added focus to e-Government design and evaluation processes.

References

1. Jorgenson, D., Vu, K.: The ICT revolution, world economic growth, and policy issues. Telecommun. Policy **40**(5), 383–397 (2016)
2. Vu, K.: ICT as a source of economic growth in the information age: empirical evidence from the 1996–2005 period. Telecommun. Policy **35**(4), 357–372 (2011)
3. Lee, S., Gholami, R., Tong, T.: Time series analysis in the assessment of ICT impact at the aggregate level – lessons and implications for the new economy. Inf. Manage. **42**(7), 1009–1022 (2005)
4. OECD: ICT and Economic Growth: Evidence from OECD countries, industries and firms (2003). http://www.oecd-ilibrary.org/science-and-technology/ict-and-economic-growth_9789264101296-en. Accessed 3 Mar 2018
5. World Bank: ICT for Greater Development Impact: World Bank Group Strategy for Information and Communication Technology, 2012–2015. World Bank, Washington, DC (2012). https://openknowledge.worldbank.org/handle/10986/27411. Accessed 3 Mar 2018
6. Erumban, A.A., Das, D.K.: Information and communication technology and economic growth in India. Telecommun. Policy **40**(5), 412–431 (2016)

7. Vicente, M., Gil-de-Bernabé, F.: Assessing the broadband gap: from the penetration divide to the quality divide. Technol. Forecast. Soc. Change **77**(5), 816–822 (2010)
8. Morrison, A., Pietrobelli, C., Rabellotti, R.: Global value chains and technological capabilities: a framework to study learning and innovation in developing countries. Oxford Dev. Stud. **36**(1), 39–58 (2008)
9. Das, A., Singh, H., Joseph, D.: A longitudinal study of e-government maturity. Inf. Manage. **54**(4), 415–426 (2017)
10. Ifinedo, P.: Factors influencing e-government maturity in transition economies and developing countries: a longitudinal perspective. Database Adv. Inf. Syst. **42**(4), 98–116 (2011)
11. Gil-García, J., Pardo, T.: E-government success factors: mapping practical tools to theoretical foundations. Gov. Inf. Q. **22**, 187–216 (2005)
12. Heeks, R.: Information systems and developing countries: failure, success and local improvisations. Inf. Soc. **18**(2), 101–112 (2002)
13. Gunawong, P., Gao, P.: Understanding e-government failure in the developing country context: a process-oriented study. Inf. Technol. Dev. **23**(1), 153–178 (2017)
14. Kanda, S., Tuamsuk, K., Chaopanon, W.: Factors affecting the development of e-government using a citizen-centric approach. J. Sci. Technol. Policy Manage. **6**(3), 206–222 (2015)
15. Shareef, M., Dwivedi, Y.: Electronic government adoption paradigms. In: Shareef, M., Kumar, V., Kumar, U., Dwivedi, Y. (eds.) Stakeholder Adoption of E-Government Services: Driving and Resisting Factors. IGI Global, Hershey (2011)
16. Grimsley, M., Meehan, A., Tan, A.: Evaluative design of e-government projects: a community development perspective. Transform. Gov. People Process Policy **1**(2), 174–193 (2007)
17. Klecun, E., Cornford, T.: A critical approach to evaluation. Eur. J. Inf. Syst. **14**, 229–243 (2005)
18. Serafeimidis, V., Smithson, S.: Information systems evaluation as an organizational institution – experience from a case study. Inf. Syst. J. **13**(2), 251–274 (2003)
19. Krishnan, S., Teo, T., Lymm, J.: Determinants of electronic participation and electronic government maturity: insights from cross-country data. Int. J. Inf. Manage. **37**, 297–312 (2017)
20. Heeks, R.: Most eGovernment-for-Development Projects Fail: How can risks be reduced? Institute for Development Policy and Management, University of Manchester (2003). http://unpan1.un.org/intradoc/groups/public/documents/NISPAcee/UNPAN015488.pdf. Accessed 23 Feb 2018
21. Pardo, T., Nam, T., Burke, G.: E-Government interoperability: interaction of policy, management, and technology dimensions. Soc. Sci. Comput. Rev. **30**(1), 7–23 (2012)
22. Shareef, M., Kumar, V., Kumar, U., Dwivedi, Y.: e-Government adoption model (GAM): differing service maturity levels. Gov. Inf. Q. **28**(1), 17–35 (2011)
23. Cordella, A., Iannacci, F.: Information systems in the public sector: the e-Government enactment framework. J. Strateg. Inf. Syst. **19**(1), 52–66 (2010)
24. Aladwani, A.: Corruption as a source of e-Government projects failure in developing countries: a theoretical exposition. Int. J. Inf. Manage. **36**, 105–112 (2016)
25. James, J.: Sharing mobile phones in developing countries: implications for the digital divide. Technol. Forecast. Soc. Change **78**(4), 729–735 (2011)
26. Morgeson, F., VanAmburg, D., Mithas, S.: Misplaced trust? exploring the structure of the E-Government-citizen trust relationship. J. Public Adm. Res. Theor. **21**, 257–283 (2011)
27. Mutula, S.: Digital divide and economic development: case study of sub-Saharan Africa. Electron. Libr. **26**(4), 468–489 (2008). https://doi.org/10.1108/02640470810893738

28. Rowley, J.: E-Government stakeholders – who are they and what do they want? Int. J. Inf. Manage. **31**(1), 53–62 (2011). https://doi.org/10.1016/j.ijinfomgt.2010.05.005

29. Helbig, N., Gil-García, J., Ferro, E.: Understanding the complexity of electronic government: implications from the digital divide literature. Gov. Inf. Q. **26**, 89–97 (2009)

30. United Nations: United Nations E-Government Survey: E-Government in support of sustainable development (2016). https://publicadministration.un.org/egovkb/en-us/reports/un-e-government-survey-2016. Accessed 3 Mar 2018

31. Carroll, J.M., Swatman, P.A.: Structured-case: a methodological framework for building theory in information systems research. Eur. J. Inf. Syst. **9**, 235–242 (2000)

32. Allan, J.: Perspectives on research in quality management. Total Qual. Manag. **9**(4–5), 1–5 (1998). https://doi.org/10.1080/0954412988451

33. Willcocks, L.: Information Management: The Evaluation of Information Systems Investment. Chapman & Hall, London (1994)

34. Beynon-Davies, P.: Business Information Systems. Macmillan Publishers Limited, Hampshire (2009)

35. Gupta, M.P., Jana, D.: E-government evaluation: a framework and case study. Gov. Inf. Q. **20**, 365–387 (2003)

36. Irani, Z., Love, P.E.D., Jones, S.: Learning lessons from evaluating eGovernment: reflective case experiences that support transformational government. J. Strateg. Inf. Syst. **17**(2), 155–164 (2008). https://doi.org/10.1016/j.jsis.2007.12.005

37. Wood, F.B., et al.: A practical approach to e-government web evaluation. IT Prof. **5**(3), 22–28 (2003)

38. Harris, R.W.: How ICT4D research fails the poor. Inf. Technol. Dev. **22**(1), 177–192 (2015)

39. Madon, S., Sahay, S., Sudan, R.: E-Government policy and health information systems implementation in Andhra Pradesh, India: need for articulation of linkages between the macro and the micro. Inf. Soc. **23**(5), 327–344 (2007)

40. Baxter, G., Sommerville, I.: Socio-technical systems: from design methods to systems engineering. Interact. Comput. **23**(1), 4–17 (2011). https://doi.org/10.1016/j.intcom.2010.07.003

41. United Nations: Transforming our world: the 2030 Agenda for Sustainable Development (2015). https://www.un.org/sustainabledevelopment/development-agenda

42. Heeks, R.: e-Government as a carrier of context. J. Public Policy **25**(1), 51–74 (2005)

43. Borrus, M., Stowsky, J.: Technology Policy and Economic Growth. In: Branscomb, L.M., Keller, J. (eds.) Investing in Innovation: Creating a Research and Innovation Policy that Works. MIT Press, Cambridge (1998)

44. Meso, P., Musa, P., Straub, D., Mbarika, V.: Information infrastructure, governance, and socio-economic development in developing countries. Eur. J. Inf. Syst. **18**, 52–65 (2009)

45. Silvano, R., Hanna, N.: New technologies for public sector transformation. J. of E-Gov. **3**(3), 3–39 (2007). https://doi.org/10.1300/J399v03n03_02

46. Krishnan, S., Teo, T.: Moderating effects of governance on information infrastructure and E-Government development. J. Am. Soc. Inf. Sci. Technol. **63**(10), 1929–1946 (2012)

47. Gil-García, J., Pardo, T., Burke, G.: Conceptualizing information integration in Government. In: Schnoll, H. (ed.) E-Government: Information, Technology and Transformation. Abingdon, Taylor & Francis Group (2015)

48. Schware, R. (ed.) E-development: From excitement to effectiveness. World Bank, Washington, DC (2005). http://documents.worldbank.org/curated/en/261151468325237852/pdf/341470EDevelopment.pdf

49. Zakareya, E., Zahir, I.: E-government adoption: architecture and barriers. Bus. Process Manage. J. **11**(5), 589–611 (2005)

50. Cresswell, A.M., Pardo, T.A., Canestraro, D.S.: Digital capability assessment for egovernment: a multi-dimensional approach. In: Wimmer, M.A., Scholl, H.J., Grönlund, Å., Andersen, K.V. (eds.) EGOV 2006. LNCS, vol. 4084, pp. 293–304. Springer, Heidelberg (2006). https://doi.org/10.1007/11823100_26

51. Kyambalesa, H.: The Quest for Technological Development: Constraints. Caveats and Initiatives. University Press of America, Lanham (2001)

52. Madu, C.: Strategic Planning in Technology Transfer to Less Developed Countries. Quorum Books, New York (1992)

53. Madon, S., Reinhard, N., Roode, D., Walsham, G.: Digital inclusion projects in developing countries: processes of institutionalization. Inf. Technol. Dev. **15**(2), 95–107 (2009)

54. Siau, K., Long, Y.: Factors affecting E-government development. J. Comput. Inf. Syst. **50** (1), 98–107 (2009)

55. Chaskin, R.: Building community capacity: a definitional framework and case studies from a comprehensive community initiative. Urban Aff. Rev. **36**(3), 291–323 (2001)

56. Grootaert, G.: Social capital: the missing link, SCI Working Paper No. 3, World Bank, Washington, DC (1998)

57. Lundvall, B.: Innovation, Growth and Social Cohesion: The Danish Model. Edward Elgar, Cheltenham, UK (2002)

58. Lall, S.: Social capital and industrial transformation. In: Fukuda-Parr, S., et al. (eds.) Capacity Development New Solutions to Old Problems, pp. 101–119. UNDP, New York (2002)

59. Field, J.: Social Capital. Routledge, London (2008)

60. Wilson, E.: The What, Why, Where, and How of National Information Initiatives (1997). http://www.ernestjwilson.com/uploads/The%20What,%20Why,%20Where%20and%20 20How%20of%20National%20Information%20Initiatives.pdf

61. Mansell, R., Wehn, U.: Knowledge Societies: Information Technology for Sustainable Development. Oxford University Press, Oxford (1998)

62. Kennes, W.: Small Developing Countries and Global Markets – Competing in the Big League. Macmillan, Basingstoke (2000)

63. Venables, A.: Geography and international inequalities: the impact of new technologies. J. Ind. Competit. Trade **1**(2), 135–159 (2001)

64. Serbin, A.: Sunset over the Islands: The Caribbean in an Age of Global and Regional Challenges. Palgrave MacMillan, Basingstoke (1998)

65. Collier, P., Pattillo, C. (eds.): Investment and Risk in Africa (Studies on the African economies). Palgrave Macmillan, London (2000)

66. Perez, C.: Technological change and opportunities for development as a moving target. In: Toye, J. (ed.) Trade and Development: Directions for the 21st Century. Edward Elgar, Cheltenham (2001)

67. Parker, D., Kirkpatrick, C.: Privatisation in developing countries: a review of the evidence and the policy lessons. J. Dev. Stud. **41**(4), 513–541 (2007)

68. Buys, P., Dasgupta, S., Thomas, T., Wheeler, D.: Determinants of a digital divide in Sub-Saharan Africa: a spatial econometric analysis of cell phone coverage. World Dev. **37**(9), 1494–1505 (2009)

69. Nishijima, M., Ivanauskas, T., Sarti, F.: Evolution and determinants of digital divide in Brazil (2005–2013). Telecommun. Policy **41**, 12–24 (2017)

70. Garbacz, C., Thompson, H.: Demand for telecommunication services in developing countries. Telecommun. Policy **31**(5), 276–289 (2007)

71. Ferro, E., Cantamessa, M., Paolucci, E.: Urban versus regional divide: comparing and classifying digital divide. In: Böhlen, M., Gamper, J., Polasek, W., Wimmer, M. (eds.)

Proceedings of the International Conference on E-Government: Towards Electronic Democracy, TCGOV 2005, Bologna, Italy (2005)

72. Haenssgen, M., Ariana, P.: The social implications of technology diffusion: uncovering the unintended consequences of people's health-related mobile phone use in rural India and China. World Dev. **94**, 286–304 (2017)

73. Khatun, F., Heywood, A., Ray, P., Hanifi, S., Bhuiya, A., Liaw, S.: Determinants of readiness to support mHealth in a rural community of Bangladesh. Int. J. Med. Inform. **84** (10), 847–856 (2015)

74. Woods, B.: Communication, Technology and the Development of People. Routledge, London (1993)

75. Rodrigo, G.: Technology, Economic Growth and Crises in East Asia. Edward Elgar, Cheltenham (2001)

76. Enos, J.: The creation of technological capability in developing countries. Pinter Publishers, London (1991)

77. Fukuda-Parr, S., Hill, R.: The network age: creating new models of technical cooperation. In: Fukuda-Parr, S., Lopes, C., Malik, K. (eds.) Capacity Development: New Solutions to Old Problems. UNDP, New York (2002)

78. Malik, K.: Towards a normative framework: technical cooperation, capacities and development. In: Fukuda-Parr, S., Lopes, C., Malik, K. (eds.) Capacity Development: New Solutions to Old Problems. UNDP, New York (2002)

79. Gunasekaran, V., Harmantzis, F.: Emerging wireless technologies for developing countries. Technol. Soc. **29**, 23–42 (2007)

80. Coleman, J.: Social capital in the creation of human capital. Am. J. Sociol. **94**, 95–120 (1988)

81. Lever, W.: Correlating the knowledge-base of cities with economic growth. Urban Stud. **39** (5–6), 859–870 (2002)

82. Jaffee, D.: Levels of Socio-Economic Development Theory. Praeger Publishers, Westport (1998)

83. Singh, H., Das, A., Joseph, D.: Country-level determinants of e-Government maturity (2004). https://pdfs.semanticscholar.org/7d1c/afd6c6010dc610898be6aa57036168b3b6f9. pdf

84. World Bank: Global Economic Prospects: Technology diffusion in the developing world. World Bank, Washington, DC (2008)

85. Fountain, J.: Social capital: its relationship to innovation in science and technology. Sci. Public Policy **25**(2), 103–115 (1998)

86. Woolcock, M.: Social capital in theory and practice: where do we stand? In: Isham, J., Kelly, T., Ramaswamy, S. (eds.) Social Capital and Economic Development: Well-being in Developing Countries. Edward Elgar, Cheltenham (2002)

87. Fukuyama, F.: Social capital and civil society. Paper prepared for delivery at the IMF Conference on Second Generation Reforms. International Monetary Fund, Washington, DC (1999)

88. Knack, S., Keefer, P.: Does social capital have an economic payoff? a cross-country investigation. Q. J. Econ. **112**(4), 1251–1288 (1997)

89. Narayan, D., Pritchett, L.: Cents and sociability: household income and social capital in rural Tanzania. Econ. Dev. Cult. Change **47**(4), 871–897 (1999)

90. Putnam, R.: The prosperous community: Social capital and public life (1993). http://prospect.org/article/prosperous-community-social-capital-and-public-life

91. Ebrahim, Z., Irani, Z.: E-Government adoption: architecture and barriers. Bus. Process Manage. J. **11**, 589–611 (2005)

92. Talero, E.: National information infrastructure in developing economies. In: Kahin, B., Wilson, E. (eds.) National Information Infrastructure Initiatives: Vision and Policy Design, pp. 287–306. MIT, Cambridge (1997)

93. Inkpen, A., Tsang, E.: Social capital, networks, and knowledge transfer. Acad. Manage. Rev. **30**(1), 146–165 (2005)

94. Bowles, S., Gintis, H.: Social capital and community governance. Econ. J. **112**(483), 419–436 (2005)

95. Smith, P., Wellenius, B.: Mitigating Regulatory Risk in Telecommunications. Viewpoint. World Bank, Washington, DC. © World Bank (1999). https://openknowledge.worldbank.org/handle/10986/11470

96. Anius, D.: Technology and Policy of a Regional Wireless Grid (unpublished doctoral thesis, Tufts University, 2004) (2005)

97. Schuller, T.: Reflections on the use of social capital. Rev. Soc. Econ. **65**(1), 11–28 (2007)

Theorizing the Relationship of Corruption in National Institutions with E-Government Maturity

Satish Krishnan[✉] and Anupriya Khan

Indian Institute of Management Kozhikode, Kozhikode 673570, Kerala, India
{satishk, anupriyak09fpm}@iimk.ac.in

Abstract. Though information and communication technologies (ICTs) are increasingly used in a range of governmental services in terms of e-government and smart government, many countries struggle to achieve a higher level of maturity owing to several challenges. In this study, we perceive corruption in a country is one such challenge, and take interest in understanding its impact on the growth and maturity of e-government. While the literature highlights a number of negative effects of corruption, its impact on e-government remains nearly unexplored, since most studies linking e-government and corruption have investigated the impact of e-government on corruption, but not the other way around. To address this void in the literature, we strive to provide a rich theoretical understanding of the mechanisms pertaining to the impact of corruption on e-government maturity. Adopting an institutional perspective to conceptualize corruption, we argue that corruption in three basic national institutions (political, legal, and media institutions) in a country can impede its e-government maturity. Specifically, we develop a conceptual framework by drawing on four key theoretical perspectives, namely, the agency theory, the control theory, the theory of X-inefficiency, and the rent-seeking theory to explain the negative influence of corruption in national institutions on e-government maturity. We believe that the proposed conceptual framework will guide further research on "corruption–e-government" phenomenon by offering theoretical insights, and help practitioners and policymakers dealing with e-government projects and initiatives.

Keywords: Corruption · E-government maturity · Institutions
Agency theory · Control theory · Theory of X-inefficiency
Rent-seeking theory · Conceptual framework

1 Introduction

The use of information and communication technologies in all facets of governmental operations and services (e-government) has evolved in the last decade to enable more effective and transparent interactions between government and citizens (G2C),

---

S. Krishnan and A. Khan—Contributed equally to the paper.

© IFIP International Federation for Information Processing 2019
Published by Springer Nature Switzerland AG 2019.
A. Elbanna et al. (Eds.): TDIT 2018, IFIP AICT 533, pp. 177–193, 2019.
https://doi.org/10.1007/978-3-030-04315-5_13

government and businesses (G2B), and among government entities (G2G) [22, 45]. Most recently, the trend appears to be shifting towards embracing smart government that seeks to leverage smart technologies and promote innovation in order to improve stakeholder participation and collaboration, government decision making, and overall governmental services and operations [50]. However, to provide the desired values, governments have to secure a higher level of online presence or e-government maturity for offering technology-enabled ways for the citizens to readily access various services and be engaged with governments [17]. E-government maturity is defined as the extent to which a government in a country has established an online presence [32, 57]. Attaining a higher level of maturity is quite challenging since it not only requires the adoption of new (smart) information technologies (IT) but also demands integration and interoperability in e-government. The current study thus focuses on understanding how e-government maturity in a country can be affected, and specifically takes interest in analyzing the impact of corruption in this context.

Corruption, defined as the misuse of entrusted power for personal or private gains [67], is one of the largest societal concerns that puts citizens in a continuous misery [31, 52]. The Transparency International [64] report notes that over two-thirds of the 176 nations surveyed scored less than 50, on a scale of 0 (highly corrupt) to 100 (very clean), indicating a severe corruption problem. Corruption in a country can disrupt its economy [42] by creating an environment of uncertainty [11], reducing investment incentives, and curbing the flow of foreign direct investment [18, 51]. Similarly, corruption in a country can be thought to affect its e-government initiatives by complicating regulations, manipulating information technology market, and actuating inefficiency in public workforce. However, theoretical underpinning explaining such predictions is quite sparse in the literature. Some studies though mention that corruption may be pivotal in affecting e-government growth and maturity [20, 27, 57], the mechanisms explaining the phenomenon are not theoretically driven [74]. This essentially incentivizes us to investigate the impact of corruption on e-government.

Corruption has gained increasing attention amongst e-government researchers of late. Broadly, two streams of research are evident that explore the linkage between corruption and e-government: (1) studies examining the impact of e-government on corruption; and (2) studies acknowledging the influence of corruption on e-government. While the first stream of research contains mixed arguments, in which, one group of studies considers e-government as an effective instrument to mitigate corruption [9, 59, 72] and another group questions its validity in reality [28, 71], this stream is reasonably well-developed as a vast amount of research falls into it. In contrast, the second stream is found to be under-developed owing to the lack of theoretical reasoning and guidance, and contains a handful of descriptive studies and anecdotes except a study by Aladwani [1]. The current study strives to address this void by contributing to this stream of research by developing an understanding of how corruption in a nation can affect its desired level of e-government maturity.

We intend to account for variation in the level of corruption across countries, and hence in line with Srivastava et al. [59], we adopt an institutional perspective to develop a more comprehensive understanding. Accordingly, we conceptualize corruption in a nation as comprising corruption in three basic national institutions— political, legal, and media institutions, and refer them as political-based, legal-based, and media-based corruption. As noted earlier, corruption is a prevalent issue across countries and affects many government operations including public welfare [36]. It is therefore reasonable to expect that corruption can also impact e-government maturity in a country. This is in line with Yoon and Chae who indicated that "corruption actually lowers the effectiveness of national e-strategy and its implementation" [73, p. 34]. Recently Aladwani [1] also reasoned that corruption could be a source of e-government failure in developing countries. Thus, acknowledging the potential impact of corruption on e-government, the key research question (RQ) that this study aims to address is:

> *RQ: How does corruption in national institutions of a country affect its e-government maturity?*

To address the above question, we propose a conceptual framework by drawing on four key theoretical perspectives: (1) the agency theory; (2) the control theory; (3) the theory of X-inefficiency; and (4) the rent-seeking theory. Specifically, the proposed framework offers rich theoretical explanations pertaining to the negative effect of corruption in national institutions on e-government maturity. We draw on the agency theory that is substantially established in the literature on corruption and information systems (IS) [59]. However, the agency problem is often identified with the lack of control by the principal [35] and control mechanisms are required for improving performance of IS projects including e-government projects; accordingly, we draw on the control theory perspective. As these two theories are more relevant under the assumption of benevolent principal, they may not be applicable for principals with non-benevolent goals [35, 36]. Hence, we use two other theories—the theory of X-inefficiency and the rent-seeking theory. Thus, in an effort to explain the "corruption–e-government" phenomenon, we develop a conceptual framework by incorporating various theoretical perspectives that are relevant and complement each other [74]. We consider that this theoretical development is necessary to make researchers, practitioners, and policymakers vigilant of the adverse impact of corruption in the context of e-government. While the trend is to make progress towards smart government and smart cities, the study indicates the potential obstruction by corruption. Further, we believe that the study will enrich our insights and encourage further scientific investigations in future.

2 Literature Review

2.1 Existing Views on E-Government Maturity

E-government is defined as "the use of information and communication technologies (ICTs) and the Internet to enhance the access to and delivery of all facets of government services and operations for the benefit of citizens, businesses, employees, and other stakeholders" [60, p. 100]. While a number of performance parameters exist to evaluate the progress of e-government, we focus on e-government maturity as it is a pre-condition for the success of smart government [17]. E-government maturity refers to the extent to which a government in a country has established an online presence. This definition entails an evolutionary approach of conceptualizing e-government maturity [2, 37], according to which, e-government proceeds through a series of stages characterized by the level of complexity and the level of online activity [10].

E-government and more specifically, smart government are expected to deliver a number of benefits ranging from improvement in governmental service delivery, accountability, transparency to collaboration and integration of processes, systems and entities. Acknowledging this, a huge amount of resources is being invested to foster its growth and maturity [33]. Despite such efforts, many countries fall short of securing these benefits since the progress of e-government maturity remains uneven across countries [68]. Further, there are constant challenges pertaining to implementation, administration, and management of e-government projects, due to which the e-government projects sometimes confront with failure in many countries [4]. A recent global study by United Nations [69], for example, mentions about the difficulty involved in attaining integration between various government institutions. And, without achieving such integration and interoperability, initiatives such as smart government may not be successful. Therefore, it remains challenging for governments across most countries to achieve the growth in e-government maturity. Motivated by this, a number of studies have identified factors, such as gross domestic product (GDP), ICT infrastructure, human capital, governance, and trust, which could influence e-government development and maturity of a country [5, 33, 57, 58]. While these are important determinants of e-government maturity, a key factor that is constantly overlooked in the literature but gaining relevance is corruption. Recently, Aladwani [1] discussed the impact of corruption in terms of e-government failure arguing that corruption misuses the resources dedicated to e-government, and called for a rigorous understanding of the issue. This study responds to that call by extending and enriching the linkages between corruption and e-government.

2.2 Existing Views on Corruption

Being a nebulous concept, corruption bears many definitions. The widely cited definition is that it is the misuse of entrusted power for personal or private gains [44, 67]. Corruption thus is a broad term and takes myriad forms, such as bribery, extortion, embezzlement, favoritism, nepotism, abuse of discretion, exploitation of conflicting interests, and improper political contributions [1, 70]. The literature attributes various political, economic, cultural, judicial, and individual reasons to corruption [12, 30, 44, 49, 55, 65]. However, there exist mixed perceptions regarding its consequences. First, some researchers [7, 24, 38] believe that corruption produces positive outcomes and aids the economy, especially under the circumstances of undue bureaucracy, complex regulation, or market restrictions. Second, as opposed to the first view, many scholars [48, 51] argue in favor of the adverse impacts of corruption and perceive that corruption increases transaction cost, consumes economic resources, complicates policies and regulations, reduces investment incentives, and hampers economic growth.

While economists largely adopt the second view and consider corruption as 'sand' in the gears of the economy, political scientists, for many years, have mostly considered it as the 'grease' [51]. However, most recent studies follow the second view as these studies are primarily influenced by the spread of democracy in the Third World, and corruption is viewed as dysfunctional under democracy [51]. Hence, consistent with these studies, we aim extending the arguments concerning the negative effects of corruption on e-government maturity as corruption can curb the operational efficiency, accountability, and morality standards of public officials, and it can be detrimental to the administrative systems supervising e-government projects and initiatives [1].

As noted earlier, we draw on the institutional theory to conceptualize corruption since our objective is to account for variation in the level of corruption across countries. Moreover, most economic and psychological theories capture corruption at the individual level and therefore may fall short of explaining the differing levels of corruption across countries [59]. Hence, we identify three basic national institutions—political, legal, and media institutions that are considered as the major pillars under which all operations and activities of a nation are performed [59]. While political institutions largely encompass the political parties and the parliament or legislature in a country, legal institutions involve mostly the legal system or judiciary as well as the police system. In essence, by grounding the discussion on the institutional perspective for construing corruption, this study aims to explore the relationships of corruption in three basic national institutions with e-government maturity.

2.3 Linking Corruption with E-Government Maturity

The literature linking e-government and corruption mostly establishes two streams of research. Within the first stream, a number of studies view that ICTs (e-government) can reduce corruption by promoting transparency and accountability in government functions [9, 59, 72]. However, some scholars raise concerns if e-government can effectively mitigate corruption in reality [28, 71], as sometimes ICTs can create opportunities for corruption [19] by enabling opportunity for overinvestment in e-government. Though this stream contains mixed arguments about the impact of e-government on corruption, it is substantially developed, as evidenced from Table 1, which provides a summary of the key extant studies. In contrast, the second stream deals with the impact of corruption on e-government and remains mostly unexplored owing to the lack of theoretical development. To address this void, we focus on the second stream and argue that corruption in three national institutions would hinder the progress of e-government because corruption is "an evolutionary hazard, a strategic impediment [...], and an organizational deficiency" [40, p. 405].

To conceptualize the negative effect of corruption on e-government maturity, we draw on four key theoretical perspectives that are grounded in corruption and IS project management literature (see, Fig. 1). First, we draw on the agency theory (also known as the principal-agent-client model), which is predominantly used in corruption as well as IS literature [30, 59]. This theory, as depicted in the disciplines of economics and political science, identifies governments as principals, who are characterized by limited control and power over agents' activities. Second, acknowledging the requirement of proper control mechanisms in IS projects to avert poor process performance and subsequent failure [26], we draw on the control theory perspective and argue that e-government projects and initiatives could fail if principals are unable to exercise adequate control over agents. These two theoretical perspectives usually hold the assumption that principals are striving for benevolent goals, which may not be quite true when there is a competition for the principal's position [35] as such competition

Table 1. Key studies on the impact of e-government on corruption

Authors	Objectives	Key findings
Andersen [3]	Econometric modeling of secondary data	Corruption was significantly reduced in non-OECD countries during the decade 1996–2006 through the use of e-government
Elbahnasawy [14]	Panel analysis of secondary data for 160 countries for a period of 1995–2009	Corruption was reduced by e-government that facilitated telecom infrastructure and online services
Garcia-Murillo [16]	Econometric modeling of secondary data for 208 countries during 2002–2005, and 2008	The perceptions of corruption were reduced because of governments' web presence
Kim et al. [28]	Case study analyzing an e-government system for anti-corruption in Seoul metropolitan government	The regulation could be most important parameter in curbing corruption. Strong leadership was also necessary
Krishnan et al. [32]	Cross-sectional analysis of archival data for 105 countries for a period of 2004–2008	E-government maturity is negatively related to corruption, which in turn affects economic prosperity and environmental degradation
Mistry [46]	Case study analyzing e-governance initiatives in India	Corruption could be mitigated through initiatives enabling transparency and accountability
Shim and Eom [54]	Statistical analysis of data for 77 countries	E-government could be useful as anti-corruption tool because it had consistent positive impact on reduction of corruption
Singh et al. [56]	Survey of 918 respondents in India, Ethiopia, and Fiji	E-governance has a positive impact on the government-citizen relationship and reducing corruption
Srivastava et al. [59]	Panel analysis of secondary data for 63 countries during 2004–2007	E-government could be helpful in alleviating corruption in some national institutions and stakeholder service systems

can put their benevolent character into question. Moreover, the agency theory assumes that the benevolent principal has total control over the legal framework [36], which may not be the case in societies in which corruption can manifest in any public institution. Accordingly, it becomes less convincing to believe that those who control the legal framework and several governmental operations stay immune to corruption [36]. The application of the agency theory to corruption thus appears to be somewhat narrow and limited in case of large-scale corruption. Hence, to complement the agency theory's arguments in this context, we draw on two other theories—the theory of X-inefficiency and the rent-seeking theory. These two theories indicate that principals with non-benevolent goals may lack commitment to serve public interests, and may be involved in evoking X-inefficiency among agents and/or creating economic rents.

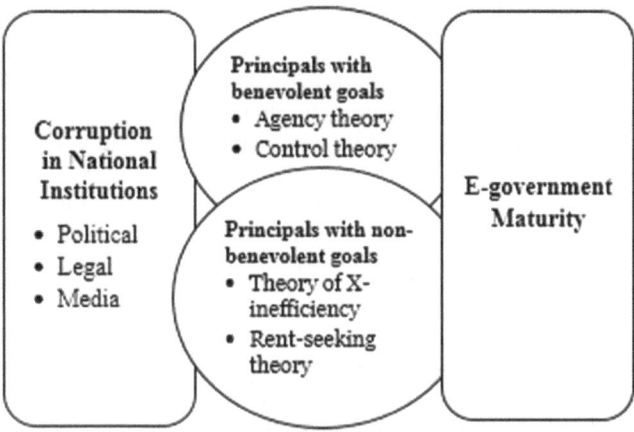

Fig. 1. Key theoretical perspectives used in this study

Agency Theory. The agency theory was initially developed to draw the relationship between private contractual parties—owners and managers, and eventually many researchers established its relevance in the context of corruption [25, 30, 48, 59]. This theory primarily underlines the role of three stakeholders—the principal, the agent, and the client, in which, the principal is usually considered as the honest government, the agents are public officials who have vested self-interest and offer services (e.g., licenses and contracts) to the clients (citizens and businesses) [30]. As per the theory, a conflict of interest arises between the principal and the agent, which further creates the agency problem [13]. While these two actors wish to maximize their own utility, the principal is said to be insufficiently skilled or have time constraints due to which tasks are delegated to the agent [35], who thus earns an informational advantage, tends to circumvent the control of principals, and works in his own self-interest. While there is some dissonance in the literature whether the self-seeking behavior of the agents can be termed as corruption or not, many scholars consider it appropriate in case of large-scale embezzlement and bribery [35]. The role of the client is also important in the agency theory as the client increases the opportunity for the agent to deceive the principal by colluding with the agent for obtaining various services (e.g., licenses and contracts). Prior studies have demonstrated the relevance of the agency theory in the context of corruption and suggested that as a result of corruption, underqualified firms are granted contracts, inappropriate projects are given priority, inefficient technologies are applied, ineffectual policies are implemented, and poor administrative decisions are made [6, 30, 48, 49, 55]. In line with the extant studies, we strive to extend these adverse impacts of corruption to the context of e-government.

Control Theory. The literature on IS project management suggests that poor process performance and management of IT projects can be effectively addressed by exercising formal and/or informal control [21, 29, 61]. Formal control comprises (a) behavior control, which is about prescribing steps and procedures of a task by the controller [29]; and (b) outcome control, which is about defining the targets to be achieved by the controlees [26]. Formal control is also about evaluating performance of the controlees —whether the appropriate steps are followed and the targets are attained [21, 29]. In contrast, informal control deals with interpersonal aspects and self-control behavior, and comprises clan and self-control. In clan control, the members of a group identify themselves with same values and work toward achieving group goals [29], whereas in self-control, a person sets his own goals, monitors it, and recognizes his efforts accordingly [21]. In line with these extant arguments, we contend that the maturity and subsequent success of e-government are contingent upon how effectively the projects and initiatives are managed by exerting proper control. Thus, if the principal fails to exercise adequate control over agents' corrupt practices and actions, the e-government maturity level could be at a disadvantage. In this study, we draw on the formal control perspective since the informal control perspective hardly refers to the involvement of controlee (as described in self-control), which makes the principal-agent relationship little relevant to the context of informal control mechanism.

Theory of X-Inefficiency. According to the theory of X-inefficiency, inefficiency could be an outcome of workers' lack of effort and motivation. This theory was initially used by Leibenstein [39] to explain efficiency losses due to minimal competition in private good markets. He argued that in a competitive environment, inefficient firms would be under pressure because the market tends to select those firms that are efficient in utilizing the factor inputs and transforming them to desired outputs. On the other hand, monopolistic firms usually do not face such pressure from market and may not pressurize the workforce to put effort and to work with efficiency. Similar situation can arise in public institutions as well. That is, when there is minimal competition for the principal's position, the principal may not be motivated enough to put effort and monitor the agents' actions. Being aware of such situation, the agents would have almost no fear of losing jobs and could become motivated towards collective non-performance [35]. While the principal is expected to rein the agents from exerting their self-interest, he may not be inclined to do so, thereby providing powerful agents more leeway to quench their self-interest. Further, in situations where there exists competition for the principal's position, a principal having corrupt agents as his resources will be at an advantage as he gets the necessary political support from these agents [35]. Hence, the principal may not be willing to stop the agents from exerting their self-interest, rather he would allow some X-inefficiency among them. The agents therefore would continue to act towards fulfilling their self-enrichment. Taken together, we argue that the principal may not be able to motivate agents to serve the public and protect their interests, and this lack of effort and motivation would result in efficiency losses in public institutions running various e-government projects and initiatives, thereby hampering the overall e-government maturity in a country.

Rent-seeking Theory. Corruption is considered as a type of rent-seeking activity in which public officials are often engaged in bending their decision upon receiving bribes. This theory encompasses various forms of seeking preferential treatment or privileged benefits from public decision-makers [36]. To benefit from such treatments, private parties compete against each other by offering bribes. The literature notes at least two views regarding the role of the government or the politician [36]. As per the traditional rent-seeking approach, politicians themselves do not seek rents or impose restrictions, rather they are pushed and lobbied into such actions by private firms [43]. Criticizing this, the other viewpoint suggests that corrupt politicians have their own incentive (e.g., financial gain); hence they need not be impelled by the private sector for imposing restrictions [23, 43]. Corruption rather influences politicians and public officials to levy restrictions so as to extort donations from the private sector; corruption thus actuates the creation of rents [36]. In this study, we concord on the traditional view of rent-seeking by considering corruption as a form of preferential treatment by public decision-makers, and also acknowledge the criticism regarding the corrupt role of politicians. We contend that public rent-seeking officials may impose restrictions, due to which the e-government project contract can be granted to an IT firm which offers a large amount of bribe without judging the firm's ability to render an effective e-government solution, thereby impeding e-government maturity. In the next section, we provide insights of the phenomenon based on these theories.

3   Relating Corruption in National Institutions to E-Government Maturity

3.1   Relating Political-Based Corruption to E-Government Maturity

The agency theory centers upon the perspective of self-interest seeking individuals in the principal–agent–client model [30], in which, the principal is the politician or the public servant (the government) in charge of the agents (other public officials) responsible for the e-government development and its service delivery to the clients (citizens and businesses). The theory indicates that the agents work in their self-interest as the principal cannot effectively monitor the agents' work of online public service development and delivery due to the information asymmetry between them. Thus, when corruption manifests in political institutions, the agents have discretion in administering e-government projects and initiatives without sufficient accountability [41, 46]. Thus, we propose that:

Proposition P1a. Political-based corruption in a country impedes its e-government maturity when there is information asymmetry between the principal and the agent.

Further, to benefit from the agents' political support, the principal would allow X-inefficiency and bureaucratic slackness among them in the political institutions [35], leading to efficiency losses which can adversely impact e-government growth and maturity. For example, the agents may lack motivation to put effort towards completion of e-government projects on time and within budget to satisfy their self-enrichment. They may also be involved in bribery that would not only affect innovation in e-government projects but also distort their decisions in various aspects of e-government development such as adopting suitable technologies, picking an IT firm, assigning the e-government project contract, and evaluating the features to be implemented on e-government platforms. Hence, we propose that:

Proposition P1b. Political-based corruption in a country hampers its e-government maturity when the principal allows X-inefficiency among the agents.

To minimize the negative effects of political-based corruption on e-government maturity, the control theory perspective suggests that the corrupt self-seeking agents require to be controlled. We assume that the principal serves as the controller of the e-government projects and initiatives, and he must exert adequate formal control mechanisms over the agents, the controlees of such projects, to improve the process performance of the projects. The agents are expected to accomplish the goals and objectives of e-government projects, and complete the targets within the scheduled time and budgeted cost. However, in a corrupt environment, the principal would fail to effectively exercise adequate formal control mechanisms over the agents' corrupt dealings as his role features limited control and power [35]. Moreover, when corruption permeates political institutions, the agents will become more powerful while principals are likely to struggle to retain their control, because politicians face competition from opposition parties and they are largely dependent on the political support of their agents to insure their own survival [35]. Further, as there can be multiple principals (owing to the division of power), the corrupt agents are more likely to occupy a strong bargaining position in favoring one principal over the other. As a result, e-government maturity in a country is likely to get hampered. So, we posit that:

Proposition P1c. *Political-based corruption in a country prevents its e-government maturity when the principal fails to exercise the formal control over the agents.*

Further, the rent-seeking theory indicates that due to corruption in political institutions, the principal may engage in imposing regulations that create artificial rents and invoke competition among private companies. The rents are useful to influence policies and rules to one's own advantage [36]. Due to the rent-seeking behaviors, an overpriced e-government contract may be awarded to an inferior IT company, which can subvert the overall development and quality of the e-government channels. Further, due to nepotism and favoritism (known as less competitive forms of rent-seeking behaviors [34, 66]) by the principal and the agents, underqualified and incompetent technical staff and administrators may be appointed to deal with the implementation and delivery of e-government services to the other stakeholders [1]. These staff might not be capable enough to understand user requirements, design appropriate features on e-government websites, and respond to user concerns; and their poor performance could eventually harm the maturity of e-government in a country. Thus, we posit that:

Proposition P1d. *Political-based corruption in a country impedes its e-government maturity when the principal and the agents engage in rent-seeking behaviors.*

3.2   Relating Legal-Based Corruption to E-Government Maturity

Corruption "could cast its dark shadows" on the legal institutions and "the prevalence of such kind of corruption has always far reaching effects on all governmental contexts including that of e-government's" [1, p. 109]. To elaborate, one of the major purposes of implementing e-government initiatives in a country is to better transparency and accountability in public institutions including the legal systems, therefore it would be difficult for the judiciary and the police personnel to derive personal gains from their corrupt dealings. In other words, as it would be hard for them to break ethical codes in a transparent and accountable legal environment of a country, corrupt judicial and police officials would be motivated to hamper its e-government development and circumvent its control [1]. According to the rent-seeking theory, corrupt judicial officials and the police, to benefit from economic rents, might work directly or indirectly by helping the principal and/or the agents, who have dominating societal powers. For example, in the context of offering an e-government project contract to a firm, while doing their background verification, the police in consultation with the principal and/or the agents, might demand a bribe to reduce the competition among the potential firms competing for the project contract [35]. In a similar vein, the corrupt judiciary might also favor the firm offering the largest bribe. That is, in exchange for successful verification, corrupt police officials and judiciary might create rents and hassle competing firms for bribe. As a result of such corrupt dealings among them, an ineffective firm might be chosen for awarding the e-government project contract, thereby hindering its overall maturity. Thus, we propose that:

Proposition P2. *Legal-based corruption in a country impedes its e-government maturity when the judiciary and the police engage in rent-seeking behaviors.*

3.3   Relating Media-Based Corruption to E-Government Maturity

The media can make corrupt governmental activities more prominent, except when the media itself encourages corrupt practicing. The ownership of media companies can be considered as a crucial factor in determining the effect of corruption in these institutions on the e-government. The coverage by state-owned media than private media is often considered to favor the government. For instance, in Kenya, the reporting of the state-controlled Kenya Broadcasting Corporation (KBC) is said to privilege its government [15]. Even as compared to private media, the state-owned media is found to be less effective in monitoring governments [62], thereby creating opportunities for the government officials to engage in the rent-seeking behavior. In other words, according to the rent-seeking theory, the government and its agents would be better off if they could exert rent-seeking behaviors in various aspects including e-government projects and initiatives; and, when the media is state-run, the government agents could exercise strong influence on it [53] in such a way that the rent-seeking and corrupt behaviors pertaining to the e-government projects are suppressed and high profile cases are stifled. As the journalists, editors and media houses are bribed for not publishing unfavorable reports [47], it is more likely that the violation of regulatory requirements in the e-government project can go unreported, which not only undermines the neutrality of the reporting but also hinders the overall growth and maturity of e-government in a country. Adding to this, as privately owned media companies may be beholden to certain political leaders, public figures and individuals having dominating power [8], it is more likely that they might prefer promoting their image and views, rather than providing awareness to the citizens in terms of e-government development and services. So, we posit that:

Proposition P3. *Media-based corruption in a country degrades its e-government maturity when it creates opportunities for the principal and the agents to engage in rent-seeking behaviors.*

In sum, we propose a conceptual framework, as shown in Fig. 2 that depicts how corruption in each of the three national institutions hinders e-government maturity.

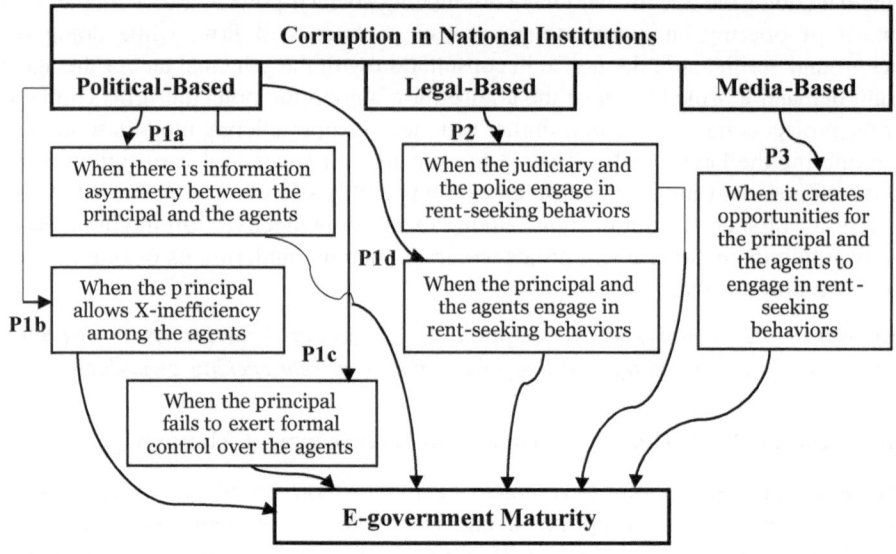

Fig. 2. Conceptual framework

4   Discussion

A recent global study on e-government by United Nations [69] indicates that though almost all countries have been able to establish an online presence, most of them have not achieved the desired maturity level. As a higher level of maturity is necessary to further technology-enabled initiatives such as smart government and smart city, it becomes imperative to understand the challenges and how they affect e-government. Our study thus analyses an important societal concern, corruption, and its impact on e-government maturity. Specifically, this study provides theoretical insights on the mechanisms concerning the adverse impact of corruption by construing corruption using institutional theory and drawing on four theoretical perspectives—the agency theory, the control theory, the theory of X-inefficiency, and the rent-seeking theory.

This study contributes to e-government research in several ways. First, while most extant studies analyzed the conventional relationship in terms of the impact of e-government on corruption, the current study views the relationship between these two in the other way (i.e., the impact of corruption on e-government), which remains nearly under-explored in the literature. Second, drawing on the aforesaid four key theoretical perspectives, this study provides an initial foundation offering rich theoretical expla-nations concerning the relationships of political-, legal-, and media-based corruption in a country with its e-government maturity. Third, guided by the institutional theory to construe corruption, the study not only depicts an understanding of the relationships of each of the three national institutions in a country with its e-government maturity but also takes into account the variation in the level of corruption across countries. With reference to practical implications, this study cautions policymakers about the aspects of corruption that are yet not contained and can hinder the progress and success of e-government and smart government initiatives in a country. Second, the theoretical reasoning presented in this study facilitates the understanding of the mechanisms through which corruption in a country can affect its e-government maturity. Specifically, our conceptual framework serves as a guide for the policymakers to enhance the maturity levels by managing corruption in each of the three national institutions, under which most government activities are run. For example, they can make policies to contain corruption in political institutions and appoint impartial and skilled professionals in the administration and management of e-government projects.

The study has a few limitations that are worthy of further research. First, though we ground our study on three national institutions, corruption can permeate many other institutions and stakeholder service systems [59, 63], which in turn can adversely affect e-government maturity. Future research may consider studying corruption in other institutions such as religious bodies, non-governmental organizations (NGOs), and business and citizen service systems to extend our framework and establish a more comprehensive understanding. Second, while we conceptualize corruption using an institutional perspective, future research can perceive corruption as a cultural variant and theorize the phenomenon accordingly. Third, though we restrict our investigation to the negative aspects of corruption, future research may look into its positive impacts as well. Despite these limitations, the current study is one among the first few studies providing theoretical insights into the negative influence of corruption in national institutions of a country on its e-government maturity. We believe that this theoretical understanding will encourage further investigations on the subject.

5   Conclusion

In conclusion, corruption has numerous adverse effects; despite that, we know considerably little about the potential impact of corruption on e-government maturity. Such understanding is essential if governments across nations are willing to make further advancements by developing smart government and smart city. As an initial step towards providing important insights into the phenomenon, the current study theorizes how corruption in political, legal, and media institutions of a country can hinder its e-government maturity, and develops a conceptual framework by taking an institutional perspective to construe corruption and drawing on the four key theoretical perspectives. The study hence contributes to e-government research and practice by theoretically explaining a potential but under-explored linkage between corruption and e-government maturity, and guiding policymakers to achieve a higher level of e-government maturity by managing corruption within each of the institutions.

References

1. Aladwani, A.M.: Corruption as a source of e-government projects failure in developing countries: a theoretical exposition. Int. J. Inf. Manag. **36**(1), 105–112 (2016)
2. Andersen, K.V., Henriksen, H.Z.: E-Government maturity models: extension of the Layne and Lee model. Gov. Inf. Q. **23**(2), 236–248 (2006)
3. Andersen, T.B.: E-government as an anti-corruption strategy. Inf. Econ. Policy **21**(3), 201–210 (2009)
4. Anthopoulos, L., Reddick, C.G., Giannakidou, I., Mavridis, N.: Why e-government projects fail? An analysis of the healthcare.gov website. Gov. Inf. Q. **33**(1), 161–173 (2016)
5. Azad, B., Faraj, S., Goh, J., Feghali, T.: What shapes global diffusion of government: comparing the influence of national governance institutions. J. Glob. Inf. Manag. **18**(2), 85–104 (2010)
6. Bardhan, P.: Corruption and development: a review of issues. J. Econ. Lit. **35**(3), 1320–1346 (1997)
7. Bayley, D.: The effects of corruption in a developing nation. West. Polit. Q. **19**(4), 719–732 (1967)
8. Centre for International Media Ethics, Media Ethics Survey. www.cimethics.org. Accessed 20 Jan 2018
9. Cho, Y.H., Choi, B.: E-government to combat corruption: the case of Seoul metropolitan government. Int. J. Public Adm. **27**(10), 719–735 (2004)
10. Das, A., Singh, H., Joseph, D.: A longitudinal study of e-government maturity. Inf. Manag. **54**(4), 415–426 (2017)
11. Dawes, S.S.: Stewardship and usefulness: policy principles for information-based transparency. Gov. Inf. Q. **27**(4), 377–383 (2010)
12. Doig, A., Theobald, R.: Corruption and Democratization. Frank Cass, London (2000)
13. Eisenhardt, K.M.: Agency theory: an assessment and review. Acad. Manag. Rev. **14**(1), 57–74 (1989)
14. Elbahnasawy, N.G.: E-government, internet adoption, and corruption: an empirical investigation. World Dev. **57**(C), 114–126 (2014)
15. Freedom House, Freedom of the Press 2012. https://freedomhouse.org/report/freedom-press/freedom-press-2012. Accessed 6 Jan 2018
16. Garcia-Murillo, M.: Does a government web presence reduce perceptions of corruption? Inf. Technol. Dev. **19**(2), 151–175 (2013)
17. Gartner, Smart Government Key Initiative Overview. https://www.gartner.com/doc/2520516/smart-government-key-initiative-overview. Accessed 6 Feb 2018
18. Habib, M., Zurawicki, L.: Corruption and foreign direct investment. J. Int. Bus. Stud. **33**(2), 291–307 (2002)
19. Heeks, R.: Information technology and public sector corruption. Information Systems for Public Sector Management Working Paper No. 4. Institute for Development Policy and Management, Manchester, CO (1998)
20. Heeks, R.: Information technology and the management of corruption. Dev. Pract. **9**(1/2), 184–189 (1999)
21. Henderson, J., Lee, S.: Managing I/S design teams: a control theories perspective. Manag. Sci. **38**(6), 757–777 (1992)
22. Hamza, H., Sehl, M., Egide, K., Diane, P.: A conceptual model for G2G relationships. In: Janssen, M., Scholl, H.J., Wimmer, M.A., Tan, Y. (eds.) EGOV 2011. LNCS, vol. 6846, pp. 285–295. Springer, Heidelberg (2011). https://doi.org/10.1007/978-3-642-22878-0_24

23. Hirshleifer, J.: Toward a more general theory of regulation: comment. J. Law Econ. **19**(2), 241–244 (1976)
24. Huntington, S.P.: Political Order in Changing Societies. Yale University Press, New Haven (1968)
25. Jain, A.K.: Models of corruption. In: Jain, A.K. (ed.) Economics of Corruption. RETH, pp. 13–34. Springer, Boston (1998). https://doi.org/10.1007/978-1-4615-4935-2_2
26. Keil, M., Rai, A., Liu, S.: How user risk and requirements risk moderate the effects of formal and informal control on the process performance of IT projects. Eur. J. Inf. Syst. **22**(6), 650–672 (2013)
27. Kim, C.: Anti-corruption initiatives and e-government: a cross-national study. Public Organ. Rev. **14**(3), 385–396 (2014)
28. Kim, S., Kim, H.J., Lee, H.: An institutional analysis of an e-government system for anti-corruption: the case of OPEN. Gov. Inf. Q. **26**(1), 42–50 (2009)
29. Kirsch, L.: Portfolios of control modes and IS project management. Inf. Syst. Res. **8**(3), 215–239 (1997)
30. Klitgaard, R.: Controlling Corruption. University of California Press, Berkeley (1988)
31. Kock, N., Gaskins, L.: The mediating role of voice and accountability in the relationship between internet diffusion and government corruption in Latin America and Sub-Saharan Africa. Inf. Technol. Dev. **20**(1), 23–43 (2014)
32. Krishnan, S., Teo, T.S., Lim, V.K.: Examining the relationships among e-government maturity, corruption, economic prosperity and environmental degradation: a cross-country analysis. Inf. Manag. **50**(8), 638–649 (2013)
33. Krishnan, S., Teo, T.S., Lymm, J.: Determinants of electronic participation and electronic government maturity: insights from cross-country data. Int. J. Inf. Manag. **37**(4), 297–312 (2017)
34. Krueger, A.: The political economy of the rent seeking society. Am. Econ. Rev. **64**(3), 291–303 (1974)
35. Lambsdorff, J.G.: How corruption in government affects public welfare: a review of theory. Discussion Paper (No. 9), Center for Globalization and Europeanization of the Economy (2001)
36. Lambsdorff, J.G.: Corruption and rent-seeking. Public Choice **113**(1/2), 97–125 (2002)
37. Layne, K., Lee, J.W.: Developing fully functional e-government: a four stage model. Gov. Inf. Q. **18**(2), 122–136 (2001)
38. Leff, N.: Economic development through bureaucratic corruption. Am. Behav. Sci. **8**(3), 8–14 (1964)
39. Leibenstein, H.: Allocative efficiency vs. "x-efficiency". Am. Econ. Rev. **56**(3), 392–415 (1966)
40. Luo, Y.: Corruption and organization in Asian management systems. Asia Pac. J. Manag. **19**(3), 405–422 (2002)
41. Mahmood, M.A., Bagchi, K., Ford, T.C.: On-line shopping behavior: cross-country empirical research. Int. J. Electron. Commer. **9**(1), 9–30 (2004)
42. Mauro, P.: Corruption and growth. Q. J. Econ. **110**(3), 681–712 (1995)
43. McChesney, F.S.: Rent extraction and rent creation in the economic theory of regulation. J. Leg. Stud. **16**(1), 101–118 (1987)
44. McMullen, M.: A theory of corruption. Sociol. Rev. **9**(2), 181–200 (1961)
45. Mellouli, S., Bousalam, F.: Multi-agent based framework for e-government. Electron. Gov. Int. J. **6**(2), 177–192 (2009)
46. Mistry, J.J.: The role of eGovernance in mitigating corruption. Account. Public Interes. **12**(1), 137–159 (2012)

47. Ristow, B.: Cash for coverage: Bribery of journalists around the world. https://www.cima. ned.org/resource/cash-for-coverage-bribery-of-journalists-around-the-world/. Accessed 12 Jan 2018
48. Rose-Ackerman, S.: Corruption - A Study in Political Economy. Academic Press, New Haven (1978)
49. Rose-Ackerman, S.: Corruption and Government: Causes, Consequences, and Reform. Cambridge University Press, Cambridge (1999)
50. Scholl, H.J., Scholl, M.C.: Smart governance: a roadmap for research and practice. In: iConference 2014 Proceedings, pp. 163–176. iSchools, Berlin (2014)
51. Seligson, M.A.: The impact of corruption on regime legitimacy: a comparative study of four Latin American countries. J. Polit. **64**(2), 408–433 (2002)
52. Senior, I.: Corruption, the government and the private sector: why it matters and what can be done. Econ. Aff. **24**(2), 22–29 (2004)
53. Servaes, J.: Communication policies, good governance and development journalism. Commun. S. Afr. J. Commun. Theory Res. **35**(1), 50–80 (2009)
54. Shim, D.C., Eom, T.H.: E-government and anti-corruption: empirical analysis of international data. Int. J. Public Adm. **31**(3), 298–316 (2008)
55. Shleifer, A., Vishny, R.W.: Corruption. Q. J. Econ. **108**(3), 599–617 (1993)
56. Singh, G., Pathak, R.D., Naz, R., Belwal, R.: E-governance for improved public sector service delivery in India, Ethiopia and Fiji. Int. J. Public Sector Manag. **23**(3), 254–275 (2010)
57. Singh, H., Das, A., Joseph, D.: Country-level determinants of e-government maturity. Commun. Assoc. Inf. Syst. **20**, 632–648 (2007)
58. Srivastava, S.C., Teo, T.S.: What facilitates e-government development? A cross-country analysis. Electron. Gov. Int. J. **4**(4), 365–378 (2007)
59. Srivastava, S.C., Teo, T.S., Devaraj, S.: You can't bribe a computer: dealing with the societal challenge of corruption through ICT. MIS Q. **40**(2), 511–526 (2016)
60. Teo, T.S., Srivastava, S.C., Jiang, L.: Trust and electronic government success: an empirical study. J. Manag. Inf. Syst. **25**(3), 99–132 (2008)
61. Tiwana, A., Keil, M.: Control in internal and outsourced systems development projects. J. Manag. Inf. Syst. **26**(3), 9–44 (2010)
62. Transparency International: Global corruption barometer 2003. https://www.transparency. org/whatwedo/publication/gcb_2003. Accessed 5 Dec 2017
63. Transparency International: Global corruption barometer 2013. https://www.transparency. org/gcb2013/report. Accessed 5 Dec 2017
64. Transparency International: Corruption perception index 2016. https://www.transparency. org/news/feature/corruption_perceptions_index_2016. Accessed 2 Dec 2017
65. Treisman, D.: The causes of corruption: a cross-national study. J. Public Econ. **76**(3), 399–457 (2000)
66. Tullock, G.: Efficient rent seeking. In: Buchanan, J.M., Tollison, R.D., Tullock, G. (eds.) Toward a Theory of the Rent-Seeking Society, pp. 97–112. Texas A&M University Press, College Station (1980)
67. UNDP (United Nations Development Programme): Tackling Corruption, Transforming Lives: Accelerating Human Development in Asia and the Pacific. Macmillan Publishers, New Delhi (2008)
68. United Nations: E-government for the people (2012 report). http://www.unpan.org/egovkb/ global_reports/08report.htm. Accessed 15 Nov 2017
69. United Nations: United Nations e-government survey 2016. http://workspace.unpan.org/ sites/Internet/Documents/UNPAN97453.pdf. Accessed 16 Nov 2017

70. UNODC: The global programme against corruption—UN anti-corruption toolkit (2004 report). https://www.unodc.org/documents/corruption/Toolkit_ed2.pdf. Accessed 20 Jan 2018
71. Wescott, C.: E-government in the Asia-Pacific region. Asia J. Polit. Sci. **9**(2), 1–24 (2001)
72. Wong, W., Welch, E.: Does e-government promote accountability? A comparative analysis of website openness and government accountability. Gov. Int. J. Policy Adm. Inst. **17**(2), 275–297 (2004)
73. Yoon, J., Chae, M.: Varying criticality of key success factors of national e-strategy along the status of economic development of nations. Gov. Inf. Q. **26**(1), 25–34 (2009)
74. Khan, A., Krishnan, S.: Investigating the impact of corruption in national institutions and national stakeholder service systems on e-government maturity. Int. J. Inf. Manag. (forthcoming)

Digital Payments Adoption Research: A Meta-Analysis for Generalising the Effects of Attitude, Cost, Innovativeness, Mobility and Price Value on Behavioural Intention

Pushp P. Patil, Nripendra P. Rana, and Yogesh K. Dwivedi[✉]

Emerging Markets Research Centre (EMaRC), School of Management,
Swansea University Bay Campus, Swansea SA1 8EN, UK
pushpppatil@gmail.com, n.p.rana@swansea.ac.uk,
y.k.dwivedi@Swansea.ac.uk

Abstract. The rapid evolution of mobile-based technologies and applications has led to the development of several different forms of digital payment methods (DPMs) but with limited enthusiasm in consumers for adopting them. Hence, several academic studies have already been conducted to examine the role of various antecedents that determines consumers' intention to adopt DPMs. The degree of effect and significance of several antecedents found to be inconsistent across different studies. This provided us a basis for undertaking a meta-analysis of existing research for estimating the cumulative effect of such antecedents. Therefore, this study aims to perform a meta-analysis of five antecedents (i.e. attitude, cost, mobility, price value and innovativeness) for confirming their overall influence on intentions to adopt DPMs. The results of this study suggest that the cumulative effect of four out of five antecedents found to be significant while influence of price value was found insignificant on behavioural intentions. The recommendations drawn from this research would help to decide if and when to use such antecedents for predicting consumer intention to adopt DPMs.

Keywords: Adoption · Cashless payments · Digital payments
Meta-analysis · Mobile payments

1 Introduction

There have been rapid advances in evolution of information and communication technologies (ICT) including wireless handheld devices such as smartphones both in terms of their technological capability and fast reduction in their purchase cost for consumers. Widespread availability of smartphones and other handheld devices with Internet connectivity is providing conducive environment for innovation development and commercialisation in various areas including digital payment methods (DPMs). In the past two decades, a wide range of new functionalities have been developed and added to mobile and portable devices supporting different forms of financial services. These include bill payments, account transfers, person-to-person transfers, electronic point of sales payment, remote payments for purchasing goods and services as well as

A. Elbanna et al. (Eds.): TDIT 2018, IFIP AICT 533, pp. 194–206, 2019.
https://doi.org/10.1007/978-3-030-04315-5_14

other types of services such as mobile marketing, ticketing, discounts or coupon etc. (Oliveira et al. 2016). Majority of consumer oriented DPMs are mobile payment (m-payment) systems, which refer to making payments for goods and services using mobile devices including wireless handsets, personal digital assistants, radio frequency devices and near-field communication based devices (Chen and Nath 2008; Slade et al. 2013; 2014).

Despite the availability of various forms of mobile based DPMs and the encouraging possibility provided by the m-payment systems, their penetration and adoption are relatively low in comparison to the other recent forms of cashless payments mode (or DPMs) including credit card and online payments. For example, only 17.1% of mobile Internet users have ever used m-payments in China whereas in the US, this figure is 12% (Gao and Waechter 2017; Garrett et al. 2014; Zhou 2014). A similar trend of low adoption rates for the m-payment systems have been witnessed in several European countries such as the UK and France (Kapoor et al. 2014a; Slade et al. 2013; 2014). Although m-payment offers a number of benefits including ubiquity, convenience and value to users, it also involves great deal of uncertainty and risk due to virtuality and lack of control (Lin et al. 2014; Yan and Yang 2014), which might have impact on consumer attitude towards emerging DPMs (Hossain and Mahmud 2016; Liebana-cabanillas 2015a, b; Schierz et al. 2010; Tian and Dong 2013). There is a cost for owning appropriate devices, having Internet connectivity and sometime there is a fee for making mobile-based transactions, which may or may not be influencing consumers' intentions towards mobile-based DPMs (Lu et al. 2011; Phonthanukitithaworn et al. 2015; Zhou 2011). Relating to cost and fee, existing research has also examined the role of price value (Oliveira et al. 2016; Slade et al. 2015a). One of the major advantages of mobile-based DPMs over other types of DPMs (such as e-banking) is its portability/mobility from one place to other place, which makes anytime, anywhere payment feasible. Some studies (e.g. Liu 2012; Schierz et al. 2010) have already examined the role of mobility for explaining consumer intention to adopt. However, a number of other studies (e.g. Liebana-cabanillas 2015a, b; Makki et al. 2016; Oliveira et al. 2016; Sam et al. 2014; Slade et al. 2015b; Thakur and Srivastava 2014; Yang et al. 2012) have argued consumer innovativeness as a significant antecedent of consumer intention to adopt DPMs. Considering the importance of such constructs, various existing adoption studies have integrated them with dominant technology adoption models (such as IDT, TAM, UTAUT and UTAUT2) for explaining consumer intention to adopt DPMs. Effects of some of these constructs have been consistent (across different studies) in terms significance but their extent of influence varies across studies. However, for some constructs both significance level and degree of influence vary across different studies.

Integration and synthesis of existing results about these constructs are essential for better understanding of the overall influence of such constructs on intention to adopt DPMs. An initial literature review suggested that there is no existing work yet that has either undertaken systematic literature review or meta-analysis around these constructs in relation to DPMs. Therefore, in order to understand the overall influence (by estimating cumulative effect size) of theoretical constructs (namely, attitude, cost, mobility, price value and innovativeness) on intention to adopt DPMs, *the aim of this study is to undertake the meta-analysis of findings reported in the existing research.* This is to be noted that although there are many other external constructs that are important for explaining intention to and usage of DPMs, the focus of this submission is to review and integrate results of aforementioned five constructs only due to space limitations. This study is part of a larger project so subsequent outputs would cover other important constructs.

The remaining part of this submission is structured as follows: Sect. 2 describes research and analysis method, which is followed by a descriptive review around constructs of interest in Sect. 3. The meta-analysis results are then presented in Sect. 4. Finally, conclusions, limitations and future research directions are presented in Sect. 5.

2   Research Method

The purpose of this study is to analyse and integrate results from existing studies. Hence, the first step was to identify relevant empirical research work on digital payment methods/systems adoption, which was undertaken by employing a keyword-based search. The following keywords were searched in the Scopus database: "Digital Payment" OR "Cashless Payment" OR "Mobile Payment" AND "Adoption" OR "Acceptance" OR "Diffusion" OR "Usage" OR "Intention" OR "Success" OR "Satisfaction". Although 109 studies appeared in initial search results, it was found that only 80 studies were directly appropriate for inclusion in the literature analyses focussed on consumer adoption and use of digital payment methods. It is important to note that some conference papers were not accessible through researcher's library, hence the total number further reduced to 75 studies. A further detailed screening and analysis was conducted to identify various independent variables (IVs) employed to determine influence on different dependent variables (DVs) such as behavioural intention (BI), usage (U), satisfaction and continuance intention. This was achieved by collecting the information regarding name of IVs and DV along with types of relationships (significant, insignificant or conceptual) reported between them (see Tables 1 and 2). Although several different relationships were identified through literature analysis, we decided to focus on 23 existing studies that had examined effects of attitude, cost, mobility, price value and innovativeness on determining intention to adopt digital payment systems. This is simply due to page limits and other reasons as discussed in the previous sections. Further details about these 23 studies have been provided in both Tables 1 and 2.

The second step of this study was to undertake a narrative review for descriptively analysing 23 studies focussing on the effect of each independent construct on behavioural intention, which is presented in Sect. 3. This was then followed by undertaking meta-analysis (quantitatively integrating and synthesising results from existing research) for the purpose of generative cumulative effect sizes and significance values (Dwivedi et al. 2011, 2017). It is a methodical alternative to a qualitative and descriptive literature analysis and praised by many researchers for being better than a literature analysis (Rana et al. 2015; Rosenthal and DiMatteo 2001; Wolf 1986). As illustrated in Table 2, we collected path coefficients relating to each relationship along with sample size in order to perform the meta-analysis, which was conducted using comprehensive meta-analysis software tool. Further details about meta-analysis and results obtained from it are described in Sect. 4.

Table 1. Existing studies that have utilised attitude, cost, mobility, price value and innovativeness as antecedents of behavioural intention

I.V.	D.V.	Sig	Non-sig	App example	Context	Respondent types
AT	BI	Tian and Dong (2013) Liebana-cabanillas (2015a, b) Hossain and Mahmud (2016) Schierz et al. (2010)	None	Mobile payment QR mobile payment system	China Spain Bangladesh Germany	University Students Civil Service College Students Consumers
CO	BI	Hongxia et al. (2011) Lu et al. (2011) Phonthanukitithaworn et al. (2015) Zhou (2011) Yang et al. (2011) Yang et al. (2012)	Yang et al. (2012)	Mobile Payment	China Finland Thailand	University Students Alipay Users Consumers
MO	BI	Liu (2012) Schierz et al. (2010)	Liebana-cabanillas (2015a, b)	Mobile Payment QR Mobile Payment System	China Germany Spain	University Students Consumers
PV	BI	None	Oliveira et al. (2016) Slade et al. (2015a)	Mobile Payment	Portugal UK	University Students Online Consumers
IN	BI	Makki et al. (2016) Slade et al. (2015b) Oliveira et al. (2016) Thakur and Srivastava (2014) Liebana-cabanillas (2015) Yang et al. (2012)	None	NFC Based MP Technology Mobile Payment QR Mobile Payment System	UK India China Portugal Spain USA	Online Consumers University Students Consumers

[Legend: ATT: Attitude; COS: Cost; D.V.: Dependant variable; INN: Innovativeness; I.V.: Independent Variable; MOB: Mobility; PV: Price Value]

3 Descriptive Review

The literature related to areas of digital payments, mobile payments and mobile banking has already been reviewed by existing studies (Patil et al. 2017; Slade et al. 2013, 2014). So, it was not considered necessary to conduct a review on digital or mobile payments in general. Rather, focus of review presented in this section is given on evaluating and summarising the role of constructs (i.e. attitude, cost, mobility, price value and innovativeness) examined in this study. As shown in Table 1, a number of existing studies have already empirically examined the role of antecedents such as

Table 2. Details of Existing studies that have utilised attitude, cost, mobility, price value and innovativeness as antecedents

#	Study	TU	IV	DV	β	p	Sample size
1	Tian and Dong (2013)	TAM, TPB, IDT	AT	BI	0.82	<0.001	178
2	Liebana-cabanillas (2015a, b)	TAM, TRA, IDT	AT	BI	0.917	<0.001	168
3	Hossain and Mahmud (2016)	TAM + AT	AT	BI	0.797	<0.001	75
4	Schierz et al. (2010)	TAM, TRA, IDT	AT	BI	0.24	<0.01	1447
5	Hongxia et al. (2011)	UTAUT	CO	BI	−0.27	< 0.01	186
6	Lu et al. (2011)	Trust Transfer Theory + IDT	PCO	BI	−0.072	< 0.05	961
7	Phonthanukitithaworn et al. (2015)	TAM, TRA, IDT	PCO	BI	−0.128	<0.05	265
8	Zhou (2011)	TAM	PCO	UI	−0.26	<0.001	277
9	Yang et al. (2011)	IDT	PFE	BI	−0.163	<0.05	157
10	Yang et al. (2012)	IDT	PFE	BI	−0.071	<0.05	483
11	Yang et al. (2012)	IDT	PFE	BI	−0.013	ns	156
12	Liu (2012)	IDT	MO	BI	0.143	<0.05	177
13	Schierz et al. (2010)	TAM, TRA, IDT	IMO	BI	0.07	<0.01	1447
14	Liebana-cabanillas (2015a, b)	TAM, TRA, IDT	IMO	BI	0.032	0.768 (ns)	168
15	Oliveira et al. (2016)	UTAUT2, IDT	PV	BI	0.03	ns	301
16	Slade et al. (2015a)	UTAUT2	PV	BI	−0.024	0.847 (ns)	244
17	Makki et al. (2016)	SE + Risk	IN	BI	0.38	<0.01	450
18	Slade et al. (2015b)	UTAUT	IN	BI	0.22	<0.001	268
19	Oliveira et al. (2016)	UTAUT2, IDT	IN	BI	0.16	<0.01	301
20	Thakur and Srivastava (2014)	TAM	PIN	BI	0.13	<0.001	803
21	Liebana-cabanillas (2015a, b)	TAM, TRA, IDT	PIN	BI	0.244	0.014	168
22	Yang et al. (2012)	IDT	PIN	BI	0.2	<0.001	483
23	Yang et al. (2012)	IDT	PIN	BI	0.263	<0.01	156

Legend: AT = Attitude; β = Path coefficient (Beta); BI = Behavioural Intention; C = Cost; DV = Dependent Variables; IDT = Innovation Diffusion Theory; IN = Innovativeness; IV = Independent Variable; IMO = Individual Mobility; MO = Mobility; ns = non-significant; p = Significance; PCO = Perceived Cost; PFE = Perceived Fee; PIN = Personal Innovativeness; PV = Perceived Value; SE = Self Efficacy; TAM = Technology Acceptance Model; TPB = Theory of Planned Behaviour; TRA = Theory of Reasoned Action; TU = Theory Used; UI = Usage Intention; UTAUT = Unified Theory of Acceptance and Usage of Technology; UTAUT2 = Extended Unified Theory of Acceptance and Use of Technology attitude, cost, mobility, price value and innovativeness. A brief discussion about these studies is provided in remaining part of this section.

As listed in Table 1, four existing studies (Hossain and Mahmud 2016; Liebana-cabanillas 2015a, b; Schierz et al. 2010; Tian and Dong 2013) have examined the role of attitude for determining consumer intention to adopt digital payment systems in the contexts of both developed (Germany) and developing (Bangladesh, China and Spain) countries. The results suggest that the attitude has significant influence on consumer intention across all four studies. This may provide the case for employing this construct for further examination of emerging digital payment systems adoption across various contexts subject to demonstrating significant cumulative effect size across all existing work. This will be in line with recommendation from a recent meta-analytic study (Dwivedi et al. 2017) that argued for considering role of attitude as a core to a modified UTAUT model.

Five studies (e.g. Lu et al. 2011; Phonthanukitithaworn et al. 2015; Zhou 2011) have examined and reported significant effect of Cost/Perceived Cost/Perceived Fee on BI but only one such study (Yang et al. 2012) has reported non-significant effect of this construct. The effect of cost has been found significant in the context of both developed (Finland) and developing (China and Thailand) countries. Contrastingly, two existing studies (Oliveira et al. 2016; Slade et al. 2015a) reported non-significant effect of a similar construct (Price Value from UTAUT2 Theory) for explaining consumer BI. This suggests a synthesis of existing results using method such as meta-analysis is needed in order to establish whether cost or perceived value is a more relevant construct for examining issues related to digital payment adoption.

The role of 'mobility' as an antecedent of consumer intention to adopt has been examined by three existing studies with two reporting significant (Liu 2012; Schierz et al. 2010) influence in the context of China and Germany and one with non-significant effect (Liebana-cabanillas 2015a, b) in a Spanish context. Given the inconsistency in existing results relating to this construct, it was deemed appropriate to estimate overall effect size and significance of this construct by employing a meta-analytic approach.

Existing literature of innovation adoption (Kapoor et al. 2014b, c) has argued and illustrated important role of 'innovativeness' towards influencing intention formation for variety of systems in various contexts. In line with this, seven existing studies (Liebana-cabanillas 2015a, b; Makki et al. 2016; Oliveira et al. 2016; Sam et al. 2014; Slade et al. 2015b; Thakur and Srivastava 2014; Yang et al. 2012) have examined the role of innovativeness for determining intention to adopt digital payment systems in various contexts namely the UK, India, China, Portugal, Spain and the USA. All these studies have suggested that innovativeness consistently exerts significant influence on BI to adopt digital payment systems in a variety of contexts. This shows that innovativeness is a relatively robust and important construct, hence should be considered by future adoption studies in this and other similar domains. Therefore, it was considered appropriate to establish its cumulative effect size using meta-analysis approach.

Literature presented in Table 1 also suggests that existing studies have mainly examined issues related to mobile-based payment methods, mobile payment devices such as smartphones, NFC, contactless mobile payments and QR mobile payment system. This suggests that other forms of digital payments[1] are yet to be examined. Hence, the term digital payments in this paper largely represents mobile payments and may have less relevance for any other forms of digital payments.

4 Meta-Analysis

Table 2 presents data (path coefficients (β), significance (p) and sample size) utilised for conducting meta-analysis for relationships between IVs (attitude, cost, price value, mobility and innovativeness) and behavioural intention to adopt digital payment methods that have occurred two or more times across 23 existing studies. Table 2 also presents different theories and models employed by the existing studies that have examined these constructs. Details of constructs and their path-coefficients with BI presented in this table suggest that these constructs were integrated with frequently utilised adoption and diffusion theories and models such as Theory of Reasoned Action (TRA), Technology Acceptance Model (TAM), Theory of Planned Behaviour (TPB), Innovation Diffusion Theory (IDT), UTAUT/UTAUT2 theories, Trust Transfer Theory and self-efficacy and risk constructs. Table 2 also suggests that in a number of studies (#1, 2, 3, 5, 7, 8, 9, 11, 12, 14, 16, 18, 21, 23 in Table 2) sample size was below 300, which is frequently recommended minimum threshold for theory testing particularly for studies that have utilised SEM as a theory testing technique. This may have impact on generalisability and validity of results reported by these studies. This provides added reason and basis for conducting the meta-analysis, which utilise cumulative sample size to overcome such problems. Table 2 also illustrates that some relationships are reported significant by some studies whilst non-significant by some other studies leading to inconsistency and lack of generalisation. In such scenario, meta-analysis helps to determine overall significance of such relationships with inconsistent p values.

Table 3 presents the results generated from the meta-analysis. In addition to the independent (IV) and dependent (DV) variables, the table presents the number of times the specific relationships were examined, total sample size (TSS) for relationships across different studies, effect size (β), 95% lower (L(β)) and upper U(β) confidence intervals and significance level for effect size (β) (i.e. p(ES)) as part of meta-analysis for all relationships examined.

The meta-analysis results indicate that four from five relationships are significant. There are relatively strong links between attitude and behavioural intention ($\beta = 0.767$, $p = 0.006$) and innovativeness and intention ($\beta = 0.227$, $p = 0.000$). Two relationships (Cost-BI and Mobility- BI) are found to be overall significant but with relatively low strength in terms of effect size. The results also demonstrate that the cost has negative influence on BI. The findings also suggest that cumulative effect of causal relationship between Perceived Value (PV) and BI was found to be non-significant. Moreover, the 95% confidence intervals for the ES(β) between MOB-BI and INN-BI presented in Table 3 indicate that their range difference (i.e. 95% High (β) - 95% Low (β)) of less

---

[1] http://cashlessindia.gov.in/digital_payment_methods.html.

Table 3. Meta-analysis results

IV	DV	TSS	#	Effect size (β)	95% L(β)	95% U(β)	p(ES)
ATT	BI	1868	4	0.767	0.279	0.940	0.006
COS	BI	2485	7	−0.135	−0.203	−0.066	0.000
MOB	BI	1792	3	0.074	0.027	0.120	0.002
PV	BI	545	2	0.006	−0.078	0.090	0.892
INN	BI	2629	7	0.227	0.152	0.300	0.000

[**Legend:** #: Number of studies; ATT: Attitude; COS: Cost; DV: Dependant variable; ES(β): Meta-analysis effect size; INN: Innovativeness/Innovation; IV: Independent Variable; LL: Lower Limit (Beta); MOB: Mobility; p(ES): Meta-analysis significance; PV: Price Value; TSS: Total sample size; UL: Upper Limit (Beta)]

than two, which is narrow enough to provide one confidence to the level of variance that could be explained.

5 Discussions

Figure 1 presents a meta-analytic model with antecedents of BI for digital payment systems. Figure 1 provides a visual representation of all relationships (strengths in terms of path coefficients and significance) examined in this study. As presented in Table 3, the model clearly indicates that attitude, cost, mobility and innovativeness are significant predictors of BI.

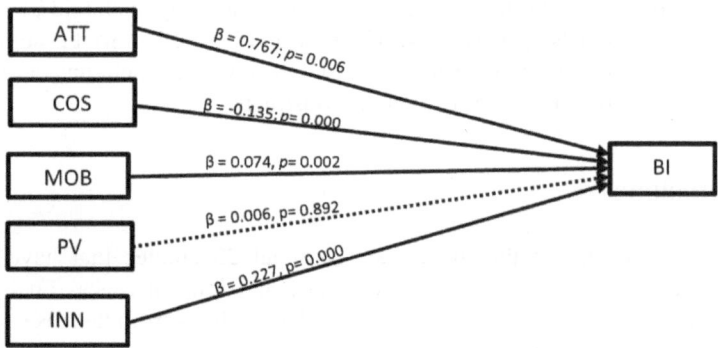

Fig. 1. Influence of attitude, cost, mobility, price value and innovativeness as per results obtained from meta-analysis

Both studies (i.e. Oliveira et al. 2016; Slade et al. 2015a) that had examined role of price value found that its effect on BI was non-significant. The meta-analysis result is in line with these two previous studies, as shown in Fig. 1 where PV has non-significant effect on BI. According to Slade et al. (2015a) effect of this construct on BI was non-significant possibly due to type of sample employed for data collection. They collected data from non-adopters of mobile payments, which possibly "unable to evaluate whether NFC MPs represent value for money" (Slade et al. 2015a, p. 218) as respondents had not experienced actual benefits that can be gained by using mobile payments. Oliveira et al. (2016) provided no reason why effect of price value was non-significant. However, it was noted that they collected data from students who were more likely to be non-adopters than adopters, and so they might have been unable to evaluate trade-off between price for acquiring and using such technologies and benefits obtained from using it. In conclusion, both studies have utilised same questions to measure this construct and similar data sample employed to collect data, which suggest a strong possibility of non-significance due to data collected from non-adopters. So in order to confirm whether this construct is still relevant for investigating digital payment adoption, it is suggested that the future studies should test its effect on BI using data collected from adopters.

Other salient finding of this meta-analysis is that attitude plays an extremely strong and central role for determining BI to adopt mobile payment systems. This is not in line with dominant adoption models such as TAM, UTAUT and UTAUT2 as they excluded attitude construct from their core model. However, the central role of attitude for influencing BI is in line with recommendations from recent studies (Dwivedi et al. 2017a, 2017b; Rana et al. 2017; 2016; Williams et al. 2015) that have found that attitude significantly influences BI in technology adoption research. Dwivedi et al. (2017a) argued that aforementioned models measure technological and environmental attributes but they lack individual attributes. They demonstrated this based on a meta-analysis of a large number studies that utilised attitude along other UTAUT constructs, which was also tested by utilising primary data and found similar results (Dwivedi et al. 2017b; Rana et al. 2016, 2017). Given that attitude is a well tried and tested construct in various domains including information systems and marketing, it should be included as an integral part of models such as TAM, UTAUT and UTAUT2. So it is suggested that future studies in mobile payment adoption should consider including attitude as an antecedent of both BI and actual behaviour constructs.

6 Conclusions

This study has performed the meta-analysis of all 23 studies that have examined influence of attitude, cost, mobility, price value and innovativeness on behavioural intention to adopt digital (m-payment) systems. The findings from this research suggest that attitude, cost, mobility and innovativeness are significant antecedents of consumers' intention to adopt digital (m-payment) systems. However, effect of price value on consumers' intention to adopt was found as non-significant. Both attitude and innovativeness emerged as stronger predictors in comparison to cost and mobility. Although effect of cost is relatively less strong (yet significant), results confirmed that it has negative influence on the intention to adopt. Hence, it is recommended that future studies employing intention-based theories/models for examining digital (mobile) payment adoption should integrate attitude and innovativeness as antecedents of intention along with other standard antecedents from respective theories/models. Cost/perceived cost/perceived fee should be considered as an external construct in an adoption model only when there is some form of charge/fee/commission being deducted per transaction either by mobile payment providers and/or their partners. Mobility construct should be carefully considered in terms of its measurements utilised to collect data and context of the study in order to gain stronger effect. Finally, it would be fruitful not to utilise price value construct if data is being collected from non-adopters due to its inconsistent and non-significant performance. Both cost and price value are conceptually similar in nature, but cost is better defined than later. For this reason, it would be better to consider cost as an alternative to price value when determining intention to adopt mobile payment systems.

6.1   Limitations and Future Research Directions

There are few limitations that need to be accounted when interpreting results of this study. Only a limited number of studies have utilised antecedents meta-analysed in this research, so results of this study may not hold in differing contexts. Therefore, further observations and analyses are needed to confirm if results of this study are applicable in diverse contexts. The future research may also increase the number of studies used for meta-analysis by considering other forms of digital payment ecosystems and emerging FinTech applications. This study has utilised only Scopus database for identifying relevant research articles so studies that are not indexed in this database would have been excluded from being considered for this meta-analysis. This study included only five antecedents of BI but there are other important antecedents and results about them, which also need to be considered in future meta-analysis based studies. A recent study by Patil et al. (2018) has conducted a meta-analysis on the role of Trust and Risk constructs on determining BI. Similarly, role of other constructs such as anxiety, privacy, security, self-efficacy and core constructs of various adoption models should also be examined. The future research can comprehensively search the related keywords across all other databases and Google Scholar to maximise the number of potential studies to perform meta-analysis. In this study, effect of each construct is individually estimated. It is recommended that future studies should also conduct meta-regression or meta-analytic structural equation modelling (MASEM) for testing effect of all constructs together at one time (See Dwivedi et al. 2017a as an example). The future research can also collect primary data for different constructs presented in the proposed conceptual model and validate the performance of the proposed research model.

References

Chen, L.-D., Nath, R.: Determinants of mobile payments: an empirical analysis. J. Int. Technol. Inf. Manag. **17**(1), 2 (2008)

Dwivedi, Y.K., Rana, N.P., Jeyaraj, A., Clement, M., Williams, M.D.: Re-examining the Unified theory of acceptance and use of technology (UTAUT): towards a revised theoretical model. Inf. Syst. Front. (2017a). https://doi.org/10.1007/s10796-017-9774-y

Dwivedi, Y.K., Rana, N.P., Janssen, M., Lal, B., Williams, M.D., Clement, R.M.: An empirical validation of a unified model of electronic government adoption (UMEGA). Govern. Inf. Q. **34**(2), 211–230 (2017)

Dwivedi, Yogesh K., Rana, Nripendra P., Chen, H., Williams, Michael D.: A meta-analysis of the unified theory of acceptance and use of technology (UTAUT). In: Nüttgens, M., Gadatsch, A., Kautz, K., Schirmer, I., Blinn, N. (eds.) TDIT 2011. IAICT, vol. 366, pp. 155–170. Springer, Heidelberg (2011). https://doi.org/10.1007/978-3-642-24148-2_10

Gao, L., Waechter, K.A.: Examining the role of initial trust in user adoption of mobile payment services: an empirical investigation. Inf. Syst. Front. **19**(3), 525–548 (2017)

Garrett, J.L., Rodermund, R., Anderson, N., Berkowitz, S., Robb, C.A.: Adoption of mobile payment technology by consumers. Fam. Consum. Sci. Res. J. **42**(4), 358–368 (2014)

Hongxia, P., Xianhao, X., Weidan, L.: Drivers and barriers in the acceptance of mobile payment in China. In: 2011 International Conference on E-Business and E-Government, pp. 1–4, May 2011

Hossain, R., Mahmud, I.: Influence of cognitive style on mobile payment system adoption: an extended technology acceptance model. In: International Conference on Computer Communication and Informatics, pp. 1–6 (2016)

Kapoor, K.K., Dwivedi, Y.K., Williams, M.D.: Examining the role of three sets of innovation attributes for determining adoption of the interbank mobile payment service. Inf. Syst. Front. **17**(5), 1039–1056 (2014a)

Kapoor, K.K., Dwivedi, Y.K., Williams, M.D.: Rogers' innovation adoption attributes: a systematic review and synthesis of existing research. Inf. Syst. Manag. **31**(1), 74–91 (2014b)

Kapoor, K.K., Dwivedi, Y.K., Williams, M.D.: Innovation adoption attributes: a review and synthesis of research findings. Eur. J. Innov. Manag. **17**(3), 327–348 (2014c)

Liébana-Cabanillas, F., Muñoz-Leiva, F., Sánchez-Fernández, J.: Influence of age in the adoption of new mobile payment systems. Revista Brasileira de Gestão de Negócios **17**(58), 1390–1407 (2015a)

Liébana-Cabanillas, F., Ramos de Luna, I., Montoro-Ríos, F.J.: User behaviour in QR mobile payment system: the QR payment acceptance model. Technol. Anal. Strat. Manag. **27**(9), 1031–1049 (2015b)

Lin, J., Wang, B., Wang, N., Lu, Y.: Understanding the evolution of consumer trust in mobile commerce: a longitudinal study. Inf. Technol. Manag. **15**(1), 37–49 (2014)

Liu, B.: Understanding consumers' intention to use mobile payment services: the perspective of university students in northern Jiangsu area. In: Proceedings of Second International Conference on Business Computing and Global Informatization, pp. 257–260 (2012)

Lu, Y., Yang, S., Chau, P.Y., Cao, Y.: Dynamics between the trust transfer process and intention to use mobile payment services: a cross-environment perspective. Inf. Manag. **48**(8), 393–403 (2011)

Makki, A.M., Ozturk, A.B., Singh, D.: Role of risk, self-efficacy, and innovativeness on behavioral intentions for mobile payment systems in the restaurant industry. J. Foodservice Bus. Res. **19**(5), 454–473 (2016)

Oliveira, T., Thomas, M., Baptista, G., Campos, F.: Mobile payment: understanding the determinants of customer adoption and intention to recommend the technology. Comput. Hum. Behav. **61**, 404–414 (2016)

Patil, P.P., Rana, N.P., Dwivedi, Y.K., Abu-Hamour, H.M.J.: The role of trust and risk in mobile payments adoption: a meta-analytic review. In: Proceedings of Pacific Asia Conference on Information Systems, Japan (2018)>

Patil, Pushp P., Dwivedi, Yogesh K., Rana, Nripendra P.: Digital payments adoption: an analysis of literature. In: Kar, A.K., Ilavarasan, P.Vigneswara, Gupta, M.P., Dwivedi, Yogesh K., Mäntymäki, M., Janssen, M., Simintiras, A., Al-Sharhan, S. (eds.) I3E 2017. LNCS, vol. 10595, pp. 61–70. Springer, Cham (2017). https://doi.org/10.1007/978-3-319-68557-1_7

Phonthanukitithaworn, C., Sellitto, C., Fong, M.: User intentions to adopt mobile payment services: a study of early adopters in Thailand. J. Internet Bank. Commer. **20**(1), 1–29 (2015)

Rana, N.P., Dwivedi, Y.K., Williams, M.D.: A meta-analysis application for synthesizing findings of existing research on citizen adoption of e-government. Inf. Syst. Front. **17**(3), 547–563 (2015)

Rana, N.P., Dwivedi, Y.K., Lal, B., Williams, M.D., Clement, M.: Citizens' adoption of an electronic government system: towards a unified view. Inf. Syst. Front. **19**(3), 549–568 (2017)

Rana, N.P., Dwivedi, Y.K., Williams, M.D., Weerakkody, V.: Adoption of online public grievance redressal system in India: toward developing a unified view. Comput. Hum. Behav. **59**, 265–282 (2016)

Rosenthal, R., DiMatteo, M.R.: Meta-analysis: recent developments in quantitative methods for literature reviews. Ann. Rev. Psychol. **52**(1), 59–82 (2001)

Sam, K.M., Chatwin, C.R., Zhang, J.X.: Adoption of near field communication for mobile payment: Evidence from Macau. In: 2014 IEEE International Conference on Industrial Engineering and Engineering Management (IEEM), pp. 1121–1125. IEEE (2014)

Schierz, P.G., Schilke, O., Wirtz, B.W.: Understanding consumer acceptance of mobile payment services: An empirical analysis. Electron. Commer. Res. Appl. **9**(3), 209–216 (2010)

Slade, E., Williams, M.D., Dwivedi, Y.K.: Mobile payment adoption: classification and review of the extant literature. Market. Rev. **13**(2), 167–190 (2013)

Slade, E., Williams, M.D., Dwivedi, Y.K.: Devising a research model to examine adoption of mobile payments: an extension of UTAUT2. Market. Rev. **14**(3), 310–335 (2014)

Slade, E., Williams, M., Dwivedi, Y., Piercy, N.: Exploring consumer adoption of proximity mobile payments. J. Strat. Market. **23**(3), 209–223 (2015a)

Slade, E.L., Dwivedi, Y.K., Piercy, N.C., Williams, M.D.: Modeling consumers' adoption intentions of remote mobile payments in the United Kingdom: extending UTAUT with innovativeness, risk, and trust. Psychol. Market. **32**(8), 860–873 (2015b)

Thakur, R., Srivastava, M.: Adoption readiness, personal innovativeness, perceived risk and usage intention across customer groups for mobile payment services in India. Internet Res. **24**(3), 369–392 (2014)

Tian, Y., Dong, H.: An analysis of key factors affecting user acceptance of mobile payment. In: Second International Conference on Informatics and Applications, pp. 240–246 (2013)

Williams, M.D., Rana, N.P., Dwivedi, Y.K.: The unified theory of acceptance and use of technology (UTAUT): a literature review. J. Enterpr. Inf. Manag. **28**(3), 443–488 (2015)

Wolf, F.M.: Meta-Analysis: Quantitative Methods for Research Synthesis. Sage, Beverly Hills (1986)

Yan, H., Yang, Z.: An empirical examination of user adoption mobile payment. In: Paper presented at the Proceedings - 2014 International Conference on Management of e-Commerce and e-Government, ICMeCG 2014, pp. 156–162 (2014). https://doi.org/10.1109/icmecg.2014.40

Yang, S., Cao, Y., Mao, W., Zhang, R., Luo, L.: Determinants of behavioral intention to mobile payment: evidence from China. In: 7th International Conference on Advanced Information Management and Service, pp. 151–154 (2011)>

Yang, S., Lu, Y., Gupta, S., Cao, Y., Zhang, R.: Mobile payment services adoption across time: an empirical study of the effects of behavioral beliefs, social influences, and personal traits. Comput. Hum. Behav. **28**(1), 129–142 (2012)

Zhou, T.: The effect of initial trust on user adoption of mobile payment. Inf. Develop. **27**(4), 290–300 (2011)

Zhou, T.: Understanding the determinants of mobile payment continuance usage. Industr. Manag. Data Syst. **114**(6), 936–948 (2014)

IT Project Management

Conceptualizing the Transition from Agile to DevOps: A Maturity Model for a Smarter IS Function

Aymeric Hemon[1(✉)], Barbara Lyonnet[1], Frantz Rowe[1,3], and Brian Fitzgerald[2]

[1] University of Nantes, LEMNA, Chemin de la Censive du Tertre, Bâtiment Erdre, 44322 Nantes, France
{aymeric.hemon,barbara.lyonnet, frantz.rowe}@univ-nantes.fr
[2] University of Limerick, LERO, Castletroy, Limerick V94 T9PX, Ireland
brian.fitzgerald@ul.ie
[3] SKEMA Business School, KTO, Sophia Antipolis, France

Abstract. Agile development approaches have become the norm for almost all software development now. While agile approaches can deliver more frequent releases of working software, it quickly became apparent in many organisations that they were not able to leverage these frequent releases due to the disconnect between the development and operations functions, with the latter typically responsible for releasing software to customers. This resulted in the move towards closer integration of these functions through the DevOps movement. As the trend towards digitalisation continues, companies are increasingly implementing DevOps. We propose a maturity model for this agile to DevOps transition with three levels: agile, continuous integration, continuous delivery. Based on an in-depth case study in an organisation which has several years' experience of DevOps, we identify a fundamental disruption in the soft skills and competences that software teams are expected to possess, and in the patterns of collaboration among teams. The latter is especially salient for release managers, project managers, production engineers and even architects. Arguably, smartness may be characterized as being flexible, teaming up with people who have a different profile, belonging to a different function, and delivering more quickly what had been designed. In light of this, we argue that DevOps leads to greater smartness for the Information Systems (IS) function.

Keywords: DevOps · Agile · Roles · Skills · Collaboration

1 Introduction

Agile methods seek to ensure a close link between the customer and developers to ensure that software meets market needs. Agile methods also strive for a more rapid release schedule. However, while agile methods can achieve a more frequent cadence of development of software, a bottleneck has emerged in that the Operations function (Ops), who coordinate the actual release of software in organizations, are typically not

© IFIP International Federation for Information Processing 2019
Published by Springer Nature Switzerland AG 2019.
A. Elbanna et al. (Eds.): TDIT 2018, IFIP AICT 533, pp. 209–223, 2019.
https://doi.org/10.1007/978-3-030-04315-5_15

aligned with the Development function (Dev). A release could take weeks to be launched. Consequently, organizations were not able to achieve faster software releases to customers. In order to solve this problem, Debois advocated a tighter integration between the Dev and Ops functions which is termed DevOps [1–3].

Emerging as it did from practice, there is not a great deal of work thus far outlining the conceptual or theoretical underpinnings of DevOps. A similar situation occurred in the case of agile methods, which was also practice-led, and some important definitional work appeared later [4]. We believe that many companies are in the transition from agile to DevOps, and we suggest three maturity levels to reflect this: Agile, Continuous Integration, Continuous Delivery. Each level builds cumulatively on the previous one. We analyse five key job roles in DevOps (Release Manager, Architect, Product Owner, Department/Project Manager and Production Engineer) and describe the key collaborations across these and other DevOps roles. We then describe the skills for each of these roles, dividing them into 'hard' and 'soft' skills [5, 6]. We consider how soft skills (SSk) vary by level of maturity.

The paper is structured as follows. In Sect. 2, we discuss other relevant work in this area. Section 3 presents our research method and Sect. 4 our findings. Finally, Sect. 5 discusses the implications of our findings for research and practice.

2 Literature

2.1 Roles, Skills and Competencies of Information Technology (IT) Jobs

"A skill is a combination of ability, knowledge and experience that enables a person to do something well" [7]. Skills are specific to a domain and developed by practice [7]. Hard skills refer to the ability to perform, to do something well, using knowledge, techniques, practices. Robles [8] defines "soft skills as intangible, nontechnical, personality-specific skills that determine one's strengths as a leader, facilitator, mediator, and negotiator" (see Table 1). This paper will focus on SSk.

Gallivan et al. [5] identify a "long history of IT-skills studies" which suggest that soft or non-technical skills are more important. Wong [6] also emphasises the relative importance of SSk – flexibility, adaptability, motivation and good communication. Non-technical skills include interpersonal, leadership, organization, independence/motivation, and creativity skills. However, studies found that non-technical skills were far less valued than technical skills in recruitment advertisements. They concluded that despite the emphasis on hiring well rounded employees with good business knowledge and SSk, the recruitment process focuses on "hard skills" because they were easier to screen. Thus, they confirmed the "recruitment gap" that had been identified earlier [9, 10]. This lack of recognition is harmful as some SSk have been identified as important in agile software teams [11]. In addition, Wiedemann et al. [12] investigated key capabilities of DevOps teams which could foster competitive advantage. They identified seven key capabilities (Change Readiness, Decision Making, Culture, Collaboration, Intrapreneurship Skills, Agile Project Management, IT Technical Skills, Continuous Skills). However, they mixed capabilities with skills without determining precisely which skills were a source of competitive advantage. In their study, they

Table 1. Soft Skills (SSk) as identified by Robles (2012)

•(CS) Communication – oral, speaking capability, written, presenting, listening
•Courtesy – manners, etiquette, business etiquette, gracious, respectful
•(FS) Flexibility – adaptability, willing to change, lifelong learner, accepts new things, adjusts, teachable
•Integrity – honest, ethical, high morals, has personal values, does what's right
•(ISk) Interpersonal Skills – nice, personable, sense of humor, friendly, nurturing, empathetic, has self-control, patient, sociability, warmth, social skills
•Positive attitude – optimistic, enthusiastic, encouraging, happy, confident
•Professionalism – businesslike, well-dressed, appearance, poised
•(RS) Responsibility – accountable, reliable, gets the job done, resourceful, self-disciplined, wants to do well, conscientious, common sense
•(TS) Teamwork – cooperative, gets along with others, agreeable, supportive, helpful
•Work Ethic – hard working, loyal, initiative, self-motivated, on time/attendance

suggested some ways to foster collaboration within DevOps team but did not specify the extent of such collaboration. In a companion study focusing on new forms of collaboration, Wiedemann [13] highlighted assimilation stages of innovation within DevOps teams but did not consider the question of the extent of the collaboration. Hence our research questions:

- To what extent are soft skills perceived as important by IS Function members transitioning from agile to DevOps?
- What are the implications for collaboration when transitioning to DevOps?

2.2   Agile, DevOps and IT Jobs

Agility is defined as "the continual readiness of an entity to rapidly or inherently, proactively or reactively, embrace change, through high quality, simplistic, economical components and relationships with its environment" [14]. Agile methods arise from the inability of conventional methods, i.e. Waterfall, to give satisfaction in a changing environment [15]. DevOps initiative was launched to extend the movement towards the agile by including Operations and Quality. The idea was to solve the problem of bottleneck present when Development teams were delivering to Operations faster and more frequently. Thus, agile methods form a base for DevOps. Agile methods impact teams as well as jobs on management styles, collaboration, control, new skills set, training or recruitment [16–18]. DevOps philosophy leads to build bridges between Development and Operations teams. DevOps foster the creation of cross-functional teams where each team member need to consider and anticipate the job to be done by other members. For example, developers need to understand real-world production environment where their colleagues will release the code. In the same way, Operations need to integrate the way Developers will produce the code, will test it and will build the delivery package. It is therefore fundamental in a DevOps configuration to increase test automation [19] to optimize end-to-end deployment processes. Indeed, "automation is the key to efficient collaboration and tight integration between development and operations" [20].

2.3 Roles, Competencies of IT Jobs in the Transition from Agile to DevOps

Humble et al. [21] presented four core values for DevOps: Culture, Automation, Measurement and Sharing. In the recent DevOps handbook, Kim et al. [22] suggest that "a high-trust culture that enables all departments to work together effectively, where all work is transparently prioritized and there is sufficient slack in the system to allow high-priority work to be completed quickly". In the IS literature, Ghobadi and Mathiassen [23] study knowledge-sharing barriers in agile software teams. Knowledge sharing is important in these teams as it is essential for collaboration across different specialties. They focus on four jobs: user representative, project manager, developer and tester. While tester can be part of development teams, they can also be considered as part of the operations. In this paper, we focus on the jobs which are a priori most impacted by DevOps in terms of skills and competencies. In consultation with industry experts, we selected five jobs of core interest: (1) product owner (a more commonly used title than user representative), (2) managers, (3) architects, (4) production engineers who perform the tests as Ops (in fact developers also perform tests in a DevOps mode), (5) release managers. We did not consider developers in this paper. Although developers are certainly also impacted in the way they share knowledge and collaborate, we did not see particular high challenges for them in moving towards DevOps, while greater challenges were identified and anticipated for others. This view was confirmed by the industry experts. The main argument was that the core activity for developers is coding and that while they would have to take into account additional factors when coding in a DevOps context, the coding role would still be central, and they would not have to evolve as much as others.

The **Product Owner (PO)** role is essential when working in agile with Scrum. POs play a dual role, as representative of the client needs, but also with a real operational role that links the business to project management. POs are responsible for optimizing the value of what development teams produce. Autonomy is essential for POs to succeed and their decisions must be respected by all stakeholders [24, 25]. There is some debate as to whether POs can also act as project managers (PM). They can definitely be managers as indicated in the Scrum guide, "Product Owner is the sole person responsible for managing the Product Backlog" [25]. However, there is no clear indication regarding project management in the Scrum method. The Scrum guide mentions that "Scrum Teams are self-organizing and cross-functional. Self-organizing teams choose how best to accomplish their work, rather than being directed by others outside the team" and "Scrum recognizes no titles for Development Team members other than Developer, regardless of the work being performed by the person" [25]. Therefore, this means implicitly that self-organization is compulsory which avoids the possibility for the team to be managed by a PM from the team or external to the team. Theoretically in the Scrum method, POs are managers, but not PM. POs are associated with business ownership and not project management even if they are accountable for the product backlog management and the final product delivery. However, in reality a PO can also assume the function of PM. Beyond, the distinction between the PO and the PM, some studies mix the PM profile with Scrum Master (SM) profile to identify Scrum Product Owner competences [26].

The notion of **Manager** (**DPM** for Department & Project Manager) is very large, and the literature contains many definitions. In our conception, a manager is a person with the responsibility to deal with resources, tangible and intangible, to serve a specific objective. The Managers may be project leaders or simply team leaders, or both. It is simply a feature of the hierarchy that often places these two roles in the same person. Others like SM are either not always present or are played by the more traditional role of developer or PM. Team Managers (TM) include different professions: development/operational or supervisory team leader, and qualification-integration manager. PM define and manage an IT project from conception to delivery to get an optimal result for customer requirements of quality, performance, cost, time and security. The **architect** (**AR**) role is evolving. The AR is often brought to develop multiple skills, whether it is a technical AR, a software-application AR, or a functional AR. On the Ops side, **Production Engineers** (**PE**) or production integrators and testers are responsible for production, operations, incident monitoring, support and user support. PEs participate in the development of architectural files and the production of applications. PEs also provide the expertise and support for incident resolution. Finally, on the Ops side, the **Release Manager** (**RM**) is key to ensuring the success of projects. RMs are responsible for the deployment processes. They follow the different versions and coordinate between the development and test teams and the deployment teams. The RM is associated, in the French context, with the function of PM Implementation. This is an essential activity but the scope is questioned by DevOps. We investigated to what extent SSk were perceived as important by these five roles when transitioning from agile to DevOps and the implications for collaboration (See Fig. 1).

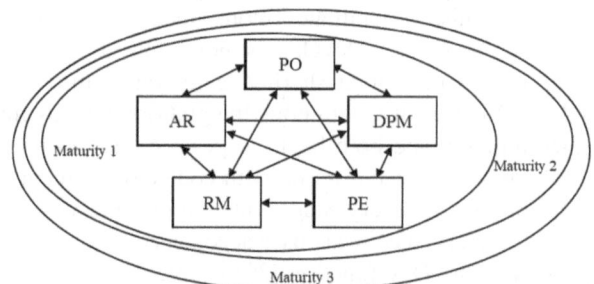

Mat.1: Agile moving towards DevOps / Mat.2: Continuous Integration /
Mat.3: Continuous Delivery

Fig. 1. Existing 5 Roles related to 3 Maturity Levels

3   Methodology

This study was conducted in a large European services firm with thousands of IT Staff using agile methods since 2010 and DevOps since 2016.

We followed case study method combining interviews, observations and documentation [27]. We studied 5 job roles and their scope of collaboration in 11 project teams, which involved 54 in-depth face to face individual interviews (these were recorded and lasted 90 min on average). About DPM, we interviewed six PM and six TM. Interviews were conducted by three interviewers and were subsequently transcribed and coded. Codification was triangulated to verify if codes were consistent and similar. This can be viewed as an embedded case study, where job roles are embedded in teams and are centered on collaborative relationships with other job roles.

First, a review of the literature identified the appropriate criteria for selecting the sample of 54 individuals. Second, we observed and interviewed four teams for 15 days (mat. 2 and 3) to compare elements in the literature and those in practice, i.e. size of the team, agile to DevOps maturity (as per our model), and level of externalization. Third, we conducted a series of interviews with 12 strategists in IS and Human Resources, to incorporate their vision and to validate the selected sample.

Three criteria were retained to select the sample: 1- the size of the project measured in terms of number of staff assigned to the project [28] with small project equal to or less than 14 people and large project larger than 15 people; 2- the outsourcing policy and more precisely the degree and nature of outsourcing on the project, e.g. we realized that fixed-price contracts can pose specific problems when working in agile mode. We contrasted two situations: some project activities carried out in work package and fixed price mode, and project without outsourcing or with an outsourced technical assistance contract; 3- the level of maturity in terms of the agile to DevOps transition as presented in Sect. 2.3 above. All theoretically possible configurations allowed us to identify 12 distinct types of projects. This document covers 11 projects whose analysis has been completed. The case of fixed-price outsourcing, maturity level 2 and large project was not completed. Then, agile stage: agile can be considered maturity level 1 in the transition to DevOps, because it facilitates more frequent releases as development becomes more iterative. However, DevOps is not realized because Dev and Ops continue to work in silos with limited sharing, common culture and automation of releases. Maturity level 2 is that of Continuous Integration: the Ops function has to be aligned with the Dev function and both begin to perform various tests (unit and non-regression tests) [29] which are synchronised with code development. Lastly, maturity level 3 is that of Continuous Delivery Stage: integration tests with the other components, end-to-end tests, performance tests, user acceptance tests are then performed by Ops and co-designed with the Dev function [30] (Table 2).

Documents, observations and interviews performed in the first stage considerably helped us in interpretation of the 54 interviews in the second stage. Collaboration scope was parsed by interviewing individuals to express with whom they worked the most. While it is susceptible to bias, we did not want to induce other biases by repeating this question for each possible job role they could have collaborated with. Collaboration enrichment was examined through responses to whether and how individuals were

Table 2. Distribution of 54 interviews per contingencies

Project Size: 25 Small (min: 5; max: 14) / 29 Large (min: 15; max: 80)
Type & Degree of Sourcing: 24 Outsourced Fixed-Price/ 30 Other (Internal or other)
Agile Maturity: Mat.1: 19 / Mat.2: 15 / Mat.3: 20

satisfied or unsatisfied in our semi-structured interview. To investigate the skills issue in the 54 interviews, we asked what skills (know-how, behaviour) were necessary for the evolution of their jobs. We then analysed SSk detecting the presence of any subcategories in keeping with Robles [8] set of SSk (cf. Table 1).

4   Findings

4.1   Changes in SSk Perceptions When Considering Maturity Levels

Codification of interviewee skill perceptions allowed us to complete nine of the ten groups of SSk identified by Robles (2012). Only half of Robles [8] 10 groups of SSk are mentioned by interviewees for each maturity level. Five groups of SSk are under-represented if not absent within representations of Agile and DevOps teams whatever the maturity level, i.e. integrity, work ethic, courtesy. Among them, positive attitude clusters various skills, i.e. being optimistic, enthusiastic, confident, encouraging, and is only cited by PO and DPM at higher level of maturity (2 and 3). Beyond these results, we came across five groups of SSk represented in each maturity level.

Communication skills (CS) refer to the ability to communicate both orally and in writing, presenting and listening, and are present at each maturity level. A RM high-lighted the importance of CS: "I think you have to know how to communicate" (RM, mat. 1). This perception is shared by many people on both sides, Dev and Ops, e.g. a PO (mat. 2): "You have to listen, so especially not having the posture of "I know, I have experience", especially today". A DPM (mat. 3) confirms the central position of communication saying that "Communication is still a fundamental basis of teamwork. And I think that often, either because we are partitioned (…) we are somewhat inclined to understand or integrate neither the constraints of the rest of the team nor other people from other teams". We noted that the perception of CS was slightly higher in terms of diversity and frequency of mentioned skills when maturity level was going up. These previous verbatim show CS at mat. 1 covering basic CS principles as to convey an information between two or more stakeholders, then CS at mat. 2 with a stress on listening skills integrating humility, and finally CS at mat. 3 with a wider coverage and a higher degree of CS incorporating large understanding skills and their usage to interact with teams and integrate their constraints.

Interpersonal skills (ISk) are related to sociability, empathy, nurturing, friendly, patience; self-control capacity. As for CS, ISk appear at each maturity level. A PO underlined the importance of ISk to satisfy different stakeholders and reach final goal: "Coordination, of course, then relational, because everyone is not going necessarily in the same direction or does not necessarily have the same objectives (…) On the one hand, the production and the operations managers ask to limit the number of releases or production launches (…) on the other hand, we have businesses that always ask for more." (PO, mat. 1), a shared vision by a DPM (mat. 3): "Stakeholders analysis! I change partners very often. So, know how to evaluate a situation quickly, if I have someone who is supportive, or if someone who is perhaps a little more reluctant (…) You are asked to get closer to a certain number of people with whom you are not used to work with (…) so it requires human qualities.". The perception of ISk was slightly larger in terms of diversity and frequency of skills when maturity level was higher.

Flexibility skills (FS) signify to be ready to change, to learn throughout the life, to accept new things, to adjust, to adapt. FS are present at all levels of maturity and on both Dev and Ops sides. Moreover, people from maturity level 3 seem to have a clearer and wider representation of FS. A PE (mat. 1) simply mentioned one sub-skill of FS group, adaptability: "Adaptation is perhaps most important, because it changes all the time, businesses, tools, applications and technologies". At a similar position, a PE (mat. 3) asserted: "Everything evolves so quickly…it is better to know how to learn than to develop know-how because that will change, it is important to be open to the novelty". A PO (mat. 2) stated that: "You have to feel and accept the error. One must accept sometimes and assume one has made a mistake, and it is a step backwards". The skill is about adaptability but with a deeper and larger interpretation of learning and adaptability. Finally, a DPM (mat. 3) on a small project suggested: "You must be humble or agree hat you don't know…your neighbor knows better and will show you. (It is better) not to impose your vision either." Meanwhile another DPM (mat. 3) confirmed this "The challenge is to change the subject - just able to juggle these topics. It necessarily requires great flexibility and adaptability. A questioning, because suddenly, you've been in the business a long time, have already proven worth in the past, and you are asked to work in an-other way". We discovered that FS perception was broader and much more important in terms of diversity and frequency of mentioned skills when maturity level was higher.

Teamwork skills (TS) indicate a capacity to cooperate, to be supportive, collaborative, helpful. TS are intimately linked to Agile Principles, i.e. "Business people and developers must work together daily throughout the project", as well as Agile Methodologies (Scrum, XP), Agile Practices (daily stand-up, sprint review) or DevOps philosophy breaking silos between Dev and Ops and building bridges and fostering new teams. As mentioned by a PO, it is important to "understand that we do not work each one in his own corner (…) it must be shared a minimum, that every-one knows where the others are (…) all the developers do not need to know where all the integrators are, but we can have a roughly correct and almost real-world view of where we are. to know how to adjust, to know how to project also." (PO, mat. 1). From the Operations side, an RM highlighted a cultural change regarding Teamwork: "We do not ask for technical expertise anymore, because we really want people to stop solving the problem technically. (We prefer) to get the problem solved by a community. It is really a different positioning". (RM, mat. 2), a vision confirmed by another Ops: "You really need to have the vision of belonging to the same team, and not to say: "Me, I do represent Production (Ops)", to feel "powerful" because we (Ops) take the decision in fine to put the application into production." (PE, mat. 3). Finally, a DPM on a small project (mat. 3) demonstrated her way to become supportive and collaborative integrating fully her team: "You also have to be ready to join this team even if you are a manager of some of them. We (the DPM) must also know when to take a back seat." When team members are really acculturated to work together, i.e. in advanced DevOps team, silos disappear. We figured out that the perception of TS was moderately larger in terms of diversity and frequency of mentioned skills when maturity level was higher.

Lastly, as a DPM (mat. 3) stated clearly: "the responsibility necessarily, to know to be responsible.", thus Responsibility skills (RS) which covers two aspects. The first one is more evoked by PE: get the job done, and well done, conscientious, accountable. The second one is more perceived by DPM: trustworthy, astute, common sense imply to get the job done, to be conscientious, accountable, reliable. These skills are mostly cited by DPM, afterwards PE and to a lesser extent RM, and then few PO and very few AR. A large and complex PM suggested: "I want to say for commitment too. If they are self-organized, they must get in deep. They take a subject, they go to the end. They bring their ideas, they apply their ideas, and then when they fail, they repair. We must assume." About conscientiousness, the sense of getting the job well done and being resourceful, a PE on a large project (mat. 3) declared: "You do not have to be an expert to find the solution. You must understand what's going on. And about the know-how-to-be well, you must listen rather than talk." We identified this same preoccupation of consciousness, reaching objectives with POs trying to stay the course: "do not do the wind vane. We can be wrong, but on the other hand, we do not return every day on what we said the day before. (…) It is disastrous for the progress of work." (PO, mat. 1) We detected that the perception of RS was decreasing in terms of diversity and frequency of mentioned skills when maturity level was higher.

To conclude, we found that Agile maturity is a factor impacting SSk perception. First, FS are much higher in team members in a more mature agile environment (mat. 3). Secondly, the higher the maturity level, the more the presence and the diversity of CS and ISk increase. Third, TS and team spirit, are more present in a mat. 3 project compared to a mat. 2 or 1, which may seem logical but not obvious, particularly when considering the fundamentals of the agile approach which require a Teamwork culture. Fourth, surprisingly, RS are more present in a lower agility context (mat. 1) and decrease when maturity is higher. This could mean that in an agile environment, the sense of responsibility is more formally distributed, and in a mature DevOps configuration, the sense of responsibility is more shared within the team. In a DevOps environment, we can explain this result with Automation that could reduce and/or transfer responsibilities and therefore responsibility skills.

Type of Outsourcing may have an impact on SSk 'perceptions'. Some competences, such as sense of responsibility or teamwork are more present when the project is internal. In contrast, outsourcing seems to be a factor which results in increasing FS and ISk. The perception of SSk seems to vary less with project size than with type of outsourcing. Overall maturity level is the most important.

4.2 Roles and Collaboration Analysis

To the question about the actors with whom they interacted the most, all interviewees cited more than 15 different co-worker's functions. For maturity 1, projects, main collaborations between Dev and Ops are less numerous (20) than those within Dev and within Ops (31). Collaborations crossing the two functions become more numerous than those internal either to Dev or to Ops (20 against 16) for projects in maturity 2, and then become balanced (31 against 32) for projects in maturity 3. This balancing with DevOps means that collaboration with members of other function are perceived as important as internal collaborations within Dev and Ops functions respectively.

Table 3 lists these main collaborations by role/profession; for example, 4 of the 10 RM reported the developer as a main co-worker. Some similarities and differences in collaborations are observed for the five key interviewed roles. As expected, the DPM reported the highest number of collaboration with different co-workers in comparison to the four other interviewed roles. This highlights their large scope of collaborations. Another important observation is the key role of the PO: all interviewed professions have mentioned their collaboration with the latter.

Table 3. Main collaborations reported by each role.

		PO (N=11)	DPM (N=12)	AR (N=10)	PE (N=11)	RM (N=10)
Main Collaborations cited → DEV	Product Owner (PO), N	2	12	10	11	10
	Department & Project Manager, N	9	12	10	11	10
	Architect (AR), N	3	1	1	4	2
	Scrum Master, N		3			
	Developer, N	8	6	8	10	4
	DevOps animator, N		1			
	Technical expert, N		1		2	1
	Quality expert, N	1				
	Multiple collaborators, N		2			
	Qualifier, N		1			
OPS ←	Production Engineer (PE), N	1	4	2	1	8
	Admin. Infrastructure Director, N			1		
	System Engineer, N				1	
	Operators, N		3	2	4	3
	Release Manager (RM), N	2	1	6	6	

In Table 3, we can see more precisely the main collaborations between Dev and Ops. From the Dev side, we highlight collaborations between PO and RM, AR with operators or DPM with PE and operators. From the Ops side, we see a strong collaboration between PE and Developers, between RM and PO and with developers. Given the question asked, in traditional developments mode or in agile (mat. 1), these collaborations would not have been considered as main collaborations.

Moreover, all respondents have highlighted an improvement of the collaboration's quality between co-workers in an agile context. As mentioned during the interviews, the setting up of daily meetings or sprint reviews, but also the use of collaboration tools (such as the Mingle) could partly explain this finding. Indeed, the setting up of these daily meetings will rhythm the collaborations in a formal way. However, the frequency of meetings can be perceived as an overwork. For each role, we also describe the different forms of collaboration and types of actors involved.

Release Manager (RM). The RM is at the center of numerous collaborations within the company and in particular with the production team. All RMs underlined interactions with the project manager, generally on a weekly basis. This collaboration is, and must be, continuous to prioritize certain tasks and thus ensure the success of projects. For example, a RM explained (mat. 3): "every week we establish a point called the "Common Work Plan of Exploitability" where we exchange. We go through all actions, all activities in progress, and … we see what has to be prioritized in the case of new actions". These collaborations are often real driving forces to create a dynamic for all teams working on the same project. In addition, almost all RMs reported collaborations with production engineers (see Table 3). Their exchanges are frequent, (RM mat. 2): "we discuss certain points between us before going to meet the project manager. Given the slightest problem, one goes to see the other and vice versa". It should be also noted that in this context, the setting-up of project group meetings provided the opportunity to gather RMs, developers and operators. The maturity level in the transition from agile to DevOps could influence the frequency of these collaborations. In fact, "The developers for me are hidden behind the project manager. But this evolves within the most advanced projects in the DevOps approach" (RM mat. 3). Thus, an advanced application level of agile and DevOps methods and concepts might naturally lead to establishing more interactions with developers.

Product Owner (PO). As expected, most POs reported collaborations with developers. Some of these interactions are required for the validation of the sprint during the demos. The maturity level in the transition from agile to DevOps has a direct impact on the frequency and quality of these interactions. Thus, a PO suggested that to feel part of an integrated team (mat. 3): "Today we are really an integrated team with marketing, developers." In the case where several POs participate in the same project, they collaborate with each other daily via email or telephone and during the weekly "sales meeting". This meeting is also a moment of exchange with the Product Manager and line managers. Moreover, some POs mentioned multiple exchanges with functional architects. In line with the various roles inherent to the PO roles, the majority of POs also reported collaborations with business sponsors or users, albeit not considered main ones. It should be noted that several POs highlighted the limited collaborative exchanges with supervisor-operators (mat. 2): "Those with whom I exchange the least, are probably exploitation"; "I have difficulties to express myself on this point, they ("supervisor-operators") are more related to developers."

Architect (AR). As in previous findings, the two main co-workers mentioned by the architects were PMs and developers (see Table 3). Most architects reported interactions with PMs to share information and views on a project. Collaborations were also reported with development team to exchange information, especially during sprint reviews and demos. An architect stressed the importance of this (mat. 3): "we have to be precise on how to proceed, and if feasible, establish a stronger, detailed collaboration with the technical manager". These exchanges take place regularly. Several architects mentioned information exchange with the RM profession, especially to agree on norms, standards and good practices (mat. 2): "The (RM) is supposed to hand over to his team, to read the technical architectural file". An AR (mat. 3) highlighted the impact of the transition to DevOps on his work and collaborating: "it's an approach allowing better understanding the role of each person involved in the project. In the end, each remains accountable; but decision-making in an architecture problem (…) will be more shared than before (…) thus, problems disappear."

Production engineer (PE). The main collaborations cited by PEs are with the PM and developers (see Table 3). Thus, most PEs agree on the existence of a significant mutual collaboration with developers (mat. 2 and 3): "we inform each other, it's natural…with the developers, we are becoming a unique team: the DevOps one."

In addition, in their daily activities the PMs must provide applications to PEs so significant collaboration with shared responsibilities have been reported. However, some difficulties of co-operation have been mentioned, for instance a PE pointed out the following (mat. 2): "I was the one who explained what I expected in terms of documentation, whereas it's their job." PEs also discussed their collaborations with RMs. However, the frequency of these collaborations can vary a lot across projects. Indeed, in a context where the RM is entirely dedicated to the team's projects, collaborations are frequent. A PE described this collaboration as follows (mat. 2): "In our organization, the role of RM was created because of administrative importance of our project, it's useful to lighten our work (…) The role of the RM is to anticipate complex operations, to be sure we do not forget anything". A PE (mat. 3) explained his view of the evolution of collaboration in a DevOps team: "the roles of PM and RM no longer exist in a DevOps team; At the development team level, the role of PM is operated by the Scrum Master; at the planning level, project management role is a crucial role covered by the team. And the role of RM is operated both by PO, technical expert, and production engineers, and operators".

Department and Project Managers (DPM). PMs are at the center of multiple collaborations, both inter and intra-team. The manager profile collaborates with many actors (see Table 3). Most also mentioned collaborations with other PM and POs, in particular to discuss budget, tracking, prioritization of items. Several Managers also highlighted a close relationship with functional architects (mat. 2): "I work early with our functional architects to define and schedule future development." In addition, although the PM is not a functional expert, he approves the conformity of the result.

To conclude, the collaborative scope within the main collaborators clearly changed and is now more balanced. The perceived greater richness of collaboration reflects a better understanding among members. This greater richness appears to be more salient when projects are in maturity 3. Consequently, considering our findings on skills and collaboration, we could describe a three levels maturity model as follow. At maturity 1, there is a lower range of collaborations which could be explained by the DevOps philosophy itself opening collaboration to a new extent between Dev and Ops while Agile limits collaboration among Dev. Because agile methodologies ask for it, communication skills are very important and responsibility skills very developed as interpersonal skills. However, surprisingly, flexibility and teamwork are less present in their discourses. At maturity 2, the extent of collaboration is thus wider than for mat. 1. All the SSk are more represented at this level, except for RS which are decreasing. At maturity 3, the extent of collaboration is similar to mat. 2 or can slightly decrease. We explain this finding because when teams reach mat. 3, they know better that anyone with who to collaborate to be more efficient, hence they limit or cancel collaboration with some stakeholders. SSk increase in comparison to mat. 2, except for RS, and this is particularly true for FS, TS and ISk.

5 Discussion and Conclusion

DevOps and Agile methods impact collaboration and existing IT skills; therefore, it is essential to understand the requirement for new skills [31] and new curricula for IT students [32, 33]. Companies struggle to determine the most important tasks for IT teams, specifically future Release/DevOps engineers [34]. Understanding the evolution of IT skills would help organizations to hire skills that fit their needs [10]. This is lacking in DevOps job advertisements which largely neglect SSk [35] and focus on hard skills, e.g. technical skills, thus confirming a recruitment gap [9, 10]. We sought to investigate what skills and competencies are required notably for the collaboration culture between Dev and Ops when a firm engages in Agile and DevOps.

Our study provides compelling evidence that the move from Agile to DevOps Maturity has an impact on perceived skills in use or in making. While all agile software projects require significant SSk, these are even greater in DevOps especially at mat. 3. Our study shows flexibility and interpersonal skills are important for agile teams [11], and also extends this to others SSk such as teamwork and communication and suggests that SSk are even more important for DevOps. Our findings are largely congruent with that of Wiedemann et al. [12] and complement with an in-depth analysis of SSk in Agile and DevOps teams. Beyond key capabilities highlighted by Wiedemann et al. [12], we identified characteristic features of DevOps teams.

Regarding collaboration, we showed that collaborative scope among the main collaborators has drastically changed and is now more balanced. Also, the perceived greater richness of collaboration reflects a better understanding of roles in the overall project. We provide greater clarity about collaborations within a DevOps team than previously available (e.g., [13]). Our findings align with Humble [21] who highlighted the importance of collaboration and shared responsibilities and more specifically with skills, experience and mindset of Ops people. This expression of greater richness seems more salient when projects are in continuous delivery (mat. 3).

Overall, these results show disruption in collaboration between agile and DevOps. The transition to DevOps facilitates the IS function becoming smart for three reasons. Firstly, adaptability is considered an indicator of smartness. Extending collaboration across functions within IS is a sign of adaptation where there is an evident need. The fact that delivery can be continuous at DevOps stage is also a sign of adaptation to a more demanding environment and of higher performance. DevOps is the agile approach whereby better sharing of information and developing a common culture can happen across different roles and jobs throughout the IS function as a whole which overcomes the traditional distinction between Dev and Ops.

References

1. Brunnert, A., et al.: Performance-oriented DevOps: a research agenda. ArXiv Prepr. ArXiv150804752 (2015)
2. Debois, P.: DevOpsDaysGhent. DevOpsDays, Ghent, Belgium (2009)
3. Debois, P.: DevOps: a software revolution in the making. J. Inf. Technol. Manag. **24**, 3–39 (2011)
4. Conboy, K., Coyle, S.: People over process: the implications of agile for IS skills and Human Resource Management. IEEE Softw. **28**, 48–57 (2009)
5. Gallivan, M.J., Truex III, D.P., Kvasny, L.: Changing patterns in IT skill sets 1988-2003: a content analysis of classified advertising. ACM SIGMIS Database DATABASE Adv. Inf. Syst. **35**, 64–87 (2004)
6. Wong, S., von Hellens, L., Orr, J.: Non-technical skills and personal attributes: the Soft Skills Matter Most. In: Proceedings of the 6th Australiasian Women in Computing Workshop, Brisbane, Australia, pp. 27–33 (2006)
7. Boyatzis, R.E., Kolb, D.A.: From learning styles to learning skills: the executive skills profile. J. Manag. Psychol. **10**, 3–17 (1995)
8. Robles, M.M.: Executive perceptions of the top 10 soft skills needed in today's workplace. Bus. Commun. Q. **75**, 453–465 (2012)
9. Todd, P.A., McKeen, J.D., Gallupe, R.B.: The evolution of IS job skills: a content analysis of IS job advertisements from 1970 to 1990. MIS Q. **19**, 1–27 (1995)
10. Trauth, E.M., Farwell, D.W., Lee, D.: The IS expectation gap: industry expectations versus academic preparation. Mis Q. **17**, 293–307 (1993)
11. Vivian, R., Tarmazdi, H., Falkner, K., Falkner, N., Szabo, C.: The development of a dashboard tool for visualising online teamwork discussions. In: IEEE/ACM 37th IEEE International Conference on Software Engineering, pp. 380–388. IEEE (2015)
12. Wiedemann, A.M., Schulz, T.: Key Capabilities of DevOps teams and their influence on software process innovation: a resource-based view. In: Proceedings of 23rd ACIS Americas Conference on Information Systems, pp. 1–10, Boston (2017)
13. Wiedemann, A.: A new form of collaboration in IT teams-exploring the DevOps phenomenon. In: Proceedings of the 21st PACIS Pacific Asia Conference on Information Systems, pp. 1–12, Langkawi (2017)
14. Conboy, K., Fitzgerald, B.: Toward a conceptual framework of agile methods: a study of agility in different disciplines. In: Proceedings of the 2004 ACM Workshop on Interdisciplinary Software Engineering Research, pp. 37–44. ACM, Newport Beach (2004)
15. Highsmith, J., Cockburn, A.: Agile software development: the business of innovation. Computer **34**, 120–127 (2001)
16. Conboy, K., Coyle, S., Wang, X., Pikkarainen, M.: People over process: key people challenges in agile development. IEEE Softw. **28**, 48–57 (2011)
17. Coram, M., Bohner, S.: The impact of agile methods on software project management. In: ECBS 2005 Proceedings, pp. 363–370. IEEE Computer Society, Greenbelt (2005)
18. Nerur, S., Mahapatra, R., Mangalaraj, G.: Challenges of migrating to agile methodologies. Commun. ACM **48**, 72–78 (2005)
19. Lwakatare, L.E., Kuvaja, P., Oivo, M.: Dimensions of DevOps. In: Lassenius, C., Dingsøyr, T., Paasivaara, M. (eds.) XP 2015. LNBIP, vol. 212, pp. 212–217. Springer, Cham (2015). https://doi.org/10.1007/978-3-319-18612-2_19
20. Wettinger, J., Breitenbücher, U., Leymann, F.: Standards-based DevOps automation and integration using TOSCA. In: Proceedings of the 2014 IEEE/ACM, pp. 59–68. IEEE Computer Society, London (2014)

21. Humble, J., Molesky, J.: Why enterprises must adopt DevOps to enable continuous delivery. Cut. IT J. **24**, 6 (2011)
22. Kim, G., Debois, P., Willis, J., Humble, J.: The DevOps Handbook: How to Create World-Class Agility, Reliability, and Security in Technology Organizations. IT Revolution, Portland (2016)
23. Ghobadi, S., Mathiassen, L.: Perceived barriers to effective knowledge sharing in agile software teams. Inf. Syst. J. **26**, 95–125 (2016)
24. Coyle, S., Conboy, K., Acton, T.: An exploration of the relationship between contribution behaviours and the decision making process in agile teams. In: Proceedings of the 36th ICIS International Conference on Information Systems, pp. 1–15, Fort Worth, TX, USA (2015)
25. Schwaber, K., Sutherland, J.: The scrum guide. Scrum Alliance 21 (2011)
26. Oomen, S., De Waal, B., Albertin, A., Ravesteyn, P.: How can Scrum be successful? Competences of the Scrum Product Owner. In: Proceedings of the 25th ECIS European Conference on Information Systems, pp. 131–142, Guimarães, Portugal (2017)
27. Yin, R.K.: Validity and generalization in future case study evaluations. Evaluation **19**, 321–332 (2013)
28. Rolland, K.H., Fitzgerald, B., Dingsøyr, T., Stol, K.-J.: Problematizing agile in the large: alternative assumptions for large-scale agile development. In: Proceedings of the 37th ICIS International Conference on Information Systems, pp. 1–21, Dublin, Ireland (2016)
29. Ståhl, D., Bosch, J.: Modeling continuous integration practice differences in industry software development. J. Syst. Softw. **87**, 48–59 (2014)
30. Chen, L.: Continuous delivery: overcoming adoption challenges. J. Syst. Softw. **128**, 72–86 (2017)
31. Tan, C.-H., Teo, H.-H.: Training future software developers to acquire agile development skills. Commun. ACM **50**, 97–98 (2007)
32. Bang, S.K., Chung, S., Choh, Y., Dupuis, M.: A grounded theory analysis of modern web applications: knowledge, skills, and abilities for DevOps. In: Proceedings of the RIIT, 2nd Annual Conference on Research in Information Technology, pp. 61–62. ACM, Orlando (2013)
33. Betz, C., Olagunju, A.O., Paulson, P.: The impacts of digital transformation, agile, and DevOps on future IT curricula. In: Proceedings of the 17th Annual Conference on Information Technology Education, p. 106. ACM, Boston (2016)
34. Kerzazi, N., Adams, B.: Who needs release and DevOps engineers, and why? In: Proceedings of the International Workshop on Continuous Software Evolution and Delivery, pp. 77–83. ACM, Austin (2016)
35. Hussain, W., Clear, T., MacDonell, S.: Emerging trends for global DevOps: a New Zealand perspective. In: Proceedings of the 12th ICGSE International Conference on Global Software Engineering, pp. 21–30. IEEE Press, Buenos Aires (2017)

Situational Incompetence: The Failure of Governance in the Management of Large Scale IT Projects

Darryl Carlton[1(✉)] and Konrad Peszynski[2]

[1] Swinburne Business School, Melbourne, Australia
dcarlton@swin.edu.au
[2] RMIT University, Melbourne, Australia
konrad.peszynski@rmit.edu.au

Abstract. Information technology (IT) projects in the government (public) sector experience significant challenges. Despite decades of research, the adoption of formal methods, the use of external suppliers and packaged software, these remediation attempts have not appeared to have reduced nor mitigated the problems faced when the public sector undertakes large IT projects. Previous studies have examined the causes of IT project failure, in particular these have focused on factor analysis. A relatively limited number of studies have investigated the contribution of IT competence, and even fewer have considered the role and contribution of non-IT executives in IT project outcomes. This study sought a deeper understanding of what drives the behaviour of large scale IT projects. Of particular note was the finding by Kruger and Dunning (2009) that 'the skills required to do the job are the same skills needed to identify competence in others'. It was this finding which was found to most influence the observed behaviours of executive leadership leading to IT project failure.

This research reports on a qualitative study that investigated 181 interviews and 5,000 pages of project data drawn from a large-scale public sector IT project which resulted in a cost overrun that exceeded AUD$1 Billion. The interview transcripts and project data were analysed using an inductive case study methodology and the research process was influenced by aspects of Grounded Theory.

A new Theory of Situational Incompetence has been developed as a result of the analysis. The research culminates in a proposed measurement instrument intended to gauge leadership competence in the context of increasing project size and complexity.

Keywords: IT project failure · Public sector waste · Failed projects
Governance · Project management · Critical success factors
Situational incompetence

© IFIP International Federation for Information Processing 2019
Published by Springer Nature Switzerland AG 2019.
A. Elbanna et al. (Eds.): TDIT 2018, IFIP AICT 533, pp. 224–244, 2019.
https://doi.org/10.1007/978-3-030-04315-5_16

1   Introduction

Information Technology projects fail, and the cost of these failures is staggering (for example; Engelbrecht et al. 2017; Hidding and Nicholas 2017; Hughes et al. 2017; Hughes et al. 2016a, 2016b; Standish Group 1994 to 2015). This concern has been highlighted and repeated for more than forty years (see; Davis 1974; Lucas 1981; Maddison et al. 1983; Avison and Fitzgerald 2003; Hoffer et al. 1998; Lauden and Lauden 1998; Hawryszkiewycz 2001; Nickerson 2001).

Research has proposed a host of different reasons to explain project failure (Prater et al. 2017; Ewusi-Mensah 1997; Baccarini et al. 2004; Al Neimat 2005; Al Ahmed et al. 2009). Recent research by the Standish Group (2017) has found that 'development projects that exceed $100 million in labor costs, only 2% are successful, meaning on-time and within budget. Another 51% are considered challenged or over budget, behind schedule or didn't meet user expectations. The rest, 47%, are seen as outright failures' (Thibodeau 2017, para 5).

One of the reasons for explaining this high rate of failure has been assumed as due to shortcomings in generic project management capacity, rather than due to attributes of IT projects in particular. For example, according to Hidding and Nicholas (2017, p. 81), 'most of the improvement efforts have focused on advancing variations of the traditional project management paradigm, such as (that which) is embodied by the Project Management Body of Knowledge'.

Two questions arise regarding IT project failure research. First, why is the success rate of IT projects so poor? And secondly, why, despite the efforts of many, the situation fails to improve? This problem is known as 'Cobb's Paradox' (Bourne 2011). Cobb's Paradox states: 'We know why projects fail; we know how to prevent their failure—so why do they still fail?'. Cobb made the observation in 1995 while attending a presentation by the Standish Group (authors of the Chaos series of reports) while working at the Secretariat of the Treasury Board of Canada. Cobb's observation that "we know why projects fail" should not be taken in a literal, completely black and white sense, rather it should be considered to be a reference to the collective body of expert commentary, opinion, research and project practitioners that have offered solutions. Despite the successful implementation of major IT projects, repeatable success continues to be elusive (Thibodeau 2017).

Cobb was not alone in observing that there is a great deal studied and written about project failure, and that consulting firms propose methodologies and remedies but little actual progress appears to have been made. The International Federation for Information Processing (IFIP) Working Party 8.6 ran a conference to address this specific issue asking 'why our scholarship has not been more effective. Is the fault one of theory and inadequate understanding? Or is the problem one of knowledge transfer, the failure to embed research knowledge in the working practices of managers and policy-makers' (Dwivedi et al. 2015a, 2015b).

This study reports on the Queensland Health payroll project. Queensland is a state of Australia, located on the north-east coast. Queensland has a population approaching five million persons and covers an area of almost two million square-kilometres. The most famous tourist attraction is the Great Barrier Reef. Queensland Health employs

65,000 persons, and has an operating budget of AUD$11 Billion annually. Queensland has more than two hundred hospitals and health care facilities.

The primary question of this research is why. Why despite all of the experience, the research, and the training that is available, the consultants and software companies focussing attention on IT projects and the billions upon billions of dollars spent, large scale IT projects continue to fail at a rate that appears little changed over the decades.

2   Findings

When examining the Queensland Health payroll project files there are clear and obvious factors, which can be identified as having either not occurred or had been executed poorly and could be considered the causes of project failure. Any objective assessment of the project would conclude that project management had failed, there was a lack of requirements definition even though it was the first contracted deliverable, and management across all layers of the project were in conflict. These are all of the issues that appear in the literature on failed projects, and appear to confirm previous research.

Of potential significance is that the evidence provided by witness statements mapped to the project chronology showed that issues related to the identified themes were raised by staff and consultants throughout the project phases, and yet they still they remained as issues that were not resolved nor remediated at the time they were raised. The evidence is that management was made aware of these failures. So it was not a lack of awareness or communication of the failure risks, and therefore highlighting these as the only contributory factors of project failure lacks explanatory completeness, as the issue related to the inability to act on the concerns suggests other contributing factors to project failure.

The incoming Executive Director who oversaw the commencement of the project and managed the first few years had the exit report from the immediately preceding whole-of-government project produced by the external consultants that provided stark warnings of how that project had failed and what was required to ensure the next project would not fail. The only conclusion that can be drawn is that this report was ignored in its totality.

To paraphrase Cobb's Paradox (Bourne 2011) the management of the Queensland Health payroll project should have known why their project was certain to end in failure, yet they failed to act appropriately thereby ensuring that the project did in fact fail, and spectacularly. As was evident from the analysis of the witness statements in the conduct of the Queensland Health Payroll project - the management was regularly informed of what was going on with their project by both staff and external consultants (WS013). Management knew that the project was facing problems (or at least should have known). The reports on the 2005 whole-of-government initiative (WS039), the KPMG Report (WS003), the KJ Ross report on testing (PD103), the IBM and Corp-Tech report to 'reconstruct' the business requirements (PD063) and the 2009 Queensland Audit Office report (PD108) all provided clear statements identifying where the project was failing and what needed to be done to remedy the situation. Yet the problems persisted until the total project costs had blown out to beyond A$1 billion.

Faced with the clear and certain statement that the project was performing badly, and with specific statements of where the project was failing, successive managements failed to act appropriately to stem the problems. The only conclusion that can be drawn from this failure to act is that senior executives of the Department, the Governance and steering committees, the Executive Director did not know what specific actions were available to them, or what they specifically needed to do in order to be effective. The management and oversight of this project were at a complete loss as to how to effectively manage an information technology project.

This research proposes that the following are the contributory factors that led to the Queensland Health Payroll project becoming a failure:

- a lack of domain expertise by senior management responsible for the project as evidenced by the inability or unwillingness to adopt appropriate governance processes;
- stakeholders remained in conflict throughout the life of the project;
- there was a complete lack of accountability for failure evident throughout the project and especially when it came to vendor and contract management.

It is not immediately obvious why this situation was allowed to unfold in the manner in which it did. The project appeared to comply with all the appropriate governance structures and reporting requirements, yet an historical or retrospective view would allow that the project was never managed effectively.

Indeed, the findings of the Commission of Inquiry (WS122) state that 'Its (Queensland Health payroll) failure, attended by enormous cost, damage to government and impact on workforce, may be the most spectacular example of all the unsuccessful attempts to impose a uniform solution on a highly complicated and individualised agency' (WS122 p. 10). The Commissions conclusion was that there were two primary causes for the failure of the payroll project (1) 'unwarranted urgency' and (2) a 'lack of diligence on behalf of State officials'. (WS122 p. 217). The Commissions Report elaborated further on lack of diligence, describing it as 'poor decisions made in scoping the Interim Solution, in their Governance of the project, and in failing to hold IBM to account' (WS122 p. 217). The Commissioner further reported that 'the problems are systemic to government and to the natural commercial self-interest of vendors' (WS122 p. 218) which supports the observation that Normalisation of Deviance (Vaughan 2016) was at play throughout the conduct of this project. However, these findings by the Commission do not explain what motivated senior management to ignore the lessons learned from immediately preceding projects, and to ignore the warnings and advice of their own personnel. It is unclear, from the Commissions' report, what specific steps a subsequent project might implement to ensure that they too did not all into these traps.

2.1 Situational Incompetence

The question of most concern to this researcher has been to uncover why, despite all of the research, publications, education, training and certification that is available to individuals and organisations undertaking project management of an information technology solution, a project could still display all of the mistakes, errors and failings that have been identified in the literature.

The theme that was the most consistent throughout the project was that senior management was repeatably made aware of project risks and failings. Reports had been written about the whole-of-government project prior to the creation of the Queensland Health project that specifically enumerated the challenges and risks that needed to be kept front of mind to the QH project team (WS003, WS004). The literature provided no plausible explanation to describe the fact that senior executives responsible for the direct execution of the project, and departmental executives with governance and oversight accountability apparently ignored all of the advice that they were presented with.

What emerged from the data was that the executives in charge of the project, those executives that operated above the hands-on technical level, were manifestly incompetent when it came to issues of information systems project management. The executives simply did not understand the information that was being presented to them, and interpreted professional concerns raised by Queensland Health team members as "personality conflicts". These executives were presented with several formal reports outlining risks and issues, and acted in a manner that, under conventional wisdom, would defy rational explanation - the witness statements and project documents provide no evidence of any action being taken to address the issues raised. On more than one occasion IBM complained that employees of Queensland Health were trying to hold IBM to its contract and make IBM meet its obligations. IBM convinced senior departmental management that these staff were interfering in the project and senior management subsequently ordered their removal from the project.

Engelbrecht et al. (2017) suggest that inexperienced managers will seek advice and guidance from inappropriate sources. Kruger and Dunning (2009) offer the observation that the unskilled and unaware (Ryvkin et al. 2012) are incapable of identifying their own failings, incapable of independently observing and learning from the competence of others, and incapable of identifying competence in others.

These findings have led this researcher to postulate a new theory: Situational Incompetence.

Situational Incompetence applies when an otherwise experienced executive is placed in a position of authority or accountability for which they lack experience, training or specific skills. In this new role they are effectively incompetent and incapable of providing reasoned advice, guidance or management.

Situational Incompetence has implication for how leaders are selected for complex tasks requiring specialist IT domain knowledge and technical competence, it may also apply to other disciplines requiring specific knowledge of unique technology in those domains (e.g.: science, technology, engineering, medicine, and maths).

3   Research Methods

The corpus of published literature on the subject of failed IT projects lacks evidence based research drawn from comprehensive case studies (Dwivedi et al. 2015b). This research addresses that gap, and aims to identify what occurred in a specific, very large project, and what led to failure in that instance. From this case study it is hoped that confirmation of previously identified contributory factors may emerge, or else that a new theory may be constructed leading to further research that might confirm these findings as being generally applicable. A single case study, even one as complex as the Queensland Health Payroll project, is still only a singular event and cannot produce outcomes which are generalisable. But this case is of 'very special interest ... and the study of (it's) particularity and complexity ... to understand its activity within important circumstances' (Stake 1995, p xi) is worthy of being undertaken.

Thus, this research needs to follow an approach that will lead to formative 'theory building' rather than the more common 'theory testing' (Eisenhardt and Graebner 2007). Theory building is more suited to a comprehensive case study approach, which would subsequently lead to future research opportunities to test any emergent or confirmatory hypothesis. The goal of this research is to "understand more about the reasons why (project failure) occurs" (Keil 1995, p. 423) and has therefore employed an inductive case study approach.

The process of 'theory building' is undertaken by examining a case in detail by starting with little or no preconceived notion of the theory that will ultimately emerge from the data (Eisenhardt 1989b). 'Induction is viewed as the key process, with the researcher moving from the data to empirical generalisation and on to theory' (Heath and Cowley 2004, p. 144). Eisenhardt (Eisenhardt 1989b) refers to this method as 'Inductive Case Oriented Research'.

For this study the observed phenomenon is the ongoing and continual failure of information technology projects where failure has been defined by the inability to deliver on time, to an agreed budget, and to meet the value and quality objectives of the enterprises that the systems are meant to serve.

The methodology being utilised to examine this case is Inductive Grounded Theory which follows the methods established by Glaser (2004), Grounded theory was designed with the intent of ensuring that 'theories systematically emerge directly from data' (Martin and Gynnild 2011, p. 20). The term 'grounded' is intended to imply that the emergent theories are grounded in the data and not generated a priori and then applied to surveys or examples. By investigating the social constructs that exist in and around the main concern, inductive case oriented research is looking to tease out answers to the question 'why?' (Charmaz 2008a).

Inductive case study methods start with collecting and analysing data for the purposes of developing theories (Charmaz 2008a). And while data analysis may be influenced by the beliefs, prior experiences, and readings of the researcher (Heath and Cowley 2004), any researcher held preconceptions as to the prevailing theories or contributory factors should be consciously suspended until theories emerge from the data (Baker et al. 1992). This does not mean that the researcher should ignore, forget, or deliberately exclude all prior knowledge and research. Ignoring everything that has gone before may lead the researcher to develop theories that are already fully exposed, or, worse, to trivialise the problem being addressed (Thornberg 2012).

For this project, the initial set of data was archival and drawn from the public records of the Queensland Royal Commission of Inquiry, supplemented by additional material requested through the Freedom-of-Information (FOI) process and comprised:

- the published files of the Queensland Commission of Inquiry (http://www. healthpayrollinquiry.qld.gov.au, 2013) into the Queensland Health Payroll Project; and
- documents obtained under freedom of information (FOI) requests to the Department of Health Queensland, and to the Queensland Treasury Department.

In total there were 355 files of which 116 were individual witness statements from the Commission of Inquiry, and the balance of 239 files have been sourced by repeated FOI requests. The documents sourced by FOI request contained multiple records in each file, bringing the sum total number of individual files and documents to be examined to approximately 1,000.

The total number of pages of witness statements amounted to 3,850. In addition there was the collection of project documentation that exceeded 5,000 pages of emails, reports, project plans and other data.

To examine the case from the perspective of a timeline of events, of data and advice that was available at the time, to the participants, the researcher must endeavour to reconstruct the project from the available information. Dekker (2014) refers to this method of investigation as being 'inside the tunnel'.

Inside the tunnel 'is the point of view of people in the unfolding situation. To them, the outcome was not known (or they would have done something else). They contributed to the direction of the sequence of events on the basis of what they saw on the inside of the unfolding situation. To understand human error, you need to attain this perspective' (Dekker 2014, p. 18). Understanding the Queensland Health payroll project from a perspective that is reflective of the experience of the project executives and team members as events unfolded is critical to the inductive case study process. In order to emerge a theory or theories that may potentially be applied to working projects it is imperative that the actions and decisions that were taken throughout Queensland Health payroll project are understood in the context within which they were experienced at the time.

The files were loaded into NVIVO software for qualitative analysis, allowing the researcher to identify nodes of interest, and to collate and identify common behaviours occurring throughout the projects life. Every document was scanned into Nvivo where it was examined and tagged with topics. Nvivo also provided the main repository for memos. Some documents were unable to be scanned into NVIVO and these were analysed manually, with memo's maintained using the same coding system as that used in NVIVO. A process of normalising the initial topics was conducted to reduce them down to a manageable data set of fifty topics. These fifty topics were then correlated to themes of which three primary themes emerged from the data.

4   Literature Review

The literature on information technology project management is vast, and stretches back over almost fifty years. 'The History of Project Management', (Kozak-Holland 2011) traces the same project management disciplines back to the time of the construction of the Great Pyramids of Giza and the Great Wall of China. In construction of the Great Wall of China, Kozak-Holland (2011) identifies the stages of planning, executing, controlling and monitoring, and closing as being evidenced in the ancient literature. When reviewing the construction of the Great Pyramids, the archeological evidence suggest the creation of an advanced sundial which divided time into 12 roughly equal segments during daylight hours and is evidence that 'scheduling was done using the day as the basic unit of measure' (Kozak-Holland 2011, p. 66).

Grenny et al. (2007, p. 2) referred to a phenomenon in project management that they called 'fact-free planning'. 'Project leaders under pressure from various stakeholders determine deadlines, scope, deliverables and budget with little or no regard for the hard facts about what will actually be required. At other times, they base their estimates on facts, only to have the estimates ignored. In either case, the result is a set of project parameters and goals that is unrealistic from the beginning'.

Jones (2004, p. 5) created a working hypothesis of the contributory factors of project failure as being '(1) poor quality control is the largest contributor to cost and schedule over-runs, and (2) poor project management is the most likely cause of inadequate quality control'.

A difference amongst studies about successful projects reported in the literature, is the criteria used in defining project success or failure. Many studies assess the success of a project as completion on time, on budget, and delivering the full scope of requirements (Andersen 2010; Baccarini et al. 2004). This is certainly the criteria that has been established by the previously discussed Chaos Reports from the Standish Group (1994 to 2015).

Part of the challenge of measuring project success or failure is the lack of consensus regarding what constitutes a successful project. The CHAOS studies measure the success of a project as on time, on budget, with the full scope of requirements (Andersen 2010; Baccarini et al. 2004). However, critical commentators find these criteria incomplete because 'they do not consider, for example, usefulness, value or user satisfaction' (Eveleens 2009, p. 7; deBakker et al. 2010; Munns and Bjeirmi 1996).

Most companies measure the success of IT projects as meeting implementation deadlines, budgets and agreed requirements. Yet, projects can be on-time and within budget and deliver no actual business value according to Marchand and Peppard (2008).

Failure, as commonly reported in the literature reviewed, is often defined by both timeliness and budget performance. In many instances success appears to be a function of finishing the project at any cost, even if some intended functionality is not delivered or is sacrificed in order to meet that deadline. On-time and on-budget are criteria, which may have little or nothing to do with whether or not the product of an information technology project will be deemed a success by the enterprise and the users of the system.

Whilst an investigation into success and failure measurement is a worthwhile endeavour, for the purposes of this research, the determination of success or failure will be the generally accepted on-time, on-budget with the agreed level of functionality - this was the criteria applied to the Queensland Health Payroll project by the Commission of Inquiry (Chesterman 2013).

Nasir and Sahbuddin (2011b) conducted a comprehensive analysis of the literature about factors contributing to IT project success. They collated data from 43 peer-reviewed papers from 1990 to 2010. They grouped by frequency of mention in order to construct a hierarchy that appears to imply that if a subject is mentioned most frequently then it must be the most important. Nasir and Sahbuddin (2011b, p. 1) claimed that 'in a result unique to our study, we found that the factors of clear and frozen requirements, realistic estimation of the schedule and budget, along with a competent project manager are the five most critical success factors of software projects'.

In very large IT projects, the type which the Standish Group (2015) have identified as having the lowest success rate, the complexity inherent in the solution being built is very great. 'Today, business processes are more complex, interconnected, interdependent and interrelated than ever before. Additionally, they reject traditional organisational structures in order to create complex communities comprised of alliances with strategic suppliers, outsourcing vendors, networks of customers and partnerships with key political groups, regulatory entities, and even competitors' (Hass Hass 2007, p. 2).

It is this level of complexity which permeates every aspect of a project (Baccarini 1996), from the internal complexity of the business problem being solved (Al Neimat 2005), to organisational complexity that complicates what should have been relatively simple (Drummond 1998). When discussing complexity in this context most projects would be looking at the complexity of the business problem to be addressed, the complexity of the technology being deployed and inter- and intra-organisational complexity of dealing with competing demands (Thomas and Mengel 2008).

Beginning in 1995 Keil observed the escalating rate of IT project failure and its cost on business and government. The generic phrase "poor project management" (Keil 1995) is far too broad to provide clarity for what actually drives project escalation and ultimately failure. Keil (1995, p. 422) adopts the definition of escalation as being "continued commitment in the face of negative information about prior resource allocations, coupled with uncertainty surrounding the likelihood of goal attainment".

According to Keil "projects are more prone to escalation when they involve a large potential payoff, when they are viewed as requiring a long-term investment in order to receive any substantial gain" (Keil 1995 p. 422). Keil touches on "psychological factors" which may impact a managers decision to continue with a project that appears doomed to failure, and suggests that "escalation is more likely to occur when managers make errors in processing information" but does not delve deeper into why managers make those errors in processing information, whether there are different outcomes associated with different "types" of managers, or whether or not there are underlying factors as to how managers process the information being presented to them.

Keil suggests (1995. p. 431) that certain psychological factors may contribute to escalation. These factors include:

- prior history of success,
- high degree of personal responsibility for the outcome of the project,
- errors in information processing, and
- emotional attachment to the project.

Prior history of success correlates to Vaughan's (2016) observations as to the contributory factors of Normalisation of Deviance. Where an organisation has not previously experienced negative outcomes they will continue to assume that taking the same actions or decisions will not produce deleterious results. The fact that failure had not occurred previously is not proof that their decision making was sound, rather it may have been just "luck" that no disaster had previously befallen them. In the specific case of the NASA Challenger space shuttle, various other launches had been successful despite components such as the O-Rings operating beyond their specified tolerances, and so it was assumed that earlier decisions to launch were sound and this decision would also prove to be sound. The most likely description is however that previous launches prior to the Challenger explosion were "lucky" that components operating outside of tolerances had not caused a disaster to occur similar to what happened with the Challenger. A decision by NASA to implement processes to ensure that O-Rings were checked on future launches (the proximal cause) would do nothing to ameliorate the underlying cause (normalization of deviance).

Optimism bias in a project management environment (Prater et al. 2017) may also account for why project managers maintain a "continued commitment in the face of negative information" (Keil 1995, p. 422). But what is absent from the literature is why an experienced manager would suffer from what amounts to a delusional optimism bias in the face of hard evidence to the contrary. Does the project executive not understand the information being presented to them? Does the project executive somehow consider that they are immune from the risks and failures that the majority of projects face? What propels a project executive to operate under the assumption that their project will somehow be one of the very few to be successful? The fact that project executives ignore negative information about project escalation is supported by the evidence. Even the fact that project executives may suffer from optimism bias fails to clarify why an executive would act in this way? What conditions or conditioning lead the project executive to ignore clear evidence that their project is doomed to fail requires a deeper investigation.

5 The Case Study

In 2002, the Queensland Government (Chesterman 2013) decided to establish a 'shared services initiative' (SSI) to provide IT services as a shared electronic payroll resource amongst most Queensland Government departments and other statutory government agencies. As part of this initiative the SSI undertook the management of the existing Lattice Payroll System in independent use by several departments, Queensland Health (QH) amongst them.

By 1st of July 2003 (Chesterman 2013, p. 10) the SSI was underway and was called CorpTech. In August 2005 CorpTech was granted A$125 million to build and operate a whole-of-government human resources and finance IT software solution. Multiple vendors were commissioned to implement the solution and support CorpTech. There were smaller numbers of contractors engaged to build an integration between SAP ECC5 to WorkBrain for payroll rostering and time and attendance recording. These multiple related system developments by different vendors were intended to be inter-operable with no discernible separation to the end user.

In March of 2006 Queensland Health (QH) had transferred responsibility for the maintenance of human resource software and hardware to CorpTech. At this time, the provision of a new computerised payroll system for QH employees was thought to be urgent because the existing system, known as LATTICE, was nearing the end of its useful life (WS122 p. 11). By 2007, an independent review known as the 'Kelliher Report' (PD015) found that the whole of Government system was significantly behind schedule.

A series of reviews and tenders were undertaken to fix the project by introducing a Prime Contractor. IBM subsequently won that tender to commence in December 2007. 'By October 2008 IBM had not achieved any of the contracted performance criteria; but it had been paid about $32 million of the revised contract price of $98 million; and it forecast that to complete what it had contracted to undertake would cost the State of Queensland $181 million' (Chesterman 2013, para 2.13).

With the QH Payroll Project, IBM had agreed to undertake a project, at a fixed price, for which no statement of work existed and no detailed planning of any description had been undertaken.

The externally engaged legal firm (WS014), in preparing their advice with respect to each of the proposals from Accenture, IBM and Logica, stated that 'we believe on balance that IBM's Offer gives rise to a greater number of material issues and less thought has gone into IBM's Offer regarding contractual mechanisms that will assist the customer or enhance the working relationship between the parties' (WS014, p. 39).

At this stage of the Queensland Health Payroll project, the Queensland Government had accepted a contract to implement an IT project to a business problems for which no business case existed and no technical solutions architecture had been provided. The IT project was shown by the evidence tabled at the Commission (Chesterman 2013) and by the analysis of documents, to be a solution to fulfil an unknown set of requirements at a fixed price and timescale, and oddly one already in government use on an existing challenged project. Furthermore, senior management was acting against the advice of their technical experts (WS085) and external legal advisors (WS014).

On 14th of March 2010 the QH payroll system finally "went live" (operational) after ten failed prior attempts. The resulting system was reported to have 35,000 payroll anomalies or processing errors (WS053) and consequently required 1,000 clerical staff to manually process fortnightly pays that otherwise was intended as the most basic core function of the new system.

After the "go live" was achieved, the Queensland Government was facing a total expenditure in the range of AUD$1.2 billion for total cost of ownership of the project. The Executive Council of the Queensland Government ordered a Commission of Inquiry into the project.

6 Discussion

'Organisational artefacts such as mission statements, goals and objectives, strategic plans and the like function as tools to reduce choice, not to guide it' (Manning 2008, p. 677). In the same manner, the specification of requirements, the business case, the architecture and solution design of the project are all intended to constrain choice to deliver 'order'. In the QH project 'order' should have been represented by a defined scope of work, a defined project plan which sets out not only what work will be done, but also what work will not be done, and by an agreed contract. None of these things existed on the QH payroll project, and any efforts to enforce them were resisted by the vendor with the support (tacit or otherwise) of departmental executives.

The issue of transparent flows of information between parties, of experts being able to make informed decisions utilising tacit information compared to less experienced people needing to 'follow the script' (Vo-Tran, 2014), of actors controlling the release of information, and of stakeholders presenting different versions of themselves across multiple stages becomes critical when one considers both the makeup of the governance and management of the QH project and the individuals involved. "The involvement of non-IT stakeholders can actually work detrimentally and confound and confuse proceedings, even causing error" (Engelbrecht et al. 2017, p. 995). Non-IT experienced management, placed in a position of authority "may be influenced by some suppliers or colleagues to whose IT knowledge they had access, and insist on a certain course of action" (ibid) which may result in confusion, delay or inappropriate decision making, and contribute to the risk of IT project failure.

An appropriate lens through which to view this performance construct is referred to as the Dunning-Kruger Effect. This effect is where the less competent an individual is with respect to a particular domain then the more they are likely to overstate their perceived knowledge and ability. This may be referred to as a 'confidence/competence dissonance'. Individuals that lack competence in a particular domain (incompetent) but are not self-aware of their lack of competence, generally perceive their performance to be not significantly inferior to those who possess significant competence, training and ability (the experts).

This phenomena has also been described as the Unskilled and Unaware Problem (UUP) (Ryvkin et al. 2012). Essentially UUP argues that individuals that are unskilled in a particular domain overestimate their own competence in both absolute terms and relative terms. Top performers underestimate their absolute and relative performance. Kruger and Dunning (Kruger and Dunning 2009) found that an unskilled person was more likely to dramatically misstate their absolute and relative competence. Ehrlinger et al. (2008) have argued that UUP is a persistent feature of decision making. Furthermore, and potentially much more concerning for complex IT projects, Kruger and Dunning (2009) determined that the skills necessary to do the job, are the same skills necessary to identify competence in others. This facet of the UUP research is particularly important when an unskilled individual is placed in a position of decision making authority, in this case with respect to an IT Project. Where an unskilled individual possesses neither the skills necessary to do the job, nor the skills necessary to identify competence in others they are not in a position to make informed decisions on complex issues. The application of this principle to the Queensland Health Payroll project would suggest that the Executive Director, the Department Secretary, and the governance boards lacked the skills needed to identify competence in others, and to comprehend informed advice when it was provided.

Engelbrecht et al. (2017 p. 5) aimed to "identify whether a causal relationship exists between the various components of business managers' IT competence and IT success". What they found was that a "business managers' IT competence can, and does, exert a substantial influence on project success" (ibid: p. 1002). They reported a 'surprising' finding where a lack of knowledge or competence was likely to have a negative impact on project outcomes, "although one would have expected a positive relationship and a positive impact, it has been reported that the involvement of non-IT stakeholders can actually work detrimentally and confound and confuse proceedings, even causing errors".

Engelbrecht et al. (2017) also found that 'business managers may be influenced by some suppliers or colleagues to whose IT knowledge they had access, and insist on a certain course of action. If that business manager is particularly influential in an organisation, then there could be similar confusions, delays, and even inappropriate decisions'. This finding is reflective of the behaviours referred to in the Witness Statements. The senior executives of Queensland Health deferred to the advice of the vendor, rather than their own staff. Having discounted the concept of "amoral actors" it is this lack of knowledge of information technology, and the executives inability to parse the information being presented that builds the foundations of a theory to explain how the Queensland Health payroll project became so dysfunctional and ended in failure.

Given the importance of information technologies to business success, and their presence in almost every endeavour, one would expect to see an increase in technically literate, skilled or experienced managements to provide effective oversight and governance. Coertze and vonSolms (2013) found that 10% of organisations had Chief Information Officer (CIO) or equivalent representation at board or executive level of organisational governing management. Only 15% of organisations had board members with any IT-related qualifications, and in their United Kingdom (UK) sample, no organisation exhibited board level oversight of organisational IT through qualified representation directly as a board member. A focus on general business competence over specific IT competence continues at the CIO level where less than 50% of CIOs in the United States of America (US) public sector had primary qualifications from technical or engineering backgrounds (Ionescu 2017).

Twenge and Foster (2010) found that 'there has been a 30% tilt towards narcissistic attitudes in US students since 1979', and that 'The Narcissism Epidemic' (Kremer 2013) breeds 'the idea that being highly self-confident is the key to success'. Twenge and Campbell (2010) were at pains to point out that there is no correlation between confidence and successful outcomes. Kremer (2013) reported that 'over 15,000 journal articles have examined the links between high self-esteem and measurable outcomes in real life, such as educational achievement, job opportunities, popularity, health, happiness and adherence to laws and social codes' and found no correlation or causation.

'Over the last 30 years confidence has replaced competence' (Kremer 2013). Positive thinking has replaced knowledge. An increase in narcissism correlates with the unskilled and unaware problem (UUP) in that 'individuals become so self-obsessed they cannot identify their own weaknesses or learn from others' (Kruger and Dunning 2009). This narcissistic self-belief and confidence may go some way to explain why an executive with little knowledge of information technology and no formal training or experience in information technology would agree to take on the responsibility of running 'the largest organisational reform undertaken within the State Government' (WS122). When it comes to the QHP payroll project, it was stated very clearly by the Deputy-Secretary of the Department that the newly appointed Executive-Director was not skilled in information technology but was a very experienced people manager with greater than 30 years in the public sector (WS026). The Executive-Director described her education and work experience as mostly being in the human resources domain (WS024).

The potential risk that this lack of (Information Technology) domain expertise causes for Information Technology projects generally, and the Queensland Health project as a specific example is encapsulated by the Dunning-Kruger Effect (2009), 'that incompetent individuals lack the metacognitive skills that enable them to tell how poorly they are performing, and as a result, they come to hold inflated views of their performance and ability'. They are therefore potentially prone to ignore mounting evidence of their contribution to project related issues, to over-estimate their own ability to diagnose and resolve issues, and to listen to and take advice from unreliable sources. All of which were evident in the witness statements.

Of even greater concern is the UUP findings (Ryvkin et al. 2012) that not only do the domain illiterate individuals tend to overestimate their own ability relative to their actual performance, they are also at risk of being deficient in identifying relevant domain competence in others, 'participants who scored in the bottom quartile were less able to gauge the competence of others than were their top-quartile counterparts' (Kruger and Dunning 2009). Furthermore, they found that 'incompetent individuals fail to gain insight into their own incompetence by observing the behaviour of other people. Despite seeing the superior performances of their peers, bottom-quartile participants continued to hold the mistaken impression that they had performed just fine' (Kruger and Dunning 2009).

A possible explanation contributing to the Queensland Health Payroll project failure is that where managers are not technically competent, but perceive themselves as managerially capable, not only are they potentially at risk of overestimating their own ability and underestimating the relative competence of the skilled workers on the project, they do not have the skills to discern the quality of advice being given to them. Essentially, the evidence suggests that they are at high risk of not being able to assess the difference between the veracity of a confident but incompetent colleague or vendor providing advice, in comparison to a competent but less-confident colleague.

These managerial perceptions about domain expertise, confidence and competence carry the risk of significant contribution to poor project management decision-making and governance with implications for overall project failure and success. The decision-making senior project manager with accountability, responsibility and authority needs to be able to assess the information provided to them in order to make well-informed decisions. It is contended in the interpretation of the QH project data presented in this study that the consequences of placing domain-challenged persons in positions of project-critical authority is likely to lead to unsatisfactory outcomes where:

- managers who lack domain expertise will act the part that they perceive they need to adopt;
- these managers tend to be incapable of identifying the skilled and competent individuals that can be trusted for expert advice;
- these managers will not have the cognitive or experiential tools to determine an appropriate course of action when faced with a project related crisis; and
- these managers are likely to confuse confidence with competence and may be subject to undue influence by other incompetent actors.

In summary, the Queensland Health Payroll project was potentially placed at significant risk by failing to appoint management, governance and oversight that comprised sufficient domain expertise appropriately matched to the size, complexity and nature of the project.

7   Testing Situational Incompetence

It has been argued in this paper that situational incompetence is allowed to persist because of normalisation of deviance (Vaughan 2016). Normalisation of deviance implies that incompetence is tolerated because it has not previously caused significant failures. It is known that smaller projects have much higher rates of success than larger projects (Standish Group 2015), and as a consequence the skills needed to effectively manage very large projects are rarely put to the test and competence deficiencies escape detection.

It is necessary therefore to provide a method of measuring the competence of leadership as it applies to a range of IT project situations. The situations being tested are those of increasing complexity and size, and the competence of leaders relative to those constructs.

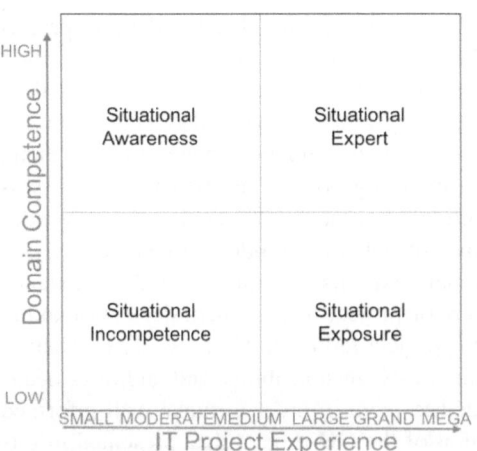

Creating a measurement instrument requires the identification and creation of an effective scale. Scale development is well established in the literature and the 'rules' for creating an effective scale are well articulated (for example: Churchill 1979; Flynn et al. 1993; Rao et al. 1999; Kimberlin and Winterstein 2008)

The 'key indicators of the quality of a measuring instrument are the reliability and validity of the measures' (Kimberlin and Winterstein 2008, p. 2276). A measure is considered 'valid' when the differences in observed scores accurately reflect differences in the construct being examined (Churchill 1979, p. 64). 'Validity is often defined as the extent to which an instrument measures what it purports to measure' (Kimberlin and Winterstein 2008, p. 2278), but an instrument can be reliable without being valid. Reliability ensures that the instrument always generates a reproducible outcome, while validity ensures that the instrument measures what it is intended to measure. In this specific instance the instrument must validly test leadership competence in a given situation, and it must do so reliably under different inputs.

The first step in creating a measurement instrument (scale development) is to create an 'item pool'. The goal is to develop a set of measures which might sample 'all possible contents which might comprise the putative trait according to all knows theories of the trait' (Flynn et al. 1993, p. 310). The domain of construct is determined by a literature search. This research has determined that the domain of construct is leadership competence in a given project situation. The instrument will be developed following the procedure outlined by Churchill (1979).

The factors which will be used for the initial version of the scale have been taken from prior research into project failure which focussed on factor analysis. In particular the leadership competence construct is been drawn from the work of Engelbrecht et al. (2017), while the software project complexity measures are being informed, principally, by the work of Fitsilis and Damasiotis (2015).

The item pool has been drawn from prior work as identified in the literature. However, the response format has been modified to ensure validity and reliability in the responses provided. The two dominant response types are dichotomous responses and scale responses based on some form of Likert-type measurement (Clark and Watson 1995, p. 312).

While some of the factors presented are of a general or generic nature, many are specific. Where the respondent is asked about their experience with and knowledge of technologies, these factors should be modified to reflect the specific project be examined. For the purposes of the initial presentation of the scale, the factors used have been framed in a generic style.

The framing of the questions has also been structured to be 'forward looking', with the intent of being able to predict how a project might be affected rather than looking backwards and analysing a previous project that has been completed.

The model being suggested is a simple X/Y plot. The 'X' scale refers to project complexity and the 'Y' scale to leadership competence in a technical domain.

8 Implications and Future Research

The implications for industry of this research is that more attention needs to be paid to the skills and competence of the individual that will have direct authority over an IT project. Specifically, the larger and more complex the project the more important that the leader be technically skilled and experienced. While an unskilled individual may not expose a small project to significant risk, the success rate of large and complex projects is so small (Standish Group 2015) that ensuring a positive project outcome for even the most skilled and experienced practitioners is challenging. Organisations cannot afford the increased risk of management not having the competence to provide effective oversight and governance.

This research reflects the findings of a single case study, albeit a very large case, but still just one instance of a failed project. The findings cannot be generalised to apply to all IT projects, however they do provide insight into what might be occurring on other projects and why research over the last thirty or more years has not resulted in a significant improvement in project outcomes. More work is required to confirm these findings on other projects. The instrument needs to be tested and applied more broadly to determine its validity to reproduce outcomes. As identified (Dwivedi et al. 2015b) more in-depth and detailed case studies are required of both failed and successful projects to identify what actually happened on these projects and what can be both avoided in the future, and what best practices can be generalised to ensure improved outcomes. The implications for future research from this study are that investigations need to go beyond factor analysis to look for underlying drivers of project failure.

9   Conclusion

This research identified that the leading cause of failure for the Queensland Health payroll project was that the project executives and governance bodies were ill-equipped to understand the complexity of an IT project. This lack of competence meant that the project executives did not have the experience to allow them to infer appropriate actions in the face of adverse circumstances. Project executives with little knowledge or skills in Information Technology were found to be unable to (i) recognise their own limitations, (ii) identify competence in others, (iii) learn from their mistakes (iv) learn from the example of others (v) and tended to favour inappropriate sources of advice and guidance. The final word on situational competence comes from the proceedings of the IFIP Conference on IT Project Failures: 'someone implementing IT needs to know which levers to pull, in which context, and at what time' (Dwivedi et al. 2015bb, 149). IT project leaders do not need to be the technical expert, but they do need sufficient knowledge and experience to recognise expertise and to take appropriate actions when the situation demands.

References

Al Neimat, T.: Why IT Projects Fail (2005). www.projectperfect.com.au

Al-Ahmad, W., Al-Fagih, K., Khanfar, K., Alsamara, K., Abuleil, S., Abu-Salem, H.: A taxonomy of an IT project failure: root causes. Int. Manag. Rev. 5(1), 93–103 (2009)

Andersen, E.S.: Are we getting any better? comparing project management in the years 2000 and 2008. Proj. Manag. J. 41(4), 4–16 (2010)

Avison, D.E., Fitzgerald, G.: Information Systems Development: Methodologies, Techniques and Tools, 3rd edn. McGraw-Hill, New York (2003)

Baccarini, D.: The concept of project complexity: a review. Int. J. Proj. Mang. 14(4), 201–204 (1996)

Baccarini, D., Salm, G., Love, P.E.D.: Management of risks in information technology projects. Ind. Manag. Data Syst. 104(4), 286–295 (2004)

Baker, C., Wuest, J., Stern, P.: Method slurring, the phenomenology/grounded theory example. J. Adv. Nurs. **17**, 1355–1360 (1992)

Bourne, L.: Cobb's Paradox is alive and well (2011). http://www.mosaicprojects.wordpress.com. Accessed 2 Sept 2016

Charmaz, K.: Constructing Grounded Theory. A Practical Guide Through Qualitative Analysis. Sage, London (2006)

Charmaz, K.: Constructionism and the Grounded Theory. In: Holstein, J.A., Gubrium, J.H. (eds.) Handbook of Constructionist Research, pp. 397–412. The Guildford Press, New York (2008a)

Charmaz, K.: Grounded theory as an emergent method. In: Hesse-Biber, S.N., Leavy, P. (eds.) Handbook of Emergent Methods, pp. 155–172. The Guildford Press, New York (2008b)

Chesterman, R.N.: Queensland Health Payroll System Commission of Inquiry", Queensland Government Gazette (2013). ISSN 0155-9370

Churchill, G.A.: A paradigm for developing better measures of marketing constructs. J. Market. Res. **XVI**, 64–73 (1979)

Clark, L.A., Watson, D.: Constructing validity: basic issues in objective scale development. Psychol. Assess. **7**(3), 309–319 (1995)

Coertze, J., von Solms, R.: A model for information security governance in developing countries. In: Jonas, K., Rai, I.A., Tchuente, M. (eds.) AFRICOMM 2012. LNICST, vol. 119, pp. 279–288. Springer, Heidelberg (2013). https://doi.org/10.1007/978-3-642-41178-6_29

Davis, G.B.: Management Information Systems: Conceptual Foundations, Structure and Development. Mcgraw Hill Inc., NY (1974)

deBakker, K., Boonstra, A., Workmann, H.: Does risk management contribute to IT project success? a meta-analysis of empirical evidence. Int. J. Proj. Manag. **28**, 493–503 (2010)

Dekker, S.: The Field Guide to Human Error Investigations. Cranfield University Press, Bedford (2014)

Drummond, H.: Riding a tiger: some lessons of taurus. Manag. Decis. **36**(3), 141–146 (1998)

Dwivedi, Y.K., Wastell, D., Henriksen, H.Z., De, R.: Guest editorial: grand successes and failures in IT: private and public sectors. Inf. Syst. Front. **17**, 11–14 (2015a)

Dwivedi, Y.K., et al.: Research on information systems failures and successes: status update and future directions. Inf. Syst. Front. **17**, 143–157 (2015b)

Ehrlinger, J., Johnson, K., Banner, M., Dunning, D., Kruger, J.: Why the unskilled are unaware: further explorations of (absent) self-insight among the incompetent. Organ. Behav. Hum. Decis. Processes **105**(1), 98–121 (2008)

Eisenhardt, K.M.: Making fast strategic decisions in high-velocity environments. Acad. Manag. J. **32**, 543–576 (1989a)

Eisenhardt, K.M.: Building theories from case study research. Acad. Manag. Rev. **14**, 532–550 (1989b)

Eisenhardt, K.M., Graebner, M.E.: Theory building from cases: opportunities and challenges. Acad. Manag. J. **50**, 25–32 (2007)

Engelbrecht, J., Johnston, K.A., Hooper, V.: The influence of business managers' IT competence on IT project success. Int. J. Proj. Manag. **35**, p994–p1005 (2017)

Eveleens, J.L., Verhoef, C.: The rise and fall of the chaos report figures. IEEE Softw. **27**(1), 30–36 (2010)

Eveleens, L.: The rise and fall of the CHAOS report figures, pp. 1–23 (2009). http://www.cs.vu.nl/equity/

Ewusi-Mensah, K.: Critical issues in abandoned information systems development projects. Commun. ACM **40**(9), 74–80 (1997)

Fitsilis, P., Damasiotis, V.: Software project's complexity measurement: a case study. J. Softw. Eng. Appl. **8**, 549–556 (2015). https://doi.org/10.4236/jsea.2015.810052

Flynn, B.B., Schroeder, R.G., Sakakibara, S.: A framework for quality management research and an associated measurement instrument. J. Oper. Manag. **11**, 339–366 (1993)

Glaser, B.G.: Remodeling grounded theory. forum: qualitative social research. **5**(2), Art. 4 (2004). http://nbn-resolving.de/urn:nbn:de:0114-fqs040245

Grenny, J., Maxfield, D., Shimberg, A.: How project leaders can overcome the crisis of silence. MIT Sloan Manag. Rev. **48**(4), 46–52 (2007)

Hass, K.B.: The blending of traditional and agile project management. PM World Today **9**(5), 1–8 (2007)

Hawryszkiewycz, I.T.: Introduction to Systems Analysis and Design, 5th edn. Prentice Hall, Frenchs Forest (2001)

Heath, H., Cowley, S.: Developing a grounded theory approach: a comparison of glaser and strauss. Int. J. Nurs. Stud. **41**, 141–150 (2004)

Hidding, G.J., Nicholas, J.M.: A new way of thinking about IT project management practices: early empirical results. J. Organ. Comput. Electron. Commer. **27**(1), 81–95 (2017)

Hoffer, J.A., Valacich, J.S., George, J.F.: Modern Systems Analysis and Design, 2nd edn. Addison-Wesley, Reading, Mass (1998)

Hughes, D.L., Dwivedi, Y.K., Rana, N.P., Simintiras, A.C.: Information systems project failure – analysis of causal links using interpretive structural modelling. Prod. Plan. Control **27**(16), 1313–1333 (2016a)

Hughes, D.L., Dwivedi, Y.K., Simintiras, A.C., Rana, N.P.: Success and Failure of IS/IT Projects. Springer Briefs in Information Systems. Springer, Cham (2016b). https://doi.org/10.1007/978-3-319-23000-9

Hughes, D.L., Rana, N.P., Simintiras, A.C.: The changing landscape of IS project failure: an examination of the key factors. J. Enterp. Inf. Manag. **30**(1), 142–165 (2017)

Humphrey, W.S.: Why big software project fail: the 12 questions. CrossTalk, J. Defense Softw. Eng. **18**(3), 25–29 (2005)

IFIP WPG 8.6: International Federation for Information Professionals, Technical Committee 8, Working Group 6. http://ifipwg86.wikidot.com. Accessed 01 Jan 2018

Ionescu, V.: The competencies of the CIO, a 2016 analysis of the United States of America Federal CIO Council Members Background. J. Defense Resour. Manag. **8**(1) (2017)

Jones, C.: Software project management practices: failure versus success. J. Defense Softw. Eng. **17**, 5–9 (2004)

Keil, M.: Pulling the Plug: software project management and the problem of Project escalation. MIS Q. **19**, 421–447 (1995)

Kimberlim, C.L., Winterstein, A.G.: Validity and reliability of measurement instruments used in research. Am. J. Health-Syst. Pharm. **65**, 2276–2284 (2008)

Kozak-Holland, M.: The History of Project Management. Multi-Media Publications, Ontario (2011)

Kremer, W.: Does Confidence Really Breed Success?. BBC World Service (2013). http://www.bbc.com/news/magazine-20756247. Accessed 01 Jan 2018

Kruger, J., Dunning, D.: Unskilled and Unaware of It: how difficulties in recognising one's own incompetence lead to inflated self-assessments. J. Pers. Soc. Psychol. **77**(6), 1121–1134 (2009)

Lauden, K.C., Lauden, J.P.: Information Systems and the Internet: A Problem-Solving Approach, 4th edn. The Dryden Press, Orlando (1998)

Lucas, H.C.: Implementation: The Key to Successful Information Systems. Columbia University Press, New York (1981)

Maddison, R.N., Baker, G.J., Bhabuta, L., Fitzgerald, G., Hindle, K., Song, J.H.T.: Information System Methodologies. Wiley Heyden on behalf of British Computer Society (1983)

Manning, P.K.: Goffman on organisations. Organ. Stud. **29**, 677–699 (2008)

Marchand, D.A., Peppard, J.: Designed to fail: why it projects underachieve and what to do about it. Research Paper, vol. 11, pp. 1–28 (2008)

Martin, V.B., Gynnild, A. (eds.): Grounded Theory: The Philosophy, Method and Work of Barney Glaser. Brown Walker Press, Florida (2011)

Munns, A.K., Bjeirmi, B.F.: The role of project management in achieving project success. Int. J. Proj. Manag. **14**(2), 81–87 (1996)

Nasir, M.H.N., Sahibuddin, S.: Addressing a critical success factor for software projects: a multi-round Delphi study of TSP. Int. J. Phys. Sci. **65**(5), 1213–1232 (2011a)

Nasir, M.H.N., Sahibuddin, S.: Critical success factors for software projects: a comparative study. Sci. Res. Essays **6**(10), 2174–2186 (2011b)

Nickerson, R.C.: Business and Information Systems, 2nd edn. Prentice Hall, NJ (2001)

Prater, J., Kirytopoulis, K., Ma, T.: Optimism bias within the project management context: a systematic quantitative literature review. Int. J. Managing Proj. Bus. **10**(2), 370–385 (2017)

Ryvkin, D., Krajc, M., Ortmann, A.: Are the unskilled doomed to remain unaware? J. Econ. Psychol. **33**, 1012–1031 (2012)

Stake, R.E.: The Art of Case Study Research. Sage Publications, Thousand Oaks (1995)

Standish Group International 1994: Chaos Technical Report. www.standishgroup.com

Standish Group International 1995: Chaos Technical Report. www.standishgroup.com

Standish Group International 1996: Chaos Technical Report. www.standishgroup.com

Standish Group International 1999: Chaos: A Recipe for Success Technical Report. www.standishgroup.com

Standish Group International 2001: Extreme Chaos. Technical Report. www.standishgroup.com

Standish Group International 2009: Chaos Summary 2009: 10 Laws of CHAOS. www.standishgroup.com

Standish Group International 2010: Chaos Summary for 2010. Technical Report. www.standishgroup.com

Standish Group International 2013: Chaos Manifesto 2013: Think Big, Act Small. www.standishgroup.com

Standish Group International 2014: Chaos Technical Report. www.standishgroup.com

Standish Group International 2015: Chaos. Technical Report. www.standishgroup.com

Subba Rao, S., Solis, L.E., Raghunathan, T.S.: A framework for international quality management research: Development and validation of a measurement instrument. Total Qual. Manag. **10**(7), 1047–1075 (1999). https://doi.org/10.1080/0954412997226

Thibodeau, P.: Pennsylvania sues IBM over troubled $110 M IT upgrade (2017). http://www.computerworld.com/article/3180325/it-industry/pennsylvania-sues-ibm-over-troubled-110m-it-upgrade.html. Accessed 01 June 2017

Thomas, J., Mengel, T.: Preparing project managers to deal with complexity – Advanced project management education. Int. J. Proj. Manag. **26**, 304–315 (2008)

Thornberg, R.: Informed grounded theory. Scand. J. Educ. Res. **56**(3), 243–259 (2012). https://doi.org/10.1080/00313831.2011.581686

Twenge, J.M., Campbell, W.K.: The Narcissism Epidemic: Living in the Age of Entitlement. Free Press, New York (2010)

Twenge, J.M., Foster, J.D.: Birth cohort increases in narcissistic personality traits among American college students, 1982–2009. Soc. Psychol. Pers. Sci. **1**(1), 99–106 (2010)

Vaughan, D.: The Challenger Launch Decision: Risky Technology, Culture, and Deviance at NASA; With a New Preface. University of Chicago Press, New York (2016)

V-Tran (2014)

Project Documents and Witness Statements

WS003_20120531_KPMG_Report_dated_31_May_2012.pdf
WS004_20120531_KPMG_Report.pdf
WS013_20130225-Statement-of-Craig-Vayo.pdf
WS014_20130225a_SWINSON,-John-signed-statement.pdf
WS017_20130227_MANDER,-Robert-signed-statement.pdf
WS024_20130228-Geoffrey-WAITE.pdf
WS026_20130301a_BRADLEY_Gerard_Statement_signed.pdf
WS032_20130305_SALOUK_witness-statement.pdf
WS039_20130307_UHLMANN,-Gary-signed-statement.pdf
WS043_20130317_BLAKENEY,-Maree-signed-statement.pdf
WS085_20130507_Margaret-Berenyi.pdf
WS104_20130523_LUCAS-Paul.pdf
WS107_20130524a-Malcolm-Grierson.pdf
WS116_20130611_Kalimnios-Shea-and-Brown.pdf
WS118_20130617-POLLOCK-Brendan.pdf
WS120_20130624_Submission-for-Contract-IBM-Australia.pdf
WS122_20130731_royal_commission_report.pdf
PD010_20070528 - HR Current System Maintenance and Support - Payroll and Rostering Risk Analysis with attachments.pdf
PD063_20080911_Prog_42.pdf
PD103_20090422-KJ-Ross-draft-report.pdf
PD108_20090501_Queensland Audit Office.pdf

Revisiting Concepts and Theories

Making Sense of Smart Living, Working, and Organizing Enhanced by Supposedly Smart Objects and Systems

Steven Alter[(✉)]

University of San Francisco, San Francisco 94117, USA
alter@usfca.edu

Abstract. The term *smart* is applied to many different types of things in today's world, leaving the question of what is meant by the title of an IFIP 8.6 workshop called "Smart Living, Working, and Organizing." This paper's goal is to provide a conceptual basis for making sense of "smart living, working, and organizing." It provides many examples of nominally smart objects and systems, presents principles related to smartness, provides a definition of smart that applies to objects and systems, presents dimensions related to four categories of smartness, and uses two brief examples to show how those dimensions might be used in thinking about how to make an object or system smarter.

Keywords: Smart living · Smart working · Smart organizing · Smart object
Smart system · Definition of smart

1 Is a Hospital Smart if Its Nurses Use Smart Thermometers?

This paper responds to the Call for Papers for the IFIP 8.6 workshop on Smart Living, Working, and Organizing by trying to make sense of the term *smart* in the context of living, working, and organizing.

An Elusive Idea. The idea of "Smart Living, Working, and Organizing" is suggestive but elusive. The CFP does not define smart, but mentions smart devices, smart homes, smart cars, smart phones, smart government, smart cities and smart organizations. Wikipedia contains articles about many other supposedly smart things, such as smart bombs, smart bullets, smart cameras, smart cards, smart clothing, smart contracts, smart doorbells, smart drinks, smart fabrics, smart farming, smart file systems, smart fluids, smart glass, smart glasses, smart grids, smart guns, smart highways, smart keys, smart labels, smart lighting, smart locks, smart manufacturing, smart materials, smart meters, smart mirrors, smart missiles, smart numbers, smart objects, smart pensions, smart power, smart speakers, smart systems, smart terminals, smart watches, and smart whiteboards. Microsoft Word 2016 touts nominally smart capabilities including smart quotes, smart lookup, smart copy and paste, smart paragraph selection, and smart cursoring. While writing this paper, I learned about competition in the world of smart toothbrushes, one version of which identifies whether specific teeth have been cleaned and transmits that information to a smart phone where it is displayed superimposed on an image of a set of teeth. The decades-old stream of research and practice related to

© IFIP International Federation for Information Processing 2019
Published by Springer Nature Switzerland AG 2019.
A. Elbanna et al. (Eds.): TDIT 2018, IFIP AICT 533, pp. 247–260, 2019.
https://doi.org/10.1007/978-3-030-04315-5_17

artificial intelligence, computer science, statistics, and other fields brings concepts, methods, experience, and a great deal of techno-hype and salesmanship related to subjects such as machine learning, big data, Internet of things, and recently, cognitive computing.

The diverse nature of those supposedly smart things illustrates why it is difficult to say something nontrivial about smartness that fits most of those examples and that helps in understanding smart living, working, and organizing. The diversity of supposedly smart things and capabilities leads to doubting whether their supposed smartness implies they have common properties. Viewed more broadly, one might wonder whether it would be fruitful, or even possible to theorize or generalize about the nature or impacts of smartness if the same concept purports to describe smart toothbrushes, smart bombs, and smart cities. Furthermore, a definition of smart that emphasizes the presence of artificial intelligence, big data, or cognitive computing would automatically disqualify many supposedly smart objects or systems that do not use those approaches.

Goal and Organization. This research essay tries to provide a conceptual basis for making sense of "smart living, working, and organizing." Making sense of smartness in that context is necessary if discussions of that topic are to move beyond scattered predictions, social criticism, and/or philosophizing based on whatever examples seem interesting or potentially profitable to whomever is writing or speaking.

The goal: Characterize smart and smartness in relation to objects and systems in a way that is useful for describing, analyzing, and designing objects and systems.

The next section identifies principles that can be applied in thinking about the concept of smartness as it might apply to smart living, working, and organizing. The principles are capability-orientation, context-dependence, multidimensionality, separability, and applicability to objects, automated systems, and sociotechnical systems. The principles lead to a definition of smartness in the context of objects and systems. The definition leads to a classification matrix for smart capabilities, which fall into four areas, information processing, internal regulation, action in the world, and knowledge acquisition. Each of those areas includes a set of capabilities that can be described on a continuum from not smart to somewhat smart to extremely smart based on the definition of smart. A concluding section describes how this multidimensional view of smartness can be applied in thinking about smartness while describing, analyzing, and designing objects and systems. Except for a brief comment near the end, this paper focuses almost entirely on understanding what smart might mean in the context of living, working, and organizing. It does not cover important topics concerning conflicting stakeholder interests such as privacy, autonomy, job satisfaction, equity, and wealth.

What About Adoption of Technology? Adoption and diffusion of technology is the traditional focus of IFIP WG 8.6. This paper's focus on defining smartness and dimensions of smartness is directly related to adoption and diffusion of smart technologies because is not meaningful to theorize or generalize about adoption and diffusion of smart things unless the concepts of smart and smartness are taken seriously.

That requires defining those terms and not just treating smart and smartness essentially as hype that serves as little more than enticement.

2   Principles Related to Smart and Smartness

This paper's view of smart and smartness is related to purposefully constructed entities including objects, sociotechnical systems, and totally automated systems. It explicitly excludes consideration of smart or smartness as a characteristic of human intellect, of groups of people, or of natural capabilities of living things. It assumes that applications of AI methods and research may or may not be related to smartness in the sense of smart living, working, and organizing.

While most significant aspects of living, working, and organizing occur within sociotechnical systems, this paper assumes that the concept of smartness must have a broader domain that includes objects and totally automated systems. That is necessary because a current sociotechnical system that happens to use objects that are currently viewed as smart may evolve into a more automated system that relies on smart objects and other systems in ways not yet imagined. The discussion of smartness needs to cover those cases, but a focus on smart living, working, and organizing calls for special emphasis on sociotechnical systems in which nominally smart technologies are used. For example, it includes uses of smart phones within sociotechnical systems that perform systematic sales work or systematic customer service work. It might include the use of smart phones to make phone calls if communication in a general sense is viewed as a sociotechnical system. It pays little attention to uses of smart phones for playing single player games while riding a bus because that type of individual activity generally is not associated with research or practice related to sociotechnical systems.

This paper's consideration of smartness in the context of sociotechnical systems is guided by the following principles, which coalesced as this paper was being written (i.e., did not come from a literature survey). The principles are introduced at this point in the paper to make it easier to understand how this paper's ideas unfold

Capability-Orientation. An entity's smartness is described in terms of its capabilities for performing types of actions that are associated with smartness. Thus, a sociotechnical system's smartness along the various dimensions of smartness can be assessed by observing how it operates.

Context-Dependence. An entity that might seem smart along some of the dimensions of smartness within a context might be totally unsmart on those dimensions in another context. For example, a sociotechnical system that seems to be smart in the context of dealing with minor variations in a highly repetitive situation might be unable to function in the presence of high variation.

Multidimensionality. Smartness is not a binary, yes/no distinction. Smartness can be viewed as a set of continuous variables or dimensions that individually range from not at all smart to extremely smart. The dimensions are assumed to be only partially independent, i.e. that smartness on one dimension often is partially dependent on smartness along another dimension. While it is always possible to combine any set of numerical dimensions into a single numerical score (e.g., the average of numerical scores for 10 dimensions), there is little reason to believe that a combined smartness score is useful for describing or comparing entities with regard to smartness.

Separability. An entity that includes or uses a nominally smart component may not be smart of its own right. For example, a hospital that uses smart thermometers may not be smart in terms of most or all of the dimensions of smartness. Similarly, having an exceptionally smart exhaust system does not imply that an entire car should be viewed as smart.

Applicability to Objects, Totally Automated Systems, and Sociotechnical Systems. Totally automated systems are increasingly evident as subsystems of sociotechnical systems. The dimensions of smartness should make sense for objects, totally automated systems, and sociotechnical systems.

3   Definition of Smart

This section defines smart and related dimensions of smartness in a way that applies both to objects and to sociotechnical systems in which smart living, working, and organizing occur. The powerful trend toward automating important parts of business operations calls for using a definition and set of dimensions that apply beyond just sociotechnical systems. As automation possibilities continue to appear, there will be many situations in which it may not be obvious whether a smartness initiative should be directed at an entire sociotechnical system or at specific components. The definition of smart and the dimensions of smartness should apply in either case.

3.1   Smart in the Context of Living, Working, and Organizing

The introduction mentioned the difficulty of trying to define smart in a way that applies in a nontrivial way to most of supposedly smart things that it mentions. Searches of Google Scholar for various "smart" things (e.g., smart phones, smart cities, etc.) did not come close to producing a consensus definition that is useful here.

A hint at a possible direction for thinking about the topic of "smart living, working, and organizing," comes from [1], a 2015 editorial in the journal *Service Science*. That editorial defines smart service system as follows:

> "a system capable of learning, dynamic adaptation, and decision making based upon data received, transmitted, and/or processed to improve its response to a future situation. The system does so through self-detection, self-diagnosing, self-correcting, self-monitoring, self-organizing, self-replicating, or self-controlled functions. These capabilities are the result of the incorporation of technologies for sensing, actuation, coordination, communication, control, etc."

Most of the nominally smart things mentioned in this paper's introduction exhibit aspects of some of those capabilities. Combining those ideas with the general spirit of the five principles mentioned earlier, smartness calls for at least some automated information processing and at least some degree of self-control, learning, adaptation, and/or decision-making related to performing activities or functions that have consequence in the world.

Definition of smartness. Purposefully designed entity X is smart to the extent to which it performs and controls functions that produce directly perceptible results for people by using automated capabilities for processing information, interpreting information, and/or learning from information that may or may not be specified by its designers.

Specific aspects of the definition should be noted:

"Purposefully designed entity." The entities under consideration are designed. They are artificial [2]. They may have evolved through many iterations that involve at least some degree of conscious design effort, either through formal projects with allocated resources or through workarounds and adaptations to overcome limitations of previously existing versions of object or system.

"Smart to the extent to which." Smartness is not a binary, yes/no variable that describes whether something is or is not smart. Instead, smartness is a continuous variable or a series of continuous variables related to different aspects of smartness.

"Performs and controls functions that produce directly perceptible results for people." This phrase is stated in a way that applies to both objects and sociotechnical systems. Specifying that the functions performed and/or controlled produce directly perceptible results for people implies greater concern about things that people can perceive and less concern for about automated activity deep within computing infrastructures that only technicians perceive. Notice that the visibility of a function does not imply that it is the most important aspect of a situation. Consistent with the principle of separability, a smart attendance system in an automobile factory would not be evidence that the factory is smart because the factory's primary functions are related to producing automobiles, not taking attendance.

"Automated capabilities for processing information." The primary components of purely social systems and noncomputerized work systems do not perform automated information processing and therefore cannot be smart in this sense. Processing information can be subdivided into capturing, storing, retrieving, transmitting, manipulating, and/or displaying information, each of which will be treated as a dimension of smartness within the category of processing information.

"Automated capabilities for interpreting information." This includes drawing conclusions from information, such as recognizing the semantics of the information and evaluating the extent to which the information is correct.

"Learning from information that may or may not be specified by its designers." This includes executing predefined scripts and capturing or creating new knowledge and internalizing that knowledge into the nominally smart entity itself.

Such careful attention to the definition of smartness might seem excessive, but actually is important for serious discussion of smart systems and devices Aside from the general benefits of defining terms, serious attention to the definition of smartness helps in separating the discourse of smart systems and devices from common uses the term smart related to whether or not people are smart and whether or not an object or system's design has convenient or otherwise beneficial features. Smart systems and devices are products of human intellect but are not a direct reflection of the intellect of any individual or group. Smartness also is not treated as a synonym of high quality, good fit to needs, or otherwise impressive or beneficial capabilities. Mixing those three views of smartness leads to confusion. A product/service that exhibits excellent quality and fits customer requirements in an extremely clever way might not exhibit smartness as defined here. Conversely, a product/service might have low quality or inadequate fit to user needs even though it exhibits some of the characteristics of smartness as defined here.

4   Classification Matrix for Smart Capabilities

Defining smartness is a step forward, but the definition provides little guidance for supporting description, analysis, and design of smart objects and systems. The next step is a classification matrix shown below Table 1, which includes a very brief description of each capability. The horizontal categories are basically different domains of smartness, i.e., smartness related to information processing, internal regulation, action in the world beyond the object or system, and knowledge acquisition. The second, third, and fourth domains rely on the first domain, but are different enough to identify separately. It is possible for an object or system to be very smart in one or several of these domains, but not smart at all in others. For example, an ability to capture information through sensors does not imply that an object or system can use that information for internal regulation, for action in the world beyond itself, or for accumulating knowledge.

The rows in Table 1 go from scripted execution of prespecified instructions through formulaic adaptation, creative adaptation, and finally, unscripted or partially scripted invention. Effective sociotechnical systems generally have capabilities in every cell of the matrix, and usually have possibilities for improvement in some of those areas. Things that are called smart objects often have capabilities in only one or several of those areas. Scripted execution, i.e., following programmed instructions, is fundamental to all computing and generally describes sociotechnical systems whose processes are highly structured and mechanical. Formulaic adaptation is common, as in the handling of repetitive exceptions within organizational routines. Creative adaptation is more challenging due to novelty and difficulty of changing established practices. It becomes especially challenging when it involves abstraction, inference, optimization, or search to develop a new adaptation that was not specified in advance. Unscripted or partially scripted invention involves producing new understandings, methods, or artifacts using inferences or extrapolations from past, current, or projected future situations. Many sociotechnical systems perform localized invention through workarounds or other unscripted or partially scripted responses to conditions that make it difficult to fulfill organizational or personal goals (e.g., see theory of workarounds [3]). Totally automated invention is far beyond current capabilities of most totally automated systems except in rare niche areas such as drug discovery.

4.1   Dimensions of Smartness

By the definition above, smartness of an object, totally automated system, or sociotechnical system is best described as a set of dimensions that are continuous

Table 1. Classification matrix for smart capabilities

	Information processing	Internal regulation	Action in the world	Knowledge acquisition
Scripted execution	Execution of prespecified instructions in a computer program	Internal regulation based on a prespecified script or method	Visible action based on a prespecified script or method	Acquisition and internalization of information based on a prespecified script or method
Formulaic adaptation	Adaptation of information processing based on prespecified inputs or conditions	Adaptation of internal regulation based on prespecified inputs or conditions	Adaptation of current action in the world based on prespecified inputs or conditions	Adaptation of knowledge acquisition based on prespecified inputs or conditions
Creative adaptation	Adaptation of information processing instructions based on unscripted or partially scripted analysis of relevant information or conditions	Adaptation of a script for internal regulation based on unscripted or partially scripted analysis of relevant information or conditions	Adaptation of a script for action in the world based on unscripted or partially scripted analysis of relevant information or conditions	Adaptation of a script for knowledge acquisition based on unscripted or partially scripted analysis of relevant information or conditions
Unscripted or partially scripted invention	Unscripted or partially scripted design and execution of a workaround or new method for processing information	Unscripted or partially scripted design and execution of a workaround or new method for internal regulation	Unscripted or partially scripted design and execution of a workaround or new method related to action in the world	Unscripted or partially scripted planning and execution of a workaround or new method related to knowledge acquisition

variables going from not at all smart to somewhat smart to extremely smart. Tables 2, 3, 4, and 5 provide an initial description the "somewhat" and "extreme" parts of those dimensions. As will be illustrated in the next section, the dimensions in those tables might be used as an aid for thinking about different ways to make an object or system smarter or less smart, either of which might be more advantageous for specific purposes and/or specific stakeholders.

The dimensions in Table 2 are the six aspects of automated information processing [4], i.e., capturing, transmitting, storing, retrieving, manipulating, and displaying information. Most of the smart things listed in this paper's introduction (e.g., smart

Table 2. Dimensions related to automated information processing in general.

Dimension	Somewhat smart	Extremely smart
Capture information	Captures predefined data items using data capture techniques designed for the data captured	Uses context-related knowledge (not prespecified knowledge) to decide which information to capture and how to capture it
Transmit information	Transmits predefined data items using transmission techniques designed for the data transmitted	Uses context-related knowledge (not prespecified knowledge) to decide where information needs to be transmitted and how to transmit it
Store information	Stores predefined information using data storage techniques designed for the data stored	Uses context-related knowledge (not prespecified knowledge) to decide how and where to store information
Retrieve information	Retrieves predefined data items using data retrieval techniques designed for the data retrieved	Uses context-related knowledge (not prespecified knowledge) to decide how to find information and how to retrieve it
Manipulate information	Manipulates predefined data items or aggregations of data items using data manipulation techniques designed for the prespecified data.	Uses context-related knowledge (not prespecified knowledge) to decide what manipulation of information is needed and how to produce that result
Display information	Displays predefined data items or aggregations of data items using data display techniques designed for the prespecified data	Uses context-related knowledge (not prespecified knowledge) to decide what information would be most valuable to display

glasses, smart locks, and smart meters) capture information and then use that information to perform their primary functions. Some of them transmit, store, or retrieve information; some do not. Most of them manipulate information, e.g. performing calculations using the information or changing the format of the information. Many entities are somewhat smart along one or more of the six dimensions. Few are extremely smart along any of those dimensions. Notice Table 2's use of the terms information, data, and knowledge. The first column uses the term information because electronic signals that are processed must be information, i.e., must have some impact in relation to the function at hand. Without such impact, the data collected and transmitted, would be considered data, not information. The second column (somewhat smart) uses the term data because the physical processing occurs through applying predefined techniques to predefined data items. The fourth column (extremely smart) uses the term knowledge because extremely smart implies a higher order of purpose and semantic mastery than is implied by merely processing data.

Table 3 presents dimensions related to internal regulation, which is increasingly important as objects and systems become more automated and more autonomous. Each dimension relies on information processing and each overlaps to some extent with

Table 3. Dimensions related to internal regulation

Dimension	Somewhat smart	Extremely smart
Self- detection	Uses prespecified data and criteria to characterize its existence as separate from but possibly related to the existence of other relevant entities	Performs non-scripted activities that establish and maintain its separate identity within the surrounding ecosystem
Self-monitoring	Uses predefined sensing techniques, criteria, and data to monitor its internal state	Uses non-scripted methods for self-monitoring in order to maintain the entity itself
Self-diagnosis	Diagnoses internal problems by applying predefined techniques and criteria to predefined data	Diagnoses internal problems by performing novel analysis not scripted in advance by designers
Self-correction	Uses predefined techniques, criteria, and data to modify internal parameters or business rules	Uses non-scripted methods for identifying deviations from past, current, or future goals and determining how to adjust or to meet those goals in the future
Self-organization	Uses predefined techniques, criteria, and data to organize its own operational structure	Uses non-scripted methods to organize different components of the entity in order to achieve its goals

Table 4. Dimensions related to action in the world

Dimension	Somewhat smart	Extremely smart
Sensing	Captures predefined data items using sensing techniques designed for the types of data that are sensed	Uses non-scripted methods to decide how to sense situations or other higher order information (e.g., work being done in a way that is not competent)
Actuation	Uses predefined methods and information to actuate activity involved in primary functions	Uses non-scripted methods for deciding what to actuate and how to perform the actuation.
Coordination	Uses predefined business rules or decision tables to support coordination of actors and/or uses of resources	Uses non-scripted methods for deciding what needs to be coordinated and how to perform the coordination
Communication	Uses predefined methods and rules for communicating with people or supporting human communication	Uses non-scripted methods for identifying communication recipients and deciding what needs to be communicated and how to perform the communication effectively
Control	Manipulates predefined data items or aggregations of data items using data manipulation techniques designed for the prespecified data.	Uses non-scripted methods for deciding what needs to be controlled and how to perform the control activities effectively

Table 5. Dimensions related to knowledge acquisition

Dimension	Somewhat smart	Extremely smart
Sensing or discovering	Uses predefined scripts to capture predefined data items	Uses context-related knowledge (not prespecified knowledge) to decide which information to capture and how to capture it
Classifying	Uses predefined scripts to classify information	Uses context-related knowledge to decide how to classify information
Compiling	Uses predefined scripts to compile information	Uses context-related knowledge to decide how to compile information to make it as useful as possible
Inferring or extrapolating from examples or statistical summaries	Uses predefined scripts to infer or extrapolate conclusions from concrete examples or statistical summaries of examples	Uses knowledge that is not specified in the form of a script to infer or extrapolate conclusions from concrete examples or statistical summaries of examples
Inferring or extrapolating from abstractions	Uses predefined scripts to infer or extrapolate conclusions from abstractions	Uses knowledge that is not specified in the form of a script to infer or extrapolate conclusions from abstractions
Testing and evaluating	Uses predefined scripts to test or evaluate hypothesized knowledge	Uses knowledge not in the form of a script to test or evaluate hypothesized knowledge

some of the dimensions in other categories. The five dimensions are based largely on the description of smart service system in [1].

The dimensions in Table 4 are related to various aspects of performing action in the world beyond the boundary of the nominally smart object or system. The dimensions in Table 4 involve applying information processing (see Table 2) to systemic purposes including sensing, actuation, coordination, communication, and control, topics from the description of smart service system mentioned earlier. The reference to non-scripted methods in the extremely smart column sets the bar very high because it calls for invention using techniques and goals that are determined dynamically based on the context at hand. Determining techniques and goals on-the-fly is often challenging for people. Imbuing that level of "smartness" into totally automated systems is far beyond current capabilities except possibly in certain niche situations.

Table 5 presents six dimensions related to knowledge acquisition. This dimension starts with sensing or discovering predefined data items. From there it moves to classifying and compiling data in a way that constitutes factual knowledge. More advanced dimensions involve inferring or extrapolating from examples, from statistical summaries, or from abstractions, and at some point testing and evaluating the knowledge acquired.

5 Using the Dimensions of Smartness for Describing, Analyzing, or Designing Objects or Systems

A test of whether the dimensions of smartness are useful is to apply them for describing, analyzing, or designing smartness into objects or systems. Lacking an empirical test at the time of this writing, the applicability of the dimensions is illustrated by using two hypothetical examples, an imagined smart water bottle (a smart object) and an imagined attempt to make a hiring system smarter.

5.1 Use Related to a Potentially Smart Object, a Water Bottle

Imagine that a company's R&D department uses Tables 2, 3, 4, and 5 to brainstorm about different forms of smartness that might apply to product X, a smart version of the type of water bottle that some people carry around and use when exercising.

Smartness Dimensions Related to Information Processing. With the necessary electronics, X could *capture* information related to the amount of water in the bottle, the amount drunk each time the bottle is used, the temperature of the water, and even characteristics of the user such as identity, temperature, or pulse rate. The data could be *stored* and *retrieved*. It could be *transmitted* wirelessly to a phone or other device could be *manipulated* and *displayed* in graphs by using a related app.

Smartness Dimensions Related to Internal Regulation. With *self-monitoring*, X could track the rate at which water was consumed. It might monitor the temperature of the water and even the presence of impurities. It might *self-diagnose* problems, such as inadequate or excessive rate of usage or presence of impurities. X might *self-correct*, if it had a way of heating, cooling, or filtering the water.

Smartness Dimensions Related to Action in the World. X's tracking data from its *sensing* capabilities might be used *actuate* a visual signal that *communicates* the user's need to drink water or the fact that the water supply was impure or almost depleted. It also might *communicate* with a phone or fitness tracker. X might tighten its opening to exert *control* to prevent the user from drinking too rapidly.

Smartness Dimensions Related to Knowledge Acquisition. X could *sense* data and then *classify* it in relation to the types of issues revealed. It would *compile* a history of usage including time, place, quantity, and other characteristics of each instance of usage. *Inference or extrapolation* from the compiled information could generate statistical knowledge about usage patterns for individuals and populations, plus details of individual or group idiosyncrasies.

I imagined the hypothetical water bottle example as a simple if unlikely illustration of how to use the smartness dimensions. Later I performed a search on "smart water bottle" and found not only product examples, but product reviews that mentioned smart capabilities but seemed to focus more on cost and features.

5.2 Use Related to a Sociotechnical System, a Hiring System

Imagine that managers of a technology company wanted to explore whether their hiring system might benefit from greater smartness. They know that their employees are smart and believe that their processes make sense. Nonetheless, they wonder whether a smarter hiring system would reduce costs and improve hiring results.

Smartness Dimensions Related to Information Processing. Their current system contains technology that seems to process information adequately. It *captures* necessary information, *stores* it in a database where it is *retrieved* easily, provides a straightforward way of *manipulating* information to generate management reports, and *displays* the information in convenient forms. Table 2's descriptions of extremely smart information processing seem like science fiction to the managers.

Smartness Dimensions Related to Internal Regulation. Looking at internal regulation highlights important problems in the system, which cannot be viewed as *self-monitoring, self-diagnosing,* or *self-correcting*. In some ways it seems *self-organizing,* but the CEO views that as a synonym of excessively improvisational. The CEO believes the system needs smarter management rather than smarter technology.

Smartness Dimensions Related to Action in the World. They see room for improvement in *sensing* the ability of applicants to work with others. Perhaps video or some other technology might help in detecting antisocial tendencies in applicants. Smarter *actuation* might produce a path for interviewing the most qualified applicants sooner. Smarter *coordination* might call for better scheduling of interviews. The *communication* dimension might lead to wondering whether more interviews could be done by video and whether interviewers could submit their comments by video. Smarter control of the process might involve better notifications of due dates and better feedback related to interview reports.

Smartness Dimensions Related to Knowledge Acquisition. Management believes that knowledge acquisition is not a significant problem. The *sensing, classification*, and *compilation* of knowledge about hiring seems adequate. They question whether knowledge from smarter *inferences* or *extrapolations* related to *examples* or *abstractions* would make any difference. They like the idea of *testing* or *evaluating* the company knowledge about specific interviewees, but they do not know how that might be done in a smarter way.

6 Conclusion

This paper presented principles related to smartness, defined smart, presented dimensions related to four categories of smartness, and used two brief examples to show how those dimensions might be used in thinking about how to make an object or system smarter. I believe that serious discussion of smart living, working, and organizing requires clarity about the topic, i.e., a definition of smart and a related series of dimensions such as those presented here. Obviously, other definitions and sets of dimensions might be proposed. Ideally, alternative perspectives on smartness should be tested in situations related to the adoption of smart things.

When and How is It Wise to Use Smart Technologies? This paper's length limitations dictated that it could not explore important topics related to the social benefits, costs, and implications of using smart technologies. Many examples show that the use of smart technologies may or may not be beneficial to direct users of those technologies and to many other stakeholders concerned with topics ranging from privacy and surveillance through employment, equity, and wealth.

Consider just several types of impacts of just one type of smart device: Reports in the *Spine Journal* [5] and in other sources have described "text neck" as a medical issue related to the stress on neck and postural muscles due to flexing the neck for extended time spans to look downward at smart phones. Texting on smart phones is associated with a substantial percentage of car crashes [6]. The social scientist Sherry Turkle "found that children now compete with their parents' devices for attention, resulting in a generation afraid of the spontaneity of a phone call or face-to-face interaction." [7]. From a different perspective, "Facebook's former president, Sean Parker, recently said the platform was designed to be addictive and to 'consume as much of your time and conscious attention as possible. …. It literally changes your relationship with society, with each other … God only knows what it's doing to our children's brains'." [7]. Impacts of other smart objects and systems could be discussed as well, with the range of topics including "surveillance capitalism" [8], algorithmic justice [9]. dangers of smart drones [10], and sometimes making everyday life more complicated and less convenient [11].

In summary, defining smartness and exploring its various aspects is one of the ways to add care and specificity to discussions of how technical developments have had major consequences to date and that likely will bring many positive and negative impacts on living, working, and organizing in the future.

References

1. Medina-Borja, A.: Editorial column—smart things as service providers: a call for convergence of disciplines to build a research agenda for the service systems of the future. Serv. Sci. **7**(1), ii–v (2015)
2. Simon, H.A.: The Sciences of the Artificial. MIT Press, Cambridge (1996)
3. Alter, S.: Theory of workarounds (2014)
4. Alter, S.: The Work System Method: Connecting People, Processes, and IT for Business Results. Work System Press, Larkspur (2006)
5. Cuéllar, J.M., Lanman, T.H.: "Text neck": an epidemic of the modern era of cell phones? Spine J. **17**(6), 901–902 (2017)
6. Gliklich, E., Guo, R., Bergmark, R.W.: Texting while driving: a study of 1211 US adults with the distracted driving survey. Prev. Med. Rep. **4**, 486–489 (2016)
7. Popescu, A.: Keep your head up: how smartphone addiction kills manners and moods. New York Times, 25 January 2018
8. Zuboff, S.: Big other: surveillance capitalism and the prospects of an information civilization. J. Inf. Technol. **30**(1), 75–89 (2015)

9. Koene, A.: Algorithmic bias: addressing growing concerns. IEEE Technol. Soc. Mag. **36**(2), 31–32 (2017)
10. ABC7News: UC Berkeley professor helps create viral video to warn about killer robots, 17 November 2017. http://abc7news.com/technology/uc-berkeley-professor-helps-create-viral-video-to-warn-about-killer-robots/2664980/
11. Chen, B.X.: In an era of 'smart' things, sometimes dumb stuff is better. New York Times, 21 February 2018

Balancing Stakeholder Interests: Socio-Technical Perspectives on Smart Working Practice

Peter M. Bednar[1,2] and Christine Welch[3(✉)]

[1] School of Computing, University of Portsmouth, Buckingham Building,
Lion Terrace, Portsmouth PO1 3HE, UK
peter.bednar@port.ac.uk
[2] Portsmouth Business School, University of Portsmouth, Portsmouth, UK
Christine.welch@port.ac.uk

Abstract. The advantages put forward for so-called Smart working may sound very appealing. However, it is unlikely that all stakeholder groups involved will benefit to the same extent, if at all. Many initiatives that seem to be aimed at development of Smart work systems can be seen to be flawed, since they are suggested to support empowerment but are expressed in terms of pre-defined 'best practice'. This inherent paradox leads to consideration of ways in which innovation could occur that would lead to genuinely Smart systems, harnessing Smart technologies and empowering engaged actors to co-create meaningful practice in pursuit of professional excellence. An open, socio-technical systems approach is suggested to be the way forward.

Keywords: Open systems · Socio-technical systems · Smart working
Human-centred design

1   Introduction

Suggestions have been made that a paradigm shift has taken place since the Millennium in the way in which work practices are organized [1]. This is said to have been characterized by willingness of managers to adopt new organizing principles; a decline in the importance of place in work activities; greater scope for collaboration; employee autonomy and talent management; and an emphasis on innovation [2]. Advantages put forward for this, new 'Smart' working include a better work-life balance, less time and money spent on travel, lower rents and running costs for organizations, attraction of new talent into the workforce and increased productivity [3–5]. At the same time, it is acknowledged that Smart working requires very careful planning and can involve a shift of costs from employer to employee. Use of collaborative and mobile technologies is suggested to support team working and innovation, even though increased isolation for employees is recognized as a drawback.

A number of questions arise in relation to this suggested shift in management thinking. First, is there concrete evidence for this apparent trend in management thinking? If so, it would be expected to be accompanied by changes in relations among

© IFIP International Federation for Information Processing 2019
Published by Springer Nature Switzerland AG 2019.
A. Elbanna et al. (Eds.): TDIT 2018, IFIP AICT 533, pp. 261–276, 2019.
https://doi.org/10.1007/978-3-030-04315-5_18

stakeholders in organizations to reflect new thinking and to deliver the suggested benefits. There have been many 'new' perspectives on change in the past that promised much but were later abandoned, e.g. Business Process Re-engineering. Secondly, if it was genuinely desired by decision-makers in an organization to promote 'Smart' working, by what means could this be accomplished? The discussion which follows is intended to address these questions.

In the next section, results of a search for evidence is set out. Some examples are examined of initiatives advertised as efforts to adopt Smart working in the interests of all stakeholders. The following section will examine how introduction of Smart working practices might be effected from a systemic, socio-technical perspective. Finally, some conclusions are drawn.

2 Smart Working Initiatives

A search for literature on, and examples of 'Smart Working Practice' produced rather disappointing results, both from Google and Google Scholar. It is to be emphasized that this was not a rigorous or scholarly attempt to uncover material but only intended to be the type of search an interested manager or business owner might undertake, having learned of this supposed paradigm shift in management thinking. Several of the documents revealed in the search were from Governmental or quasi-governmental bodies and contained useful advice for other organizations wishing to pursue a Smart Working paradigm. Others were produced by consultants or commercial organizations wishing to encourage use of their services, e.g. Cisco who supply network technologies. Few examples of actual Smart working initiatives in organizations emerged.

2.1 The UK Government

The UK Government provides one example of an espoused wish for Smart working. It has launched an initiative for its services that it terms 'The Way We Work (TW3)' [4] and has set out a set of principles of 'best practice for Smart working', suggesting that in future the Civil Service will: focus on outcomes not process; be empowered by technology, work flexibly and cost-effectively; collaborate more effectively with other teams in their own department and other departments; maximize productivity and innovation, while reducing environmental impact. These aims and principles are discussed on the Civil Service Blog (2018) [6]. There seems little apparent awareness of any paradox between publication of 'best practice' for benchmarking on the one hand, and a statement of intent to promote flexibility, empowerment and autonomous innovation on the other. A case study of success is set out, relating to changes in practice at the Defence Science & Technology Laboratories (DSTL). However, we note that this is a section of the Civil Service whose whole purpose is to bring about innovation. How far such policies have met with success in, say, the Treasury, is a matter for conjecture.

2.2   The European Commission

A guide promoted by the EC on its Website was actually produced by Transport for London, in conjunction with a not-for-profit organization 'Work Wise UK' and dated 2007 [7]. The document offers advice to organizations wishing to embark on changes towards a Smart working paradigm. Examples are given, such as the Nationwide Building Society's move towards 'Flexible Working'.

The suggested policies on 'How to Implement Smarter Working' in this guide suggest, inter alia: *'It is important to assess business needs first, as production and service delivery dictate to a degree the choices that can be offered to staff ... It is important to assess business needs first, as production and service delivery dictate to a degree the choices that can be offered to staff'* (2007, p. 16).

2.3   Flexibility.co.uk

A Smart Working Handbook [8] is available on-line from flexibility.co.uk. The organization is stated to bring together expertise from research and opinion, drawing upon experience and working with large organizations, some of whom are listed as sponsors. This is more up-to-date and contains useful examples of real organizational initiatives, but these take the form of snapshots of particular aspects of practice from, e.g. Volkswagen Financial Services, Credit Suisse, Vodafone, Ofsted. It is stated to underpin and inform the UK Government TW3 document (see above). The advice and examples may be useful to those contemplating changing their practice, but not sufficient to enable to realistic evaluation for anyone less convinced.

2.4   Cisco IBSG

The report published by CISCO is persuasive about the suggested paradigm shift [1]. It refers to a global survey of more than 2,500 'end-users and key decision takers'. Smart Working is said to be the end of an evolutionary process in which technological developments have enabled organizations to reduce the importance of place in their activities. Their survey suggests that employees desire to work more flexibly but that IT-professional capability to deliver Smart systems lags behind. This is not a surprising conclusion from a company that sells networks. A number of successful initiatives are cited as examples (presumably from among Cisco customers) but it is interesting that these focus on enabling systems, e.g. Smart Work Centres in Amsterdam; a women's professional network 'GreenBizStartup'; community Smart work services in Belgium. The only large organization given as an example of Smart strategy is Cisco itself.

Discussion of Smart working in these technical and business publications refers to benefits as if these are both automatic and uncontentious, while occasionally acknowledging a downside, e.g. isolation or higher running costs for employees. However, any strategy involves choices between the interests of particular stakeholder groups – customers, employees, investors and society more generally.

2.5   The Automobile Association

An example of conflicting interests among stakeholders can be seen in the history of the Automobile Association in the UK. [9] The AA was originally a members' organization formed in 1905, funded by motorists' subscriptions. Uniformed patrol staff provided roadside services such as breakdown cover. Over a period of some 90 years, membership grew from 100 to over 15 million, and the range and quality of services was expanded until there was a fleet of more than 3,500 breakdown vehicles providing national coverage. The AA became instantly recognizable as a safe and reliable brand. During the 1990s and early 2000s, further products and services were added, including publications, a transport information services 'AA Roadwatch' and insurance. In 1999, members voted to end mutuality and sell to a commercial venture. Almost immediately, the AA was sold on to private equity capital. It became clear that these new owners had different priorities [9, 10]. Return on investment was prioritized. The workforce was cut by over 3,000. The number of patrol vehicles was cut from 3,500 to 1,100. Instead of in-house, recognizable patrolmen, members were likely to receive assistance from any available local garage sub-contracted by the company. People, particularly women, no longer felt the same trust in the service. Wachman [11] reports anecdotal evidence of people being left waiting at the side of the road for hours on end following a request for assistance. Meanwhile, staff were subjected to greater and greater pressure with close monitoring of all aspects of work and rigid timing of meal or comfort breaks. Morale became very low and staff turnover high. However, investors received a high yield and were very satisfied. Shortly afterwards, the company was sold on again at a profit.

Thus, it can be seen that the AA appeared to be a successful business for many, often institutional investors requiring a high return on capital. However, use of networking, electronic communication and remote working delivered benefits to neither customers nor employees [12].

2.6   Discussion

A number of the examples revealed in the rudimentary Web search described above relate to enabling initiatives. It is not difficult to see how small business centres offering Smart facilities would be attractive to self-employed entrepreneurs, who wish to operate in an agile way, e.g. keeping in close touch with actual and potential customers using mobile technologies. However, is this a genuine example of paradigm change?

Barber and Campbell [13] create a discussion on the drive from investors for companies to reduce their costs in order to generate a short-term surplus. Such strategies are not sustainable in the longer-term, but this is not the objective. Such imperatives might be cloaked under suggestions for Smart working. It is recognized, of course, that there are some industries in which it is possible to produce economies of scope by investing in new technologies to replace people (e.g. oil, banking, telecommunications), but in others human talent and engagement is key to pursuing excellence and revenue generation as can easily be seen in, e.g. software development, pharmaceuticals or fashion [13]. Policies that might, on the surface, appear to be 'Smart' may not survive beyond the short-term interests of a particular interests of a particular stakeholder group.

In any organization, there will be a strategic balance to be achieved. Clearly, an organization must be sustainable in many dimensions – financial, ecological and (socio) technical. Pursuit of effectiveness in delivering products and services requires professional education and commitment from staff, but is also dependent upon the financial viability of the processes involved, at least in the short-term. However, sustainability in the longer term requires attention to the so-called 'Triple Bottom-line' [14, 15]. The AA, for instance, may be able to deliver a service that is more flexible by getting rid of dedicated patrolmen and instead buying in services from local garages. As we have seen, when they attempted to do so, efficiency gains pleased only investors – customers and employees became disaffected. Smart working requires an optimal balance of skills, engagement and supporting technologies. Thus, the AA may be able to provide a better service to members by utilizing a computer-aided dispatch system to direct the closest and best-equipped patrolman to a particular stranded motorist. At the same time, the patrolmen may have less stress by travelling shorter distances and the AA fuel costs may be reduced. As an academic, it is easy to recognize that these benefits may emerge in such a context. Whether they will emerge, however, depends crucially upon the perceptions and perspectives of the engaged actors within a system of professional service delivery, and the extent to which they have an opportunity to explore and express them. Social networks can be viewed as intwined aspects of cultural behaviour. Proposed change that is not culturally feasible within particular socio-technical environments is unlikely to succeed [16, 17].

An important point that must be recognized when considering pursuit of benefits from Smart working is that every engaged stakeholder (customer, investor or employee) will have a personal, unique view of what is desired in context, and this also will be subject to redefinition and change over time. Desire by individuals to participate in, and facilitate change in pursuit of excellence must be a key to genuinely Smart work systems that deliver benefits to all [18, 19].

The next section of the paper will consider how genuinely Smart work systems might be co-created.

2.7 Systemic, Socio-Technical Perspectives

Effectiveness in any purposeful activity is a socio-technical phenomenon. People use tools in order to be productive. Tools are designed for use. Systems for the effective use of tools by people, to bring about desired outcomes, requires social and technical elements to be considered together. Thus, a modern, socio-technical approach does not pursue two separate (social and technical) strands for examination, but one, integrated whole. Mohr and van Amelsvoort [20] have defined a modern, socio-technical approach to comprise: '*The participative, multidisciplinary study and improvement of how jobs, single organizations, networks, and ecosystems function internally and in relation to their environmental context, with a special focus on the mutual interactions of the entity's ... value-creation processes*' (2016, p. 2). This definition is not entirely satisfactory, however, since it tends to ignore the participation of real human beings, whose contextual understandings, skills and desires are crucial to the achievement of 'value-creation processes'.

Any effort to bring about change in an organization in order to develop Smart working practices must be considered from a socio-technical perspective. A relevant question to pose is how far traditional ideas of 'organization' can be useful in an age of Smart living and working. Much of the business literature suggests that an 'organization' was identifiable by its corporate status, brand, distinctive culture and carefully managed activities. Organizations were associated with formally-defined missions, such as profit-making or religious observance, and tended to be associated with place– land and buildings. Any given organizations will have unique characteristics making it distinctive. As other organizations attempt benchmarking and copying 'best practice', they will probably acquire some of the first organization's market share or reputation assets; but those organizations that achieve sustained success are likely to do so through continuous innovation. As has famously been pointed out [21], the only sustainable source of competitive advantage for organizations in the long-run is the 'know-how' of those who work in them (p. 15). Thus, organizations perceived to be successful are those within which employee enthusiasm, creativity and team working are continually engaged. A journey of co-creation is undertaken by engaged profes- sionals seeking to achieve excellence in their practice, supported and facilitated by leaders. To what extent is the concept of 'Smart working' relevant to such a journey?

Nowadays it is common to consider business activities in terms of webs of value, often generated through a loose-knit collection of partner companies and individuals who come together to source, produce and/or deliver a collection of benefits perceived as a product/service. As Za et al. [22] suggest, gradual blurring of organizational, social and temporal boundaries has been supported by evolution of new 'digital ecosystems', allowing new products and services across multi-connected, transformative systems of collaboration, co-operation and learning. Joint ventures, collaborations and out-sourced activities are increasingly the norm.

It becomes increasingly difficult to express organizational boundaries with clarity – when someone logs into a social networking site such as FaceBook or LinkedIn, for instance, are they engaging in business or social activity? Or a combination of both? Only an engaged individual can tell where such boundaries lie, for them and from moment-to-moment. What sort of 'organization' is Airbnb, for instance? Who are its members – renters, owners, facilitators? When people engage in purposeful activity, they often desire to become 'organized' so that activities are not missed or duplicated, methods and channels are chosen, etc. Does this mean that 'an organization' has come into being? Possibilities for Smart working and living have created an environment in which many things become possible at short notice, with little capital outlay and collaboration can be supported over wide distances. 'Organization' becomes an increasingly temporary and informal concept. Pop-up restaurants, festivals and galleries are common examples of ephemeral 'organization'. Community life may be enhanced within Smart cities, that enable factors such as government services, transport and leisure to be 'organized' as integrated socio-technical systems. Personal life can be enhanced through Smart homes that support advanced communication with devices via an Internet of Things [23]. Where is the boundary between personal and professional life to be drawn? It may be that the mental model of 'an organization' is less helpful than an alternative view of 'work systems' in which actors collaborate, communicate and use available technologies for particular purposes.

2.8 Dynamic, Open Systems Approach

In contemplating design of work and/or organization, a systemic perspective is needed. Checkland [24] discusses emergence in systems. Originally a chemist, he uses the analogy with chemical elements. The distinctive smell of the household cleaner ammonia has little to do with the properties of nitrogen and hydrogen atoms, which are involved in ammonia's chemical structure (NH3) – the whole is more than just a combination of its parts. Thus, an organization might be seen as a purposeful whole, made up of smaller, interacting elements combined in an organized way to bring about a desired transformation of some kind (see Fig. 1). Since definition depends essentially on an observer who describes a phenomenon, it follows that purposeful activity systems will be defined differently according to the perspectives (or what Checkland calls Weltanschauungen) of the individuals who view them. Thus, a system's emergent properties exist only as a reflection of the mind of a person who contemplates them (p. 671) and chooses to draw a particular boundary around a system of interest [25]. Attempts to define a system from a particular perspective at a given moment in time can only result in a 'snapshot' view, meaningful to a particular observer only.

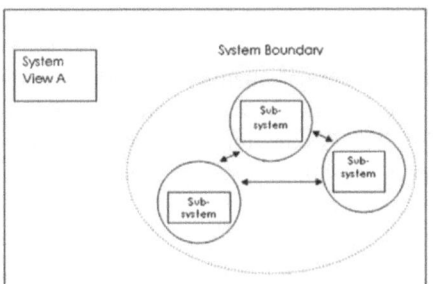 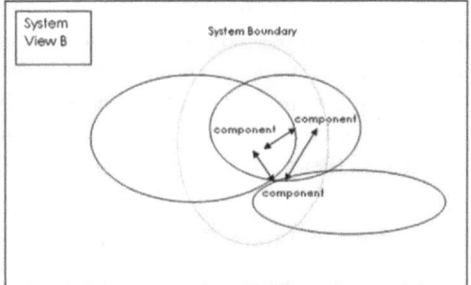

Fig. 1. System Views: A – organization as an emergent whole comprising hierarchical subsystems (adapted from Checkland, 1999), contrasted with View B – organization as an emergent property of interactions among individual actors (adapted from Bednar, 2007; 2008).

When a systemic lens is turned upon the nature of organization, it is possible to perceive that a higher order of complexity is involved. As Mumford [26] points out, organizations can be perceived as dynamic and open systems – elements continually entering, interacting and/or leaving over time. Thus, an organizational system's uniqueness derives from the qualities of the individual people who create and recreate it on an on-going basis by their participation and mutual interactions. Furthermore, as Bednar [27, 28] suggests, individual emergence is worthy of special consideration in relation to organizational systems, since it would be naïve to regard people simply as interchangeable 'units' of labour. Uniquely of all systemic elements, human beings may exhibit emergent properties greater than those of the whole system within which they interact, since human lives transcend any particular organizational context and human life is reflexive – we recreate 'ourselves' on an ongoing basis through experience and learning. Participants' roles, relations and perspectives in organization overlay one another and subsist in a constant state of flux. An organization may be viewed, therefore, as a complex social-technical system, affected by aspirations, behaviour and values of individuals within it [29]. Indeed, it is the interactions among engaged actors on an on-going basis that co-creates and re-creates which is recognizable as 'organization' (Fig. 1, System View B). Schein uses the term 'organizational culture' to reflect these recognizable characteristics.

All of this demonstrates the challenges involved in design of flexible, dispersed organizational systems to promote creativity and autonomous, continual innovation. Furthermore, attempts to separate technologies underpinning Smart living and working from the activities of the individuals whose desires are supported seem increasingly unhelpful. Kappelman et al. [30] point to a study carried out by the Society for Information Management, in which it is established that business-IT alignment is still the first concern of senior managers of companies around the world. Such 'alignment' has been a focus of discussion in IS circles for a generation [31]. However, in the early years of the IS discipline, Langefors [32] had already pointed out that a need for reporting was a crucial feature of management roles, and that it was therefore impossible to draw a meaningful distinction between Information System and organization – the latter's structure being crucially influenced by the former (p. 53). Since Langefors time, technological developments have gone far beyond reporting of management data, to pervade production and delivery of desired outcomes. It is suggested, therefore, that a concept of alignment between separate organizational sub-systems is not a useful construct. The idea is now receiving recognition that dynamic co-evolution of socio-technical elements is more relevant [33, 34]. A contemporary socio-technical approach is therefore required to support an on-going journey towards excellence.

2.9   Creating Smart Work Systems

A contemporary Socio-Technical perspective can be seen as a cornerstone of discussions about the human agency in the pursuit of Smart working. Phenomena such as human use and engagement with mobile technologies, the Internet of Things, or social networking as an intertwined aspect of mainstream cultural behaviour are factors all that have potential to promote or inhibit major changes in organizations and in society [35]. These changes, however, must be designed and created. Such design must focus on individuals and groups, according to a philosophy of human-centred design [36], and by taking into account systemic interactions among people and technologies [26, 37, 38]. Technical systems must be seen to be intrinsically incomplete, and therefore continually open to design and redesign in relation to human engagement [39]. It is possible to point to a double-helix relationship of use and reflection-upon-use in relation to IT artefacts, driving this process onwards [40]. Thus, design and re-design of socio-technical systems must be conceived as a continuous process involving innovators and recipients dealing with complex and evolving artefacts [26]. This process cannot be decoupled from soft, social, cultural and even psychological components of individual and organizational experience [35, 41]. Conceptually, we can distinguish between design of a new artefact, and design of systems for use of that type of artefact in real-world contexts, by real people, pursuing their own desired activities.

In practice, socio-technical systems are indivisible as they form dynamic, evolving 'wholes' through human agency.

It can therefore be demonstrated that human action, and interface with changes in personal and organizational life, are driven by desire. Too often, this crucial factor has been overlooked in efforts to develop and exploit new ideas for IT artefacts and systems [18]. Too often, consultation about 'requirements', followed by a phase of 'beta testing' have been considered all that was necessary as engagement with human motivation to use designed products. However, if organizations wish to achieve innovation through a process of autonomous evolution in working practices, human desire must become a central focus. There are motivating factors for use of mobile and Smart artefacts that might be described as 'fun', e.g. to be able to keep in touch with friends via social media, play games or to stream music and film. People may be motivated by factors equally compelling in the work environment, i.e. to engage with fellow professionals in carrying out tasks effectively to achieve professional excellence [17].

While designers may give adequate attention to the technical workings of artefacts and the ways in which they can be exploited for Smart working, this is often limited to a perspective we might term first order. Here, a socio-technical system, incorporating mobile devices, intelligent agents, and including human use of that system, form what is understood as a system of work. The boundary of this system is perceived as limited by the extent of artefacts, direct human use and interaction. It may be relevant here to reflect upon Alvesson's commentary on emptiness [42] in contemporary social systems. People seeking for growth in satisfaction sometimes focus not on real, economic improvements or improved utility in products, but rather on relative or positional satisfiers – e.g. 'my mobile phone has a better camera than yours'. Those who wish to support design of genuinely Smart working and living environments need to avoid a similarly empty response, as people engage with rhetoric and policy, rather than genuine professional commitment.

It is suggested that system design requires specific attention to the factor of desire-for-use. This can only be achieved within a second-order interpretation of relevant socio-technical systems. Here first order elements are considered together with other, further, inter-human communication within a work system (or other human activity systems in social contexts such as communities and groups) [19]. Viewed in this way, a work system (organization) can be seen to be both ephemeral and limited only by perceived boundaries of social networks out of which it is created. Desire to engage with such a system can only arise through opportunities for human agents to create and explore these boundaries for themselves. Designers then take the role of interested and supportive 'by-standers', taking a holistic approach in supporting actors to build systems that can contribute to empowerment for use [19, 43]. If human agents are to be supported to pursue excellence in their professional environments, then they need appropriate support to create purposeful revisions of contextuality – to explore and shape the contextual dependencies inherent in their working lives [16], and to design innovation in working practices from a socio-technical perspective. Every aspect of socio-technical change requires a human-centred design perspective, whether work systems comprise people-to-people interactions, machine-to-machine interactions, or combinations of both [44]. Professionals are distinguished by their ability to reflect upon practice of a professed skill set in context, and to relate these reflections to a body of standards and values transcending their immediate job role, and to interact with other professionals in doing so. Often, this involves membership of wider 'landscapes of practice' – formal and informal [45]. It is these interactions, and those of professionals with other stakeholders within and outside of work environments, that continually co-(-re)create 'organization'. Engaged professionals pursuing excellence will engage in extra role behaviour, e.g. experimenting, making suggestions for improvements, innovating methods or making efforts to help others in their professional roles. They are likely to bring experiences from other socio-cultural dimensions of life into their reflections upon practice [46]. It is through such attachment to a transcendent system of values, standards and experience that we recognize a professional at work.

Unfortunately, the world of business is full of examples where a human focus is not apparent [47]. In banking, for instance, there are examples of whole processes becoming automated through use of intelligent agents that can read and assimilate text rapidly and can also observe human-customer interactions in order to learn by experience. This, managers and system designers claim, frees human staff members to deal with the more complex issues needing experience and discretion to solve [48, 49]. Bank directors may consider this to be contributing towards Smart Working. However, a question arises how in future human agents will acquire deep knowledge of task performance in order to be able to develop experience, use discretion and/or promote innovation. Such attempts appear to be grounded in first order thinking.

Even where there is a focus upon human agents as part of a socio-technical system, innovations are not always designed in such a way as to support collaborative pursuit of excellence. An example is explored by Solon [50], who relates how Amazon have patented a bracelet to be worn by staff working in its warehouses. This uses ultrasonic tracking to identify the precise location of each worker's hands. A buzzing sensation against the hand alerts the wearer when moving away from the target warehouse bin. It is intended to speed up the picking process against certain performance measures. In public statements, the company asserts that this technology will be helpful to employees – saving them time and freeing their hands from scanners and their eyes from screens. Suggestions that performance monitoring is the real purpose of the wristband is dismissed by the company as 'misguided speculation'. Interestingly, however, examination of the actual registered US patent describes the purpose of the device as 'radio frequency based tracking of a worker's hands to monitor performance of inventory tasks' [51]. Thus, it can be seen that Smart working does not always produce rewards for all involved stakeholders.

Leaders of organizations may seem to recognize that investment in enabling technologies must be combined with redesign of whole working systems [3]. However, it becomes ever more necessary to ask the question from whose point of view resultant systems may be regarded as Smart, genuinely socio-technical or supportive of a journey towards professional or organizational excellence? Such initiatives often appear to be motivated by a wish to achieve cost savings, yielding greater returns for investors, rather than developing excellence through Smart working. It may be worthwhile to reflect, here, that efficiencies are often an expensive luxury in practice – achieved only by sacrifice of other, valuable assets. Too often, it appears that policies suggested to encourage innovation and Smart working are not translated into effective change [42]. Smart working practices are not always rewarded in practice, but rather incentives are applied in such a way as to create disorder and unintended, negative consequences. We see this in personal life as individuals become attached to Smart mobile devices and social media to an extent that may amount to addiction. The intended opportunities to stay connected, access leisure facilities and eCommerce can lead to fear of 'missing out' on desired contacts and an unreasonable focus on artefact use. In organizations, people may wish to be seen to carry out policies promoting innovation, rather than genuinely understanding or desiring beneficial outcomes from those policies. The resultant distortions in practice may lead to the opposite of excellence. Ciborra [52], drawing on Heidegger, distinguishes between two types of indication discernible in organizational life and discourse. The first, he terms illusory appearances: the set of ideas and models that are readily espoused in the domain of organizational theories or consulting models (p. 176). These can lead to taken-for-granted assumptions that are not challenged, stifling responsiveness and innovation [53]. The second he labels apparitions, which belong to a space that cannot be filled by any model, surfacing in informal communication that host 'the unexpected aspects of organizational life' (p. 177). Only the latter that can actually illuminate investigations into the desires of engaged actors for beneficial change. Again, it is clear that those who desire the benefits of Smart working within co-evolving socio-technical systems need support to engage in inquiry into contextual dependencies and thus unveil their desires and possibilities from use of innovative processes.

Efforts to assess the benefits of any particular innovation need to take into account both the positive and negative factors that may arise [54]. However, it is possible that those who seek for beneficial change will ask the question 'What are the negatives of the current system/behaviour?' in conjunction with the question 'What are the benefits to be expected from the posited future system/behaviour?' and use this as the basis to initiate action. However, in doing so they have neglected to ask the questions 'What are the negatives of the future system/behaviour?' and 'What are the positives of the current system/behaviour?' Both of these questions are relevant to consider in taking an open systems perspective, and their neglect is likely to detract from achievement of desired outcomes [55] (p. 44). Such a problem seems likely to occur when managers have published policies for 'best' practice in advance of any particular innovation in pursuit of Smart working.

In pursuit of professional effectiveness, the potential to go beyond the basic requirements of a role in order to create new boundaries involves a higher order of reflection. It becomes possible only through commitment to on-going reflection upon competence (Bateson)64 in which the individual concerned is reflecting not only upon experience, but upon the process of reflecting on exercise of judgment. This development of a learning 'spiral' may be regarded as an exercise in practical philosophy. In a socio-technical context, such a spiral must be generated through collaborative inquiry. Figure 2 provides a summary of a contemporary, socio-technical approach to design of Smart working systems. It shows how individuals interact within an organizing space, each with unique experiences of inherent contextual dependencies arising around their professional roles, and bringing their unique life experiences into the space. This figure therefore reflects multiple boundaries drawn from the perspectives of different human actors within the space. Recognition is given to individual emergence, showing how human lives transcend the space that forms current system(s) of interest.

Individuals interact within an organized working system, continually creating and recreating it. This system of interest is open and dynamic as different people, in multiple roles and with unique perspectives join, interact in and leave the system. These interactions overlap with a co-created system of inquiry into meaningful action that supports continual (re)co-creation through interaction, reflection and learning [17, 46].

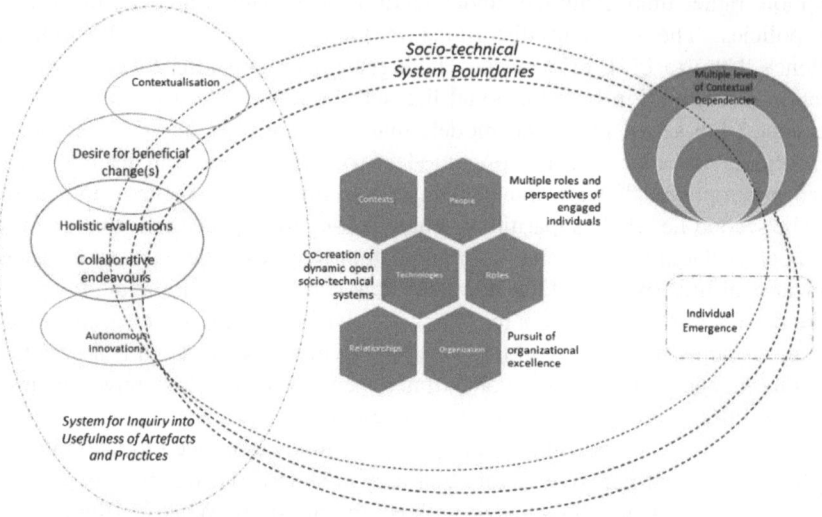

Fig. 2. A contemporary socio-technical approach to engagement with smart working

3   Conclusion

The evidence of a paradigm shift towards Smart working practice in organizations is not entirely convincing. It is important to recognize the potential benefits that such a shift might realize for different stakeholder groups, but at the same time to understand that Smart working strategy requires a balancing between differing interests. Benefit realization is not automatic. Desire for the benefits of Smart working may genuinely exist within an organization, but inertia may mean that such aspirations are not translated into action. Where desire for Smart working does exist, even the greatest advocates may inadvertently sabotage realization of these aims in practice [56]. Such phenomena have been well documented in the past, e.g. the (1928) comment of American Justice Louis Brandeis on the role of governments, inscribed in the Capitol Building 'The greatest dangers to liberty lurk in the insidious encroachment by men of zeal, well-meaning but without understanding' (Brandeis). People may desire to engage in Smart working, resulting in demand for greater access to supportive services. How is such demand to be articulated, assessed and acted upon? Organizational leaders may be ambitious to support Smart innovation. However, consideration of support for mean-ingful practice, and learning for meaningful practice are required in order to bring about such a transformation [17, 57, 58] and this aspect is frequently over-looked. Argyris

[56] suggests: '*It is not possible for human beings to engage de novo the full complexity of the environment in which they exist. Life would pass them by. Human beings deal with the challenge by constructing theories of action that they can use to act in concrete situations*' (p. 8).

It can be seen that a rational planning model to expand organizational choices involves an inherent paradox. Since any observation must, by definition, be made by a particular observer, adoption of a 'neutral' stance cannot be achieved in practice. This means that those who espouse rational planning are unaware that any data they gather about a dynamic and constantly recreated problem space is inherently misleading. In particular, the concept of 'best practice' is a dangerous one. It is possible to observe the practice of others, consider it in relation to our own contextual experiences and desires, and learn from it. However, attempts to copy practice from one unique context to another are unlikely to yield unsatisfactory results. Only a human-centred stance, recognizing that organizations subsist from moment-to-moment as self- creating, dynamic and open systems, is likely to lead to success in Smart innovation (see Fig. 2). Thus, if expressions of aspiration for Smart working are to lead to design of socio-technical systems that are experienced as Smart by professional human agents, support for professionals to explore their contextuality in pursuit of excellence must be more appropriate than policies setting out principles for supposed 'best' practice.

References

1. Boorsma, B., Mitchell, S.: Work-Life Innovation Smart Work—A Paradigm Shift Transforming How, Where, and When Work Gets Done. Ciscoo IBSG Point of View (2011). https://www.cisco.com/c/dam/en_us/about/ac79/docs/ps/WorkLife_Innovation_Smart_Work.pdf. Accessed 21 Apr 2018
2. Hamel, G.: The Future of Management. Harvard Business School Press, Cambridge (2007)
3. Gastaldi, L., Corso, M., Raguseo, E., Neirotti, P., Paolucci, E., Martini, A.: Smart working: rethinking work practices to leverage employees' innovation potential. In: Proceedings of 15th CINet Conference 'Operating Innovation – Innovating Operations', Budapest (Hungary), 7–9 September, pp. 337–347 (2014)
4. HM Government (UK): PAS 3000:2015. ICS 03.100.01 Committee ZZ/3, Smart Working. Code of Practice, 30 November 2015, BSI (2015)
5. Dominguez, A.: Do you know what Smart Working is? eHorus, 22 August 2017. https://ehorus.com/smart-working/. Accessed 14 Feb 2018
6. Civil Service Blog: Transforming the Way We Work (2018). https://civilservice.blog.gov.uk/2015/01/22/transforming-the-way-we-work/. Accessed 14 Feb 2018
7. Transport for London: Smarter Working Guide (2007). https://ec.europa.eu/energy/intelligent/projects/sites/ieeprojects/files/projects/documents/astute_smarter_working_guide_en.pdf. Accessed 14 Apr 2018
8. Lake, A.: Smart Working Handbook (2015). www.flexibility.co.uk. Accessed 14 Apr 2018
9. Millward, D.: For one day only, the saluting AA patrolman is back. The Telegraph, 11 April 2006. http://www.telegraph.co.uk/news/uknews/1515359/For-one-day-only-the-saluting-AA-patrolman-is-back.html. Accessed 21 Feb 2018
10. Teather, D., Treanor, J.: Private equity: the human cost. The Guardian on-line, 23 Feb 2007. https://www.theguardian.com/business/2007/feb/23/privateequity1. Accessed 21 Feb 2018

11. Wachman, R.: A sorry Saga at the AA? Private equity is back in the headlight. The Guardian on-line, 1 July 2007. https://www.theguardian.com/business/2007/jul/01/privateequity.observerbusiness. Accessed 21 Feb 2018
12. Williams, C.: How the wheels came off at the AA. The Telegraph on-line, 5 August 2017. http://www.telegraph.co.uk/business/2017/08/05/wheels-came-aa/. Accessed 21 Feb 2018
13. Barber, F., Campbell, D.: Layoffs: creating or destroying shareholder value? Ivy Bus. J., September/October 2001. https://iveybusinessjournal.com/publication/layoffs-creating-or-destroying-shareholder-value/. Accessed 21 Feb 2018
14. Elkington, J.: Cannibals with Forks: the Triple Bottom Line of 21st Century Business, Capstone (1997)
15. Willard, B.: The New Sustainability Advantage: Seven Business Case Benefits of a Triple Bottom Line. New Society Publishers (2012)
16. Bednar, P.M.: A contextual integration of individual and organizational learning perspectives as part of IS analysis. Inf. Sci. J. Emerg. Transdiscipline 3(3), 145–156 (2000)
17. Bednar, P.M., Welch, C.: Learning for professional competence in an IS context. In: Lundh Snis, U. (ed.) SCIS 2016. LNBIP, vol. 259, pp. 163–175. Springer, Cham (2016). https://doi.org/10.1007/978-3-319-43597-8_12
18. Bednar, P.M., Welch, C.: Incentive and desire: covering a missing category. In: MCIS 2006, Proceedings of the Mediterranean Conference on Information Systems, Università degli Studi di Trento, San Servolo, Venice, Italy, 5–9 October 2006
19. Bednar, P.M., Welch, C.: Inquiry into Informing Systems: critical systemic thinking in practice, Chap. 14. In: Gill, G. (ed.) Foundations of Informing Science: 1999–2008, pp. 459–501. Informing Science Press, Santa Rosa (2016)
20. Mohr, B.J., van Amelsvoort, P.: Co-Creating Humane and Innovative Organizations: Evolutions in the Practice of Socio-technical System Design. Global STS-D Network Press, Portland (2016)
21. Davenport, L., Prusak, L.: Working Knowledge: How Organisations Manage What They Know. Harvard Business Press, Cambridge (2000)
22. Za, S., Spagnoletti, P., North-Samardzic, A.: Organisational learning as an emerging process: The generative role of digital tools in informal learning practices. Br. J. Edu. Technol. 45(6), 1023–1035 (2014)
23. Carillo, K., Scornavacca, E., Za, S.: The role of media dependency in predicting continuance intention to use ubiquitous media systems. Inf. Manag. 54(3), 317–335 (2017)
24. Checkland, P.: Systems Thinking, Systems Practice: A 30-year Retrospective. Wiley, Chichester (1999)
25. Checkland, P.B.: OR and the systems movement: mappings and conflicts. J. Oper. Res. 34(8), 661–675 (1983)
26. Mumford, E.: The study of socio-technical design: reflections on its successes, failures and potential. Inf. Syst. J. 16, 317–342 (2006)
27. Bednar, P.M. (2007). Individual emergence in contextual analysis. Problems of individual emergence. In: Proceedings of Dutch Systems Society 12th Bi-Annual 'Problems of…' Systems Conference, Systemica, vol. 14(1-7) (2007)
28. Bednar, P.M.: Contextual analysis – a multiperspective inquiry into emergence of complex socio-cultural systems. In: Minati, G., Abram, M., Pessa, E. (eds.) Processes of Emergence of Systems and Systemic Properties: Towards a General Theory of Emergence. World Scientific (2008)
29. Schein, E., Schein, P.: Organizational Culture and Leadership, 5th edn. Jossey Bass, Thousand Oaks (2016)
30. Kappelman, L., McLean, E., Johnson, V., Torres, R., Nguyen, Q., Maurer, C., Snyder, M.: The 2016 SIM IT issues and trends study. MIS Q. Executive 16(1), 47–80 (2017)

31. Henderson, J.C., Venkatraman, N.: Strategic alignment: leveraging information technology for transforming organisations. IBM Syst. J. **32**(1), 472–484 (1993)
32. Langefors, B., Dahlbom, B. (eds.): Essays on Infology. Studentlitteratur, Lund (1995)
33. Kahle, C., Hoffmann, D., Ahlemann, F.: Beyond business-IT alignment - digital business strategies as a paradigmatic shift: a review and research agenda. In: Proceedings of the 50th Hawaii International Conference on System Sciences, Hilton Waikoloa Village, Hawaii, 4–7 January 2017, pp. 4706–4715 (2017). https://aisel.aisnet.org/hicss-50/os/digital_innovation/2/. Accessed 21 Feb 2018
34. Amarilli, F., van Vliet, M., Van Den Hooff, B.: An Explanatory Study on the Co-evolutionary Mechanisms of Business IT Alignment. Proceedings of International Conference on Information Systems, Seoul, S. Korea, 10–13 December 2017
35. Bednar, P.M., Welch, C.: The innovation-diffusion cycle: time for a sociotechnical agenda. In: Proceedings of IFIP WG8.6 Working Conference: Re-Imagining Diffusion of Information Technology and Systems: Opportunities and Risks, University of Minho, School of Engineering, Gilmaraes, Portugal, 5 June 2017 (2017)
36. Shin, D.: A socio-technical framework for Internet-of-Things design: a human- centered design for the Internet of Things. Telematics Inf. **31**(4), 519–531 (2014)
37. Kling, R., Lamb, R.: IT and organizational change in digital economies: a socio- technical approach. ACM SIGCAS, Comput. Soc. **29**(3), 17–25 (1999)
38. Lyytinen, K., Yoo, Y., Boland Jr., R.J.: Digital product innovation within four classes of innovation networks. Inf. Syst. J. **26**(1), 47–75 (2016)
39. Kallinikos, J., Aaltonen, A., Marton, A.: The ambivalent ontology of digital artifacts. MIS Q. **37**(2), 357–370 (2013)
40. Nissen, H.-E., Bednar, P., Welch, C.: Double helix relationships in use and design of IS: lessons to learn from phenomenology and hermeneutics. In: Nissen, H.-E., Bednar, P., Welch, C. (eds.) Use and Redesign in IS: Double Helix Relationships? Informing Science: Journal of an Emerging Transdiscipline, vol. 10(Monograph), pp. 1–19 (2007)
41. Silver, M.S., Markus, M.L.: Conceptualizing the Socio-Technical (ST) artifact. Syst. Signs Actions **7**(1), 82–89 (2013)
42. Alvesson, M.: The Triumph of Emptiness: Consumption, Higher Education, and Work Organization. Oxford University Press, Oxford (2014)
43. Friis, S.: User Controlled Information Systems Development – problems and possibilities towards Local Design Shops. Dept of Information and Computer Science, Lund University Publications, Sweden (1991)
44. Bednar, P.M., Welch, C.: Enid Mumford: the ETHICS methodology and its legacy, Chap. 15. In: Mohr, B.J., van Amelsvoort, P. (eds.) Co-Creating Humane and Innovative Organizations Evolutions in the Practice of Socio-technical System Design, pp. 274–288. Global STS-D Network Press, Portland (2016)
45. Wenger-Trayner, E.: Learning in Landscapes of Practice. Routledge, Abingdon (2015)
46. Bednar, P.M., Welch, C.: Paradoxical relationships in collaboration, competition and innovation: a critical systemic perspective. In: Proceedings of WOA 2009. The 10th Workshop of Italian scholars on Organization Studies, Università degli Studi di Cagliari, Cagliari, Sardinia, Italy 29–30 April 2009 (2009)
47. Bednar, P.M., Welch, C.: Stepping on the cracks – transcending the certainties of Big Data analytics. In: Proceedings of the 14th conference of the Italian Chapter of AIS (itAIS2017), University of Milano Bicocca, 6th–7th October 2017, Milan, Italy (2017)
48. Flinders, K.: Interview: how Swedish bank prepared robot for customer services. Computer Weekly, 28 October 2016 (2016). www.computerweekly.com/news/450401647. Accessed 31 May 2017

49. Haaramo, E.: Robotic automation takes off in the Nordics. Computer Weekly, 19 April 2017 (2017). www.computerweekly.com/news/450417014. Accessed 31 May 2017

50. Solon, O.: Amazon patents wristband that tracks warehouse workers' movements, 1 February 2018. The Guardian on-line (2018). https://www.theguardian.com/technology/2018/jan/31/amazon-warehouse-wristband-tracking. Accessed 20 Feb 2018

51. United States Patent Office: Patent No. 9,881,277 - Wrist band haptic feedback system (2018)

52. Ciborra, C.U.: The Labyrinths of Information: Challenging the Wisdom of Systems. Oxford University Press, Oxford (2002)

53. Alvesson, M., Spicer, A.: A stupidity-based theory of organizations. J. Manage. Stud. **49**(7), 1194–1220 (2012)

54. Bednar, P.M., Welch, C.: A case for multi criteria benefit analysis. In: Spagnoletti, P. (ed.) Organizational Change and Information Systems: Working and Living Together in New Ways. LNISO, vol. 2, pp 337–344. Springer, Heidelberg (2013). https://doi.org/10.1007/978-3-642-37228-5_33

55. Bednar, P.M.: The Socio-Technical Toolbox, vol. 12.3. Craneswater Press, Portsmouth (2018)

56. Argyris, C.: Reasons and Rationalisations. Oxford University Press, Oxford (2004)

57. Bednar, P., Welch, C.: A double helix metaphor for use and usefulness in Informing Systems. In: Nissen, H.-E., Bednar, P., Welch, C. (eds.) Use and Redesign in IS: Double Helix Relationships? Informing Science: Journal of an Emerging Transdiscipline, vol. 10 (Monograph), pp. 272–295 (2007)

58. Bednar, P.M., Welch, C., Milner, C.: Excellence in practice through a socio-technical, open systems approach to process analysis and design. Int. J. Syst. Soc. **3**(1), 110–118 (2016)

Use of 'Habit' Is not a Habit in Understanding Individual Technology Adoption: A Review of UTAUT2 Based Empirical Studies

Kuttimani Tamilmani[✉], Nripendra P. Rana, and Yogesh K. Dwivedi

Emerging Markets Research Centre (EMaRC), School of Management,
Swansea University Bay Campus, Swansea SA1 8EN, UK
kuttimani.tamilmani@gmail.com, ykdwivedi@gmail.com,
n.p.rana@swansea.ac.uk, y.k.dwivedi@swansea.ac.uk

Abstract. 'Habit' was the most important theoretical addition into UTAUT2 to challenge the role of behavioural intention as a lone predictor of technology use. However, systematic review and meta-analysis of Price value the other UTAUT2 additional construct revealed major inconsistency of the model with just 41% UTAUT2 based studies including the construct in their research. Thus, the aim of this research is to understand the appropriateness of 'habit' construct usage among UTAUT2 based empirical studies and their reason for omission or inclusion. The findings from 66 empirical studies revealed only 23 studies a meagre (35%) utilised 'habit' construct and the remaining massive 43 studies (65%) excluded the construct from their research model. The major reason for studies not including "habit" construct was they were examining users of new technology at early stage of adoption where sufficient time hasn't elapsed for users to form habit. Moreover this study caution the use of experience as an alternative for habit. Since experience can be gained under mandatory settings which is not sufficient enough to form habit that occurs more naturally under voluntary settings. This study also provided number of recommendations for theory and practice based on the findings.

Keywords: Meta-analysis · Habit · UTAUT2

1   Introduction

Understanding why individuals accept or reject information technology (IT) is a mature stream in the contemporary information systems (IS) arena and constantly examined for two reasons: new technologies are rapidly evolving and finding their place both in organisations and society; and the IS failure rate continued to be high [1]. Unified theory of acceptance and use of technology (UTAUT) developed in the organisational context emphasising on the utilitarian value (extrinsic motivation) through exhaustive review, mapping and integration of constructs from eight dominant technology adoption models is the most comprehensive model in explaining individual technology acceptance and use [see 2 for review]. The latest extended version of UTAUT popularly referred to as UTAUT2 comprises of three new constructs such as hedonic motivation, price value and habit focused on consumer context emphasising on hedonic

© IFIP International Federation for Information Processing 2019
Published by Springer Nature Switzerland AG 2019.
A. Elbanna et al. (Eds.): TDIT 2018, IFIP AICT 533, pp. 277–294, 2019.
https://doi.org/10.1007/978-3-030-04315-5_19

value (intrinsic motivation) of technology users to be more relevant to emerging consumer technologies. However, in the UTAUT2, voluntariness of use was dropped as a moderator since consumers have no organisational mandate and in many situations, consumer behaviour is voluntary [see 3 for review]. The predictive ability of UTAUT2 theory was much higher explaining about 74 percent of the variance in consumers' behavioural intention to use a technology and 52 percent of the variance in consumers' technology use [4].

The UTAUT2 model has already garnered more than 2500 citations despite its recent introduction in the year 2012, spanning from IS field and beyond emphasising on its predictive ability. However, systematic review of 650 UTAUT2 citations revealed 77% of the studies cited UTAUT2 for generic purpose without employing its constructs whereas the remaining 23% of studies, even if they utilised UTATU2, did so in combination with external theories omitting some of its original constructs with rare inclusion of moderators [see 5 for review]. Moreover, extant literature review on UTAUT2 additional constructs such as Price value have revealed major inconsistency on its usage with just 41% studies including the construct in their research model [see 6 for review]. 'Habit' was the most important new theoretical construct added into UTAUT2 model as a key predicator of technology use to challenge the role of behavioural intention as a lone predictor of technology use. To that extent habit as an key alternative mechanism in predicting consumer behaviour is lauded in the Journal of the Association for Information Systems (JAIS) special issue on the technology acceptance model (TAM) [3]. Thus, integrating 'habit' into the UTAUT2 will act as overarching mechanism and complement the focus of theory on intention as key driver of use behaviour. 'Habit' is function of both behavioural intention (BI) and use behaviour (UB) in the UTAUT2 model. HA → UB path was based on Habit/automaticity perspective (HAP) [7], which states use behaviour occur automatically as a result of past habits without formation of evaluation and intention. Whereas, HA → BI path was based on the instant activation perspective (IAP) [8] where use behaviour is considered as accelerated form of conscious use and perceived as function of behavioural intention such that past use habit will not weaken evaluation → intention → usage relationship.

Given the preceding discussion on centrality of habit construct as a key predicator of technology use and inconsistency among usage of UTAUT2 model on its entirety. This study is intend to evaluate appropriateness of habit construct usage among UTAUT2 based studies and aims to provide guidelines to future researchers on suitability of various context to operationalize 'habit' construct in their research. This study intends to achieve this through fulfilment of the following objectives:

- Identify studies that used UTAUT2 model as their underpinning theory and omitted 'habit' in their research model and reason for omission.
- Identify various antecedents/dependant variables of 'habit' and their significance.
- To conduct meta-analysis of the empirical studies to understand the convergence and divergence of various 'habit' path relationships and their performance.

The next section of this paper i.e. Section 2 describes the research method employed in this study; Sect. 3 will present the findings of meta-analysis and narrative review from empirical studies that utilized 'habit' construct. This will be followed by discussion in Sect. 4 and conclusion in Sect. 5.

2   Research Method

This study employed combination of "narrative review", "citation reference search" and "meta-analysis" approach to synthesize the existing research findings that operationalized 'habit' from the UTAUT2 model in understanding individual technology adoption [4, 9, 10]. Meta-analysis enables to establish true effect size of various relationships of population through accumulation of effect sizes from individual studies facilitated by statistical techniques [10–13]. It allows to discover new knowledge that is undetectable otherwise in the isolated parcels of data scattered amongst individual "primary" studies [14]. Cited reference search for Venkatesh, Thong [3] article in Scopus and Web of Science database from March 2012 to March 2017 resulted in 1,320 papers (823 from Scopus; 497 from Web of Science). On further scrutiny, it was identified that 452 citations were common in both databases resulting in 868 unique citations for UTAUT2. Out of 868 articles, 650 were fully downloadable and 147 utilized at least one UTAUT2 construct whereas the remaining 503 articles just citied UTAUT2 for generic reason [see 5 for review]. Out of 147 studies, only 66 studies were empirical in nature to perform meta-analysis and hence the remaining studies were discarded from the scope of this research since they were neither empirical in nature nor did they report relevant data for meta-analysis. This leads us to the next stage of this study to screen 66 UTAUT2 based empirical studies to identify operationalization of 'habit' construct and appropriateness of its usage.

3   Findings

This section presents narrative review and meta-analysis findings of the 66 UTAUT2 based empirical studies based on the usage of habit construct. The findings resulted in classification of 66 studies broadly into two categories: (1) studies not utilizing habit– 43 studies; and (2) Studies utilizing habit – 23 studies.

3.1   Review of Studies not Using 'Habit'

Majority of the 66 UTAUT2 based empirical studies (i.e. 43) did not operationalize 'habit' in their research. Out of 43 studies that did not use 'habit' in their research model only 10 studies employed use behaviour (UB) [e.g. 15, 16] as their outcome variable with all of them utilizing behavioural intention (BI) as their immediate antecedent. Whereas BI was the most operated outcome variable with 31 studies hypothesizing BI [e.g. 17, 18] as their final outcome variable. Finally, there were couple of studies that employed radically new outcome variables apart from BI and UB such as: (1) Location disclosure on location based social networking applications [19] and (2) Disclosure of information about others in social network sites [20].

Table 1 presents findings of in-depth examination of these 43 studies across various contexts such as respondent types and system/technology examined to ascertain their convergence and divergence. This resulted in advent of eight broader categories based on the system/technology examined with 20 studies mobile technologies emerged as the topmost category. Social networking sites emerged as the second most studied category with five examinations. Whereas, five categories such as (1) Education, (2) Internet banking, (3) Music as a service, (4) Smart home devices and (5) Wearables jointly occupied the third category spot with two examinations each. Finally, the 'others category' involved eight studies that were not able be classified readily under any of the above seven categories as seen form Table 1.

In terms of respondents, the researchers examined six different types of technological users across 43 studies. Consumers emerged as the most researched user type with as large as 25 examinations. Students were the second most examined respondent's type with 14 studies involving them to validate their research model on range of technology use. For instance, students were used as respondents to evaluate people willingness to pay for music as services [21] and information disclosure about others in social network sites to mention a few [19, 20] see Table 1 for exhaustive list. Finally, the remaining four respondents' types were examined on one instance each: (1) "Tourists" responses to mobile augmented reality travel guide [22]; (2) "Citizens" adoption of e-government [23]; (3) "Teachers and Students" difference in podcasting acceptance on campus [24]; and (4) "Software developers" adoption intention to use existing software products [25].

3.2   Reason for Studies not Using 'Habit'

This section explains the reason behind 43 studies that adapted UTAUT2 as underpinning theory for their research and excluded one of its core constructs 'habit' from their final research model. Five major categories emerged as reason for studies not using 'habit' construct as seen from Table 2. The basis for classification of these five categories are explained in detail along with instances of quotes from actual studies in italics.

3.2.1   New Technology at Early Stage of Adoption

Twelve studies fell under this category as they did not use 'habit' since they were examining new technologies in introduction stage of the product life cycle with usage only among early adopters. Consumers tend to generate habit for particular technology or product after prolonged use especially during growth stages of product life cycle. For that reason few researchers examining early adopters recommended usage of "habit" construct in future (three such studies [21, 29, 39]) after sufficient time has lapsed from product launch and users developed habit for technology under investigation. For instance, Oliveira et al. [28] study on understanding consumer intention towards mobile payment in Portugal excluded 'habit' for the following reason:

> *"The habit construct was not included in the research model since mobile payment is a relatively new technology that has not yet gained sufficiently widespread use among consumers to generate a habit"*

Whereas Ramantoko et al. [48] study on exploring consumers behavioural intention to use home digital services in Indonesia omitted 'habit' stating the following reason:

> *"….the authors seek to understand characteristics in the early stage of adoption, where factor Habit was not taken into consideration. The authors' prejudice considers that Habit did not exist among the respondents during the time of study"*

Table 1. Classification of studies not using habit construct

S N	Themes/Technology examined (with frequency)	Respondents type (with frequency)	Citations
1	Mobile technologies (20)		
	Mobile payments (7)	Consumers (6)	Jia et al. [26]; Koenig-Lewis et al. [27]; Oliveira et al. [28]; Qasim and Abu-Shanab [29]; Shaw [30]; Slade et al. [17]
		Students (1)	Teo et al. [31]
	Smart phone adoption (3)	Consumers(3)	Choudrie et al. [32]; Gao et al. [33]; Gao et al. [34]
	Mobile learning (2)	Students (1)	Bere [35]
		Consumers (1)	Wong et al. [36]
	Mobile banking (2)	Consumers (2)	Alalwan et al. [15]; Mahfuz et al. [37]
	Interactive mobile technologies (IMT) in hotels (1)	Students (1)	Wendy Zhu and Morosan [38]
	Mobile advertising (1)	Students (1)	Wong et al. [18]
	Mobile applications (1)	Consumers (1)	Lu et al. (2017)
	Mobile Augmented Reality (1)	Tourists (1)	Kourouthanassis et al. [22]
	Telebanking (1)	Consumers (1)	Alalwan et al. [16]
	Usage of Mobile devices in private clubs (1)	Consumers (1)	Morosan and DeFranco [39]
2	Social Networking sites (5)		
	Information sharing in SNS (1)	Students (1)	Hajli and Lin [40]
	Location disclosure on LB-SNAs (1)	Students (1)	Koohikamali et al. [19]
	Information disclosure in SNS (1)	Students (1)	Koohikamali et al. [20]
	Facebook usage (1)	Students (1)	Lallmahomed et al. [41]
	Purchase intention in Social networking sites (1)	Students (1)	Sharifi fard et al. [42]
3	Education (2)		
	Informal learning context (1)	Students (1)	Lai et al. [43]
	Podcasting in higher education (1)	Teacher and Students (1)	Lin et al. [24]
4	Internet banking (2)	Consumers (2)	Chaouali et al. [44]; Salim et al. [45]
5	Music as a service (2)	Consumers (1)	Wagner et al. [46]
		Students (1)	Wagner and Hess [21]

(continued)

Table 1. (*continued*)

S N	Themes/Technology examined (with frequency)	Respondents type (with frequency)	Citations
6	Smart home devices (2)		
	Household Technology acceptance (1)	Consumers (1)	Ahn et al. [47]
	Home Digital Services (1)	Consumers (1)	Ramantoko et al. [48]
7	Wearables (2)		
	Wearable healthcare technology	Consumers (1)	Gao et al. [49]
	Pervasive Information Systems (Google glass)	Consumers(1)	Segura and Thiesse [50]
8	Others (8)		
	Online shopping intention for agricultural products (1)	Students (1)	An et al. [51]
	Crime prevention using IS (1)	Consumers (1)	Cvijikj et al. [52]
	Purchase intention of electric vehicles (1)	Consumers (1)	Degirmenci and Breitner [53]
	E-government adoption (1)	Citizens (1)	Lallmahomed et al. [23]
	Biometric e-gates in airports (1)	Consumers (1)	Morosan [54]
	Broadband Technology Use (1)	Students (1)	Muraina et al. [55]
	Software reuse adoption individual perspective (1)	Software developers (1)	Stefi [25]
	E-books (1)	Students (1)	Yoo and Roh [56]

The study of Wagner and Hess [21] on freemium usage of Music as a Services of students in Germany was one of the three instance when 'habit' was recommended to be used in future studies stating the following reason:

"... results indicate that separating free and premium products can increase people's intention to use the premium version. However, lock-in effects resulting from the free version may also have a positive effect on users' willingness to pay. Future studies should therefore focus on habit and the resulting lock-in effect in detail"

Table 2. Reason for studies not using habit construct

Category type	Frequency	Description	Example citations
1. New technology at early stage of adoption	12	Studies in this category examined users at nascent stages technology adoption to with some of them recommending usage of habit in future.	Alalwan et al. [15], Alalwan et al. [16], Oliveira et al. [28], Ramantoko et al. [48]; Wagner and Hess [21]
2. Alternative construct	1	This study used construct similar to habit.	Lin et al. [24]
3. Extensive usage of habit	1	Habit construct extensively studied in this research context.	Ahn et al. [47]
4. Out of Scope	1	This category perceived habit construct as an inappropriate context for technology under investigation.	Mahfuz etb al. [37]
5. No reason	28	These studies did not provide any reason for not including habit in their structural model	Bere [35], Hajli and Lin [40], Salim et al. [45], Slade et al. [17]

3.2.2   Alternative Construct

Lin et al. [24] only study in this category examined difference in perspective of "Teachers and Students" podcasting acceptance on campus in Germany included prior experience a construct similar to habit stating the below reason:

> *".....as an individual learns by doing, prior experiences with a technology is likely to impact perceptions of the amount of effort required to subsequently use the technology."*

3.2.3   Extensive Usage of Habit

Ahn et al. [47] lonely study in this category examined consumers sustainable household technology acceptance in the USA and found 'habit' among extensively studied construct to justify their exclusion from their research model. Their reason for exclusion is as follows:

> *".....household energy saving has been studied by environmental psychologists with the topics of motivations, behaviours, habits and interventions"*

3.2.4   Out of Scope

Mahfuz et al. [37] is the last of single study category that omitted habit along with hedonic motion since they perceived both these constructs were out of scope of mobile banking adoption in their research of cultural dimensions and website quality influence on Consumers Mobile banking services in Bangladesh. Their reason for exclusion is as follows:

> *".....author omitted hedonic motivation and habit from the conceptual mode due not directly related to the mobile banking adoption..."*

3.2.5   No Reason

Majority of the studies (i.e. 28) fell under category 5. Studies under this category although utilized UTAUT2 as their underpinning theory and developed their model without 'habit', they did not provide any reason for omitting the construct from their research model. Such instances include but not limited to understanding determinants of students mobile learning technology acceptance and use in South Africa [35] and factors affecting consumers Internet banking implementation in Sudan [45].

3.3   Review of Studies Using 'Habit'

Unlike UTAUT2 based empirical studies that did not utilize 'habit', more than half of the studies that utilized 'habit' (i.e. 13 out of 23 studies) employed use behaviour as their outcome variable. All these 13 studies mapped 'habit' as an antecedent of both behavioural intention and Use behaviour in similar lines of UTAUT2 to research technologies in growth/mature stages of product life cycle rather than nascent stage since users develop habit over a period of time after product utilization. Such instances include examining actual adopters habitual behaviour towards Internet banking adoption in Jordan [57] and examination of students habitual use of learning management system in Malaysia that received limited attention [58]. Whereas, habit was mapped only to BI in seven studies that operated BI as outcome variable with instances ranging from understanding consumers' Omni channel purchase intention behaviour in Spain [59] to students usage of Facebook as learning tool in Spain [60]. Apart from BI and UB, three studies employed completely new outcome variables such as: (1) Job offer success [61]; (2) Consumerization [62]; and (3) Job seeker unemployment duration [63]. Table 3 summarizes the various path relationships of 'habit' against various dependant variables, independent variables and moderators with their significance across 23 studies. Apart from being an antecedent on most instances, 'habit' also has few antecedents acting as a dependant variable.

3.3.1   Habit as an Antecedent

'Habit' served as an antecedent of six dependant variables across the span of 23 studies where it was used. It most often served as an antecedent of Behavioural Intention (BI) with 18 studies employing HA $\rightarrow$ BI path relationship in examining a range of technology adoption. Out of 18 studies, 15 studies found the path relationship HA BI to be significant [e.g. 57, 64, 65] whereas the remaining three studies [58, 59, 66] reported insignificant values for this path. Use Behaviour is the second most examined

Table 3. Summary of habit path relationships

S N	I.V.	D. V. (Mod)	Total	Sig	Citations (Sig)	In. Sig	Citations (In. Sig)
1	HA	BI	18	15	Alalwan et al. [57], Ali et al. [64], Baptista and Oliveira [65]	3	Ain et al. [58], Juaneda-Ayensa et al. [59], Raman and Don [66]
2	HA	UB	13	11	Järvinen et al. [68], Nair et al. [69], Chong [73]	2	Ain et al. [58], Raman and Don [66]
3	HA	BI (Gen)	3	0	None	3	Baptista et al. [74], Wong et al. [75], Ramírez-Correa et al. [76]
4	HA	BI (Age)	2	0	None	2	Baptista et al. [74], Ramírez-Correa et al. [76]
5	HA	BI (Exp)	1	0	None	1	Ramírez-Correa et al. [76]
6	HA	UB (Gen)	2	0	None	2	Baptista et al. [74], Ramírez-Correa et al. [76]
7	HA	UB (Age)	2	0	None	2	Baptista et al. [74], Ramírez-Correa et al. [76]
8	HA	UB(Exp)	1	0	None	1	Ramírez-Correa et al. [75]
9	HA	PE	1	1	Herrero and San Martín [70]	0	None
10	HA	CN	1	1	Dernbecher et al. [62]	0	None
11	HA	PR	1	1	Escobar-Rodríguez and Carvajal-Trujillo [77]	0	None
12	HA	CN(SI)	1	0	None	1	Dernbecher et al. [62]
13	HA	DCC	1	1	Morosan and DeFranco [71]	0	None
14	MSUH	BI	1	1	Jia et al. [72]	0	None
15	MPUH	BI	1	1	Jia et al. [72]	0	None
16	OSH	BI	1	0	None	1	Jia et al. [72]
17	CPUH	BI	1	0	None	1	Jia et al. [72]
18	OSH	MPUH	1	1	Jia et al. [72]	0	None
19	MSUH	MPUH	1	1	Jia et al. [72]	0	None

(*continued*)

Table 3. (*continued*)

S N	I.V.	D. V. (Mod)	Total	Sig	Citations (Sig)	In. Sig	Citations (In. Sig)
20	CPUH	MPUH	1	1	Jia et al. [72]	0	None
21	EE	HA	1	1	Herrero and San Martín [70]	0	None
22	SE	HA	1	1	Dernbecher et al. [62]	0	None
23	PI	HA	1	1	Dernbecher et al. [62]	0	None
24	NS	HA	1	1	Morosan and DeFranco [71]	0	None
25	HM	HA	1	1	Herrero and San Martín [70]	0	None

[**Legend:** BI: Behavioural Intention; CN: Consumerization; CPUH: Cellphone usage habit; D.V.: Dependant Variable; DCC: Degree of co-creation; EE: Effort expectancy; Exp: Experience; Gen: Gender; HA: Habit; HM: Hedonic motivation; I.V.: Independent Variable; In. Sig: Number of insignificant path values; Mod: Moderator; MPUH: Mobile payment usage habit; MSUH: Mobile service usage habit; NS: Novelty seeking; OSH: Online shopping habit; PE: Performance Expectancy; PI: Personal Innovativeness; PR: Perceived relevance; SE: Self-efficacy; Sig: Number of significant path values; SN: Serial Number; UB: Use Behaviour]

dependant variable with 13 studies utilizing 'habit' as its antecedent. The path relationship HA → UB reported significant results on 11 instances [67–69] and the remaining two studies [58, 66] reported insignificant path values.

'Habit' is used as an antecedent of four other constructs apart from BI and UB, such as: (1) Performance expectancy (PE) in understanding consumer's intention to share user generated content in social network sites [70], (2) Consumerization (CN) of information technology among European university students [62], (3) Perceived relevance (PR) of Facebook as a social media learning platform [60], and (4) Degree of co-creation (DCC) in understating consumers co-creation of value in hotels using mobile devices [71]. The path relationship was significant on all the four instances and need more examination in future to improve the validity. Age, gender, experience and social influence (SI) moderated the path relationships among the path HA → BI, HA → UB and HA → CN on various combinations and found to be insignificant on all instance as seen from Table 3.

In the pursuit, to understand effect of consumers technology use habits on their continuous intention to use mobile payments the study of Jia et al. [72] employed four different forms of consumer habits: (1) Mobile service usage habit (MSUH), (2) Mobile payment usage habit (MPUH), (3) Online shopping habit (OSH), and (4) Cell phone usage habit (CPUH). These four constructs had various path relationships between themselves and BI as seen from Table 3. Out of seven different paths, five were significant except for two paths between OSH → BI and CPUH → BI that were found to be insignificant. Thus, consumers Online shopping habit and cell phone usage habit does not translate into their intention to use mobile payments that need further examination [72].

3.3.2   Antecedents of Habit

There were also five antecedents for habit such as: (1) Novelty seeking (NS) in consumer value co-creation in hotels through mobile devices [71], (2) Effort expectancy (EE), (3) Hedonic motivation (HM) in evaluating consumer's intention to share user generated content in social network sites [60] and (4) Self-Efficacy (SE), (5) Personal Innovativeness (PI) in examining consumerization of IT [62] across span of three studies. The results of three studies found all five relationships of 'habit' and their antecedents to be significant.

3.4   Meta-Analysis of Studies Using Habit Construct

Meta-analysis allows both significant and insignificant effects to be analysed through accumulation of various results taking the relative sample and effect size into consideration enabling more accurate and credible results due to the overarching span of the analysis [9]. This study conducted meta-analysis of various dependant, independent and moderating variables and their relationships with 'habit' explored in two or more times across 23 studies [e.g., 9, 12, 78]. Only six path relationships fulfilled this criterion and were eligible for meta-analysis. Table 4 presents summary on meta-analysis path coefficients (β) results.

Table 4. Meta-analysis of 'Habit' path coefficients (β) (Adapted from [9])

S N	I.V.	D.V.(Mod)	#	TSS	p(ES)	Meta(β)	95% L(β)	95% H(β)
1	HA	BI	18	8501	0.000	0.276	0.186	0.362
2	HA	UB	13	6820	0.000	0.273	0.157	0.382
3	HA	BI(Gen)	3	1020	0.886	−0.005	−0.066	0.057
4	HA	BI(Age)	2	827	0.213	0.043	−0.025	0.111
5	HA	UB(Gen)	2	827	0.975	−0.001	−0.069	0.067
6	HA	UB(Age)	2	827	0.378	0.031	−0.038	0.099

[**Legend:** #: Number of studies; D.V.: Dependant variable; Gen: Gender; H (β): Highest (beta); In. Sig(β): Number of insignificant path values; I.V.: Independent Variable; L(β): Lowest (Beta); Meta(β): Meta-analysis path coefficient; Mod: Moderator; p(ES): Estimated value of p; TSS: Total sample size]

The results revealed only two relationships using 'habit' as an antecedent, i.e. HA $\rightarrow$ BI and HA $\rightarrow$ UB emerged as significant relationships at p < 0.000 level. Whereas all the remaining four habit based relationships with behavioural intention and use behaviour moderated by age and gender were insignificant. HA $\rightarrow$ BI emerged as the strongest path with meta-analysis (β) of 0.276 very closely followed by HA $\rightarrow$ UB with meta-analysis (β) of 0.273. The 95% confidence interval for HA $\rightarrow$ BI was the narrowest with Low (β) – 0.186 and High(β) – 0.362, revealing the range is narrow enough to provide at least one confidence in the extent of variance that could be explained. Whereas 95% confidence interval for HA $\rightarrow$ UB was bit wider with Low (β) – 0.157 and High (β) – 0.382.

4   Discussion

The purpose of this study was to have deeper understanding on appropriateness of 'habit' construct usage among 66 empirical studies that used UTAUT2 as their underpinning theory in their research. The findings revealed 43 studies (65%) did not operationalize habit in their research model with 31 of the 43 studies (72%) employing BI as their outcome variable rather than UB. Habit is an outcome of consumers prolonged experience in using particular technology and strengthened as result of repeated behaviour [79]. Majority of the studies that did not utilize 'habit' were those that conducted their research on mobile technologies. The studies that omitted 'habit' dealt with technologies in introduction stage of product life cycle and felt consumers did not have enough experience to formulate habitual behaviour for technology under investigation. Thus, it was more appropriate for them to measure behavioural intention than use behaviour. However, consumers tend to form habit after using technology for prolonged period and 'habit' is a critical factor in predicting the use of technology rather than its initial acceptance [7, 79]. This was quite evident as 13 out of 23 studies (52%) that operationalized 'habit' in their research model employed use behaviour as their outcome variable against 10 out of 43 (23%) non-habit related studies.

No reason emerged as the top category among studies that did not utilize 'habit' with 28 out of 43 studies (65%) not providing any reason for exclusion. 12 out of the remaining 15 studies excluded 'habit' since they examined users of "new technology at early stage of adoption with three studies explicitly recommending use of habit construct in future studies. The reason for final three studies to exclude 'habit' were: (1) Alternative construct, (2) Extensive usage of habit and 3) Out of scope across various research context. Researchers should be cautious in using prior experience as a proxy to measure habit. Although experience in using technology is necessary to form habit, experience alone is not a sufficient condition for the formation of habit. Moreover, experience in using technology over passage of time can form differing level of habits among users depending upon user's familiarity and degree of interaction with target technology [3].

In terms of studies that used 'habit', it mostly served as antecedent of BI (18 studies) and UB (13 studies). The path relationships HA $\rightarrow$ BI and HA $\rightarrow$ UB were together found insignificant only in three studies. Two of these insignificant studies were on mandatory settings rather than on voluntary settings such as: (1) Examination of student's use of learning management system [58] and (2) Students' acceptance of learning management software (Moodle) [66]. The plausible reason for insignificant relationships of 'habit' in such mandatory settings could be because students might have performed educational activities out of compulsion and social pressure [58], which is driven by extrinsic motivation rather than intrinsic motivation. This reveals mandatory settings can enable user to gain experience of operating technologies that not necessarily translate into habit which occurs more naturally in voluntary settings. Whereas, habit was used as an antecedent of four other dependant variables such as: (1) Performance expectancy (PE), (2) Consumerization (CN), (3) Perceived relevance (PR) and (4) Degree of co-creation (DCC) on one instance each and the relationship was found significant on all four variables.

Furthermore, meta-analysis results revealed only two 'habit' based relationships i.e. HA → BI and HA → UB to be significant at p < 0.000 level. This underscores the dominance of BI and UB as predictors in understanding consumer technology acceptance and use. However, all the four moderator relationships of habit with BI and UB were found to be insignificant in meta-analysis. This is a significant departure from the original UTAUT2 model of Venkatesh, Thong [3] that had significant results for moderators' (i.e. age, gender, experience) influence on HA → BI and HA → UB. To that extent Venkatesh et al. [4] omitted the moderators' effects in their multi-level framework for measuring individual technology acceptance and use. They rather merged moderators into individual level contextual factors including user attributes and prescribed them to be used based on context [4]. Finally, 'habit' apart from being an antecedent to dependant variables also have antecedents of its own with all-significant effects. The antecedents of 'habit' need further examination so that practitioners can leverage them in order to build habit among technological users.

5   Conclusion

This study aimed to understand appropriateness of the construct 'habit' among the UTAUT2 based empirical studies. The findings revealed 43 out of 66 studies did not operationalize 'habit' in their study with all of them focusing on introduction stage of product life cycle having early adopters as their users. Hence, 'habit' is not an appropriate construct in examining new to market technologies where sufficient time has not elapsed for users to develop habitual behaviour. In addition, 'habit' is not an appropriate construct in mandatory settings such as student's use of learning man-agement system where they are compelled to use technology driven by extrinsic motivation. Moreover, the meta-analysis results confirmed the effects of moderators to be completely insignificant on 'habit' based relationships with its dependant variables. Future studies should be cautious in operationalizing 'habit' and their moderators in the above-mentioned scenarios. Further, studies should refrain from using experience as proxy for measuring 'habit'. Since experience is a necessary but not a sufficient con-dition to form 'habit'. However, 'habit' emerged as a very strong predictor of BI and UB. 'Habit' is a valid construct for studies to examine products after introduction stages in the voluntary settings driven through consumer intrinsic motivation. This study found five antecedents of 'habit' all having significant impact, future research should focus on these antecedents to understand its impact as a key predicator of technology use. Finally, none of existing studies used longitudinal data collection method to measure the impact of habit construct in their structural model. Since habitual behaviour for a technology develops after prolonged usage future studies should focus on longitudinal data collection for measuring habit.

References

1. Dwivedi, Y.K., Wastell, D., Laumer, S., Henriksen, H.Z., Myers, M.D., Bunker, D., Elbanna, A., Ravishankar, M.N., Srivastava, S.C.: Research on information systems failures and successes: status update and future directions. Inf. Syst. Front. **17**(1), 143–157 (2015)
2. Venkatesh, V., Morris, M.G., Davis, G.B., Davis, F.D.: User acceptance of information technology: toward a unified view. MIS Q. **27**(3), 425–478 (2003)
3. Venkatesh, V., Thong, J.Y., Xu, X.: Consumer acceptance and use of information technology: extending the unified theory of acceptance and use of technology. MIS Q. **36**(1), 157–178 (2012)
4. Venkatesh, V., Thong, J.Y., Xu, X.: Unified theory of acceptance and use of technology: a synthesis and the road ahead. J. Assoc. Inf. Syst. **17**(5), 328–376 (2016)
5. Tamilmani, K., Rana, N.P., Dwivedi, Y.K.: A systematic review of citations of UTAUT2 article and its usage trends. In: Kar, A.K., et al. (eds.) I3E 2017. LNCS, vol. 10595, pp. 38–49. Springer, Cham (2017). https://doi.org/10.1007/978-3-319-68557-1_5
6. Tamilmani, K., Rana, N.P., Dwivedi, Y.K., Sahu, G.P., Roderick, S.: Exploring the role of 'Price Value' for understanding consumer adoption of technology: a review and meta-analysis of UTAUT2 based empirical studies. In: Twenty-Second Pacific Asia Conference on Information Systems, Japan (2018)
7. Kim, S.S., Malhotra, N.K., Narasimhan, S.: Research note—two competing perspectives on automatic use: a theoretical and empirical comparison. Inf. Syst. Res. **16**(4), 418–432 (2005)
8. Ajzen, I., Fishbein, M.: Attitudes and the attitude-behavior relation: reasoned and automatic processes. Eur. Rev. Soc. Psychol. **11**(1), 1–33 (2000)
9. King, W.R., He, J.: A meta-analysis of the technology acceptance model. Inf. Manag. **43**(6), 740–755 (2006)
10. Dwivedi, Y.K., Rana, N.P., Jeyaraj, A., Clement, M., Williams, M.D.: Re-examining the Unified Theory of Acceptance and Use of Technology (UTAUT): towards a revised theoretical model. Inf. Syst. Front. 1–16 (2017). https://doi.org/10.1007/s10796-017-9774-y
11. Field, A.P.: Meta-analysis of correlation coefficients: a Monte Carlo comparison of fixed-and random-effects methods. Psychol. Methods **6**(2), 161–180 (2001)
12. Wu, J., Du, H.: Toward a better understanding of behavioral intention and system usage constructs. Eur. J. Inf. Syst. **21**(6), 680–698 (2012)
13. Grinstein, A.: The relationships between market orientation and alternative strategic orientations: a meta-analysis. Eur. J. Mark. **42**(1/2), 115–134 (2008)
14. Schmidt, F.L.: What do data really mean? Research findings, meta-analysis, and cumulative knowledge in psychology. Am. Psychol. **47**(10), 1173 (1992)
15. Alalwan, A.A., Dwivedi, Y.K., Rana, N.P.: Factors influencing adoption of mobile banking by Jordanian bank customers: Extending UTAUT2 with trust. Int. J. Inf. Manage. **37**(3), 99–110 (2017)
16. Alalwan, A.A., Dwivedi, Y.K., Williams, M.D.: Customers' intention and adoption of telebanking in Jordan. Inf. Syst. Manage. **33**(2), 154–178 (2016)
17. Slade, E.L., Dwivedi, Y.K., Piercy, N.C., Williams, M.D.: Modeling consumers' adoption intentions of remote mobile payments in the United Kingdom: extending UTAUT with innovativeness, risk, and trust. Psychol. Mark. **32**(8), 860–873 (2015)
18. Wong, C.-H., Tan, G.W.-H., Tan, B.-I., Ooi, K.-B.: Mobile advertising: the changing landscape of the advertising industry. Telematics Inform. **32**(4), 720–734 (2015)
19. Koohikamali, M., Gerhart, N., Mousavizadeh, M.: Location disclosure on LB-SNAs: the role of incentives on sharing behavior. Decis. Support Syst. **71**, 78–87 (2015)

20. Koohikamali, M., Peak, D.A., Prybutok, V.R.: Beyond self-disclosure: disclosure of information about others in social network sites. Comput. Hum. Behav. **69**, 29–42 (2017)
21. Wagner, T.M., Hess, T.: What drives users to pay for freemium services? Examining people's willingness to pay for music services. In: Proceedings of the Nineteenth American Conference on Information Systems, Chicago, Illinois (2013)
22. Kourouthanassis, P., Boletsis, C., Bardaki, C., Chasanidou, D.: Tourists responses to mobile augmented reality travel guides: the role of emotions on adoption behavior. Pervasive Mobile Comput. **18**, 71–87 (2015)
23. Lallmahomed, M.Z., Lallmahomed, N., Lallmahomed, G.M.: Factors influencing the adoption of e-Government Services in Mauritius. Telematics Inform. **34**(4), 57–72 (2017)
24. Lin, S., Zimmer, J.C., Lee, V.: Podcasting acceptance on campus: the differing perspectives of teachers and students. Comput. Educ. **68**, 416–428 (2013)
25. Stefi, A.: Do Developers make unbiased decisions?-The effect of mindfulness and not-invented-here bias on the adoption of software components. In: Paper presented at the ECIS (2015)
26. Jia, L., Hall, D., Sun, S.: Trust building in consumer learning process and its effect on consumers' behavioral intention toward mobile payments. In: Proceedings of Twenty-first Americas Conference on Information Systems, Puerto Rico (2015)
27. Koenig-Lewis, N., Marquet, M., Palmer, A., Zhao, A.L.: Enjoyment and social influence: predicting mobile payment adoption. Serv. Ind. J. **35**(10), 537–554 (2015)
28. Oliveira, T., Thomas, M., Baptista, G., Campos, F.: Mobile payment: Understanding the determinants of customer adoption and intention to recommend the technology. Comput. Hum. Behav. **61**, 404–414 (2016)
29. Qasim, H., Abu-Shanab, E.: Drivers of mobile payment acceptance: the impact of network externalities. Inf. Syst. Front. **18**(5), 1021–1034 (2016)
30. Shaw, N.: The mediating influence of trust in the adoption of the mobile wallet. J. Retail. Consum. Serv. **21**(4), 449–459 (2014)
31. Teo, A.-C., Tan, G.W.-H., Ooi, K.-B., Hew, T.-S., Yew, K.-T.: The effects of convenience and speed in m-payment. Ind. Manage. Data Syst. **115**(2), 311–331 (2015)
32. Choudrie, J., Pheeraphuttharangkoon, S., Zamani, E., Giaglis, G.: Investigating the adoption and use of smartphones in the UK: a silver-surfers perspective. In: Hertfordshire Business School Working Paper (2014)
33. Gao, S., Krogstie, J., Yang, Y.: Differences in the adoption of smartphones between middle aged adults and older adults in China. In: Zhou, J., Salvendy, G. (eds.) ITAP 2015. LNCS, vol. 9193, pp. 451–462. Springer, Cham (2015). https://doi.org/10.1007/978-3-319-20892-3_44
34. Gao, S., Yang, Y., Krogstie, J.: The adoption of smartphones among older adults in China. In: Liu, K., Nakata, K., Li, W., Galarreta, D. (eds.) ICISO 2015. IAICT, vol. 449, pp. 112–122. Springer, Cham (2015). https://doi.org/10.1007/978-3-319-16274-4_12
35. Bere, A.: Exploring determinants for mobile learning user acceptance and use: An application of UTAUT. In: 11th International Conference on IEEE Information Technology: New Generations (ITNG) (2014)
36. Wong, C.-H., Tan, G.W.-H., Loke, S.-P., Ooi, K.-B.: Adoption of mobile social networking sites for learning? Online Inf. Rev. **39**(6), 762–778 (2015)
37. Mahfuz, M.A., Hu, W., Khanam, L.: The Influence of Cultural Dimensions and Website Quality on m-banking Services Adoption in Bangladesh: Applying the UTAUT2 Model Using PLS. WHICEB (2016)
38. Wendy Zhu, W., Morosan, C.: An empirical examination of guests' adoption of interactive mobile technologies in hotels: revisiting cognitive absorption, playfulness, and security. J. Hospitality Tourism Technol. **5**(1), 78–94 (2014)

39. Morosan, C., DeFranco, A.: When tradition meets the new technology: an examination of the antecedents of attitudes and intentions to use mobile devices in private clubs. Int. J. Hospitality Manage. **42**, 126–136 (2014)

40. Hajli, N., Lin, X.: Exploring the security of information sharing on social networking sites: the role of perceived control of information. J. Bus. Ethics **133**(1), 111–123 (2016)

41. Lallmahomed, M.Z., Rahim, N.Z.A., Ibrahim, R., Rahman, A.A.: Predicting different conceptualizations of system use: acceptance in hedonic volitional context (Facebook). Comput. Hum. Behav. **29**(6), 2776–2787 (2013)

42. Sharifi fard, S., Tamam, E., Hj Hassan, M.S., Waheed, M., Zaremohzzabieh, Z.: Factors affecting Malaysian university students' purchase intention in social networkingsites. Cogent Bus. Manage. **3**(1) (2016). http://dx.doi.org/10.1080/23311975.2016.1182612

43. Lai, C., Wang, Q., Li, X., Hu, X.: The influence of individual espoused cultural values on self-directed use of technology for language learning beyond the classroom. Comput. Hum. Behav. **62**, 676–688 (2016)

44. Chaouali, W., Yahia, I.B., Souiden, N.: The interplay of counter-conformity motivation, social influence, and trust in customers' intention to adopt Internet banking services: the case of an emerging country. J. Retail. Consum. Serv. **28**, 209–218 (2016)

45. Salim, B.F., Mahmoud, M.H., Khair, H.M.: Perceived factors affecting the internet banking implementation in sudan: an application of (UTAUT2). Int. J. Appl. Bus. Econ. Res. **14**(1), 1–16 (2016)

46. Wagner, T.M., Benlian, A., Hess, T.: Converting freemium customers from free to premium—the role of the perceived premium fit in the case of music as a service. Electron. Markets **24**(4), 259–268 (2014)

47. Ahn, M., Kang, J., Hustvedt, G.: A model of sustainable household technology acceptance. Int. J. Consum. Stud. **40**(1), 83–91 (2016)

48. Ramantoko, G., Putra, G., Ariyanti, M., Sianturi, N.V.: Early adoption characteristic of consumers': a behavioral intention to use home digital services in Indonesia. In: 3rd International Seminar and Conference on Learning Organization (ISCLO) (2015)

49. Gao, Y., Li, H., Luo, Y.: An empirical study of wearable technology acceptance in healthcare. Ind. Manage. Data Syst. **115**(9), 1704–1723 (2015)

50. Segura, A.S., Thiesse, F.: Extending UTAUT2 to explore pervasive information systems. In: Paper presented at the ECIS (2015)

51. An, L., Han, Y., Tong, L.: Study on the factors of online shopping intention for fresh agricultural products based on UTAUT2. In: 2nd Information Technology and Mechatronics Engineering Conference (2016)

52. Pletikosa Cvijikj, I., Kadar, C., Ivan, B., Te, F.: Prevention or panic: design and evaluation of a crime prevention IS. In: Proceedings of the 2015 International Conference on Information Systems (2015)

53. Degirmenci, K., Breitner, M.H.: Consumer purchase intentions for electric vehicles: is green more important than price and range? Transp. Res. Part D Transp. Environ. **51**, 250–260 (2017)

54. Morosan, C.: An empirical examination of US travelers' intentions to use biometric e-gates in airports. J. Air Transport Manage. **55**, 120–128 (2016)

55. Muraina, I.D., Osman, W.R.B.S., Ahmad, A.: The roles of some antecedents of broadband user behavioural intention among students in the rural areas through PLS-SEM. Am. J. Appl. Sci. **12**(11), 820–829 (2015)

56. Yoo, D.K., Roh, J.J.: Use and uptake of e-books in the lens of unified theory of acceptance and use of technology. In: Paper presented at the Proceedings of Pacific Asia Conference on Information Systems (PACIS) (2016)

57. Alalwan, A.A., Dwivedi, Y.K., Rana, N.P., Lal, B., Williams, M.D.: Consumer adoption of Internet banking in Jordan: Examining the role of hedonic motivation, habit, self-efficacy and trust. J. Financ. Serv. Mark. **20**(2), 145–157 (2015)

58. Ain, N., Kaur, K., Waheed, M.: The influence of learning value on learning management system use: an extension of UTAUT2. Inf. Dev. **32**(5), 1306–1321 (2016)

59. Juaneda-Ayensa, E., Mosquera, A., Murillo, Y.S.: Omnichannel customer behavior: key drivers of technology acceptance and use and their effects on purchase intention. Front. Psychol. **7**(1117) (2016). https://doi.org/10.3389/fpsyg.2016.01117

60. Escobar-Rodrguez, T., Carvajal-Trujillo, E., Monge-Lozano, P.: Factors that influence the perceived advantages and relevance of Facebook as a learning tool: An extension of the UTAUT. Australas. J. Educ. Technol. **30**(2), 136–151 (2014)

61. Buettner, R.: Getting a job via career-oriented social networking sites: the weakness of ties. In: 49th Hawaii International Conference on System Sciences (2016)

62. Dernbecher, S., Beck, R., Weber, S.: Switch to your own to work with the known: an empirical study on consumerization of IT. In: Proceedings of the Nineteenth American Conference on Information Systems, Chicago (2013)

63. Huang, K.-Y., Chuang, Y.-R.: A task–technology fit view of job search website impact on performance effects: An empirical analysis from Taiwan. Cogent Bus. Manage. **3**(1), 1–18 (2016)

64. Ali, F., Nair, P.K., Hussain, K.: An assessment of students' acceptance and usage of computer supported collaborative classrooms in hospitality and tourism schools. J. Hospitality Leisure Sport Tourism Educ. **18**, 51–60 (2016)

65. Baptista, G., Oliveira, T.: Understanding mobile banking: the unified theory of acceptance and use of technology combined with cultural moderators. Comput. Hum. Behav. **50**, 418–430 (2015)

66. Raman, A., Don, Y.: Preservice teachers' acceptance of learning management software: an application of the UTAUT2 model. Int. Educ. Stud. **6**(7), 157–168 (2013)

67. Chong, A.Y.-L., Ngai, E.W.: What influences travellers' adoption of a location-based social media service for their travel planning? In: PACIS (2013)

68. Järvinen, J., Ohtonen, R., Karjaluoto, H.: Consumer acceptance and use of Instagram. In: 49th Hawaii International Conference on System Sciences (2016)

69. Nair, P.K., Ali, F., Leong, L.C.: Factors affecting acceptance & use of ReWIND: validating the extended unified theory of acceptance and use of technology. Interact. Technol. Smart Educ. **12**(3), 183–201 (2015)

70. Herrero, Á., San Martín, H.: Explaining the adoption of social networks sites for sharing user-generated content: a revision of the UTAUT2. Comput. Hum. Behav. **71**, 209–217 (2017)

71. Morosan, C., DeFranco, A.: Co-creating value in hotels using mobile devices: a conceptual model with empirical validation. Int. J. Hospitality Manage. **52**, 131–142 (2016)

72. Jia, L., Hall, D., Sun, S.: The effect of technology usage habits on consumers' intention to continue use mobile payments. In: Proceedings of the 20th Americas Conference on Information Systems. AIS. Savannah (2014)

73. Chong, A.Y.-L.: A two-staged SEM-neural network approach for understanding and predicting the determinants of m-commerce adoption. Expert Syst. Appl. **40**(4), 1240–1247 (2013)

74. Baptista, G., Baptista, G., Oliveira, T., Oliveira, T.: Why so serious? Gamification impact in the acceptance of mobile banking services. Internet Res. **27**(1), 118–139 (2017)

75. Wong, C.-H., Wei-Han Tan, G., Loke, S.-P., Ooi, K.-B.: Mobile TV: a new form of entertainment? Ind. Manage. Data Syst. **114**(7), 1050–1067 (2014)

76. Ramírez-Correa, P.E., Rondán-Cataluña, F.J., Arenas-Gaitán, J.: An empirical analysis of mobile Internet acceptance in Chile. Inf. Res. **19**(3), 19-3 (2014)
77. Escobar-Rodríguez, T., Carvajal-Trujillo, E.: Online purchasing tickets for low cost carriers: An application of the unified theory of acceptance and use of technology (UTAUT) model. Tour. Manage. **43**, 70–88 (2014)
78. Rana, N.P., Dwivedi, Y.K., Williams, M.D.: A meta-analysis of existing research on citizen adoption of e-government. Inf. Syst. Front. **17**(3), 547–563 (2015)
79. Limayem, M., Hirt, S.G., Cheung, C.M.: How habit limits the predictive power of intention: the case of information systems continuance. MIS Q. **31**(4), 705–737 (2007)

Searching the Identity of Information Systems: A Study from Interdisciplinary Contexts

Paolo Rocchi[1,2(✉)] and Andrea Resca[2]

[1] IBM, via Shangai 53, Rome, Italy
[2] LUISS Guido Carli Univ., via Romania 32, Rome, Italy
{procchi,aresca}@luiss.it

Abstract. Purpose: The present paper addresses the problem of the information systems (IS) identity, in particular it makes an attempt to identify the intellectual causes that hinder the research about the core of IS and suggests how to remove them.

Design/methodology/approach: Authors who argue on the cultural core of IS sometimes relate this argument to the 'reference disciplines' of IS such as economics and sociology. Authors rarely examine what happens in parallel domains of knowledge usually labeled as 'cognate disciplines' of IS. We fixed to extend inquiries on the close domains, in particular we have analyzed the literature of artificial intelligence, information retrieval, medical informatics, digital humanities and software engineering.

Findings: Bibliographical evidence shows how these disciplines struggle with the 'identity crisis' as IS do; more precisely thinkers share non-trivial difficulties when they argue about broad topics connected to the information technology such as the possibilities and limits of computer systems, the transfer and diffusion of technology etc.

Research implications: We recall how normally philosophy and science progress side to side and cooperate. Instead, the modern literature shows how computer science illustrates all the technical details but does not provide effective explanations to philosophers of post-computation disciplines. Several narrow theories underpin computer systems that prove to be futile to thinkers who address broad arguments. An apparent cause-effect relationship emerges between the fragmentary notions of computer science and the current 'identity crisis' of IS and cognate disciplines.

Originality/value: This study leads to a ground-breaking conclusion. In the first stage, the solution to the identity problem should not be searched inside IS but outside. Secondly as soon as possible noteworthy efforts should be made in order to improve the theoretical basis of informatics. More precisely computing theorists should develop a unified cultural frame or, at least, should make significant progress toward this direction.

Keywords: IS identity · Foundational issues · Interdisciplinary research
Computing theories

Published by Springer Nature Switzerland AG 2019.
A. Elbanna et al. (Eds.): TDIT 2018, IFIP AICT 533, pp. 295–305, 2019.
https://doi.org/10.1007/978-3-030-04315-5_20

1 Introduction

The identity issue of the information systems (IS) discipline involves various arguments such as the intellectual core of IS, its relationship with other domains of knowledge, its social meaning, the possibilities and limits of the information technology (IT) etc. Theoretical research started in the 1960s and Sage pinpointed how attention should primarily be drawn to issues about engineering and computation [1]. Börje Langefors provided a model of IS as a combination of software, hardware, data, and procedures while people lie in the background [2]. Some pioneers even made attempts to conceptualize IS, like Reisig who developed an abstract meta-model derived from information theory [3]. The IS discipline evolved and still continues to evolve under the impulse of the technology, and the impact of computer technology on IS comes in and out of focus for researchers over the years. Kenneth and Laudon [4] offer an overview by defining five classes of IS, which emerged one after the other over time, as a result of advances in electronics.

Starting from the eighties of the past century, authors progressively highlighted the multiple features that characterize the nature of information systems. For instance, the Frisco Report—compiled by a working group of the international federation for information processing (IFIP)—built on a semiological description of IS [5]. Cybernetics theorists extended the notion of IS to the biological domain. Experts of management information systems (MIS) looked into the organizational sides of IS, such as Lucey (2005), who provided an extensive illustration to clarify the close interrelations between business and information systems [6].

Writers became aware that the IS domain encompasses a variety of elements that go beyond the purely technical stance. Thinkers have acquired a more complex perspective that includes economical, organizational and social themes. Some of the views may not easily be reconciled and writers endeavored to integrate these various intellectual stances. Wood-Harper and others suggested the 'multiview' of information systems and may be cited as one of the first efforts to set up a multifold interpretation of IS [7]. This prismatic concern raised epistemological discussion; in fact, experts of information systems often borrow theories, methods, and good practices pertaining to various sectors. The identification and relationships with the *'reference disciplines'* – e.g. economics and sociology [8] – attract the attention of Baskerville and Myer [9], who ask: Is the domain of IS simply a net importer of knowledge from other disciplines? Does IS not have any research tradition of its own?

Baskerville and Myer analyze the complex texture of topics dealing with IS, the multi-fold stances, the qualified amount of works etc. For instance, they quote the special issue of the MIS Quarterly that aims to make the reader aware of the intensive inquiries conducted in the present territory [10]. Baskerville and Myer conclude that it is time to pass from the discussion of the reference disciplines to the presentation of IS as a reference discipline [9].

Unfortunately, the progress of IT, the wealth of arguments, the flexibility to adapt to the changing environment, and the complexity of human interferences do not make the life of those who mean to follow the recommendations of Baskerville and Myer easier. Experts see the streams of research about the IS core to be somewhat intricate and seek a survey of the arguments under discussion. Lee observes how IS are intellectually linked to some key concepts, including 'information,' 'theory,' 'system,' 'organization,' and 'relevance' [11]. Banker and Kauffman offer a resume of the IS research in the past 50 years [12], and identify the ensuing streams of study:

1. *Decision support and design science* explore the application of computers in control and managerial decision making;
2. *Value of information* reflects on the importance of information as a commodity in the management of firms;
3. *Human–Computer interaction* focuses on the cognitive basis for effective systems design;
4. *IS organization and strategy* examine the value of IS investments at a strategic level;
5. *Economics of IS and IT* investigates the impact of computer applications from managerial perspectives.

Sidorova and colleagues look into the intellectual core of IS and identify five areas in the light of the bibliographical studies published by top IS journals from 1985 through 2006 [13]. The inventoried streams of research, which turn out to be self-explanatory, are *information technology and organizations; IS development; IT and individuals; IT and markets*; and *IT and groups*.

In summary, several authors agree on the prismatic nature of IS and on the importance of IT, but the questions remain open [14]. The considerations present distinct traits and there is no uniform consensus about the cultural identity of IS. The variety of positions reflects different intellectual influences and waves as the work of Whitley and colleagues underlines [15].

2   What Does Happen in the Close Domains?

Interdisciplinary Viewpoint
Traditionally, authors recognize research in information systems is interdisciplinary in nature [16]. Scholars while confronting IS' identity issue take account of the influence of the *reference disciplines* such as economics, sociology and management science – e.g. [8, 9] – but we note how thinkers rarely analyse what happens in the close domains of IS, for example artificial intelligence and digital biology. These fields together with IS are usually labeled as *cognate disciplines* since all of them have been inaugurated in consequence of the expansion of computer systems in the world; it may be said that they have a common ancestor.

Alvesson and Sandberg [17] underline the advantages of the research strategy which crosses various fields and generates more imaginative and influential results. Gibbons [18], Alderman [19] and others explain how the association of scholars belonging to different sectors is desirable since, for instance, it prevents double efforts, it makes validation easier, and enables cross-checks. The discussion held in a large community has an edge over one only held among a small circle. We personally agree that a joint intellectual effort is appropriate for the identity issue which covers a broad area of study and requires deep insights and considerations. The interdisciplinary perspective looks like an 'overhead point of view' from which one can watch the large domain influenced by the digital technologies. As an airplane pilot observes the most relevant elements in the territory from aloft and overlooks the details, so a research extended to the cognate disciplines of IS should allow scholars to grasp the most significant questions and eventually to discover their root-causes. The interdisciplinary approach is consistent with the purposes of the present work.

Some Areas of Study.

We decided to look into the following cognate fields: digital humanities (DH), information retrieval (IR), medical informatics (MI), software engineering (SE), and artificial intelligence (AI).

Digital humanities is an area of study concerned with the wide-ranging application of computational technologies to the humanities [20]. Robinson and others explore the boundaries of DH [21]. Hockey argues on the limit of machines in handling data [22], while the relations between science and humanities influence the identity problems of digital humanities according to McCarty [23]. Bod believes that the cultural roots of DH—that is to say, the humanist erudition—should enlighten most foundational questions and should provide solid answers [24].

The term *'information retrieval'* usually denotes the process of recovering specific information from stored data. Presently, this activity is connected to various techniques such as big data and search engines. The early years saw a heavy debate over the disparate technologies for retrieval as well as over some basic topics. Theorists tackle the questions of why, and in what sense the notion of information can be critical in IR. They even try to discern whether IR can be seen either as a field of study or as one among several research traditions concerned with information storage and retrieval [25]. Lancaster claims that the basic problems of IR are of intellectual nature and cannot be easily solved by technology alone [26]. Ellis [27] and Ingwersen [28] develop two conceptual schemes to clarify the structure of the IR field.

The earliest IT projects in medicine emerged in the 1950s. Many names have been given to *medical informatics*, for example *health informatics, healthcare informatics, nursing informatics*, and *biomedical informatics*; and in a sense, the list mirrors the dynamic life of this ever-expanding professional field. Lazakidou and Siassiakos [29] pinpoint how the development of electronic appliances makes it possible to cure illnesses that have never treated before. Digital systems furnish material to Kalet [30] and to Greenes and Shortliffe [31], who aim to establish medical informatics as a discipline.

The origins of the term *'software engineering'* seem to date back to 1968 when a group of scholars meant to define a new distinct engineering sector, but Smith and Ali [32], Kruchten [33] and many others raise doubts whether it is really a form of engineering. Denning and Freeman [34] notice that the unanswered questions about software computation are not confined to the intellectual concerns but are also directly relevant to practitioners. In fact, statistical surveys conducted worldwide show how, yearly, more than half of the IT projects in diverse application areas are late, over-budget, unreliable, and unsatisfactory for customers (read the Standish Group Chaos Report http://blog.standishgroup.com/). Beizer [35] and Herbsleb [36] relate these failures to vexed issues on the essence of software programming.

The term *'artificial intelligence'* covers a lot of disparate problem areas, including natural language processing, automatic programming, robotics, machine vision, automatic theorem proving, and knowledge engineering. The areas of AI are mainly united by the fact that they involve complex input and output information that is extremely difficult to compute. The number and the size of these areas, which are continuously expanding, challenges authors like Kirsh (1992) who aims to describe the common and fundamental ideas of the AI sector [37]. The very name 'artificial intelligence' implies that an explicit relationship connects or should connect an AI application to the human brain. The history written by McCorduck [38] demonstrates how, since the times of Turing, AI has captured the imagination of many scientists who are still addressing issues such as defining what intelligence is, and discovering how AI can bridge the gulf between technology and the human mind.

In summary, the current literature proves that the debates on foundational arguments are not exclusive to IS. All the mentioned post-computation disciplines struggle with the 'identity crisis' in the same manner as IS. This concern has become increasingly prevalent in recent years since none succeeds in defining a conclusive frame so far.

Significant Arguments

The approach, which involves various domains of knowledge, offers an 'overhead point of view' from which one grasps the most ponderous elements of discussion and can overlook the details: What does the interdisciplinary bibliography indicate as the most significant arguments?

The nature and roles of computing – just mentioned in Introduction – emerge amongst the knottiest foundational themes of inquiry. Let us briefly analyse three shared arguments:

(i) *Impact of computers on people.* Human factors represent one of the most often vexed themes underpinning information systems and cognate disciplines (read the series [39]). For example, effective technology transfer often requires adaptation of work practices, reskilling, and organizational change far beyond what was initially apparent. Even a trivial fault in this area can frustrate the introduction of new software into an organization or a social group [40]. Lindgaard looks into the risk factors and the barriers to success in IT transfer, he also analyses the strategies for addressing them because of the assortment of users, customers, stakeholders, managers and technologists [41]. The literature on IS ascribes great value to the identification and dissemination of information on best practices for people [42]. Hsu and colleagues aim at evaluating the impact of digital technology in MI [43]. Specifically, they aim to understand the perception of computer use and patients' satisfaction. Russel and Norvig discuss current research of AI related to reasoning under uncertainty and knowledge representation [44]. They make comments on how specific software techniques are used in the real environment, how successful they are, and why they fail with people. In a recent book, Berry and Fagerjord [45] hold that computers challenge the way in which we think about culture, society and what it is typically human: areas traditionally explored by humanities.

(ii) *Possibility and limits of automated systems.* On one side, machines prove to be more efficient than people in processing data; on the other side systems are programmed, notably they depend on humans in a substantial manner: Will the machine substitute the human mind?

Rivers of ink are still flowing about this argument, which is central to AI [46]. Amongst the skeptical we cite Peek and Newby who observe how linguistic aspects of basic importance to DH are still unanswerable [47]. For example, current computing is unable to recognize metaphor, word play, and irony. In the face of automated systems for decision assist, IS researchers seek to understand what can limit the freedom of decision-making, what can orient, influence and hamper the choice made by one or more persons [48] while Orliski and Iacono warn how the nature of the IT artifact is still unclear [49]

(iii) *Present and future trends in technology.* Researchers discuss a very broad assortment of technical topics such as Rech and Althoff [51] who explore the next trends of artificial intelligence and software engineering that have many commonalities. Larsen and others forecast incoming challenges in DH and emphasize the role that the humanist culture will play [50]. Charikar and colleagues [52] address the document clustering optimization problem in order to enhance the performance of IR while 'big data' is a new challenge topic of inquiry for IR [53]. Mahler expects the increasing diffusion of open standards to meet the challenges facing global society [54].

3   Philosophy and Science Progress Side to Side

The literature demonstrates how the authors dealing with topics (i), (ii) and (iii) struggle with broad and substantial arguments. Several issues are open since decades and the authors give the impression of being at a deadlock, so we mean to draw the reader's attention to the cooperation that should take place between science and philosophy.

Scientists and thinkers usually progress side to side as they learn from each other. The former often acquire methodological guide and impulses to establish universal principles from philosophy. On the other hand, philosophy draws from scientific discoveries fresh strength and material for conceptual generalizations. It is not rare that philosophers of science unravel intricate arguments with the aid of empirical data and the theoretical models set up by mathematicians. Unfortunately, this is not the case under discussion. Philosophers of post-computation disciplines wait to be effectively assisted by computer theorists who should explain or contribute to explain topics (i), (ii) and (iii), instead this collaboration turns out to be rather problematic: Why?

Fragmentary Explanations
Computer science makes plain all the technical details of systems but has narrow constructions. The partial constructs of theoretical computer science (TCS) back practitioners, such as software programmers and systemists, but are far less useful to

philosophers who argue on themes of general interest. Knuth was one of the first to complain about the cultural state of computer science [55]. Eden [56], Baldwin [57] and Hayes [58] look into various aspects related to the uncertain foundations of computing. They pinpoint how CS does not yet have a clear comprehensive frame, notwithstanding the large number of mathematical models in use. Tedre [59] shows how there is a great variety of different approaches, definitions, and outlooks in computer science. Denning seeks the determination of appropriate principles which should explain the essence of computing [60]. Hassan observes that what differentiates a discipline from a multidisciplinary field of interest is the development of a unique and consistent discourse [61]. More recently Rocchi [62] holds that the theories underpinning computer science exhibit the following features:

- They are *narrow*, in the sense that each one explores a particular topic;
- They are *self-referential*, in that they are scarcely connected, either logically or causally, or by shared characteristics. For example, the theory of computation and relational algebra are both involved in programming but are unrelated in point of logic;
- They are often *abstract*, such that constructions have faint relations with physical reality and the experimental control of the results turns out to be somewhat unachievable;
- Sometimes, they are *contradictory*, for example, Shannon's theory rejects semantics, whereas semioticians inquire into the making of meanings and their interpretation in communication;
- They are *uncertain*, since many theories have been put forward for a single topic but those theories have not yet undergone accurate scrutiny. For example, there are over thirty theories of information which present irreconcilable characters and the concept of information is still puzzling.

In summary, TCS provides assistance to specialists but turns out to be rather ineffective from the intellectual stance. There are several scientific explanations, but they often mismatch one another, and the consistent, exhaustive illustration of computing is missing. We wonder: How can philosophers clarify the intellectual profile of the disciplines that computers have generated whether the very studies of computers turn out to be rather confusing?

The contradiction is self-evident. The relationship between the fragmentary concepts of computing and the open problems of post-computation disciplines seems undeniable in the present context, thus the solution to the identity problem should not be searched inside IS but outside, more precisely in theoretical computing. TCS presents apparent limits from the philosophical stance and as a logical consequence, computing theorists should develop a unified frame or, at least, should make significant progress toward this direction. Noteworthy efforts should be made in order to improve the theoretical basis of informatics.

Speaking in general, discovering the root-cause of an issue makes experts aware of the true reasons that create an obstacle and enables those experts to remove it. Hence the advance of TCS promises to cancel the current difficulties met by authors about the cultural core of IS, MI, DI and other domains.

4   Conclusion

Several scholars inquire into the information systems identity and the present paper makes an attempt to identify the intellectual causes that currently hamper those investigations.

Research in information systems is interdisciplinary in nature, however most scholars who look into the cultural core of IS are inclined to maintain an inward-looking perspective. They tend to overlook what happens in the *cognate disciplines* such as artificial intelligence, digital humanities and others. So we decided to cross those domains and have found that also cognate disciplines confront foundational issues, which appear symmetrical to those tackled in the information systems. In particular, thinkers argue on broad issues about IT, and debate, for example, how technical progress challenges present and future research.

Authors raise significant arguments but theoretical computer science does not back them. The theories underpinning systems turn out to be fragmentary, uncertain and even contradictory. Those constructions pursue specialist purposes and do not meet the broad themes dealt by philosophers of post-computation disciplines. How can philosophers progress if the basic and comprehensive notions about computing are missing?

The present sad state of TCS can be regarded as a cultural root-cause of the 'identity crisis'; hence the solution to this crisis cannot be obtained inside IS, but outside IS, more precisely should be found in TCS. This field should provide such explanations as to enable philosophers of science to untangle vexed problems.

We have also driven inquiries toward this direction and concluded that the multiple themes of CS are not disjoined but a logical thread connects them [63, 64].

References

1. Sage, S.M.: Information systems: a brief look into history. Datamation **11**, 63–69 (1968)
2. Langefors, B.: Some approaches to the theory of information systems. BIT **3**, 229–254 (1963)
3. Reisig, G.H.R.: Information-system structure by communication-technology concepts: a cybernetic model approach. Inf. Process. Manage. **14**(6), 405–417 (1978)
4. Laudon Kenneth, C., Laudon, J.P.: Management Information Systems: Managing the Digital Firm. Prentice Hall/CourseSmart, Upper Saddle River (2009)
5. Falkenberg, E.D., et al.: A Framework for Information Systems Concepts, the FRISCO Report (1988). (web edition) http://www.mathematik.uni-marburg.de/~hesse/papers/fri-full.pdf. Accessed Mar 2017
6. Lucey, T.: Management Information System, 9th edn. Thomson Publ., London (2005)
7. Wood-Harper, A.T., Antill, L., Avison, D.E.: Information Systems Definition: The Multiview Approach. Blackwell Scientific Publications Ltd., Oxford (1985)
8. Grover, V., Ayyagari, R., Gokhale, R., Lim, J.: A citation analysis of the evolution and state of information systems within a constellation of reference disciplines. J. AIS **7**, 270–325 (2006)
9. Baskerville, R., Myers, D.: Information systems as a reference discipline. MIS Q. **26**, 1–14 (2002)

10. Markus, M.L., Lee, A.S.: Special issue on intensive research in information systems: using qualitative, interpretive, and case methods to study information technology. MIS Q. **23**(1), 35–38 (1999). MIS Q. **24**(1), 1–2 (2000a). MIS Q. **24**(3), 473–474 (2000b)

11. Lee, A.L.: Retrospect and prospect: information systems research in the last and next 25 years. J. Inf. Technol. **25**, 336–348 (2010)

12. Banker, R.D., Kauffman, R.J.: 50th anniversary article: the evolution of research on information systems: a fiftieth-year survey of the literature in management science. Manage. Sci. **50**(3), 281–298 (2004)

13. Sidorova, A., Evangelopoulos, N., Valacich, J.S., Ramakrishnan, T.: Uncovering the intellectual core of the information systems discipline. MIS Q. **32**(3), 467–482 (2008)

14. Benbasat, I., Zmud, R.W.: The identity crisis within the IS discipline: defining and communicating the discipline's core properties. MIS Q. **27**(2), 183–194 (2003)

15. Whitley, E.A., Gal, U., Kjaergaard, A.: Who do you think you are? A review of the complex interplay between information systems, identification and identity. Eur. J. Inf. Syst. **23**(1), 17–35 (2014)

16. Roberts, N., Galluch, P.S., Dinger, M., Grover, V.: Absorptive capacity and information systems research: review, synthesis, and directions for future research. MIS Q. **36**(2), 625–648 (2012)

17. Alvesson, M., Sandberg, J.: Habitat and habitus: boxed-in versus box-breaking research. Organ. Stud. **35**(7), 967–987 (2014)

18. Gibbons, M., Limoges, C., Nowotny, H., Schwartzman, S., Scott, P., Trow, M.: The New Production of Knowledge: The Dynamics of Science and Research in Contemporary Society. Sage Publications, London (1997)

19. Alderman, N., Ivory, C., Mcloughlin, I., Vaughan, R.: Managing Complex Projects: Networks, Knowledge and Integration. Routledge, New York (2014)

20. Thaller, M.: From History to Applied Computer Science in the Humanities. Historical Social Research, Supplement 29 (2017)

21. Robinson L., Priego E., Bawden D.: Library and information science and digital humanities: two disciplines, joint future? In: Pehar, F., Schlögl, C., Wolff, C. (eds.) Re-inventing Information Science in the Networked Society, Verlag, pp. 44–54 (2015)

22. Hockey, S.: Electronic Texts in the Humanitie. Oxford University Press, New York (2000)

23. McCarty, W.: Humanities computing: essential problems, experimental practice. Lit. Linguist. Comput. **17**(1), 103–125 (2002)

24. Bod, R.: A New History of the Humanities: The Search for Principles and Patterns from Antiquity to the Present. Oxford University Press, Oxford (2013)

25. Salton, G.: Automatic Text Processing: The Transformation, Analysis, and Retrieval of Information by Computer. Addison-Wesley Longman Publishing Co., Boston (1989)

26. Lancaster, F.W., Warner, A.J.: Information Retrieval Today. Info Resources Publ., Arlington (1993). Revised edition

27. Ellis, D.: A Behavioural approach to information retrieval design. J. Doc. **46**(3), 318–338 (1989)

28. Ingwersen, P.: Cognitive perspectives of information retrieval interaction. J. Doc. **52**(1), 3–50 (1996)

29. Lazakidou, A.A., Siassiakos, K.M.: Handbook of Research on Distributed Medical Informatics and E-Health. Medical Information Science Reference Publisher, New York (2008)

30. Kalet, I.J.: Principles of Biomedical Informatics. Academic Press, Amsterdam (2008)

31. Greenes, R.A., Shortliffe, E.H.: Medical informatics: an emerging discipline with academic and institutional perspectives. J. Am. Med. Assoc. **263**(8), 1114–1120 (1990)

32. Smith, P., Ali, S.: Is software engineering really engineering? In: Brebbia, C.A., Ferrante, A. J. (eds.) Reliability and Robustness of Engineering Software II, pp. 85–95. Springer, Dordrecht (1991). https://doi.org/10.1007/978-94-011-3026-4_7

33. Kruchten, P.: Putting the engineering into software engineering. Innovations **4**(1), 23–24 (2000)

34. Denning, P.J., Freeman, P.: Computing's paradigm. Commun. ACM **52**(1), 28–30 (2009)

35. Beizer, B.: Software is different. Ann. Softw. Eng. **10**(1–4), 293–310 (2000)

36. Herbsleb, J.D.: Beyond computer science. In: Proceedings of the 27th International Conference on Software Engineering, pp. 23–27 (2005)

37. Kirsh, D. (ed.): Foundations of Artificial Intelligence. MIT Press, Cambridge (1992)

38. McCorduck, P.: Machines who Think: A Personal Inquiry into the History and Prospects of Artificial Intelligence. AK Peters Ltd., Natick (2004)

39. Snodgrass, C.R., Szewczak, E.J. (eds.) Human Factors in Information Systems. IRM Press, Hershey (2002). Carey, J. (ed.) Intellect Books (1997), (1995), (1991)

40. Donnellan, B., Larsen, T., Levine, L., DeGross, J. (eds.): The Transfer and Diffusion of Information Technology for Organizational Resilience. Springer, New York (2006). https://doi.org/10.1007/0-387-34410-1

41. Lindgaard, G.: Some important factors for successful technology transfer. In: Levin, L. (ed.) Diffusion Transfer and Implementation of Information Technology, pp. 53–66. Elsevier, Amsterdam (1994)

42. Baskerville, R., Pries-Heje, J.: Diffusing best practices: a design science study using the theory of planned behavior. In: Bergvall-Kåreborn, B., Nielsen, P.A. (eds.) TDIT 2014. IAICT, vol. 429, pp. 35–48. Springer, Heidelberg (2014). https://doi.org/10.1007/978-3-662-43459-8_3

43. Hsu, J., Huang, J., Fung, V., Robertson, N., Jimison, H., Frankel, R.: Health information technology and physician-patient interactions: impact of computers on communication during outpatient primary care visits. J. Am. Med. Inf. Assoc. **12**(4), 474–480 (2005)

44. Russel, R.J., Norvig, P.: Artificial Intelligence: A Modern Approach. Prentice Hall, Upper Saddle River (2009)

45. Berry, D.M., Fagerjord, A.: Digital Humanities: Knowledge and Critique in a Digital Age. Wiley, Hoboken (2017)

46. Gershenfeld, N.: When Things Start to Think. Hodder & Stoughton, London (1999)

47. Peek, R.P., Newby, G.B. (eds.): Scholarly Publishing: The Electronic Frontier. MIT Press, Cambridge (1996)

48. Salles, M.: Decision-Making and the Information System. Wiley, Hoboken (2015)

49. Orlikowski, W.J., Iacono, C.S.: Research commentary: desperately seeking the "IT" in IT research - a call to theorizing the IT artifact. Inf. Syst. Res. **12**(2), 121–134 (2001)

50. Larsen, S.E., et al.: No future without humanities: literary perspectives. Humanities **4**, 13–148 (2015)

51. Rech, J., Althoff, K.D.: Artificial intelligence and software engineering: status and future trends. Künstliche Intelligenz **18**, 5–11 (2004)

52. Charikar, M., Chekuri, C., Feder, T., Motwani, R.: Incremental clustering and dynamic information retrieval. SIAM J. Comput. **33**(6), 1417–1440 (2004)

53. Chen, H., Chiang, R.H.L., Storey, V.C.: Business intelligence and analytics: from big data to big impact. MIS Q. **36**(4), 1165–1188 (2012)

54. Mahler, T.: Governance models for interoperable electronic identities. J. Int. Commer. Law Technol. **8**(2), 148–159 (2013)

55. Knuth, D.: The Art of Computer Programming, vol. 1, 2nd edn. Addison Wesley Longman Publishing Co., Redwood City (1973)

56. Eden, A.H.: Three paradigms of computer science. Minds Mach. Spec. Issue Philos. Comput. Sci. **17**(2), 135–167 (2007)
57. Baldwin, D.: Is computer science a relevant academic discipline for the 21st century? IEEE Comput. **44**(12), 81–83 (2011)
58. Hayes, B.: Cultures of code. Am. Sci. **103**(1), 10–13 (2015)
59. Tedre, M.: Computing as a science: a survey of competing viewpoints. Mind. Mach. **21**, 361–387 (2011)
60. Denning, P.J.: Is computer science? Commun. ACM **48**(4), 27–31 (2005)
61. Hassan, N.R.: Is information systems a discipline? Foucauldian and Toulminian insights. Eur. J. Inf. Syst. **20**(4), 456–476 (2011)
62. Rocchi, P.: "Informatics and electronics: some educational remarks" Guest editorial. IEEE Trans. Educ. **59**(3), 233–239 (2016)
63. Rocchi, P.: Technology + Culture = Software. IOS Press, Amsterdam (2000)
64. Rocchi, P.: Logic of Analog and Digital Machines. Nova Science Publishers, New York (2013). Revised Edition

Author Index